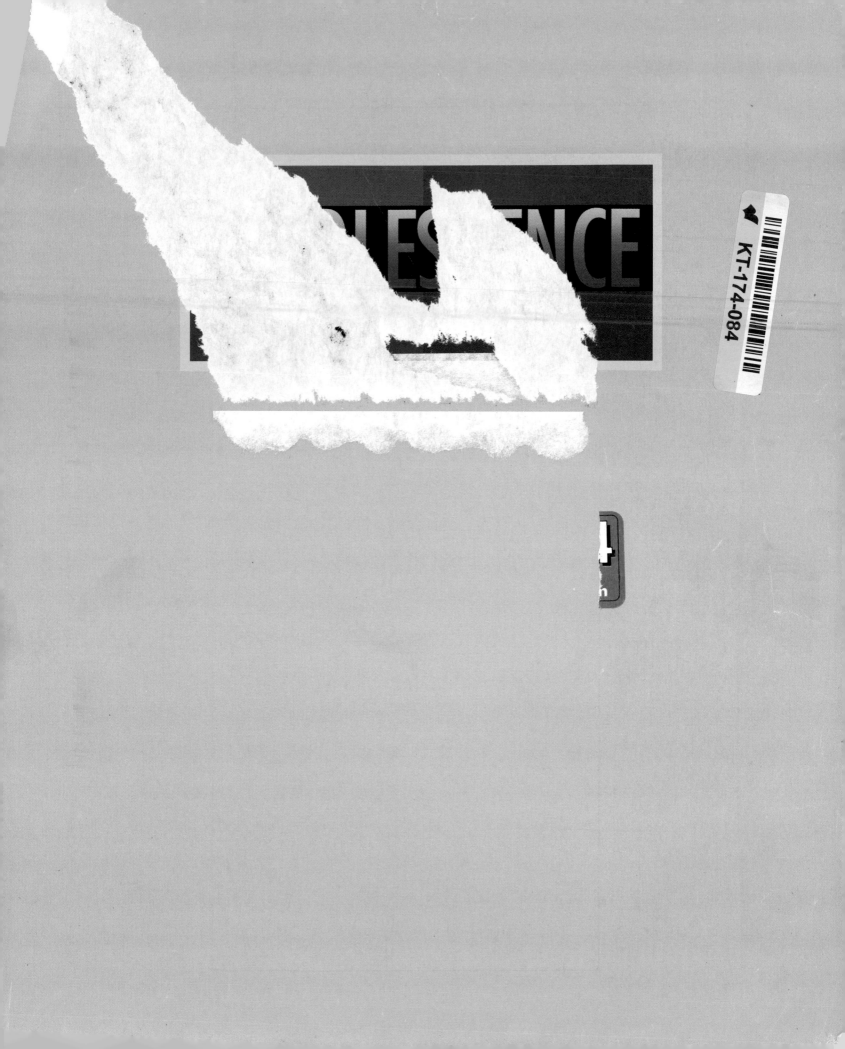

ADOLESCENCE

9TH EDITION

JOHN W. SANTROCK

UNIVERSITY OF TEXAS AT DALLAS

Boston   Burr Ridge, IL   Dubuque, IA   Madison, WI   New York   San Francisco   St. Louis
Bangkok   Bogotá   Caracas   Kuala Lumpur   Lisbon   London   Madrid   Mexico City
Milan   Montreal   New Delhi   Santiago   Seoul   Singapore   Sydney   Taipei   Toronto

McGraw-Hill Higher Education

*A Division of The **McGraw-Hill** Companies*

ADOLESCENCE, NINTH EDITION

Published by McGraw-Hill, a business unit of The McGraw-Hill Companies, Inc., 1221 Avenue of the Americas, New York, NY 10020. Copyright © 2003, 2001, 1998 by The McGraw-Hill Companies, Inc. All rights reserved. No part of this publication may be reproduced or distributed in any form or by any means, or stored in a database or retrieval system, without the prior written consent of The McGraw-Hill Companies, Inc., including, but not limited to, in any network or other electronic storage or transmission, or broadcast for distance learning.

Some ancillaries, including electronic and print components, may not be available to customers outside the United States.

This book is printed on acid-free paper.

International   1 2 3 4 5 6 7 8 9 0 QPD/QPD 0 9 8 7 6 5 4 3 2
Domestic   1 2 3 4 5 6 7 8 9 0 QPD/QPD 0 9 8 7 6 5 4 3 2

ISBN 0–07–249199–X
ISBN 0–07–121297–3 (ISE)

Vice president and editor-in-chief: *Thalia Dorwick*
Publisher: *Stephen D. Rutter*
Senior sponsoring editor: *Rebecca H. Hope*
Senior marketing manager: *Chris Hall*
Project manager: *Richard H. Hecker*
Production supervisor: *Enboge Chong*
Coordinator of freelance design: *Michelle D. Whitaker*
Cover/interior designer: *Diane Beasley*
Cover image: *David Young-Wolff/Getty Images, Inc.*
Lead photo research coordinator: *Carrie K. Burger*
Photo research: *LouAnn K. Wilson*
Senior supplement producer: *David A. Welsh*
Media technology producer: *Ginger Warner*
Compositor: *GAC–Indianapolis*
Typeface: *10.5/12 Minion*
Printer: *Quebecor World Dubuque, IA*

The credits section for this book begins on page C-1 and is considered an extension of the copyright page.

Library of Congress Cataloging-in-Publication Data

Santrock, John W.
     Adolescence / John W. Santrock. — 9th ed.
          p.   cm.
     Includes bibliographical references and indexes.
     ISBN 0–07–249199–X (alk. paper) — ISBN 0–07–121297–3 (ISE : alk. paper)
     1. Adolescence. 2. Adolescent psychology. I. Title.

   HQ796 .S26   2003
   305.235—dc21   2002022713
                                                                   CIP

INTERNATIONAL EDITION ISBN 0–07–121297–3
Copyright © 2003. Exclusive rights by The McGraw-Hill Companies, Inc., for manufacture and export. This book cannot be re-exported from the country to which it is sold by McGraw-Hill. The International Edition is not available in North America.

www.mhhe.com

TO TRACY AND JENNIFER,
WHO, AS THEY HAVE MATURED,
HAVE HELPED ME APPRECIATE
THE MARVELS OF
ADOLESCENT DEVELOPMENT

ABOUT THE AUTHOR

■

JOHN W. SANTROCK received his Ph.D. from the University of Minnesota in 1973. He taught at the University of Charleston and the University of Georgia before joining the psychology department at the University of Texas at Dallas. He has been a member of the editorial boards of *Developmental Psychology* and *Child Development.* His research on father custody is widely cited and used in expert witness testimony to promote flexibility and alternative considerations in custody disputes. John has also authored these exceptional McGraw-Hill texts: *Child Development,* Ninth Edition, *Life-Span Development,* Eighth Edition, *Children,* 7th Edition, *Psychology,* Seventh Edition, and *Educational Psychology,* First Edition.

John Santrock has been teaching an undergraduate course on adolescent development every year since 1981 and continues to teach this course and a range of other undergraduate courses at the University of Texas at Dallas.

BRIEF CONTENTS

CONTENTS

SECTION 2

BIOLOGICAL AND COGNITIVE DEVELOPMENT   73

CHAPTER 3
PUBERTY, HEALTH, AND BIOLOGICAL FOUNDATIONS   75

SECTION 3
THE CONTEXTS OF ADOLESCENT DEVELOPMENT   145

CHAPTER 6
PEERS   185

CHAPTER 7
SCHOOLS   219

THE
NATURE OF
ADOLESCENT
DEVELOPMENT

□

*In no order of things is adolescence the
simple time of life.*

—Jean Erskine Stewart
American Writer, 20th Century

Adolescence is a transitional period in the
human life span, linking childhood and
adulthood. Understanding the meaning of
adolescence is important because
adolescents are the future of any society.
This first section contains two chapters:
chapter 1, "Introduction," and chapter 2,
"The Science of Adolescent Development."

CHAPTER
1

CHAPTER MAP

HISTORICAL PERSPECTIVE

- Early History
- A Positive View of Adolescence
- The Twentieth Century
- Stereotyping Adolescents

TODAY'S ADOLESCENTS

- The Current Status of Adolescents
- Social Policy and Adolescents' Development

THE NATURE OF DEVELOPMENT

- Processes and Periods
- Developmental Issues
- Developmental Transitions

UNDERSTANDING ADOLESCENCE: WHAT MATTERS?

- Biological Processes Matter
- Critical Thinking Matters
- Cognitive Processes Matter
- Science Matters
- Contexts Matter
- Problems and Disorders Matter
- Social and Personality Development Matters

INTRODUCTION

A few years ago, it occurred to me that, when I was a teenager, in the early Depression years, there were no teenagers! Teenagers have sneaked up on us in our own lifetime, and yet it seems they always have been with us. . . . The teenager had not yet been invented, though, and there did not yet exist a special class of beings, bounded in a certain way—not quite children and certainly not adults.

—P. Musgrove
American Writer, 20th Century

◼ THE YOUTHS OF JEFFREY DAHMER AND ALICE WALKER

Jeffrey Dahmer had a troubled childhood and adolescence. His parents constantly bickered before they divorced. His mother had emotional problems and doted on his younger brother. He felt that his father neglected him, and he had been sexually abused by another boy when he was 8 years old. But the vast majority of people who suffered through a painful childhood and adolescence never go on to commit the grisly crimes that Dahmer committed in the 1970s to 1990s. Dahmer murdered his first victim in 1978 with a barbell and went on to kill 16 other individuals.

A decade before Dahmer's first murder, Alice Walker, who would later win a Pulitzer Prize for her book *The Color Purple,* spent her days battling racism in Mississippi. Walker knew the brutal effects of poverty, born the eighth child of Georgia sharecroppers. Despite the counts against her, she went on to become an award-winning novelist. Walker writes about people who, as she puts it, "make it, who come out of nothing. People who triumph."

What leads one adolescent, so full of promise, to commit brutal acts of violence and another to turn poverty and trauma into a rich literary harvest? How can we attempt to explain how one adolescent can pick up the pieces of a life shattered by tragedy, such as a loved one's death, whereas another one seems to come unhinged by life's minor hassles? Why is it that some adolescents are whirlwinds—successful in school, involved in a network of friends, and full of energy—while others hang out on the sidelines, mere spectators of life? If you have ever wondered what makes adolescents tick, you have asked yourself the central question we explore in this book.

Jeffrey Dahmer's senior portrait in high school.

Alice Walker

(*a*) The Roaring Twenties was a time when adolescents began to behave more permissively. Adults began to model the styles of youth. Adolescent drinking increased dramatically. (*b*) In the 1940s, many youth served in World War II. Military service exposed many youth to life-threatening circumstances and allowed them to see firsthand the way people in other countries live. (*c*) In the 1950s, many youth developed a stronger orientation toward education. Television was piped into many homes for the first time. One of the fads of the 1950s, shown here, was seeing how many people could squeeze into a phone booth. (*d*) In the late 1960s, many youth protested U.S. participation in the Vietnam War. Parents became more concerned about adolescent drug use as well. (*e*) Since the 1970s, much of the radical protest of youth quieted down. Today's adolescents are achievement-oriented, more likely to be working at a job, experiencing adult roles earlier, showing more interest in equality of the sexes, and heavily influenced by the media.

For many years, barriers prevented many females and ethnic minority individuals from entering the field of adolescent development. Females and ethnic minority individuals who obtained doctoral degrees were very dedicated and overcame considerable bias. One pioneering female was Leta Hollingworth, who conducted important research on adolescent development, mental retardation, and gifted children (see

FIGURE 1.1
Leta Hollingworth

Women have often been overlooked in the history of psychology. In the field of adolescence, one such overlooked individual is Leta Hollingworth. She was the first individual to use the term *gifted* to describe youth who scored exceptionally high on intelligence tests (Hollingworth, 1916). She also played an important role in criticizing theories of her time that promoted the idea that males were superior to females (Hollingworth, 1914). For example, she conducted a research study refuting the myth that phases of the menstrual cycle are associated with a decline in performance in females,

figure 1.1). Pioneering African American psychologists included Kenneth and Mamie Clark, who conducted research on the self-esteem of African American children (Clark & Clark, 1939). And in 1932, George Sanchez documented cultural bias in intelligence tests for children and adolescents.

We have described some important sociohistorical circumstances experienced by adolescents, and we have evaluated how society viewed adolescents at different points in history. Next we will explore why caution needs to be exercised in generalizing about the adolescents of any era.

Stereotyping Adolescents

It is easy to stereotype a person, groups of people, or classes of people. A **stereotype** *is a broad category that reflects our impressions and beliefs about people. All stereotypes refer to an image of what the typical member of a particular group is like.* We live in a complex world and strive to simplify this complexity. Stereotyping people is one way we do this. We simply assign a label to a group of people—for example, we say that youth are *promiscuous.* Then we have much less to consider when we think about this set of people. Once we assign stereotypes, it is difficult to abandon them, even in the face of contradictory evidence.

Stereotypes about adolescents are plentiful: "They say they want a job, but when they get one, they don't want to work"; "They are all lazy"; "They are all sex fiends"; "They are all into drugs, every last one of them"; "Kids today don't have the moral fiber of my generation"; "The problem with adolescents today is that they all have it too easy"; "They are a bunch of egotistical smart alecks"; and so it goes.

Indeed, during most of the twentieth century, adolescents have been described as abnormal and deviant, rather than normal and nondeviant. Consider Hall's image of storm and stress. Consider also media portrayals of adolescents as rebellious, conflicted, faddish, delinquent, and self-centered—*Rebel Without a Cause* in the late 1950s, and *Easy Rider* in the 1960s, for example. Consider also the image of adolescents as

stereotype

A broad category that reflects our impressions and beliefs about people. All stereotypes refer to an image of what the typical member of a particular group is like.

In case you're worried about what's going to become of the younger generation, it's going to grow up and start worrying about the younger generation.

—Roger Allen
Contemporary American Writer

adolescent generalization gap
Adelson's concept of widespread generalizations about adolescents based on information about a limited, highly visible group of adolescents.

Teens Only!
Three Teenagers
Profile of America's Youth
Trends in the Well-Being of
America's Youth
Youth Information Directory
http://www.mhhe.com/santrocka9

stressed and disturbed, from *Sixteen Candles* and *The Breakfast Club* in the 1980s to *Boyz N the Hood* in the 1990s.

Such stereotyping of adolescents is so widespread that adolescence researcher Joseph Adelson (1979) called it the **adolescent generalization gap**, *meaning that widespread generalizations about adolescents have developed that are based on information about a limited, often highly visible group of adolescents.*

A Positive View of Adolescence

The negative stereotyping of adolescents is overdrawn (Howe & Strauss, 2000; Stepp, 2000). In a cross-cultural study by Daniel Offer and his colleagues (1988) no support for such as negative view of adolescence was found. The self-images of adolescents around the world—in the United States, Australia, Bangladesh, Hungary, Israel, Italy, Japan, Taiwan, Turkey, and West Germany—were sampled. A healthy self-image characterized at least 73 percent of the adolescents studied. They were moving toward adulthood with a healthy integration of previous experiences, self-confidence, and optimism about the future. Although there were some differences in the adolescents, they were happy most of the time, they enjoyed life, they perceived themselves as able to exercise self-control, they valued work and school, they expressed confidence about their sexual selves, they showed positive feelings toward their families, and they felt they had the capability to cope with life's stresses—not exactly a storm-and-stress portrayal of adolescence.

Old Centuries and New Centuries   Beginning with G. Stanley Hall's portrayal of adolescence as a period of storm and stress, for much of this century in the United States and other Western cultures, adolescence has unfortunately been perceived as a problematic period of the human life span that youth, their families, and society had to endure. But as the research study just described indicated, a large majority of adolescents are not nearly as disturbed and troubled as the popular stereotype of adolescence suggests.

The end of old centuries and the beginning of new centuries have a way of stimulating reflections on what was and visions of what could be and should be. In the field of psychology in general, like its subfield of adolescent development, this has meant a look back at a century in which the field of psychology became too negative (Larson, 2000; Santrock, 2003; Seligman & Csikszentmihalyi, 2000). Psychology had become an overly grim science with people too often characterized as passive and victimized. The calling now is for a new focus on the positive side of psychology and greater emphasis on such topics as hope, optimism, positive individual traits, creativity, and positive group and civic values, such as responsibility, nurturance, civility, and tolerance.

As you read earlier in the chapter, in psychology's subfield of adolescent development, at the beginning of the twentieth century, G. Stanley Hall (1974) proposed a negative, storm-and-stress view of adolescents that strongly influenced perceptions of adolescence for much of that century. Now at the beginning of the twenty-first century, as we look back on the twentieth century, adolescents were stereotyped too negatively.

Generational Perceptions and Memories   Adults' perceptions of adolescents emerge from a combination of personal experience and media portrayals, neither of which produce an objective picture of how normal adolescents develop (Feldman & Elliott, 1990). Some of the readiness to assume the worst about adolescents likely involves the short memories of adults. Many adults measure their current perceptions of adolescents by memories of their own adolescence. Adults often portray today's adolescents as more troubled, less respectful, more self-centered, more assertive, and more adventurous than they were.

However, in matters of taste and manners, the youth of every generation have seemed radical, unnerving, and different from adults—different in how they look, how they behave, the music they enjoy, their hairstyles, and the clothing they choose. It is an enormous error to confuse adolescents' enthusiasm for trying on new identities and enjoying moderate amounts of outrageous behavior with hostility toward parental and societal standards. Acting out and boundary testing are time-honored ways in which adolescents move toward accepting, rather than rejecting, parental values.

Practical Resources and Research
Youth Information Directory
Adolescent Issues
Profile of America's Youth
American Youth Policy Forum
http://www.mhhe.com/santrocka9

At this point we have examined many ideas about the historical perspective on adolescence. This review should help you to reach your learning goals related to this topic.

☐ FOR YOUR REVIEW

Learning Goal 1
Explain the historical perspective on adolescence

- Plato said that reasoning first develops in adolescence and Aristotle argued that self-determination is the hallmark of adolescence. In the Middle Ages, knowledge about adolescence moved a step backward: children were viewed as miniature adults and developmental transformations in adolescence were ignored. Rousseau provided a more enlightened view of adolescence, including an emphasis on different phases of development.
- Between 1890 and 1920, a cadre of psychologists, urban reformers, and others began to mold the concept of adolescence.
- G. Stanley Hall is the father of the scientific study of adolescence. In 1904, he proposed the storm-and-stress view of adolescence, which has strong biological foundations.
- In contrast to Hall's biological view, Margaret Mead argued for a sociocultural interpretation of adolescence. In the inventionist view, adolescence is a sociohistorical invention. Legislation was enacted early in the twentieth century that ensured the dependency of adolescents and delayed their entry into the workforce. From 1900 to 1930, there was a 600 percent increase in the number of high school graduates in the United States.
- Adolescents gained a more prominent place in society from 1920 to 1950. By 1950, every state had developed special laws for adolescents. Barriers prevented many ethnic minority individuals and females from entering the field of studying adolescent development in the early and middle part of the twentieth century. Leta Hollingworth was a pioneering female, and Kenneth and Mamie Clark and George Sanchez were pioneering ethnic minority individuals in studying adolescents.

Learning Goal 2
Discuss stereotyping adolescents and a positive view of adolescence

- Negative stereotyping of adolescents in any historical era has been common.
- Joseph Adelson described the concept of the "adolescent generalization gap," which states that widespread generalizations are often based on a limited set of highly visible adolescents.
- For too long, adolescents have been viewed in negative ways. Research shows that a considerable majority of adolescents around the world have positive self-esteem. The majority of adolescents are not highly conflicted but rather are searching for an identity.

Now that we have explored the history of interest in adolescents, let's turn our attention to today's adolescents. Our discussion of today's adolescents will especially focus on how adolescents are characterized by heterogeneity and diversity.

TODAY'S ADOLESCENTS

Now that we have discussed historical perspectives on adolescents and stereotyping adolescents, let's explore the current status of adolescents.

The Current Status of Adolescents

In many ways, it is both the best of times and the worst of times for today's adolescents. Their world possesses powers and perspectives inconceivable less than a century ago: computers; longer life expectancies; the entire planet accessible through television,

TODAY'S ADOLESCENTS

The Current Status of Adolescents

Social Policy and Adolescents' Development

Growing up has never been easy. However, adolescence is not best viewed as a time of rebellion, crisis, pathology, and deviance. A far more accurate vision of adolescence describes it as a time of evaluation, of decision making, of commitment, and of carving out a place in the world. Most of the problems of today's youth are not with the youth themselves. What adolescents need is access to a range of legitimate opportunities and to long-term support from adults who deeply care about them. *What might some of these opportunities be?*

satellites, and air travel. However, today the temptations and hazards of the adult world descend upon children and adolescents so early that too often they are not cognitively and emotionally ready to handle them effectively.

Crack, for example, is far more addictive than marijuana, the drug of an earlier generation. Strange fragments of violence and sex flash out of the television set and lodge in the minds of youth. The messages are powerful and contradictory. Rock videos suggest orgiastic sex. Public health officials counsel safe sex. Various talk-show hosts present sensationalized accounts of exotic drugs and serial murders. Television pours a bizarre version of reality into the imaginations of adolescents.

Every stable society transmits values from one generation to the next. That is civilization's work. In today's world, a special concern is the nature of the values being communicated to adolescents. Only half a century ago, two of three families consisted of a father who was the breadwinner, a mother, and the children and adolescents they were raising. Today, less than one in five families fits that description. Phrases such as *quality time* have found their way into the American vocabulary. Absence is a motif in the lives of many adolescents—absence of authority, limits, emotional commitment (Morrow, 1988).

In many ways, today's adolescents are presented with an environment that is less stable than that of adolescents several decades ago (Weissberg & Greenberg, 1998). High divorce rates, high adolescent pregnancy rates, and increased geographic mobility of families contribute to this lack of stability. The rate of adolescent drug use in the United States is the highest in the industrialized world.

Copyright © 1986, Washington Post Writers Group. Reprinted with permission.

However, growing up has never been easy. In many ways, the developmental tasks of today's adolescents are no different from those of adolescents in the 1950s. Adolescence is not a time of rebellion, crisis, pathology, and deviance for a large majority of youth. It is far more accurate to see adolescence as a time of evaluation, of decision making, of commitment, and of carving out a place in the world.

Our discussion underscores an important point about adolescents. They are not a homogeneous group. Most adolescents successfully negotiate the lengthy path to adult maturity, but a large minority do not. Socioeconomic, ethnic, cultural, gender, age, and lifestyle differences influence the developmental trajectory of every adolescent.

Of special interest today in the study of adolescents is how contexts influence their development (Bronfenbrenner, 2000; Eccles, 2002; Lerner, 2000). **Contexts** *are the settings in which development occurs; settings influenced by historical, economic, social, and cultural factors.* To sense how important contexts are in understanding adolescent development, consider a researcher who wants to discover whether today's adolescents are more racially tolerant than those of a decade or two ago. Without reference to the historical, economic, social, and cultural aspects of race relations, adolescents' racial tolerance cannot be fully understood. Each adolescent's development occurs against a cultural backdrop of contexts (McLoyd, 1998, 2000). These contexts or settings include families, peers, schools, churches, neighborhoods, communities, university laboratories, the United States, China, Mexico, Egypt, and many others, each with meaningful historical, economic, social, and cultural legacies.

Contexts will be given special attention in this book. All of section 3 is devoted to contexts, with separate chapters on families, peers, schools, and culture. As we will see next, some experts argue that the social policy of the United States should place a stronger emphasis on improving the contexts in which adolescents live.

Social Policy and Adolescents' Development

Social policy *is a national government's course of action designed to influence the welfare of its citizens.* A current trend is to conduct adolescent development research that will lead to wise and effective decision making in the area of social policy (Bogenschneider, 2002; Carlson & McLanahan, 2002; Edelman, 1997; Ferber, 2002; Lerner, Fisher, & Weinberg, 2000; Shonkoff, 2000). Because more than 20 percent of adolescents are giving birth, because the use and

We need every human gift and cannot afford to neglect any gift because of artificial barriers of sex or race or class or national origin.

—Margaret Mead
American Anthropologist, 20th Century

contexts

The settings in which development occurs. These settings are influenced by historical, economic, social, and cultural factors.

social policy

A national government's course of action designed to influence the welfare of its citizens.

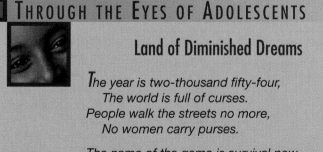

THROUGH THE EYES OF ADOLESCENTS

Land of Diminished Dreams

The year is two-thousand fifty-four,
The world is full of curses.
People walk the streets no more,
No women carry purses.

The name of the game is survival now—
Safety is far in the past.
Families are huge, with tons of kids
In hopes that one will last.

Drugs are no longer looked down on,
They are a way of life.
They help us escape the wrenching stress
Of our fast world's endless strife . . .

I wake up now—it was only a dream,
But the message was terribly clear.
We'd better think hard about the future
Before our goals and our dreams disappear.

—Jessica Inglis, Age 16

CAREERS IN ADOLESCENT DEVELOPMENT

Peter Benson
Director, Search Institute

Peter Benson has been the Director of the Search Institute in Minneapolis since 1985. The Search Institute is an indepen-

Peter Benson, talking with adolescents.

dent, nonprofit organization whose mission is to advance the well-being of adolescents. The Institute conducts applied scientific research, provides information about many aspects of improving adolescents' lives, gives support to communities, and trains people to work with youth.

Peter obtained his undergraduate degree in psychology from Augustana College, master's degree in the psychology of religion from Yale University, and Ph.D. in social psychology from the University of Denver. Peter directs a staff of 80 individuals at the Search Institute, lectures widely about youth, and consults with a number of communities and organizations on adolescent issues.

Under Peter's direction, the Search Institute has determined through research that a number of assets (such as family support and good schools) serve as a buffer to prevent adolescents from developing problems and increase the likelihood that adolescents will competently make the transition from adolescence to adulthood. We will further discuss these assets in chapter 14, "Adolescent Problems."

As we face a new century and a new millennium, the overarching challenge for America is to rebuild a sense of community and hope and civility and caring for all of our children and youth.

—Marian Wright Edelman
Contemporary American Lawyer and Child Advocate

Children's Defense Fund
http://www.mhhe.com/santrocka9

generational inequity
The unfair treatment of younger members of an aging society in which older adults pile up advantages by receiving inequitably large allocations of resources, such as Social Security and Medicare.

abuse of drugs is widespread among adolescents, and because the specter of AIDS is spreading, the United States needs revised social policy related to adolescents.

Marian Wright Edelman, president of the Children's Defense Fund, has been a tireless advocate of children's rights. Especially troublesome to Edelman (1997) are the indicators of social neglect that place the United States at or near the bottom of industrialized nations in the treatment of children and adolescents. Edelman says that parenting and nurturing the next generation of children and youth is our society's most important function and that we need to take it more seriously than we have in the past. She points out that we hear a lot from politicians these days about "family values," but that when we examine our nation's policies for families, they don't reflect the politicians' words. Edelman says that we need a better health-care system for families, safer schools and neighborhoods, better parent education, and improved family support programs.

Who should get the bulk of government dollars for improved well-being? Children? Adolescents? Their parents? The elderly? **Generational inequity** *is the unfair treatment of younger members of an aging society in which older adults pile up advantages by receiving inequitably large allocations of resources, such as Social Security and Medicare.* Generational inequity raises questions about whether the young should have to pay for the old and whether an "advantaged" older population is using up resources that should go to disadvantaged children and adolescents. The argument is that older adults are advantaged because they have publicly provided pensions, health care, food stamps, housing subsidies, tax breaks, and other benefits that younger groups do not have. While the trend of greater services for the elderly has been occurring, the percentage of children and adolescents living in poverty has been rising. Adolescents have especially been underserved by the government.

Bernice Neugarten (1988) says the problem should not be viewed as one of generational inequity, but rather as a major shortcoming of our broader economic and social policies. She believes we should develop a spirit of support for improving the range of options of all people in society. Also, it is important to keep in mind that children will one day become older adults and in turn be supported by the efforts of their children.

perience have
lescence. No g
with only a ge
ings, and beha
blueprint, chi
ences determi
Keep in mind
ment between
issue of conti
pears shortly.

A definit
age and also
earlier discus
tionist view o
adolescence
tion between
cognitive, an
and historica
exact age ran
cultures toda
13 years of
for most ind
emotional ch
ment of sexu

Develop
riods. **Early**
years and in
ter half of th
often more j
study adole:
lescents or a

The ol
transition r
study of ad
tions, the c
sequence o
& Peterson
berty and :
adolescenc
sitional ev

Today,
2000; Balte
ber that d
course and
some uniq
velopmen
the develo

Adult Deve
geneous
adult dev
adulthoo
It is a tim
becomes
Our
middle a
age and e

If there was no Social Security system, in many instances adult children would have to bear the burden of supporting their older parents, which would reduce their ability to spend resources on educating their own children (Schaie, 2000).

In the twenty-first century, the well-being of adolescents should be one of America's foremost concerns. The future of our youth is the future of our society. Adolescents who do not reach their full potential, who are destined to make fewer contributions to society than it needs, and who do not take their place as productive adults diminish our society's future.

In one recent effort to capture what is needed for more positive youth development, Reed Larson (2000) argued that adolescents need more opportunities to develop the capacity for initiative. This involves becoming self-motivated and expending effort to reach challenging goals. Too often adolescents find themselves bored with life. To counter this boredom and help adolescents develop more initiative, Larson especially believes that structured voluntary activities such as sports, arts, and participation in organizations are important contexts.

At this point we have examined many ideas about today's adolescents. This review should help you reach your learning goals related to this topic.

☐ FOR YOUR REVIEW

Learning Goal 3
Evaluate today's adolescents

- Adolescents are heterogeneous. Although a majority of adolescents successfully make the transition from childhood to adulthood, too large a percentage do not and are not provided with adequate opportunities and support. Different portraits of adolescents emerge depending on the particular set of adolescents being described.
- Contexts, the settings in which development occurs, play important roles in adolescent development. These contexts include families, peers, schools, and culture.
- Social policy is a national government's course of action designed to influence the welfare of its citizens. The U.S. social policy on adolescents needs revision to provide more services for youth.
- Some experts argue that adolescents as an age group have been underserved by the government and that a generational inequity has evolved with a much greater percentage of government support going to older adults.

So far in this chapter we have examined the history of interest in adolescence and today's adolescents. Next, we will explore the nature of development.

THE NATURE OF DEVELOPMENT

Each of us develops in certain ways like all other individuals, like some other individuals, and like no other individuals. Most of the time, our attention focuses on our individual uniqueness, but researchers who study development are drawn to our shared as well as our unique characteristics. As humans, each of us travels some common paths. Each of us—Leonardo da Vinci, Joan of Arc, George Washington, Martin Luther King, Jr., you, and I—walked at about the age of 1, talked at about the age of 2, engaged in fantasy play as a young child, and became more independent as a youth.

What do we mean when we speak of an individual's development? **Development** *is the pattern of change that begins at conception and continues through the life span. Most development involves growth, although it also includes decay (as in death and dying).* The pattern of movement is complex because it is the product of several processes.

Processes and Periods

Adolescent development is determined by biological, cognitive, and socioemotional processes. Development also is often described in terms of periods.

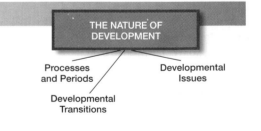

development
The pattern of change that begins at conception and continues through the life span. Most development involves growth, although it also includes decay (as in death and dying).

■ THINKING CRITICALLY

The Importance of Asking Questions— Exploring Your Own Development as an Adolescent

Asking questions reflects our active curiosity. Children— especially young children—are remarkable for their ability to ask questions. When my granddaughter Jordan was 4 years old, one of her favorite words was "Why?" As strong as question-asking is early in our lives, many of us ask far fewer questions as adults.

Asking questions can help us engage in critical thinking about adolescent development, including our own development as adolescents. As you go through this course, you might want to ask yourself questions about how you experienced a particular aspect of development. For example, consider your experiences in your family as you were growing up. Questions you could pose to yourself might include these: "How did my parents bring me up? How did the way they reared me influence what I'm like today? How did my relationship with my brothers or sisters affect my development?" Consider also questions like these about your experiences with peers and at school: "Did I have many close friends while I was growing up? How much time did I spend with my peers and friends at various points in childhood and adolescence compared with the time I spent with my parents? What were my schools like? How good were my teachers? How did the schools and teachers affect my achievement orientation today?"

Be curious. Ask questions. Ask your friends or classmates about their experiences as they were growing up and compare them with yours.

nature-nurture issue
Involves the debate about whether development is primarily influenced by nature or nurture. Nature refers to an organism's biological inheritance, nurture to its environmental experiences.

reaching adulthood involves more than just being a specific chronological age.

In sum, at some point in the late teens through the early twenties, individuals reach adulthood. In becoming an adult, they accept responsibility for themselves, become capable of making independent decisions, and gain financial independence (Arnett, 2000).

What we have said so far about the determinants of adult status mainly addresses individuals in industrialized societies, especially Americans. Are the criteria for adulthood the same in developing countries as they are in the United States? In developing countries, marriage is often a more significant marker for entry into adulthood and this usually occurs much earlier (Arnett, 2000; Davis & Davis, 1989).

So far in our coverage of the nature of development, we have focused on processes and periods in development, as well as developmental transitions. Next, we will explore some important issues in development.

Developmental Issues

A number of issues are raised in the study of adolescent development. The major issues include these: Is development due more to nature (heredity) or more to nurture (environment)? Is development more continuous and smooth or more discontinuous and stagelike? Is development due more to early experience or more to later experience?

Nature and Nurture The **nature-nurture issue** *involves the debate about whether development is primarily influenced by nature or nurture. Nature refers to an organism's biological inheritance, nurture to its environmental experiences.* "Nature" proponents claim that the most important influence on development is biological inheritance. "Nurture" proponents claim that environmental experiences are the most important influence.

According to the nature advocates, just as a sunflower grows in an orderly way— unless flattened by an unfriendly environment—so does the human grow in an orderly way. The range of environments can be vast, but the nature approach argues that the genetic blueprint produces commonalities in growth and development. We walk before we talk, speak one word before two words, grow rapidly in infancy and less so in early childhood, experience a rush of sexual hormones in puberty, reach the peak of our physical strength in late adolescence and early adulthood, and then physically decline. The nature proponents acknowledge that extreme environments—those that are psychologically barren or hostile—can depress development. However, they believe that basic growth tendencies are genetically wired into humans.

By contrast, other psychologists emphasize the importance of nurture, or environmental experiences, in development. Experiences run the gamut from the individual's biological environment—nutrition, medical care, drugs, and physical accidents—to the social environment—family, peers, schools, community, media, and culture.

Some adolescent development researchers believe that, historically, too much emphasis has been placed on the biological changes of puberty as determinants of adolescent psychological development (Montemayor & Flannery, 1991). They recognize that biological change is an important dimension of the transition from childhood to adolescence, one that is found in all primate species and in all cultures throughout the world. However, they believe that social contexts (nurture) play important roles in adolescent psychological development as well, roles that until recently have not been given adequate attention.

■ FIGU
Biological,

Changes in
socioemotid
adolescent

biological
Physical cha

cognitive
Changes in
intelligence

socioemo
Changes in
people, em
contexts.

prenatal
The time fr

infancy
The develd
to 18 or 24

early chi
The develd
of infancy
called the

middle a
The devel
6 to abou
called the

Continuity and Discontinuity   Think about your development for a moment. Was your growth into the person you are today a gradual growth, like the slow, cumulative growth of a seedling into a giant oak, or did you experience sudden, distinct changes in your growth, like the way a caterpillar changes into a butterfly (see figure 1.4)? For the most part, developmentalists who emphasize experience have described development as a gradual, continuous process; those who emphasize nature have described development as a series of distinct stages.

The **continuity-discontinuity issue** *focuses on the extent to which development involves gradual, cumulative change (continuity) or distinct stages (discontinuity).* In terms of continuity, a child's first word, while seemingly an abrupt, discontinuous event, is actually the result of weeks and months of growth and practice. Puberty, while also seemingly an abrupt, discontinuous occurrence, is actually a gradual process occurring over several years.

In terms of discontinuity, each person is described as passing through a sequence of stages in which change is qualitatively, rather than quantitatively, different. As the oak moves from seedling to giant tree, it becomes *more* oak—its development is continuous. As a caterpillar changes into a butterfly, it does not become more caterpillar; it becomes a *different kind* of organism—its development is discontinuous. For example, at some point a child moves from not being able to think abstractly about the world to being able to. This is a qualitative, discontinuous change in development, not a quantitative, continuous change.

Early and Later Experience   Another important developmental topic is the **early-later experience issue,** *which focuses on the degree to which early experiences (especially early in childhood) or later experiences are the key determinants of development.* That is, if infants or young children experience negative, stressful circumstances in their lives, can those experiences be overcome by later, more positive experiences in adolescence? Or are the early experiences so critical, possibly because they are the infant's first, prototypical experiences, that they cannot be overridden by a later, more enriched environment in childhood or adolescence?

The early-later experience issue has a long history and continues to be hotly debated among developmentalists. Some believe that unless infants experience warm, nurturant caregiving in the first year or so of life, their development will never be optimal (Bowlby, 1989; Main, 2000; Sroufe, 1996). Plato was sure that infants who were rocked frequently became better athletes. Nineteenth-century New England ministers told parents in Sunday sermons that the way they handled their infants would determine their children's future character. The emphasis on the importance of early experience rests on the belief that each life is an unbroken trail on which a psychological quality can be traced back to its origin.

The early-experience doctrine contrasts with the later-experience view that, rather than achieving statuelike permanence after change in infancy, our development continues to be like the ebb and flow of a river. The later-experience advocates argue that children and adolescents are malleable throughout development and that later sensitive caregiving is just as important as earlier sensitive caregiving. A number of life-span developmentalists, who focus on the entire life span rather than only on child development, stress that too little attention has been given to later experiences in development (Baltes, 1987, 2000). They accept that early experiences are important contributors to development, but no more important than later experiences. Jerome Kagan (1992) points out that even children who show the qualities of an inhibited temperament, which is linked to heredity, have the capacity to change their behavior. In his research, almost one-third of a group of children who had an inhibited temperament at 2 years of age were not unusually shy or fearful when they were 4 years of age (Kagan, Snidmar, & Arcus, 1995).

People in Western cultures, especially those steeped in the Freudian belief that the key experiences in development are children's relationships with their parents in the first five years of life, have tended to support the idea that early experiences are more important than later experiences (Chan, 1963). In contrast, the majority of people in

continuity-discontinuity issue

The issue regarding whether development involves gradual, cumulative change (continuity) or distinct stages (discontinuity).

early-later experience issue

This issue focuses on the degree to which early experiences (especially early in childhood) or later experiences are the key determinants of development.

■ **FIGURE 1.4**
Continuity and Discontinuity in Development

Is human development like a seedling gradually growing into a giant oak? Or is it more like a caterpillar suddenly becoming a butterfly?

the world do not share this belief. For example, people in many Asian countries believe that experiences occurring after about 6 to 7 years of age are more important aspects of development than earlier experiences are. This stance stems from the long-standing belief in Eastern cultures that children's reasoning skills begin to develop in important ways in the middle childhood years.

Continuity and Discontinuity
http://www.mhhe.com/santrocka9

Evaluating the Developmental Issues As we consider further these three salient developmental issues—nature and nurture, continuity and discontinuity, and early and later experience—it is important to realize that most developmentalists recognize that it is unwise to take an extreme position on these issues. Development is not all nature or all nurture, not all continuity or discontinuity, and not all early experience or all later experience. Nature and nurture, continuity and discontinuity, and early and later experience all affect our development through the human life span. For example, in considering the nature-nurture issue, the key to development is the interaction of nature and nurture rather than either factor alone (Loehlin, 1995, 2000). An individual's cognitive development, for instance, is the result of heredity-environment interaction, not heredity or environment alone. Much more about the role of heredity-environment interaction appears in chapter 3.

Consider also the behavior of adolescent males and females (Feldman & Elliott, 1990). Nature factors continue to influence differences between adolescent boys and girls in such areas as height, weight, and age at pubertal onset. On the average, girls are shorter and lighter than boys and enter puberty earlier. However, some previously well-established differences between adolescent females and males are diminishing, suggesting an important role for nurture. For example, adolescent females are pursuing careers in math and science in far greater numbers than in the past, and are seeking autonomy in a much stronger fashion. Unfortunately, adolescent females also are increasing their use of drugs and cigarette smoking compared to adolescent females in earlier eras. The shifting patterns of gender similarities and differences underscore the belief that simplistic explanations based only on biological or only on environmental causes are unwise.

Although most developmentalists do not take extreme positions on the developmental issues we have discussed, this consensus has not meant the absence of spirited debate about how strongly development is determined by these factors. Continuing with our example of the behavior of female and male adolescents, are girls less likely to do well in math because of their "feminine" nature or because of society's masculine bias? Consider also adolescents who, as children, experienced poverty, parental neglect, and poor schooling. Could enriched experiences in adolescence overcome the "deficits" they encountered earlier in development? The answers developmentalists give to such questions reflect their stance on the issues of nature and nurture, continuity and discontinuity, and early and later experiences. The answers also influence public policy about adolescents and how each of us lives through the human life span.

At this point we have examined many ideas about the nature of development. This review should help you to reach your learning goals related to this topic.

☐ FOR YOUR REVIEW

Learning Goal 4
Define development and describe processes and periods in development

- Development is the pattern of movement or change that occurs throughout the life span.
- Biological processes involve physical changes in the individual's body. Cognitive processes consist of changes in thinking and intelligence. Socioemotional changes focus on changes in relationships with people, in emotion, in personality, and in social contexts.
- Development is commonly divided into these periods: prenatal, infancy, early childhood, middle and late childhood, adolescence, early adulthood, middle adulthood, and late adulthood. Adolescence is the developmental period of transition between childhood and adulthood that involves biological, cognitive, and

socioemotional changes. In most cultures, adolescence begins at approximately 10 to 13 years of age and ends at about 18 to 22 years of age. Developmentalists increasingly distinguish between early adolescence and late adolescence.

Learning Goal 5
Discuss transitions and issues in development

- Two important transitions in development are from childhood to adolescence and adolescence to adulthood. In the transition from childhood to adolescence, pubertal change is prominent, although cognitive and socioemotional changes occur as well. It sometimes has been said that adolescence begins in biology and ends in culture. The concepts of youth and emerging adulthood have been proposed to describe the transition from adolescence to adulthood. Among the criteria for determining adulthood are self-responsibility, independent decision making, and economic independence.
- Three important issues in development are (1) the nature-nurture issue (Is development mainly due to heredity [nature] or environment [nurture]?), (2) the continuity-discontinuity issue (Is development more gradual, cumulative [continuity] or more abrupt and sequential [discontinuity]?), (3) the early-later experience issue (Is development due more to early experiences, especially in infancy and early childhood, or to later [more recent and current] experiences)? Most developmentalists do not take extreme positions on these issues although they are extensively debated.

So far in this chapter we have focused on the history of interest in adolescence, today's adolescents, and the nature of development. Next, we will explore what matters in adolescence, which will provide you with a menu of the main topics in the remainder of the book.

UNDERSTANDING ADOLESCENCE: WHAT MATTERS?

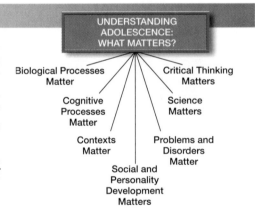

In adolescence, what matters? What is involved in understanding adolescence? What is at work when adolescents make a healthy journey from childhood to adulthood? What goes wrong when they fall off course and are not on track to reach their full potential? In thinking about what really matters in adolescence, let's examine some of the main themes of this book and explore contemporary thinking about these themes. For an understanding of adolescence, these things matter: biological processes, cognitive processes, contexts, social and personality development, problems and disorders, science, and critical thinking. Studying these aspects of adolescence scientifically and thinking critically about them also can substantially improve our understanding of adolescent development.

Biological Processes Matter

Earlier in the chapter, we examined the nature-nurture issue. Recall that this issue raises the question of how strongly adolescents' biological (nature) makeup influences their behavior and development.

Controversy swirls about this topic. In the early views of Hall and Freud, biology was dominant. Today we continue to believe that biology plays a key role in the adolescent's development, although current theorizing often seeks to determine how heredity and environment work together in producing adolescent development.

A current trend is to examine how evolution might have played a role in determining the nature of adolescent development (Buss, 1998, 2000; Buss & others, 2001; Csikszentmihalyi & Schmidt, 1998). The field of evolutionary psychology, the most recent major theoretical view in psychology, seeks to examine how adaptation, reproduction, and "survival of the fittest" can help to explain behavior and development. We especially evaluate evolution's role in chapter 3, "Puberty, Health, and Biological Foundations," and chapter 10, "Gender."

There also is considerable interest today in studying how heredity is involved in behavior and development (Lewis, 2002; Wahlsten, 2000). Scientists are making considerable progress in charting the role of genes in various diseases and disorders. We will explore heredity more extensively in chapter 3.

The health of today's adolescents is a special concern. Far too many adolescents engage in health-compromising behaviors, such as smoking, excessive drinking, and risk-taking adventures. We will examine adolescents' health throughout the book, but especially focus on it in chapter 3.

Cognitive Processes Matter

How important is the adolescent's mind in what she or he does? Adolescents not only are biological beings, they are mental beings. Considerable changes take place in cognition during adolescence (Byrnes, 2001; Kuhn, 2000). Adolescents have more sophisticated thinking skills than children, although there are considerable individual variations from one adolescent to another. Advances in adolescent thinking not only help them solve difficult academic problems in areas such as mathematics but change the way they examine their social lives as well. Increasingly, developmentalists are interested in learning more about adolescents' decision making and how it can be improved to help them adapt more competently. They also are motivated to find out ways to help adolescents think more critically and deeply about problems and issues. Another contemporary interest is determining what the components of intelligence are and creating educational programs that address these components (Torff, 1999). We will study cognitive processes in much greater detail in chapter 4, "Cognitive Development."

Contexts Matter

Earlier we described the increasing trend of examining contexts or settings to better understand adolescent development. Especially important contexts in adolescents' lives

Why do contexts matter in understanding adolescent development?

are their family, peer, school, and cultural contexts (Eccles, 2002; Harkness & Super, 2002). Families have a powerful influence on adolescent development, and today large numbers of researchers are charting many aspects of family life, such as conflict, attachment, and divorce, to determine how they affect adolescent outcomes (Buchanan, 2000; Dunn & others, 2001; Hetherington & Stanley-Hagan, 2002; Rutter, 2002). We will explore these and many other aspects of families in chapter 5.

Like families, peers play powerful roles in adolescents' lives. Researchers are studying how peer status (such as being isolated, rejected, or popular), friends, cliques, and dating and romantic relationships are involved in the adolescent's development (Brown, 2002). We will examine these and other aspects of peer relations in chapter 6.

Schools are another important context in adolescents' lives (Eccles & Wigfield, 2000; Pierce & Kurtz-Costes, 2001; Sadker & Sadker, 2003). Currently there is a great deal of concern about the quality of secondary education for adolescents. There also is controversy about the best way to teach adolescents (Ferrari, 2002). A current trend is for teachers to act as guides in providing adolescents with learning opportunities in which they can actively construct their understanding of a topic or issue (Cobb, 2000; Santrock, 2001). We will examine such concerns and trends in chapter 7, "Schools."

The Search Institute
http://www.mhhe.com/santrocka9

The culture in which adolescents live is another important context in their development (Greenfield, 2000, 2002; Triandis, 2000). Many researchers are comparing how adolescents in the United States are similar to or different from adolescents in other countries. And there is a special concern that far too many American adolescents are growing up in poverty (Fuligni & Yoshikawa, 2003; Magnuson & Duncan, 2002; McLoyd, 2000). In recent years, there also has been a considerable increase in studying the role of ethnicity in adolescent development (Cushner, McClelland, & Safford, 2003; Wong & Rowley, 2001). Another important aspect of culture today is technology (Calvert, 1999; Murray, 2000). We will examine these and many other aspects of culture in chapter 8, "Culture."

Social and Personality Development Matters

Other important aspects of adolescents' lives involve their social and personality development, such as their self and identity, gender, sexuality, moral development, and achievement. A key aspect of adolescents' development, especially for older adolescents, is their search for identity (Adams, Abraham, & Markstrom, 2000; Comas-Díaz, 2001). Researchers are interested in determining the contextual and developmental factors that promote healthy or unhealthy identity development (Rodriquez & Quinlan, 2002). We will examine these and many other aspects of the self and identity in chapter 9.

Gender is a pervasive aspect of adolescent development. Researchers are motivated to find out how contexts influence gender development, the role that sexuality plays in gender development during adolescence, how adolescence might be a critical juncture in gender development (especially for girls), gender similarities and differences, and adolescent male and female issues (Bumpas, Crouder, & McHale, 2001; Eagly, 2000). We will examine these and many other aspects of gender in chapter 10.

Sexuality has long been described as a key dimension of adolescent development. In adolescence, boys and girls

◻ CAREERS IN ADOLESCENT DEVELOPMENT

Luis Vargas
Child Clinical Psychologist

Luis Vargas is Director of the Clinical Child Psychology Internship Program and a professor in the Department of Psychiatry at the University of New Mexico Health Sciences Center. He also is Director of Psychology at the University of New Mexico Children's Psychiatric Hospital.

Luis got an undergraduate degree is psychology from St. Edwards University in Texas, a master's degree in psychology from Trinity University in Texas, and his Ph.D. in clinical psychology from the University of Nebraska–Lincoln.

His main interests are cultural issues and the assessment and treatment of children, adolescents, and families. He is motivated to find better ways to provide culturally responsive mental health services. One of his special interests is the treatment of Latino youth for delinquency and substance abuse. He recently co-authored (with Joan Koss-Chioino) *Working with Latino Youth* (Koss-Chioino & Vargas, 1999), which spells out effective strategies for improving the lives of at-risk Latino youth.

Luis Vargas, counseling an adolescent girl.

CHAPTER MAP

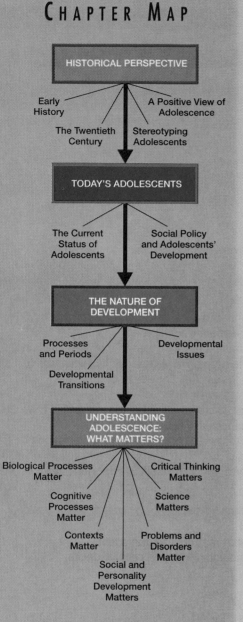

REACH YOUR LEARNING GOALS

At the beginning of the chapter, we stated six learning goals and encouraged you to review material related to these goals at four points in the chapter. This is a good time to return to these reviews and use them to guide your study and help you to reach your learning goals.

Page 13

Learning Goal 1   Explain the historical perspective on adolescence

Learning Goal 2   Discuss stereotyping adolescents and a positive view of adolescence

Page 17

Learning Goal 3   Evaluate today's adolescents

Page 24

Learning Goal 4   Define development and describe processes and periods in development

Learning Goal 5   Discuss transitions and issues in development

Page 29

Learning Goal 6   Know what matters in understanding adolescent development

KEY TERMS

storm-and-stress view 7
inventionist view 8
stereotype 11
adolescent generalization gap 12
contexts 15
social policy 15
generational inequity 16
development 17
biological processes 18
cognitive processes 18
socioemotional processes 18
prenatal period 18
infancy 18

early childhood 18
middle and late childhood 18
adolescence 19
early adolescence 19
late adolescence 19
early adulthood 19
middle adulthood 19
late adulthood 20
youth 21
nature-nurture issue 22
continuity-discontinuity issue 23
early-later experience issue 23

KEY PEOPLE

G. Stanley Hall 7
Margaret Mead 7
Leta Hollingworth 10
Kenneth and Mamie Clark 11
George Sanchez 11

Daniel Offer 12
Marian Wright Edelman 16
Bernice Neugarten 16
Reed Larson 17
Kenneth Kenniston 21

RESOURCES FOR IMPROVING THE LIVES OF ADOLESCENTS

Children's Defense Fund

> 25 E Street, NW
> Washington, DC 20001
> 202–628–8787

The Children's Defense Fund, headed by Marian Wright Edelman, exists to provide a strong and effective voice for children and adolescents who cannot vote, lobby, or speak for themselves.

Great Transitions

> (1995) by the Carnegie Council on Adolescent Development
> New York: Carnegie Corporation

This report by the Carnegie Council on Adolescent Development covers a wide range of topics, including reengaging families with their adolescents, educating adolescents, promoting adolescent health, strengthening communities, and redirecting the pervasive power of the media.

Search Institute

> Thresher Square West
> 700 South Third Street, Suite 210
> Minneapolis, MN 55415
> 612–376–8955

The Search Institute has available a large number of resources for improving the lives of adolescents. The brochures and books available address school improvement, adolescent literacy, parent education, program planning, and adolescent health, and include resource lists. A free quarterly newsletter is available.

Securing the Future

> (2000) by Sheldon Danziger and Jane Waldfogel (Eds.)
> New York: Russell Sage Foundation

This book includes articles from scholars in a number of different disciplines (such as economics, psychology, and sociology) to explore effective ways to improve social policy for children and youth.

TAKING IT TO THE NET

1. About a century ago, G. S. Hall wrote that adolescence was an especially stressful period of time, a stereotype that continues today as evidenced in media representations of adolescence as well as in literary works. Adolescents often are portrayed as interested only in drugs, engaging in promiscuous and risky sex, and as alcohol abusers. *What is the evidence about the percentages of adolescents in these categories that you can cite to refute the stereotype?*

2. You are a student teacher for Ms. Masterson, who teaches tenth-grade English. She is trying to capitalize on the vast store of information on the Web by helping students integrate Web resources into their papers. Knowing that it is important to think critically when gleaning information from the Web, Ms. Masterson asks you

http://www.mhhe.com/santrocka9

to help her formulate guidelines students can use to evaluate websites. *What clues will you suggest Ms. Masterson provide her classes to help the students evaluate website information?*

3. Our version of adolescence evolved because of a variety of social reforms, including child labor laws that limit adolescent involvement in the workforce. When you took your first job, you likely were limited in the kind of work you could do because of these laws. *Do you think they are fair? How would you argue for a more individual case-by-case application of these laws?*

Connect to *http://www.mhhe.com/santrocka9* to research the answers and complete these exercises. In some cases, you'll also find further instructions on this site.

CAREERS IN ADOLESCENT DEVELOPMENT

Some of you may be quite sure about what you plan to make your life's work. Others of you may not have decided on a major yet and are uncertain about which career path you want to follow. Each of us wants to find a rewarding career and enjoy the work we do. The field of adolescent development offers an amazing breadth of career options that can provide extremely satisfying work.

If you decide to pursue a career in adolescent development, what career options are available to you? There are many. College and university professors teach courses in many different areas of adolescent development, education, family development, and medicine. Teachers impart knowledge, understanding, and skills to adolescents. Counselors, clinical psychologists, and physicians help adolescents to cope more effectively with their lives and well-being. Various professionals work with families with adolescents to improve the quality of family functioning.

Although an advanced degree is not absolutely necessary in some areas of adolescent development, you usually can expand your opportunities (and income) considerably by obtaining a graduate degree. Many careers in adolescent development pay reasonably well. For example, psychologists earn well above the median salary in the United States. Also, by working in the field of adolescent development you can guide youth in improving their lives, understand yourself and others better, possibly advance the state of knowledge in the field, and have an enjoyable time while you are doing these things.

If you are considering a career in adolescent development, as you go through this term, try to spend some time with adolescents of different ages. Observe their behavior. Talk with them about their lives. Think about whether you would like to work with youth in your life's work.

Another important aspect of exploring careers is to talk with people who work in various jobs. For example, if you have some interest in becoming a school counselor, call a school, ask to speak with a counselor, and set up an appointment to discuss the counselor's career and work.

Something else that should benefit you is to work in one or more jobs related to your career interests while you are in college. Many colleges and universities have internships or work experiences for students who major in such fields as development. In some instances, these opportunities are for course credit or pay; in others, they are strictly on a volunteer basis. Take advantage of these opportunities. They can provide you with valuable experiences to help you decide if this is the right career area for you and they can help you get into graduate school, if you decide you want to go.

In the following sections, we will profile a number of careers in three areas: education/research; clinical/counseling/medical; and families/relationships. These are not the only career options in the field of adolescent development, but they should provide you with an idea of the range of opportunities available and information about some of the main career avenues you might pursue. In profiling these careers, we will address the amount of education required, the nature of the training, and a description of the work.

EDUCATION/RESEARCH

There are numerous career opportunities in adolescent development that involve education and/or research. These range from being a college professor to being a school psychologist.

regard to adolescen
age group, such as

Psychiatrist

Psychiatrists obtai
school takes appro
four years. Unlike
minister drugs to

Like clinical p
and/or adolescent
teaching and resea
ministering drugs
chiatrists also ma

Psychiatric Nur

Two to five years
psychiatric nurse
nursing care, psy
tings. Psychiatri
and work close
specialist in ad
nursing.

Counseling P

Counseling psy
gists, although
Counseling psy
must go throu
to the designat
clinical psycho
instances, cou
severe mental

School Cour

School couns
veloping acad
dents cope v
small groups
school admi
selors usuall

High sc
ments for c
ate vocation

Career Co

Career cou
and guide t
university.
logical test
that fit th
fessional r

College/University Professor

Courses in adolescent development are taught in different programs and schools in college and universities, including psychology, education, child and family studies, social work, and medicine. A Ph.D. or master's degree almost always is required to teach in some area of adolescent development in a college or university. Obtaining a doctoral degree usually takes four to six years of graduate work. A master's degree requires approximately two years of graduate work. The professorial job might be at a research university with one or more master's or Ph.D. programs in development, at a four-year college with no graduate programs, or at a community college.

The training involves taking graduate courses, learning to conduct research, and attending and presenting papers at professional meetings. Many graduate students work as teaching or research assistants for professors in an apprenticeship relationship that helps them to become competent teachers and researchers. The work that college professors do includes teaching courses either at the undergraduate or graduate level (or both), conducting research in a specific area, advising students and/or directing their research, and serving on college or university committees. Some college instructors do not conduct research as part of their job but instead focus mainly on teaching. In many instances, research is most likely to be part of the job description at universities with master's and Ph.D. programs.

If you are interested in becoming a college or university professor, you might want to make an appointment with your instructor in this class on adolescent development to learn more about the profession and what his or her career/work is like.

Researcher

Some individuals in the field of adolescent development work in research positions. In most instances, they will have either a master's or Ph.D. in some area of adolescent development. The researchers might work at a university, in some cases in a university professor's research program, in government at such agencies as the National Institute of Mental Health, or in private industry. Individuals who have full-time research positions in development generate innovative research ideas, plan studies, carry out the research by collecting data, analyze the data, and then interpret it. Then, they will usually attempt to publish the research in a scientific journal. A researcher often works in a collaborative manner with other researchers on a project and may present the research at scientific meetings, where she or he also learns about other research. One researcher might spend much of his or her time in a laboratory while another researcher might work out in the field, such as in schools, hospitals, and so on.

Secondary School Teacher

Becoming a secondary school teacher requires a minimum of an undergraduate degree. The training involves taking a wide range of courses with a major or concentration in education as well as completing a supervised practice-teaching internship. The work of a secondary school teacher involves teaching in one or more subject areas, preparing the curriculum, giving tests, assigning grades, monitoring students' progress, conducting parent-teacher conferences, and attending in-service workshops.

Exceptional Children (Special Education) Teacher

Becoming a teacher of exceptional children requires a minimum of an undergraduate degree. The training consists of taking a wide range of courses in education and a concentration of courses in educating children with disabilities or children who are gifted. The work of a teacher of exceptional children involves spending concentrated time with individual children who have a disability or are gifted. Among the children a teacher of exceptional children might work with are children with learning disabilities, ADHD (attention deficit hyperactivity disorder), mental retardation, or a physical disability

CHAPTER
2

CHAPTER MAP

THEORIES OF ADOLESCENT
DEVELOPMENT

Psychoanalytic
Theories

Cognitive
Theories

Behavioral and
Social Cognitive
Theories

An Eclectic
Theoretical
Orientation

Ecological,
Contextual
Theory

EXPLORING RESEARCH

Why Research
on Adolescent
Development
Is Important

The Field of Adolescent
Development Research

The Scientific
Research Approach

RESEARCH METHODS

Participants

Measures

Correlational
and Experimental
Strategies

Time Span
of Research

Multiple Measures,
Sources, and Contexts

RESEARCH
CHALLENGES

Ethics

Gender

Ethnicity
and Culture

Being a Wise
Consumer of
Information
About
Adolescent
Development

THE SCIENCE OF ADOLESCENT DEVELOPMENT

◼ THE YOUTHS OF ERIKSON AND PIAGET

Two important developmental theorists, whose views are described later in this chapter, are Erik Erikson and Jean Piaget. Let's examine a portion of their lives as they were growing up, to discover how their experiences might have contributed to the theories they developed.

Erik Homberger Erikson (1902–1994) was born near Frankfurt, Germany, to Danish parents. Before Erik was born, his parents separated, and his mother left Denmark to live in Germany. At age 3, Erik became ill, and his mother took him to see a pediatrician named Homberger. Young Erik's mother fell in love with the pediatrician, married him, and named Erik after his new stepfather.

Erik attended primary school from age 6 to 10 and then the *gymnasium* (high school) from ages 11 to 18. He studied art and a number of languages rather than science courses such as biology and chemistry. Erik did not like formal schooling, and this was reflected in his grades. Rather than go to college, at age 18 the adolescent Erikson wandered around Europe, keeping a diary of his experiences. After a year of travel through Europe, he returned to Germany and enrolled in an art school, became dissatisfied, and enrolled in another.

Jean Piaget (1896–1980) was born in Neuchâtel, Switzerland. Jean's father was an intellectual who taught young Jean to think systematically. Jean's mother was also very bright. His father had an air of detachment from his mother, whom Piaget described as prone to frequent neurotic outbursts.

At the age of 22, Piaget went to work in the psychology laboratory at the University of Zurich. There he was exposed to the insights of Alfred Binet, who developed the first intelligence test. By the time Piaget was 25, his experience in varied disciplines had helped him to see important links between philosophy, psychology, and biology.

These excerpts from Erikson's and Piaget's lives illustrate how personal experiences might influence a theorist's direction. Erikson's wanderings and search for self contributed to his theory of identity development, and Piaget's intellectual experiences with his parents and schooling contributed to his emphasis on cognitive development.

> *Truth is arrived at by the painstaking process of eliminating the untrue.*
> —Arthur Conan Doyle
> *British Physician and Detective-Story Writer, 20th Century*

SOME INDIVIDUALS HAVE DIFFICULTY THINKING OF adolescent development as being a science in the same way that physics, chemistry, and biology are sciences. Can a discipline that studies pubertal change, parent-adolescent relationships, and adolescent thinking be equated with disciplines that investigate how gravity works and the molecular structure of compounds? Science is not defined by *what* it investigates but by *how* it investigates. Whether you are studying photosynthesis, butterflies, Saturn's moons, or adolescent development, it is the way you study that makes the approach scientific or not. By the time you have completed this chapter you should be able to reach these learning goals:

1. Discuss psychoanalytic theories

2. Know about cognitive theories

3. Explain behavioral and social cognitive theories

4. Understand ecological, contextual theory and an eclectic theoretical orientation

5. Explore research

6. Describe how participants are selected and measures

7. Understand the distinction between correlational and experimental strategies and know about the time span of research

8. Elaborate on research challenges

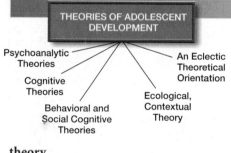

theory

An interrelated, coherent set of ideas that helps to explain and make predictions.

psychoanalytic theory

Describes development as primarily unconscious and heavily colored by emotion. Behavior is merely a surface characteristic. It is important to analyze the symbolic meanings of behavior. Early experiences are important in development.

THEORIES OF ADOLESCENT DEVELOPMENT

As researchers formulate a problem to study, they often draw on *theories*. A **theory** *is an interrelated, coherent set of ideas that helps to explain and make predictions.* We will briefly explore four major kinds of theories of adolescent development: psychoanalytic, cognitive, behavioral and social learning, and ecological. The diversity of theories makes understanding adolescent development a challenging undertaking. Just when one theory appears to correctly explain adolescent development, another theory crops up and makes you rethink your earlier conclusion. Remember that adolescent development is complex and multifaceted. Although no single theory has been able to account for all aspects of adolescent development, each theory has contributed an important piece to the puzzle. Although the theories sometimes disagree about certain aspects of adolescent development, much of their information is *complementary* rather than contradictory. Together, the various theories let us see the total landscape of adolescent development in all its richness.

Psychoanalytic Theories

Psychoanalytic theory *describes development as primarily unconscious—that is, beyond awareness—and is heavily colored by emotion. Psychoanalytic theorists believe that behavior is merely a surface characteristic and that, to truly understand development, we have to analyze the symbolic meanings of behavior and the deep inner workings of the mind. Psychoanalytic theorists also stress that early experiences with parents extensively shape our development.* These characteristics are highlighted in the main psychoanalytic theory, that of Sigmund Freud.

Freud's Theory   Freud (1856–1939) developed his ideas about psychoanalytic theory from work with mental patients. A medical doctor who specialized in neurology, he spent most of his years in Vienna, though he moved to London near the end of his career because of the Nazis' anti-Semitism.

Personality Structure Freud (1917) believed that personality has three structures: the id, the ego, and the superego. The *id* is the Freudian structure of personality that consists of instincts, which are an individual's reservoir of psychic energy. In Freud's view, the id is totally unconscious; it has no contact with reality. As children experience the demands and constraints of reality, a new structure of personality emerges—the *ego*, the Freudian structure of personality that deals with the demands of reality. The ego is called the "executive branch" of personality because it makes rational decisions. The id and the ego have no morality—they do not take into account whether something is right or wrong. The *superego* is the Freudian structure of personality that is the moral branch of personality. The superego takes into account whether something is right or wrong. Think of the superego as what we often refer to as our "conscience." You probably are beginning to sense that both the id and the superego make life rough for the ego. Your ego might say, "I will have sex only occasionally and be sure to take the proper precautions because I don't want a child to interfere with the development of my career." However, your id is saying, "I want to be satisfied; sex is pleasurable." Your superego is at work too: "I feel guilty about having sex."

Remember that Freud considered personality to be like an iceberg. Most of personality exists below our level of awareness, just as the massive part of an iceberg is beneath the surface of the water. Figure 2.1 illustrates this analogy.

Freud believed that adolescents' lives are filled with tension and conflict. To reduce this tension, adolescents keep information locked in their unconscious mind, said Freud. He believed that even trivial behaviors have special significance when the unconscious forces behind them are revealed. A twitch, a doodle, a joke, a smile—each might have an unconscious reason for appearing, according to Freud. For example, 17-year-old Barbara is kissing and hugging Tom. She says, "Oh, *Jeff*, I love you so much." Tom pushes her away and says, "Why did you call me Jeff? I thought you didn't think about him anymore. We need to have a talk!" You probably can remember times when these *Freudian slips* came out in your own behavior.

Defense Mechanisms The ego resolves conflict between its demands for reality, the wishes of the id, and the constraints of the superego by using *defense mechanisms*. They are unconscious methods the ego uses to distort reality and protect itself from anxiety. In Freud's view, the conflicting demands of the personality structures produce anxiety. For example, when the ego blocks the id's pleasurable pursuits, we feel anxiety. This diffuse, distressed state develops when the ego senses that the id is going to cause harm to the individual. The anxiety alerts the ego to resolve the conflict by means of defense mechanisms.

Repression is the most powerful and pervasive defense mechanism, according to Freud. It pushes unacceptable id impulses out of awareness and back into the unconscious mind. Repression is the foundation from which all other defense mechanisms work; the goal of every defense mechanism is to repress, or push, threatening impulses out of awareness. Freud said that our early childhood experiences, many of which he believed are sexually laden, are too threatening and stressful for us to deal with consciously, and that we reduce the anxiety of this conflict through repression.

Both Peter Blos (1989), a British psychoanalyst, and Anna Freud (1966), Sigmund Freud's daughter, believe that defense mechanisms provide considerable insight into adolescent development. Blos states that regression during adolescence is actually not defensive at all, but rather an integral, normal, inevitable, and universal aspect of puberty. The nature of regression may vary from one adolescent to the next. It may involve childhood autonomy,

Sigmund Freud, the pioneering architect of psychoanalytic theory. *How did Freud believe each individual's personality is organized?*

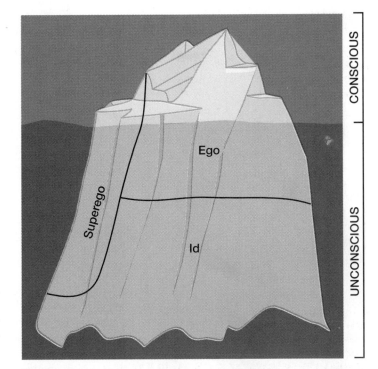

◻ FIGURE 2.1
The Conscious and Unconscious Mind: The Iceberg Analogy

The analogy of the conscious and unconscious mind to an iceberg is often used to illustrate how much of the mind is unconscious in Freud's theory. The conscious mind is the part of the iceberg above water, the unconscious mind the part below water. Notice that the id is totally unconscious, while the ego and superego can operate at either the conscious or unconscious level.

Anna Freud, Sigmund Freud's daughter. *How did her view differ from her father's?*

compliance, and cleanliness, or it may involve a sudden return to the passiveness that characterized the adolescent's behavior during childhood.

Anna Freud (1966) developed the idea that defense mechanisms are the key to understanding adolescent adjustment. She believes that the problems of adolescence are not to be unlocked by understanding the id, or instinctual forces, but instead are to be discovered in the existence of "love objects" in the adolescent's past. She argues that the attachment to these love objects, usually parents, is carried forward from the infant years and merely toned down or inhibited during the latency years. During adolescence, these pregenital urges might be reawakened, or, worse, newly acquired genital (adolescent) urges might combine with the urges that developed in early childhood.

Two final points about defense mechanisms are important. First, they are unconscious; adolescents are not aware that they are calling on defense mechanisms to protect their ego and reduce anxiety. Second, when used in moderation or on a temporary basis, defense mechanisms are not necessarily unhealthy. For the most part, though, individuals should not let defense mechanisms dominate their behavior and prevent them from facing the demands of reality.

GENITAL STAGE

LATENCY STAGE

Adolescence and Adulthood

6 Years to Puberty

PHALLIC STAGE

ANAL STAGE

3 to 6 Years

ORAL STAGE

1½ to 3 Years

0 to 1½ Years

■ **FIGURE 2.2**
Freudian Stages

Psychosexual Stages As Freud listened to, probed, and analyzed his patients, he became convinced that their problems were the result of experiences early in life. Freud believed that we go through five stages of psychosexual development, and that at each stage of development we experience pleasure in one part of the body more than in others (see figure 2.2).

The *oral stage* is the first Freudian stage of development, occurring during the first 18 months of life, in which the infant's pleasure centers around the mouth. Chewing, sucking, and biting are the chief sources of pleasure. These actions reduce tension in the infant.

The *anal stage* is the second Freudian stage of development, occurring between 1½ and 3 years of age, in which the child's greatest pleasure involves the anus or the eliminative functions associated with it. In Freud's view, the exercise of anal muscles reduces tension.

The *phallic stage* is the third Freudian stage of development, which occurs between the ages of 3 and 6; its name comes from the Latin word, *phallus,* which means "penis." During the phallic stage, pleasure focuses on the genitals as the child discovers that self-manipulation is enjoyable.

In Freud's view, the phallic stage has a special importance in personality development because it is during this period that the Oedipus complex appears.

This name comes from Greek mythology, in which Oedipus, the son of the King of Thebes, unwittingly kills his father and marries his mother. The *Oedipus complex,* in Freudian theory, is the young child's intense desire to replace the parent of the same sex and enjoy the affections of the opposite-sex parent. Freud's concept of the Oedipus complex has been criticized by some psychoanalysts and writers.

Freud's Theory
Horney's Theory
Erikson's Theory
http://www.mhhe.com/santrocka9

How is the Oedipus complex resolved? At about 5 to 6 years of age, children recognize that their same-sex parent might punish them for their incestuous wishes. To reduce this conflict, the child identifies with the same-sex parent, striving to be like him or her. If the conflict is not resolved, though, the individual can become fixated at the phallic stage.

The *latency stage* is the fourth Freudian stage of development, which occurs between approximately 6 years of age and puberty; the child represses all interest in sexuality and develops social and intellectual skills. This activity channels much of the child's energy into emotionally safe areas and helps the child forget the highly stressful conflicts of the phallic stage.

The *genital stage* is the fifth and final Freudian stage of development, occurring from puberty on. The genital stage is a time of sexual reawakening; the source of sexual pleasure now becomes someone outside of the family. Freud believed that unresolved conflicts with parents reemerge during adolescence. When these are resolved, the individual is capable of developing a mature love relationship and functioning independently as an adult.

Revisions of Freud's Theory   Freud's theory has undergone significant revisions by a number of psychoanalytic theorists (Luborsky, 2000; Westen, 2000). Many contemporary psychoanalytic theorists place less emphasis on sexual instincts and more emphasis on

Karen Horney

Nancy Chodorow

▣ FIGURE 2.3
Feminist-Based Criticisms of Freud's Theory

The first feminist-based criticism of Freud's theory was proposed by psychoanalytic theorist Karen Horney (1967). She developed a model of women with positive feminine qualities and self-evaluation. Her critique of Freud's theory included reference to a male-dominant society and culture. Rectification of the male bias in psychoanalytic theory continues today. For example, Nancy Chodorow (1978, 1989) emphasizes that many more women than men define themselves in terms of their relationships and connections to others. Her feminist revision of psychoanalytic theory also stresses the meaningfulness of emotions for women, as well as the belief that many men use the defense mechanism of denial in self-other connections.

cultural experiences as determinants of an individual's development. Unconscious thought remains a central theme, but most contemporary psychoanalysts believe that conscious thought makes up more of the iceberg than Freud envisioned. Feminist criticisms of Freud's theory have also been made (see figure 2.3 on p. 43). Next, we explore the ideas of an important revisionist of Freud's ideas—Erik Erikson.

Erikson's Theory   Erik Erikson (1902–1994) recognized Freud's contributions but believed that Freud misjudged some

Erikson's Stages	Developmental Period
Integrity versus despair	Late adulthood (60s–)
Generativity versus stagnation	Middle adulthood (40s, 50s)
Intimacy versus isolation	Early adulthood (20s, 30s)
Identity versus identity confusion	Adolescence (10 to 20 years)
Industry versus inferiority	Middle and late childhood (elementary school years, 6 years to puberty)
Initiative versus guilt	Early childhood (preschool years, ages 3 to 5)
Autonomy versus shame and doubt	Infancy (1 to 3 years)
Trust versus mistrust	Infancy (first year)

■ FIGURE 2.4
Erikson's Eight Life-Span Stages

Erikson's theory
He proposed that people go through eight stages of development with each stage consisting of a unique developmental task that confronts individuals with a crisis that must be faced.

important dimensions of human development. For one, Erikson (1950, 1968) said we develop in *psychosocial stages,* in contrast to Freud's *psychosexual stages.* For Freud, the primary motivation for human behavior was sexual in nature, for Erickson it was social and reflected a desire to affiliate with other people. Erickson emphasized developmental change throughout the human life span, whereas Freud argued that our basic personality is shaped in the first five years of life. In **Erikson's theory** *eight stages of development unfold as we go through the life span* (see figure 2.4). *Each stage consists of a unique developmental task that confronts individuals with a crisis that must be faced.* According to Erikson, this crisis is not a catastrophe but a turning point of increased vulnerability and enhanced potential. The more an individual resolves the crises successfully, the healthier that individual's development will be (Hopkins, 2000).

Trust versus mistrust is Erikson's first psychosocial stage, which is experienced in the first year of life. A sense of trust requires a feeling of physical comfort and a minimal amount of fear and apprehension about the future. Trust in infancy sets the stage for a lifelong expectation that the world will be a good and pleasant place to live.

Autonomy versus shame and doubt is Erikson's second stage of development, occurring in late infancy and toddlerhood (ages 1 to 3). After gaining trust in their caregivers, infants begin to discover that their behavior is their own. They start to assert their sense of independence or autonomy. They realize their will. If infants are restrained too much or punished too harshly, they are likely to develop a sense of shame and doubt.

Initiative versus guilt is Erikson's third stage of development, occurring during the preschool years. As preschool children encounter a widening social world, they are challenged more than when they were infants. Active, purposeful behavior is needed to cope with these challenges. Children are asked to assume responsibility for their bodies, their behavior, their toys, and their pets. Developing a sense of responsibility increases initiative. Uncomfortable guilt feelings may arise, though, in children who are irresponsible and are made to feel too anxious. Erikson has a positive outlook on this stage. He believes that most guilt is quickly compensated for by a sense of accomplishment.

Industry versus inferiority is Erikson's fourth developmental stage, occurring approximately in the elementary school years. Children's initiative brings them in contact with a wealth of new experiences. As they move into middle and late childhood, they direct their energy toward mastering knowledge and intellectual skills. At no other time is the child more enthusiastic about learning than at the end of early childhood's period of expansive imagination. The danger in the elementary school years is the development of a sense of inferiority—of feeling incompetent and unproductive. Erikson believes that teachers have a special responsibility for children's development of industry. Teachers should "mildly but firmly coerce children into the adventure of finding out that one can learn to accomplish things which one would never have thought of by oneself" (Erikson, 1968, p. 127).

Identity versus identity confusion is Erikson's fifth developmental stage, which individuals experience during the adolescent years. At this time individuals are faced with finding out who they are, what they are all about, and where they are going in life. Adolescents are confronted with many new roles and adult statuses—vocational and romantic, for example. Parents need to allow adolescents to explore many different roles and different paths within a particular role. If the adolescent explores such roles in a healthy manner and arrives at a positive path to follow in life, then a positive identity will be achieved. If an identity is pushed on the adolescent by parents, if the adolescent does not adequately explore many roles, and if a positive future path is not defined, then identity confusion reigns.

Intimacy versus isolation is Erikson's sixth developmental stage, which individuals experience during the early adulthood years. At this time, individuals face the developmental task of forming intimate relationships with others. Erikson describes intimacy as finding oneself yet losing oneself in another. If the young adult forms healthy friendships and an intimate close relationship with another individual, intimacy will be achieved; if not, isolation will result.

Generativity versus stagnation is Erikson's seventh developmental stage, which individuals experience during middle adulthood. A chief concern is to assist the younger generation in developing and leading useful lives—this is what Erikson meant by generativity. The feeling of having done nothing to help the next generation is *stagnation.*

Integrity versus despair is Erikson's eighth and final developmental stage, which individuals experience during late adulthood. In our later years, we look back and evaluate what we have done with our lives. Through many different routes, the older person may have developed a positive outlook in most or all of the previous developmental stages. If so, the retrospective glances reveal a life well spent, and the person feels a sense of satisfaction—integrity is achieved. If the older adult resolved many of the earlier developmental stages negatively, the retrospective glances likely will yield doubt or gloom—the despair Erikson talks about.

Erikson does not believe that the proper solution to a stage crisis is always completely positive in nature. Some exposure or commitment to the negative end of a person's bipolar conflict is sometimes inevitable—you cannot trust all people under all circumstances and survive, for example. Nonetheless, positive resolutions to stage crises should dominate for optimal development (Hopkins, 2000).

Evaluating the Psychoanalytic Theories
The contributions of psychoanalytic theories include their emphases on these factors:

- Early experiences play an important part in development.
- Family relationships are a central aspect of development.
- Personality can be better understood if it is examined developmentally.

Erik Erikson with his wife, Joan, who is an artist. Erikson generated one of the most important developmental theories of the twentieth century. *What is the nature of his theory?*

Jean Piaget, the famous Swiss developmental psychologist, changed the way we think about the development of children's minds. *What are some key ideas in Piaget's theory?*

Piaget's theory
He proposed that individuals actively construct their understanding of the world and go through four stages of cognitive development.

- The mind is not all conscious; unconscious aspects of the mind need to be considered.
- Changes take place in the adulthood as well as the childhood years (Erikson).

These are some of the criticisms of psychoanalytic theories:

- The main concepts of psychoanalytic theories have been difficult to test scientifically.
- Much of the data used to support psychoanalytic theories come from individuals' reconstruction of the past, often the distant past, and are of unknown accuracy.
- The sexual underpinnings of development are given too much importance (especially in Freud's theory).
- The unconscious mind is given too much credit for influencing development.
- Psychoanalytic theories present an image of humans that is too negative (especially Freud).

Cognitive Theories

Whereas psychoanalytic theories stress the importance of adolescents' unconscious thoughts, cognitive theories emphasize their conscious thoughts. Three important cognitive theories are Piaget's theory, Vygotsky's theory, and information-processing theory.

Piaget's Theory

The famous Swiss psychologist Jean Piaget (1896–1980) proposed an important theory of cognitive development. **Piaget's theory** *states that individuals actively construct their understanding of the world and go through four stages of cognitive development.* Two processes underlie this cognitive construction of the world: organization and adaptation. To make sense of our world, we organize our experiences. For example, we separate important ideas from less important ideas. We connect one idea to another. But not only do we organize our observations and experiences, we also *adapt* our thinking to include new ideas because additional information furthers understanding.

Piaget (1954) also believed that we go through four stages in understanding the world (see figure 2.5). Each of the stages is age-related and consists of distinct ways of thinking. Remember, it is the *different* way of understanding the world that makes one stage more advanced than another; knowing *more* information does not make the child's thinking more advanced in the Piagetian view. This is what Piaget meant when he said the child's cognition is *qualitatively* different in one stage compared to another. What are Piaget's four stages of cognitive development like?

The *sensorimotor stage,* which lasts from birth to about 2 years of age, is the first Piagetian stage. In this stage, infants construct an

FORMAL OPERATIONAL STAGE

The adolescent reasons in more abstract, idealistic, and logical ways.

11 Years of Age Through Adulthood

CONCRETE OPERATIONAL STAGE

The child can now reason logically about concrete events and classify objects into different sets.

7 to 11 Years of Age

PREOPERATIONAL STAGE

The child begins to represent the world with words and images. These words and images reflect increased symbolic thinking and go beyond the connection of sensory information and physical action.

2 to 7 Years of Age

SENSORIMOTOR STAGE

The infant constructs an understanding of the world by coordinating sensory experiences with physical actions. An infant progresses from reflexive, instinctual action at birth to the beginning of symbolic thought toward the end of the stage.

Birth to 2 Years of Age

◼ FIGURE 2.5
Piaget's Four Stages of Cognitive Development

understanding of the world by coordinating sensory experiences (such as seeing and hearing) with physical, motoric actions—hence the term sensorimotor. At the beginning of this stage, newborns have little more than reflexive patterns with which to work. At the end of the stage, 2-year-olds have complex sensorimotor patterns and are beginning to operate with primitive symbols.

The *preoperational stage,* which lasts approximately from 2 to 7 years of age, is the second Piagetian stage. In this stage, children begin to represent the world with words, images, and drawings. Symbolic thought goes beyond simple connections of sensory information and physical action. However, although preschool children can symbolically represent the world, according to Piaget, they still lack the ability to perform *operations,* the Piagetian terms for internalized mental actions that allow children to do mentally what they previously did physically.

The *concrete operational stage,* which lasts from approximately 7 to 11 years of age, is the third Piagetian stage. In this stage, children can perform operations, and logical reasoning replaces intuitive thought as long as reasoning can be applied to specific or concrete examples. For instance, concrete operational thinkers cannot imagine the steps necessary to complete an algebraic equation, which is too abstract for thinking at this stage of development.

The *formal operational stage,* which appears between the ages of 11 and 15, is the fourth and final Piagetian stage. In this stage, individuals move beyond concrete experiences and think in abstract and more logical terms. As part of thinking more abstractly, adolescents develop images of ideal circumstances. They might think about what an ideal parent is like and compare their parents with this ideal standard. They begin to entertain possibilities for the future and are fascinated with what they can be. In solving problems, formal operational thinkers are more systematic, developing hypotheses about why something is happening the way it is, then testing these hypotheses in a deductive fashion. We will have much more to say about Piaget's theory in chapter 4, "Cognitive Development."

Vygotsky's Theory

Vygotsky's Theory   Like Piaget, Russian Lev Vygotsky (1896–1934) also believed that children actively construct their knowledge. **Vygotsky's theory** *is a sociocultural cognitive theory that emphasizes developmental analysis, the role of language, and social relations.* Vygotsky was born in Russia in the same year as Piaget, but he died much earlier, at the age of 37. Both Piaget's and Vygotsky's ideas remained virtually unknown to American scholars for many years, not being introduced to American audiences through English translations until the 1960s. In the last several decades, American psychologists and educators have shown increased interest in Vygotsky's (1962) views.

Three claims capture the heart of Vygotsky's view (Tappan, 1998): (1) children's and adolescents' cognitive skills can be understood only when they are developmentally analyzed and interpreted; (2) cognitive skills are mediated by words, language, and forms of discourse, which serve as psychological tools for facilitating and transforming mental activity; and (3) cognitive skills have their origins in social relations and are embedded in a sociocultural backdrop.

For Vygotsky, taking a developmental approach means that in order to understand any aspect of the child's and adolescent's cognitive functioning, one must examine its origins and transformations from earlier to later forms. Thus, a particular mental act cannot be viewed accurately in isolation but should be evaluated as a step in a gradual developmental process.

Vygotsky's second claim, that to understand cognitive functioning it is necessary to examine the tools that mediate and shape it, led him to believe that language is the most important of these tools. Vygotsky argued that language is a tool that helps the child and adolescent plan activities and solve problems.

Vygotsky's third claim was that cognitive skills originate in social relations and culture. Vygotsky portrayed the child's and adolescent's development as inseparable from social and cultural activities. He believed that the development of memory, attention, and reasoning involves learning to use the inventions of society, such as language, mathematical systems, and memory strategies. In one culture, this might consist of

There is considerable interest today in Lev Vygotsky's sociocultural cognitive theory of child development. *What were Vygotsky's three basic claims about children's development?*

Vygotsky's theory
He proposed a sociocultural cognitive theory that emphasizes developmental analysis, the role of language, and social relations.

Piaget's Theory
Vygotsky's Theory
http://www.mhhe.com/santrocka9

learning to count with the help of a computer. In another, it might consist of counting on one's fingers or using beads.

Vygotsky's theory has stimulated considerable interest in the view that knowledge is *situated* and *collaborative* (Greeno, Collins, & Resnick, 1996; Kozulin, 2000; Rogoff, 1998). That is, knowledge is distributed among people and environments, which include objects, artifacts, tools, books, and the communities in which people live. This suggests that knowing can best be advanced through interaction with others in cooperative activities.

Within these basic claims, Vygotsky articulated unique and influential ideas about the relation between learning and development. These ideas especially reflect his view that cognitive functioning has social origins. We will have much more to say about Vygotsky's theory in chapter 4, "Cognitive Development." Now that we have learned some basic ideas about Piaget's theory and Vygotsky's theory, we will examine a third cognitive theory—information processing.

information-processing approach
Emphasizes that individuals manipulate information, monitor it, and strategize about it. Central to information process are the processes of memory and thinking.

The Information-Processing Approach

The **information-processing approach** *emphasizes that individuals manipulate information, monitor it, and strategize about it. Central to this approach are the processes of memory and thinking.* According to the information-processing approach, individuals develop a gradually increasing capacity for processing information, which allows them to acquire increasingly complex knowledge and skills (Bjorklund & Rosenbaum, 2000; Chen & Siegler, 2000). Unlike Piaget's cognitive developmental theory, the information-processing approach does not describe development as stagelike.

Although a number of factors stimulated the growth of the information-processing approach, none was more important than the computer, which demonstrated that a machine could perform logical operations. Psychologists began to wonder if the logical operations carried out by computers might tell us something about how the human mind works. They drew analogies to computers to explain the relation between cognition or thinking and the brain. The physical brain is described as the computer's hardware, cognition as its software. Although computers and software are not perfect analogies for brains and cognitive activities, the comparison contributed to our thinking about the mind as an active information-processing system.

Robert Siegler (1998), a leading expert on children's information processing, believes that thinking is information processing. He says that when individuals perceive, encode, represent, store, and retrieve information, they are thinking. Siegler especially thinks that an important aspect of development is to learn good strategies for processing information. For example, in becoming a better reader this might involve learning to monitor the key themes of the material being read.

THROUGH THE EYES OF ADOLESCENTS

The Cobwebs of Memory

I think the point of having memories is to share them, especially with close friends or family. If you don't share them, they are just sitting inside your brain getting cobwebs. If you have a great memory of Christmas and no one to share it with, what's the point of memories?

Before he shares memories

After he shares memories

X-ray   Cobwebs

No cobwebs

Seventh-Grade Student
West Middle School
Ypsilanti, Michigan

Evaluating the Cognitive Theories

Among the contributions of the cognitive theories are these:

• The cognitive theories present a positive view of development, emphasizing individuals' conscious thinking.
• The cognitive theories (especially Piaget's and Vygotsky's) emphasize the individual's active construction of understanding.
• Piaget's and Vygotsky's theories underscore the importance of examining developmental changes in children's thinking.
• The information-processing approach offers detailed descriptions of cognitive processes.

Among the criticisms of the cognitive theories are these:

- There is skepticism about the pureness of Piaget's stages.
- The cognitive theories do not give adequate attention to individual variations in cognitive development.
- The information processing approach does not provide an adequate description of developmental changes in cognition.
- Psychoanalytic theorists argue that the cognitive theories do not give enough credit to unconscious thought.

At this point we have examined psychoanalytic and cognitive theories. The following review should help you to reach your learning goals related to these topics.

Learning Goal 1
Discuss psychoanalytic theories

- In Freud's theory, personality is made up of three structures: id, ego, and superego. The conflicting demands of these structures produce anxiety. Most of children's thoughts are unconscious, according to Freud. Freud was convinced that problems develop because of early experiences. Individuals go through five psychosexual stages: oral, anal, phallic, latency, and genital.
- In Erikson's theory, eight psychosocial stages are emphasized: trust versus mistrust, autonomy versus shame and doubt, initiative versus guilt, industry versus inferiority, identity versus identity confusion, intimacy versus isolation, generativity versus stagnation, and integrity versus despair.
- Among the contributions of psychoanalytic theory is an emphasis on a developmental framework; among the criticisms is a lack of scientific support.

Learning Goal 2
Know about cognitive theories

- Piaget proposed a cognitive developmental theory. Children go through four stages: sensorimotor, preoperational, concrete operational, and formal operational.
- Vygotsky's theory consists of three basic claims about development: (1) cognitive skills need to be interpreted developmentally, (2) cognitive skills are mediated by language, and (3) cognitive skills have their origin in social relations and culture.
- The information-processing approach emphasizes that individuals manipulate information, monitor it, and strategize about it. The development of computers stimulated interest in this approach.
- Among the contributions of the cognitive approach is the active construction of understanding; among the criticisms is that too little attention is given to individual variations.

Now that we have discussed psychoanalytic and cognitive theories, we will turn our attention to another set of important theories about adolescent development: behavioral and social cognitive.

Behavioral and Social Cognitive Theories

Seventeen-year-old Tom is going steady with 16-year-old Ann. Both have warm, friendly personalities, and they enjoy being together. Psychoanalytic theorists would say that their warm, friendly personalities are derived from long-standing relationships with their parents, especially their early childhood experiences. They also would argue that the reason for their attraction to each other is unconscious; they are unaware of how their biological heritage and early life experiences have been carried forward to influence their personalities in adolescence.

Behaviorists and social learning theorists would observe Tom and Ann and see something quite different. They would examine their experiences, especially their most recent ones, to understand the reason for Tom and Ann's attraction to each other. Tom would be described as rewarding Ann's behavior, and vice versa, for example. No reference would be made to unconscious thoughts, the Oedipus complex, stages of development, and defense mechanisms. The **behavioral and social cognitive theories**

Skinner's View
Albert Bandura
http://www.mhhe.com/santrocka9

behavioral and social cognitive theories
Theories that emphasize the importance of studying environmental experiences and observable behavior. Social cognitive theorists emphasize person/cognitive factors in development.

emphasize the importance of studying environmental experiences and observable behavior to understand adolescent development. Social cognitive theorists emphasize person/cognitive factors in development.

Skinner's Behaviorism

Behaviorism emphasizes the scientific study of observable behavioral responses and their environmental determinants. In the behaviorism of B. F. Skinner (1904–1990), the mind, conscious or unconscious, is not needed to explain behavior and development. For him, development is behavior. For example, observations of Sam reveal that his behavior is shy, achievement oriented, and caring. Why is Sam's behavior this way? For Skinner (1938) rewards and punishments in Sam's environment have shaped him into a shy, achievement-oriented, and caring person. Because of interactions with family members, friends, teachers, and others, Sam has *learned* to behave in this fashion.

Since behaviorists believe that development is learned and often changes according to environmental experiences, it follows that rearranging experiences can change development (Adams, 2000; Hayes, 2000). For behaviorists, shy behavior can be transformed into outgoing behavior; aggressive behavior can be shaped into docile behavior; lethargic, boring behavior can be turned into enthusiastic, interesting behavior.

Social Cognitive Theory

Some psychologists believe that the behaviorists are basically right when they say that personality is learned and influenced strongly by environmental factors. But they think Skinner went too far in declaring that characteristics of the person or cognitive factors are unimportant in understanding development. *Social cognitive theory* states that behavior, environment, and person/cognitive factors are important in understanding development.

Albert Bandura (1986, 1997, 2000) and Walter Mischel (1973, 1995) are the architects of the contemporary version of social cognitive theory, which initially was labeled *cognitive social learning theory* by Mischel (1973). As shown in figure 2.6, Bandura says that behavior, environment, and person/cognitive factors interact in a reciprocal manner. Thus, in Bandura's view, the environment can determine a person's behavior (which matches up with Skinner's view), but there is much more to consider. The person can act to change the environment. Person/cognitive factors can influence a person's behavior and vice versa. Person/cognitive factors include self-efficacy (a belief that one can master a situation and produce positive outcomes), plans, and thinking skills. We will have much more to say about self-efficacy in chapter 13, "Achievement, Careers, and Work."

Bandura believes observational learning is a key aspect of how we learn. Through observational learning, we form ideas about the behavior of others and then possibly adopt this behavior ourselves (Zimmerman & Schunk, 2002). For example, a boy might observe his father's aggressive outbursts and hostile exchanges with people; when the boy is with his peers, he interacts in a highly aggressive way, showing the same characteristics as his father's behavior.

Like Skinner's behavioral approach, the social cognitive approach emphasizes the importance of empirical research in studying development. This research focuses on the processes that explain development—the socioemotional and cognitive factors that influence what we are like as people.

Evaluating the Behavioral and Social Cognitive Theories

These are some of the contributions of the behavioral and social cognitive theories:

- An emphasis on the importance of scientific research
- A focus on the environmental determinants of behavior
- An underscoring of the importance of observational learning (Bandura)
- An emphasis on person and cognitive factors (social cognitive theory)

B
Behavior

P/C
**Person and
cognitive factors**

E
Environment

■ FIGURE 2.6
Bandura's Social Cognitive Theory

Bandura's social cognitive theory emphasizes reciprocal influences of behavior, environment, and person/cognitive factors.

These are some of the criticisms of the behavioral and social cognitive theories:

- Too little emphasis on cognition (Pavlov, Skinner)
- Too much emphasis on environmental determinants
- Inadequate attention to developmental changes
- Too mechanical and inadequate consideration of the spontaneity and creativity of humans

The behavioral and social cognitive theories emphasize the importance of environmental experiences in human development. Next we will turn our attention to another approach that underscores the importance of environmental influences on development—ecological, contextual theory.

Ecological, Contextual Theory

Urie Bronfenbrenner (1917–   ) has proposed a strong environmental view of children's development that is receiving increased attention. **Ecological, contextual theory** is Bronfenbrenner's view of development. It consists of five environmental systems, ranging from the fine-grained inputs of direct interactions with social agents to the broad-based inputs of culture. The five systems in Bronfenbrenner's ecological theory are the microsystem, mesosystem, exosystem, macrosystem, and chronosystem. Bronfenbrenner's (1986, 1995, 2000; Bronfenbrenner & Morris, 1998) ecological, contextual model is shown in figure 2.7 on page 52.

The *microsystem* in Bronfenbrenner's ecological, contextual theory is the setting in which an individual lives. This context includes the person's family, peers, school, and neighborhood. It is in the microsystem that most of the direct interactions with social agents take place—with parents, peers, and teachers, for example. The individual is viewed not as a passive recipient of experiences in these settings, but as someone who helps construct the settings. Bronfenbrenner points out that most of the research on sociocultural influences has focused on microsystems.

The *mesosystem* in Bronfenbrenner's ecological, contextual theory involves relations between microsystems, or connections between contexts. Examples are the relation of family experiences to school experiences, school experiences to work experiences, and family experiences to peer experiences. For instance, adolescents whose parents have rejected them may have difficulty developing positive relations with teachers. Developmentalists increasingly believe that it is important to observe behavior in multiple settings—such as family, peer, and school contexts—to obtain a more complete picture of adolescent development.

The *exosystem* in Bronfenbrenner's ecological, contextual theory is involved when experiences in another social setting—in which the individual does not have an active role—influence what the individual experiences in an immediate context. For example, work experiences might affect a woman's relationship with her husband and their adolescent. The woman might receive a promotion that requires more travel, which might increase marital conflict and change patterns of parent-adolescent interaction. Another example of an exosystem is city government, which is responsible for the quality of parks, recreation centers, and library facilities for children and adolescents.

The *macrosystem* in Bronfenbrenner's ecological, contextual theory involves the culture in which individuals live. Culture refers to the behavior patterns, beliefs, and all other products of a group of people that are passed on from generation to generation. *Cross-cultural studies*—the comparison of one culture with one or more other cultures—provide information about the generality of adolescent development.

The *chronosystem* in Bronfenbrenner's ecological, contextual theory involves the patterning of environmental events and transitions over the life course and sociohistorical circumstances. For example, in studying the effects of divorce on children, researchers have found that the negative effects often peak in the first year after the divorce and the effects are more negative for sons than for daughters

ecological, contextual theory
Bronfenbrenner's view of development, involving five environmental systems—microsystem, mesosystem, ecosystem, macrosystem, and chronosystem. These emphasize the role of social contexts in development.

Bronfenbrenner's Theory
Bronfenbrenner and a
Multicultural Framework
http://www.mhhe.com/santrocka9

THROUGH THE EYES OF PSYCHOLOGISTS

Urie Bronfenbrenner
Cornell University

"Perhaps even more in developmental science than in other fields, the pathways to discovery are not easy to find."

BIOLOGICAL AND COGNITIVE DEVELOPMENT

I think that what is happening to me is so wonderful and not only what can be seen on my body, but all that is taking place inside. I never discuss myself with anybody; that is why I have to talk to myself about them.

—Anne Frank
German Jewish Diarist, 20th Century

Adolescence, the transition from childhood to adulthood, involves biological, cognitive, and socioemotional development. These strands of development are interwoven in the adolescent's life. This section focuses on adolescents' biological and cognitive development and consists of two chapters: chapter 3, "Puberty, Health, and Biological Foundations," and chapter 4, "Cognitive Development."

PUBERTY, HEALTH, AND BIOLOGICAL FOUNDATIONS

■ PUBERTY'S MYSTERIES AND CURIOSITIES

I am pretty confused. I wonder whether I am weird or normal. My body is starting to change, but I sure don't look like a lot of my friends. I still look like a kid for the most part. My best friend is only 13, but he looks like he is 16 or 17. I get nervous in the locker room during PE class because when I go to take a shower, I'm afraid somebody is going to make fun of me since I'm not as physically developed as some of the others.

—*Robert, age 12*

I don't like my breasts. They are too small, and they look funny. I'm afraid guys won't like me if they don't get bigger.

—*Angie, age 13*

I can't stand the way I look. I have zits all over my face. My hair is dull and stringy. It never stays in place. My nose is too big. My lips are too small. My legs are too short. I have four warts on my left hand, and people get grossed out by them. So do I. My body is a disaster!

—*Ann, age 14*

I'm short and I can't stand it. My father is 6 feet tall, and here I am only five foot four. I'm 14 already. I look like a kid, and I get teased a lot, especially by other guys. I'm always the last one picked for sides in basketball because I'm so short. Girls don't seem to be interested in me either because most of them are taller than I am.

—*Jim, age 14*

The comments of these four adolescents in the midst of pubertal change underscore the dramatic upheaval in our bodies following the calm, consistent growth of middle and late childhood. Young adolescents develop an acute concern about their bodies.

PUBERTY'S CHANGES ARE PERPLEXING to adolescents. Although these changes bring forth doubts, fears, and anxieties, most adolescents survive them quite well. By the time you have completed this chapter you should be able to reach these learning goals:

1 Understand pubertal change

2 Know about developmental changes in the brain

3 Evaluate adolescent health

4 Explain heredity and environment

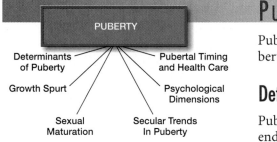

puberty

A period of rapid physical maturation involving hormonal and bodily changes that take place primarily in early adolescence.

PUBERTY

Puberty involves a number of complex factors. We will begin our exploration of puberty by focusing on its determinants.

Determinants of Puberty

Puberty can be distinguished from adolescence. For virtually everyone, puberty has ended long before adolescence is exited. Puberty is often thought of as the most important marker for the beginning of adolescence. **Puberty** *is a period of rapid physical maturation involving hormonal and bodily changes that take place primarily in early adolescence.*

Among the most important factors involved in puberty are *heredity;* hormones; and weight, body fat, and leptin.

Heredity   Puberty is not an environmental accident. Programmed into the genes of every human being is a timing for the emergency of puberty (Adair, 2001). Puberty does not take place at 2 or 3 years of age and it does not occur in the twenties. In the future, we are likely to see molecular genetic studies that identify specific genes which are linked to the onset and progression of puberty. Nonetheless, as you will see in our further discussion of puberty, within the boundaries of about 9 to 16 years of age, environmental factors can influence the onset and duration of puberty.

Hormones   Behind the first whisker in boys and the widening of hips in girls is a flood of hormones. Let's explore the nature of these hormonal changes.

Hormones *are powerful chemical substances secreted by the endocrine glands and carried through the body by the bloodstream.* Two classes of hormones have significantly different concentrations in males and females. **Androgens** *are the main class of male sex hormones.* **Estrogens** *are the main class of female hormones.* It is important to note that although these hormones function more strongly in one sex or the other that they are produced by both males and females.

Testosterone is an androgen that plays an important role in male pubertal development. Throughout puberty, increasing testosterone levels are associated with a number of physical changes in boys—development of external genitals, increase in height, and voice changes. *Estradiol* is an estrogen that plays an important role in female pubertal development. As estradiol level rises, breast development, uterine development, and skeletal changes occur. In one study, testosterone levels increased 18-fold in boys but only 2-fold in girls across puberty; estradiol levels increased 8-fold in girls but only 2-fold in boys across puberty (Nottelman & others, 1987).

The level of sex hormones is low in the early part of childhood. As we have just seen, during puberty, the level of sex hormones rises. Next, we will explore how the endocrine system functions to maintain a certain concentration of sex hormones.

The Endocrine System   The endocrine system's role in puberty involves the interaction of the hypothalamus, the pituitary gland, and the gonads (sex glands) (see figure 3.1). The *hypothalamus* is a structure in the higher portion of the brain that monitors eating, drinking, and sex. The *pituitary gland* is an important endocrine gland that controls growth and regulates other glands. The *gonads* are the sex glands—the testes in males, the ovaries in females.

hormones

Powerful chemicals secreted by the endocrine glands and carried through the body by the bloodstream.

androgens

The main class of male sex hormones.

estrogens

The main class of female sex hormones.

Biological Changes
http://www.mhhe.com/santrocka9

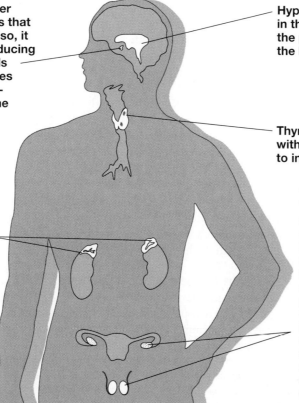

Pituitary gland: This master gland produces hormones that stimulate other glands. Also, it influences growth by producing growth hormones; it sends gonadotropins to the testes and ovaries and a thyroid-stimulating hormone to the thyroid gland. It sends a hormone to the adrenal gland as well.

Adrenal gland: It interacts with the pituitary gland and likely plays a role in pubertal development, but less is known about its function than about sex glands. Recent research, however, suggests it may be involved in adolescent behavior, particularly for boys.

Hypothalamus: It is a structure in the brain that interacts with the pituitary gland to monitor the bodily regulation of hormones.

Thyroid gland: It interacts with the pituitary gland to influence growth.

The gonads, or sex glands: These consist of the testes in males, ovaries in females. The sex glands are strongly involved in the appearance of secondary sex characteristics, such as facial hair in males and breast development in females. The general class of hormones called estrogens is dominant in females, while androgens are dominant in males. More specifically, testosterone in males and estradiol in females are key hormones in pubertal development.

■ **FIGURE 3.1**

The Major Endocrine Glands Involved in Pubertal Change

How does the endocrine system work? The pituitary gland sends a signal via gonadotropins (hormones that stimulate the testes and ovaries) to the appropriate gland to manufacture the hormone. Then the pituitary gland, through interaction with the hypothalamus, detects when the optimal level of hormones is reached and responds by maintaining gonadotropin secretion.

Levels of sex hormones are regulated by two hormones secreted by the pituitary gland: *FSH* (follicle-stimulating hormone) and *LH* (luteinizing hormone). FSH stimulates follicle development in females and sperm production in males. LH regulates estrogen secretion and ovum development in females and testosterone production in males (Hyde & DeLamater, 2000). Also, a substance called *GnRh* (gonadotropin-releasing hormone) is secreted by the hypothalamus.

These hormones are regulated by a *negative feedback system*. What this means is that if the level of sex hormones rises too high, the hypothalamus and pituitary gland reduce stimulation to the gonads and thus decrease production of sex hormones. If the level of sex hormones goes too low, then production of the hormones increases.

Figure 3.2 shows how the feedback system works. In males, the pituitary gland's production of LH stimulates the testes to produce testosterone. When testosterone levels get too high, the hypothalamus decreases its production of GnRH and the pituitary's production of LH is then also decreased. When the level of testosterone falls, the hypothalamus produces GnRH and the cycle starts again. The negative feedback system works similarly in females, involving LH, GnRH, the ovaries, and estrogen.

The negative feedback system in the endocrine system works much like a thermostat-furnace system. If a room is cold, the thermostat signals the furnace to turn on. The action of the furnace warms the air in the room, which eventually becomes warm enough to signal the furnace to turn off. Subsequently, the room temperature gradually falls off and the thermostat once again signals the furnace to produce more warm air, repeating the cycle. This is called a *negative* feedback loop because a *rise* in temperature turns *off* the furnace, while a *decrease* in temperature turns *on* the furnace.

We indicated earlier that the level of sex hormones is low in the early part of childhood but increases as puberty proceeds. In the analogy of the sex hormone system to a thermostat, it is as if the thermostat had been set at 50°F earlier in childhood and now becomes set at 80°F in puberty. At this higher level, the gonads have to produce more sex hormones, and that is what happens during puberty.

Growth Hormone   Not only does the pituitary gland release gonadotropins that stimulate the testes and ovaries, but through interaction with the hypothalamus the pituitary gland also secretes hormones that either directly lead to growth and skeletal maturation or produce growth effects through interaction with the *thyroid gland*, located in the neck region (see figure 3.1).

Growth hormone initially is secreted at night during puberty and subsequently also is secreted during the day, although daytime levels are usually very low (Susman, Dorn, & Schiefelbein, in press). Other endocrine factors can influence growth, such as cortisol, which is secreted by the adrenal cortex. Testosterone and estrogen also facilitate growth during puberty.

Adrenarche and Gonadarche   Puberty has two phases that are linked with hormonal changes: adrenarche and gonadarche (Susman, Dorn, & Schiefelbein, in press). *Adrenarche* involves hormonal changes in the adrenal glands, which are located just above the kidneys. These changes occur surprisingly early, from about 6 to 9 years of age and before what we generally consider to be the beginning of puberty. Adrenal androgens are secreted by the adrenal glands during adrenarche and continuing on through puberty.

Gonadarche is what most people think of as puberty and it follows adrenarche by approximately two years (Archibald, Graber, & Brooks-Gunn, in press). Gonadarche involves sexual maturation and the development of reproductive maturity. Gonadarche begins at approximately 9 to 10 years of age in non-Latino White girls, and 8 to 9 years in African American girls in the United States (Grumach & Styne, 1992). Gonadarche

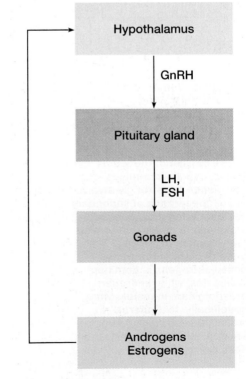

■ **FIGURE 3.2**
The Feedback System of Sex Hormones

begins at about 10 to 11 years of age in boys. The culmination of gonadarche in girls is **menarche,** *a girl's first menstrual period,* and in boys **spermarche,** *a boy's first ejaculation of semen.*

Weight, Body Fat, and Leptin

One view is that critical body mass must be attained before puberty, especially *menarche* is attained. Some scientists even have proposed that a body weight of 106 ±3 pounds can trigger menarche and the end of the pubertal growth spurt (Friesch, 1984). However, this specific weight target is not well documented (Susman, 2001).

Other scientists have hypothesized that the onset of menarche is influenced by the percentage of body fat in total body weight with a minimum of 17 percent of body weight comprised of body fat required for menarche to occur. As with body weight, this specific percentage has not been consistently verified.

However, both anorexic adolescents whose weight drops dramatically and females who participate in certain sports (such as gymnastics and swimming) may become amenorrheic (having an absence or suppression of menstrual discharge). Undernutrition also may delay puberty in boys (Susman, Dorn, and Schiefelbein, in press).

The hormone *leptin* has been proposed as a possible signal of the beginning and progression of puberty (Mantzoros, 2000; Mantzoros, Flier, & Rogol, 1997). Leptin may be one of the messengers which signals the adequacy of fat stores for reproduction and

menarche
A girl's first menstrual period.

spermarche
A boy's first ejaculation of semen.

What are some of the differences in the ways girls and boys experience pubertal growth?

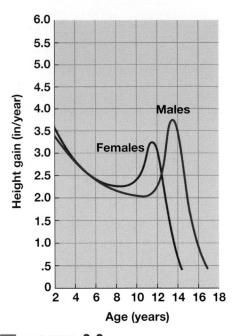

▣ FIGURE 3.3
Pubertal Growth Spurt

On the average, the peak of the growth spurt that characterizes pubertal change occurs 2 years earlier for girls (11½) than for boys (13½).

maintenance of pregnancy at puberty (Kiess & others, 1999). Leptin concentrations are higher in girls than in boys. They also are related to the amount of fat in girls and androgen concentrations in boys (Roemmrich & others, 1999). Changes in leptin have not yet been studied in relation to adolescent behavior.

In sum, the determinants of puberty include heredity and hormones. Next, we will turn our attention to the growth spurt that characterizes puberty.

Growth Spurt

Growth slows throughout childhood, and puberty ushers in the most rapid increases in growth since infancy. As indicated in figure 3.3, the growth spurt associated with puberty occurs approximately two years earlier for girls than for boys. The mean beginning of the growth spurt is 9 years of age for girls and 11 years of age for boys. The peak of pubertal change occurs at 11.5 years for girls and 13.5 years for boys. During their growth spurt, girls increase in height about 3½ inches per year, boys about 4 inches.

Boys and girls who are shorter or taller than their peers before adolescence are likely to remain so during adolescence. In our society, there is a stigma attached to being a short boy. At the beginning of adolescence, girls tend to be as tall as or taller than boys of their age, but by the end of the middle school years most boys have caught up with, or in many cases even surpassed, girls in height. And even though height in elementary school is a good predictor of height later in adolescence, as much as 30 percent of the height of individuals in late adolescence is unexplained by height in the elementary school years.

The rate at which adolescents gain weight follows approximately the same developmental timetable as the rate at which they gain height. Marked weight gains coincide with the onset of puberty. Fifty percent of adult body weight is gained during adolescence (Rogol, Raemmich, & Clark, 1998). At the peak of weight gain during puberty, girls gain an average of 18 pounds in one year at about 12 years of age (approximately six months after their peak height increase). Boys' peak weight gain per year (20 pounds in one year) occurs at about the same time as their peak increase in height (about 13 to 14 years of age). During early adolescence, girls tend to outweigh boys, but, just as with height, by about 14 years of age, boys begin to surpass girls in weight.

In addition to increases in height and weight, changes in hip and shoulder width occur. Adolescent girls experience a spurt in hip width while boys undergo an increase in shoulder width. Increased hip width is linked with an increase in estrogen in girls. Increased shoulder width in boys is associated with an increase in testosterone.

The later growth spurt of boys also produces greater leg length in boys than is experienced by girls. Also, in many cases, the facial structure of boys becomes more angular during puberty while that of girls becomes more round and soft.

Sexual Maturation

Think back to the onset of your puberty. Of the striking changes that were taking place in your body, what was the first change that occurred? Researchers have found that male pubertal characteristics develop in this order: increase in penis and testicle size, appearance of straight pubic hair, minor voice change, first ejaculation (spermarche—this usually occurs through masturbation or a wet dream), appearance of kinky pubic hair, onset of maximum growth, growth of hair in armpits, more detectable voice changes, and growth of facial hair. Three of the most noticeable areas of sexual maturation in boys are penis elongation, testes development, and growth of facial hair. The normal range and average age of development for these sexual characteristics, along with height spurt, are shown in figure 3.4 on page 81. Figure 3.5 on page 82 shows the typical course of male sexual development during puberty.

What is the order of appearance of physical changes in females? First, either the breasts enlarge or pubic hair appears. Later, hair appears in the armpits. As these changes occur, the female grows in height, and her hips become wider than her shoulders. Her first menstruation (menarche) occurs rather late in the pubertal cycle.

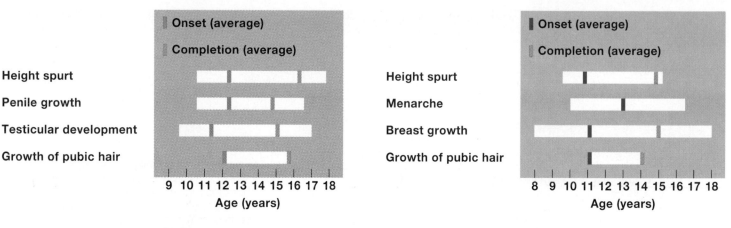

MALES   FEMALES

FIGURE 3.4
Normal Range and Average Development of Sexual Characteristics in Males and Females

Initially, her menstrual cycles may be highly irregular. For the first several years, she might not ovulate every menstrual cycle. In some instances, she does not become fertile until two years after her period begins. No voice changes comparable to those in pubertal males occur for pubertal females. By the end of puberty, the female's breasts have become more fully rounded. Two of the most noticeable aspects of female pubertal change are pubic hair and breast development. Figure 3.4 shows the normal range and average development of these sexual characteristics and also provides information about menarche and height gain. Figure 3.5 on page 82 shows the typical course of female sexual development during puberty.

It is important to understand that there may be wide individual variations in the onset and progression of puberty. The pubertal sequence may begin as early as 10 years of age or as late as 13½ for boys. It may end as early as 13 years or as late as 17. The normal range is wide enough that, given two boys of the same chronological age, one might complete the pubertal sequence before the other one has begun it. For girls, the age range of menarche is even wider. It is considered within a normal range when it occurs between 9 and 15 years of age.

Secular Trends in Puberty

Imagine a toddler displaying all the features of puberty—a 3-year-old girl with fully developed breasts or a boy just slightly older with a deep male voice. That is what we would see by the year 2250 if the age at which puberty arrives would have been getting younger at the rate at which it was occurring for much of the twentieth century.

The term *secular trends* refers to patterns over time, especially across generations. For example, in Norway, menarche now occurs at just over 13 years of age compared to 17 years of age in the 1840s (de Muinich Keizer, 2001; Petersen, 1979). In the United States—where children physically mature up to a year earlier than in European countries—the average age of menarche declined an average of two to four months per decade for much of the twentieth century (see figure 3.6 on p. 83). In the United States, menarche occurred at an average of 15 years of age compared to about 12½ years today.

The earlier onset of puberty in the twentieth century was likely due to improved health and nutrition. One speculation about the earlier onset of puberty involves the increase of girlhood obesity. For example, in one recent study, the more sexually developed that girls were, the greater was their body mass (Kaplowitz & others, 2001). We will have more to say about obesity in adolescence.

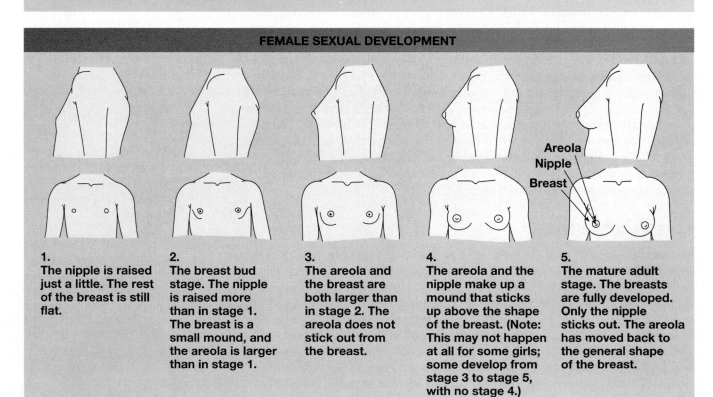

MALE SEXUAL DEVELOPMENT

1.
No pubic hair. The testes, scrotum, and penis are about the same size and shape as those of a child.

2.
A little soft, long, lightly colored hair, mostly at the base of the penis. This hair may be straight or a little curly. The testes and scrotum have enlarged, and the skin of the scrotum has changed. The scrotum, the sack holding the testes, has lowered a bit. The penis has grown only a little.

3.
The hair is darker coarser, and more curled. It has spread to thinly cover a somewhat larger area. The penis has grown mainly in length. The testes and scrotum have grown and dropped lower than in stage 2.

4.
The hair is now as dark, curly, and coarse as that of an adult male. However, the area that the hair covers is not as large as that of an adult male; it has not spread to the thighs. The penis has grown even larger and wider. The glans (the head of the penis) is bigger. The scrotum is darker and bigger because the testes have gotten bigger.

5.
The hair has spread to the thighs and is now like that of an adult male. The penis, scrotum, and testes are the size and shape of those of an adult male.

Penis
Scrotum
Testes
Glans (head)

FEMALE SEXUAL DEVELOPMENT

1.
The nipple is raised just a little. The rest of the breast is still flat.

2.
The breast bud stage. The nipple is raised more than in stage 1. The breast is a small mound, and the areola is larger than in stage 1.

3.
The areola and the breast are both larger than in stage 2. The areola does not stick out from the breast.

4.
The areola and the nipple make up a mound that sticks up above the shape of the breast. (Note: This may not happen at all for some girls; some develop from stage 3 to stage 5, with no stage 4.)

5.
The mature adult stage. The breasts are fully developed. Only the nipple sticks out. The areola has moved back to the general shape of the breast.

Areola
Nipple
Breast

■ **FIGURE 3.5**
The Five Pubertal Stages of Male and Female Sexual Development

Keep in mind that we are unlikely to see pubescent toddlers in the future because there are some genetic limits on just how early puberty can come. So far we have been concerned mainly with the physical dimensions of puberty. However, as we see next, the psychological dimensions of puberty also involve some important changes.

Psychological Dimensions

A host of psychological changes accompany an adolescent's pubertal development (Sarigiani & Petersen, 2000). Try to remember when you were beginning puberty. Not only did you probably think of yourself differently, but your parents and peers also probably began acting differently toward you. Maybe you were proud of your changing body, even though you were perplexed about what was happening. Perhaps your parents no longer perceived you as someone they could sit in bed with to watch television or as someone who should be kissed goodnight.

There has been far less research on the psychosocial aspects of male pubertal transitions than on those of females, possibly because of the difficulty in defining when the male transitions occur. Wet dreams are one such marker, yet there has been little research on this topic (Susman & others, 1995).

Body Image   One psychological aspect of physical change in puberty is certain: Adolescents are preoccupied with their bodies and develop individual images of what their bodies are like. Perhaps you looked in the mirror on a daily and sometimes even hourly basis to see if you could detect anything different about your changing body. Preoccupation with one's body image is strong throughout adolescence, but it is especially acute during puberty, a time when adolescents are more dissatisfied with their bodies than in late adolescence (Wright, 1989).

There are gender differences in adolescents' perceptions of their bodies. In general, girls are less happy with their bodies and have more negative body images, compared to boys, throughout puberty (Brooks-Gunn & Paikoff, 1993; Henderson & Zivian, 1995). Also, as pubertal change proceeds, girls often become more dissatisfied with their bodies, probably because their body fat increases, while boys become more satisfied as they move through puberty, probably because their muscle mass increases (Seiffge-Krenke, 1998).

A current major concern about adolescent girls is their motivation to be very thin and that many adolescent girls believe they can't be too thin. This motivation has especially been fueled by the media's portrait of extremely thin as beautiful. We will have much more to say about this topic in chapter 14, "Adolescent Problems," where we will discuss eating disorders.

Hormones and Behavior   Are there links between concentrations of hormones and adolescent behavior? Hormonal factors are thought to account for at least part of the increase in negative and variable emotions that characterize adolescents (Archibald, Graber, & Brooks-Gunn, in press; Dorn, Williamson, & Ryan, 2002). Researchers have found that higher levels of androgens are associated with violence and acting-out problems in boys (van Goozen & others, 1998; Susman & others, 1987). Few studies have focused on estrogens; however, there is some indication that increased levels of estrogens are linked with depression in adolescent girls (Angold & others, 1999).

It is important to understand that hormonal factors alone are not responsible for adolescent behavior (Ge & Brody, 2002; Susman, Schiefelbein, & Heaton, 2002). For example, in one study, social factors accounted for two to four times as much variance as hormonal factors in young adolescent girls' depression and anger (Brooks-Gunn &

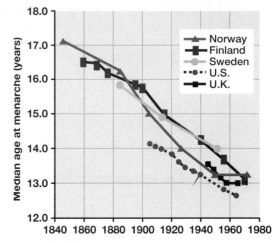

■ **FIGURE 3.6**

Median Ages at Menarche in Selected Northern European Countries and the United States from 1845 to 1969

Notice the steep decline in the age at which girls experienced menarche in five different countries. Recently the age at which girls experience menarche has been leveling off.

Adolescents show a strong preoccupation with their changing bodies and develop images of what their bodies are like. *Why might adolescent males have more positive body images than adolescent females?*

Warren, 1989). Stress, eating patterns, sexual activity, and depression can activate or suppress various aspects of the hormone system.

Menarche and the Menstrual Cycle

The onset of puberty and menarche has often been described as a "main event" in most historical accounts of adolescence (Erikson, 1968; Freud, 1917/1958; Hall, 1904). Basically, these views suggest that pubertal changes and events such as menarche produce a different body that requires considerable change in self-conception, possibly resulting in an identity crisis. Only recently has there been empirical research directed at understanding the female adolescent's adaptation to menarche and the menstrual cycle (Brooks-Gunn, Graber, & Paikoff, 1994).

In one study of 639 girls, a wide range of reactions to menarche appeared (Brooks-Gunn & Ruble, 1982). However, most of the reactions were quite mild, as girls described their first period as a little upsetting, a little surprising, or a little exciting and positive. In this study, 120 of the fifth- and sixth-grade girls were telephoned to obtain more personal, detailed information about their experience with menarche. The most frequent theme of the girls' responses was positive—namely, that menarche was an index of their maturity. Other positive reports indicated that the girls could now have children, were experiencing something that made them more like adult women, and now were more like their friends. The most frequent negative aspects of menarche reported by the girls were its hassle (having to carry supplies around) and its messiness. A minority of the girls also indicated that menarche involved physical discomfort, produced behavioral limitations, and created emotional changes.

Questions also were asked about the extent to which the girls communicated with others about the appearance of menarche, the extent to which the girls were prepared for menarche, and how the experience was related to early/late maturation. Virtually all of the girls told their mothers immediately, but most of the girls did not tell anyone else about menarche, with only one in five informing a friend. However, after two or three periods had occurred, most girls had talked with girlfriends about menstruation. Girls not prepared for menarche indicated more negative feelings about menstruation than those who were more prepared for its onset. Girls who matured early had more negative reactions than average- or late-maturing girls. In summary, menarche initially may be disruptive, especially for unprepared and early-maturing girls, but it typically does not reach the tumultuous, conflicting proportions described by some early theoreticians.

For many girls, menarche occurs on time, but for others it occurs early or late. Next, we examine the effects of early and late maturation on both boys and girls.

Early and Late Maturation

Some of you entered puberty early, others late, and yet others on time. When adolescents mature earlier or later than their peers, might they perceive themselves differently? In the Berkeley Longitudinal Study some years ago, early-maturing boys perceived themselves more positively and had more successful peer relations than did their late-maturing counterparts (Jones, 1965). The findings for early-maturing girls were similar but not as strong as for boys. When the late-maturing boys were studied in their thirties, however, they had developed a stronger sense of identity than had the early-maturing boys (Peskin, 1967). Late-maturing boys may have had more time to explore a wide variety of options. They may have focused on career development and achievement that would serve them better in life than their early-maturing counterparts' emphasis on physical status.

More-recent research, though, confirms that, at least during adolescence, it is advantageous to be an early-maturing rather than a late-maturing boy (Petersen, 1987). Roberta Simmons and Dale Blyth (1987) studied more than 450 individuals for five years, beginning in the sixth grade

THROUGH THE EYES OF ADOLESCENTS

Attractive Blond Females and Tall Muscular Males

When columnist Bob Greene (1988) called Connections in Chicago, a chatline for teenagers, to find out what young adolescents were saying to each other, the first things the boys and girls asked for—after first names—were physical descriptions. The idealism of the callers was apparent. Most of the girls described themselves as having long blond hair, being 5 feet 5 inches tall, and weighing 110 pounds. Most of the boys said that they had brown hair, lifted weights, were 6 feet tall, and weighed 170 pounds.

and continuing through the tenth grade, in Milwaukee, Wisconsin. Students were individually interviewed, and achievement test scores and grade point averages were obtained. The presence or absence of menstruation and the relative onset of menses were used to classify girls as early, middle, or late maturers. The peak of growth in height was used to classify boys according to these categories.

In the Milwaukee study, more mixed and complex findings emerged for girls (Simmons & Blyth, 1987). Early-maturing girls had more problems in school, were more independent, and were more popular with boys than late-maturing girls were. The time at which maturation was assessed also was a factor. In the sixth grade, early-maturing girls were more satisfied with their body image than late-maturing girls were, but by the tenth grade, late-maturing girls were more satisfied (see figure 3.7). Why? Because by late adolescence, early-maturing girls are shorter and stockier, while late-maturing girls are taller and thinner. The late-maturing girls in late adolescence have body images that more closely approximate the current American ideal of feminine beauty—tall and thin.

In the last decade an increasing number of researchers have found that early maturation increases girls' vulnerability to a number of problems (Brooks-Gunn & Paikoff, 1993; Sarigiani & Petersen, 2000; Stattin & Magnusson, 1990). Early-maturing girls are more likely to smoke, drink, be depressed, have an eating disorder, request earlier independence from their parents, and have older friends; and their bodies likely elicit responses from males that lead to earlier dating and earlier sexual experiences. In one study, early-maturing girls had lower educational and occupational attainment in adulthood (Stattin & Magnusson, 1990). Apparently as a result of their social and cognitive immaturity, combined with early physical development, early-maturing girls are easily lured into problem behaviors, not recognizing the possible long-term effects on their development (Petersen, 1993).

Complexity of On-Time and Off-Time Pubertal Events in Development   Being on-time or off-time in terms of pubertal events is a complex affair (Scholte & Dubas, 2002). For example, the dimensions can involve not just biological status and pubertal age, but also chronological age, grade in school, cognitive functioning, and social maturity (Petersen, 1987). Adolescents can be at risk when the demands of a particular social context do not match the adolescents' physical and behavioral characteristics (Lerner, 1993). Dancers whose pubertal status develops on time are one example. In general peer comparisons, on-time dancers should not show adjustment problems. However, they do not have the ideal characteristics for being a dancer, which generally are those associated with late maturity—a thin, lithe body build. The dancers, then, are on time in terms of pubertal development for their peer group in general, but there is an asynchrony to their development in terms of their more focused peer group—dancers.

Are Puberty's Effects Exaggerated?   Some researchers have begun to question whether puberty's effects are as strong as once believed (Montemayor, Adams, & Gulotta, 1990). Have the effects of puberty been exaggerated? Puberty affects some adolescents more strongly than others, and some behaviors more strongly than others. Body image, dating interest, and sexual behavior are quite clearly affected by pubertal change. In one study, early-maturing boys and girls reported more sexual activity and delinquency than did late maturers (Flannery, Rowe, & Gulley, 1993). The recent questioning of puberty's effects, however, suggests that, if we look at overall development and adjustment in the human life span, puberty and its variations have less-dramatic effects for most individuals than is commonly thought. For some young adolescents, the transition through puberty is stormy, but for most it is not. Each period of the human life span has its stresses. Puberty is no different. It imposes new challenges resulting from emerging developmental changes, but the vast majority of adolescents weather these stresses effectively. In addition, there are not only biological

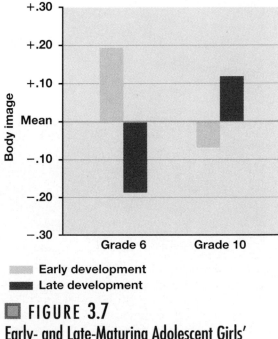

◼ FIGURE 3.7
Early- and Late-Maturing Adolescent Girls' Perceptions of Body Image in Early and Late Adolescence

CAREERS IN ADOLESCENT DEVELOPMENT

Anne Petersen
Researcher and Administrator

Anne Petersen has had a distinguished career as a researcher and administrator with a main focus on adolescent development. Anne obtained three degrees (B.A., M.A., and Ph.D.) from the University of Chicago in math and statistics. Her first job after she obtained her Ph.D. was as a research associate/professor involving statistical consultation, and it was on this job that she was introduced to the field of adolescent development, which became the focus of her subsequent work.

Anne moved from the University of Chicago to Pennsylvania State University, where she became a leading researcher in adolescent development. Her research included a focus on puberty and gender. Anne also has held numerous administrative positions. In the mid-1990s, Anne became Deputy Director of the National Science Foundation and since 1996 has been Senior Vice-President for programs at the W. K. Kellogg Foundation.

Anne says that what inspired her to enter the field of adolescent development and take her current position at the Kellogg Foundation was her desire to make a difference for people, especially youth. In her position at Kellogg, Anne is responsible for all programming and services provided by the foundation for adolescents. Her goal is to make a difference for youth in this country and around the world. She believes that too often adolescents have been neglected.

Anne Petersen, interacting with adolescents.

influences on adolescent development, but also cognitive and social or environmental influences (Sarigiani & Petersen, 2000). As with all periods of human development, these processes work in concert to produce who we are in adolescence. Singling out biological changes as the dominating change in adolescence may not be a wise strategy.

Although extremely early and late maturation may be risk factors in development, we have seen that the overall effects of early or late maturation are often not great. Not all early maturers will date, smoke, and drink, and not all late maturers will have difficulty in peer relations. In some instances, the effects of school grade are stronger than maturational timing effects are (Petersen & Crockett, 1985). Because the adolescent's social world is organized by grade rather than by pubertal development, this finding is not surprising. However, this does not mean that maturation has no influence on development. Rather, we need to evaluate puberty's effects within the larger framework of interacting biological, cognitive, and socioemotional contexts (Brooks-Gunn, 1992; Sarigiani & Petersen, 2000).

Pubertal Timing and Health Care

What can be done to identify off-time maturers who are at risk for health problems? Many adolescents whose development is extremely early or extremely late are likely to come to the attention of a physician—such as a boy who has not had a spurt in height by the age of 16 or a girl who has not menstruated by the age of 15. Girls and boys who are early or late maturers but are well within the normal range are less likely to be taken to a physician because of their maturational status. Nonetheless, these boys and girls may have fears and doubts about being normal that they do not raise unless a physician, counselor, or other health-care provider takes the initiative. A brief discussion outlining the sequence and timing of events and the large individual variations in them may be all that is required to reassure many adolescents who are maturing very early or very late.

Health-care providers may want to discuss the adolescent's off-time development with the adolescent's parents as well. Information about the peer pressures of off-time development can be beneficial. Especially helpful to early-maturing girls is a discussion of peer pressures to date and to engage in adultlike behavior at an early age. The transition to middle school, junior high school, or high school may be more stressful for girls and boys who are in the midst of puberty than for those who are not (Brooks-Gunn, 1988).

If pubertal development is extremely late, a physician may recommend hormonal treatment. In one study of extended pubertal delay in boys, hormonal treatment worked to increase the height, dating interest, and peer relations in several boys but resulted in little or no improvement in other boys (Lewis, Money, & Bobrow, 1977).

In sum, most early- and late-maturing individuals weather puberty's challenges and stresses competently. For those who do not, discussions with sensitive and knowledgeable health-care providers and parents can improve the off-time maturing adolescent's coping abilities.

Since the last review, we have discussed many aspects of puberty. This review should help you to reach your learning goals related to this topic.

☐ FOR YOUR REVIEW

Learning Goal 1
Understand pubertal change

- Puberty is a period of rapid physical maturation involving hormonal and bodily changes that take place primarily in early adolescence. Puberty's determinants include heredity, hormones, and possibly weight, percent of body fat, and leptin. Two classes of hormones that are involved in pubertal change and have significantly different concentrations in males and females are androgens and estrogens. The endocrine system's role in puberty involves the interaction of the hypothalamus, pituitary gland, and gonads. FSH and LH, which are secreted by the pituitary gland, are important aspects of this system. So is GnRH produced by the hypothalamus. A negative feedback system characterizes the way the sex hormone system works. Growth hormone also contributes to pubertal change. Puberty has two phases: adrenarche and gonadarche. The culmination of gonadarche in boys is spermarche and in girls is menarche.

- The initial onset of pubertal growth occurs on the average at 9 years for girls and 11 years for boys. The peak of pubertal changes for girls is at 11.5 years while for boys it is at 13.5 years. Girls grow an average of 3½ inches per year during puberty, boys 4 inches. Sexual maturation is a key feature of pubertal change. Individual variation in puberty is extensive and within a wide range is considered to be normal. Secular trends in puberty took place in the twentieth century with puberty coming earlier.

- Adolescents show heightened interest in their bodies and body images. Younger adolescents are more preoccupied with these images than older adolescents are. Adolescent girls often have more negative body images than adolescent boys do. Researchers have found connections between pubertal change and behavior but environmental influences need to be taken into account. Menarche and the menstrual cycle produce a wide range of reactions in girls. Early maturation often favors boys, at least during early adolescence, but as adults, late-maturing boys have a more positive identity than early-maturing boys. Early-maturing girls are at risk for a number of developmental problems. Being on-time or off-time in pubertal development is complex. Some scholars have expressed doubt that puberty's effects on development are as strong as once envisioned. Most early- and late-maturing adolescents weather the challenges of puberty competently. For those who do not, discussions with knowledgeable health-care providers and parents can improve the coping abilities of off-time adolescents.

In our discussion of hormonal changes in puberty, we indicated that the hypothalamus and pituitary gland play important roles in regulating the level of sex hormones. Next, we will focus on further changes in the brain during adolescence.

THE BRAIN

Until recently, little research had been conducted on developmental changes in the brain during adolescence. While research in this area is still in its infancy, an increasing number of research studies are being carried out. Scientists now believe that the adolescent's brain is different than the child's brain and that during adolescence the brain is still growing (Crews, 2001).

THE BRAIN

Neurons   Brain Structure

Neurons

Neurons, *or nerve cells, are the nervous system's basic units.* The three basic parts of the neuron are the cell body, the dendrites, and the axon (see figure 3.8 on p. 88). The

neurons
Nerve cells, which are the nervous system's basic units.

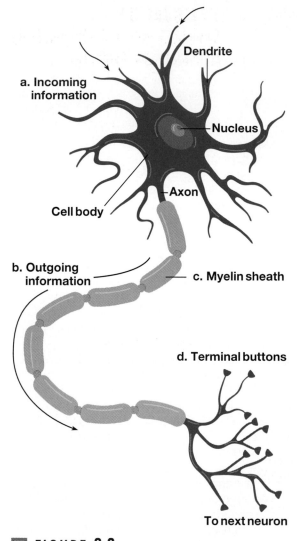

FIGURE 3.8
The Neuron

(*a*) The dendrites of the cell body receive information from other neurons, muscles, or glands through the axon. (*b*) Axons transmit information away from the cell body. (*c*) A myelin sheath covers most axons and speeds information transmission. (*d*) As the axon ends, it branches out into terminal buttons.

Neural Processes
Neuroimaging
Internet Neuroscience Resources
http://www.mhhe.com/santrocka9

dendrite is the receiving part of the neuron while the *axon* carries information away from the cell body to other cells. A *myelin sheath,* which is a layer of fat cells, encases most axons. The myelin sheath helps to insulate the axon and speeds up the transmission of the nerve impulse.

How do neurons change in adolescence? Researchers have found that cell bodies and dendrites do not change much during adolescence but that axons continue to develop through adolescence (Pfefferbaum & others, 1994; Rajapakse & others, 1996). The growth of axons is likely due to increased myelination (Giedd, 1998). Researchers have found that dendritic growth can continue even in older adults (Coleman, 1986), so further research may find more growth in dendrites during adolescence than these early studies are discovering.

In addition to dendritic spreading and the encasement of axons through myelination, another important aspect of the brain's development at the cellular level is the dramatic increase in connections between neurons (a process that is called synaptogenesis) (Ramey & Ramey, 2000). *Synapses* are gaps between neurons and are where connections between axons and dendrites take place.

Researchers have discovered an interesting aspect of synaptic connections. Nearly twice as many of these connections are made than will ever be used (Huttenlocher & others, 1991; Huttenlocher & Dabholkar, 1997). The connections that are used become strengthened and will survive, while the unused ones will be replaced by other pathways or disappear. That is, these connections will be "pruned" in the language of neuroscience. Figure 3.9 on page 89 vividly illustrates the dramatic growth and later pruning of synapses in the visual, auditory, and prefrontal cortex areas of the brain (Huttenlacher & Dabholkar, 1997). These are areas that are critical for higher-order cognitive functioning such as learning, memory, and reasoning.

As shown in figure 3.9, the time course for synaptic "blooming and pruning" varies considerably by brain region in humans. For example, the peak of synaptic overproduction in the visual cortex takes place at about the fourth postnatal month, following by a gradual retraction until the middle to end of the preschool years (Huttenlocher & Dabholkar, 1997). In areas of the brain involved in hearing and language, a similar although somewhat later course is detected. However, in the prefrontal cortex (the area of the brain where higher-level thinking and self-regulation occur), the peak of overproduction takes place at about 1 year of age and it is not until middle to late adolescence that the adult density of synapses is achieved.

What determines the timing and course of synaptic overproduction and subsequent retraction? Both heredity and experience are thought to be influential (Greenough, 2000; Greenough & Black, 1992).

Brain Structure

Neurons do not simply float in the brain. Connected in precise ways, they compose the various structures in the brain. Among structures of the brain that have recently been the focus of research in adolescent development are the brain's four lobes in the highest part of the brain—the cerebral cortex (see figure 3.10 on p. 89). The *occipital lobe* is involved in visual functioning. The *temporal lobe* is involved in hearing. The *parietal lobe* is involved in bodily sensations. The *frontal lobe* is involved in the control of voluntary muscles, personality, and intelligence. Another structure of the brain that has been studied during adolescent development is the *amygdala,* which is involved in emotion.

One of the main reasons that scientists only recently have begun to study brain development in adolescence is the lack of technology to do so. However, the creation of

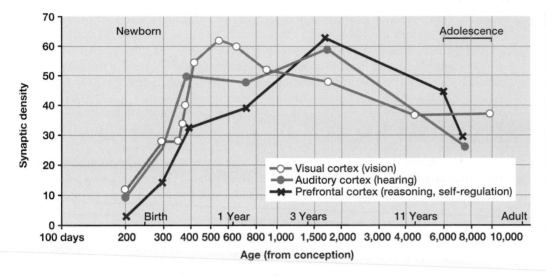

Synaptic Density in the Human Brain from Infancy to Adulthood

The graph shows the dramatic increase and then pruning in synaptic density for three regions of the brain: visual cortex, auditory cortex, and prefrontal cortex. Synaptic density is believed to be an important indication of the extent of connectivity between neurons.

sophisticated brain scanning devices, such as magnetic resonance imaging (MRI), is allowing better detection of brain changes during adolescence (Blumenthal & others, 1999). Magnetic resonance imaging consists of creating a magnetic field around a person's body and using radio waves to construct images of the brain's tissues and biochemical activities.

Using MRIs, scientists recently have discovered that children's and adolescents' brains undergo significant anatomical changes between 3 and 15 years of age (Thompson & others, 2000). By repeatedly obtaining brain scans of the same individuals for up to four years, it was discovered that rapid, distinct spurts of growth in the brain occur. The amount of brain material in some areas can nearly double within as little as one year of time, followed by a drastic loss of tissue as unneeded cells are purged and the brain continues to reorganize itself. In this research, the overall size of the brain did not change from 3 to 15 years of age. However, what did change dramatically were local patterns within the brain.

In this research, the most rapid growth from 3 to 6 years of age occurred in the frontal lobe areas that involve planning and organizing new actions, and in maintaining attention to tasks. From age 6 through puberty, the most growth took place in the temporal and parietal lobes, especially in the area of those lobes that function in language and spatial relations.

In one study, researchers used MRIs to discover if the brain activity of adolescents (10 to 18 years of age) differed from that of adults (20 to 40 years of age) during the processing of emotional information (Baird & others, 1999). In this study, the participants were asked to view pictures of faces displaying fearful expressions while undergoing an MRI. When adolescents (especially younger ones) processed emotional information, brain activity in the amygdala was more pronounced than in the frontal lobe but the reverse occurred in adults. As we indicated earlier, the amygdala is involved in emotion, while the frontal lobes are involved in higher level reasoning and thinking. The researchers interpreted these findings in this way: adolescents may respond with "gut" reactions to emotional stimuli while adults are more likely to respond in rational, reasoned ways. They also concluded that these changes are linked with growth in the frontal lobe of the brain from adolescence to adulthood. However, more research is needed to clarify these findings on

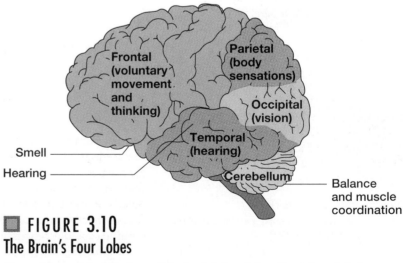

The Brain's Four Lobes

Shown here are the locations of the brain's four lobes: frontal, occipital, temporal, and parietal.

possible developmental changes in brain activity (Dahl, 2001; DeBellis & others, 2001; Spear, 2000).

In the next decade, we are likely to see far more research studies on brain development in adolescence. So far in this chapter we have studied puberty and the brain. Next, we will explore another very important topic in adolescence: health.

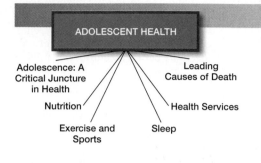

ADOLESCENT HEALTH

We will begin our discussion of adolescent health by evaluating why adolescence may be a critical juncture in the health of many individuals. Other topics we will examine include nutrition, exercise and sports, sleep, and the leading causes of death in adolescence.

Adolescence: A Critical Juncture in Health

Adolescence is a critical juncture in the adoption of behaviors relevant to health (Maggs, Schulenberg, & Hurrelmann, 1997; Roth & Brooks-Gunn, 2000). Many of the factors linked to poor health habits and early death in the adult years begin during adolescence.

The early formation of healthy behavioral patterns, such as eating foods low in fat and cholesterol and engaging in regular exercise, not only has immediate health benefits but contributes to the delay or prevention of major causes of premature disability and mortality in adulthood—heart disease, stroke, diabetes, and cancer (Jessor, Turbin, & Costa, 1998, in press).

Even though America has become a health-conscious nation, many adults and adolescents still smoke, have poor nutritional habits, and spend too much of their lives as couch potatoes.

Many adolescents often reach a level of health, strength, and energy that they will never match during the remainder of their lives. They also have a sense of uniqueness and invulnerability that leads them to think that poor health will never enter their lives, or that if it does, they will quickly recoup from it. Given this combination of physical and cognitive factors, it is not surprising that many adolescents have poor health habits.

Many health experts believe that improving adolescent health involves far more than trips to a doctor's office when sick. The health experts increasingly recognize that whether adolescents will develop a health problem or be healthy is primarily based on their behavior. The goals are to (1) reduce adolescents' *health-compromising behaviors,* such as drug abuse, violence, unprotected sexual intercourse, and dangerous driving, and (2) increase *health-enhancing behaviors,* such as eating nutritiously, exercising, wearing seat belts, and getting adequate sleep.

THROUGH THE EYES OF PSYCHOLOGISTS

Susan Millstein
University of California, San Francisco

"Identifying adolescents' unmet needs and setting goals for health promotion are important steps to take in maximizing adolescent development."

Adolescent Health
National Longitudinal Study of Adolescent Health
http://www.mhhe.com/santrocka9

basal metabolism rate (BMR)
The minimum amount of energy an individual uses in a resting state is the BMR.

Nutrition

The recommended range of energy intake for adolescents takes into account the different needs of adolescents, their growth rate, and their level of exercise. Males have higher energy needs than females. Older adolescent girls also have slightly lower energy needs than younger adolescent girls. Some adolescents' bodies burn energy faster than others. **Basal metabolism rate (BMR)** *is the minimum amount of energy an individual uses in a resting state.* As shown in figure 3.11 on page 91, BMR gradually declines from the beginning of adolescence through the end of adolescence.

Concern is often expressed over adolescents' tendency to eat between meals. However, the choice of foods is much more important than the time or place of eating. Fresh vegetables and fruits as well as whole-grain products are needed to complement the foods high in energy value and protein that adolescents commonly choose.

A special concern in American culture is the amount of fat in our diet. Many of today's adolescents virtually live on fast-food meals, which contributes to the increased fat levels in their diet. Most fast-food meals are high in protein, especially meat and dairy products. But the average American adolescent does not have to worry about getting enough protein. What should be of concern is the vast number of adolescents who consume large quantities of fast foods that are not only high in protein but high in fat.

Medical personnel and psychologists have become increasingly concerned with the health hazards associated with obesity. Eating patterns established in childhood and adolescence are highly associated with obesity in adulthood—80 percent of obese adolescents become obese adults. Obesity is estimated to characterize 25 percent of today's American adolescents. We will further explore adolescent obesity in chapter 14, "Adolescent Problems."

In this section, we have focused on adolescent nutrition and obesity. In chapter 14, "Adolescent Problems," we will discuss two disorders that have increasingly characterized adolescent females—anorexia nervosa and bulimia. Next, we will continue to explore adolescent health by examining exercise and sports.

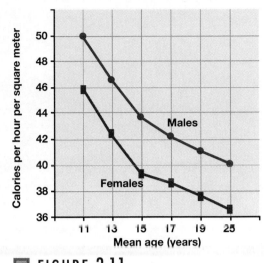

FIGURE 3.11
Basal Metabolic Rates (BMRs) for Adolescent Females and Males

Exercise and Sports

Do American adolescents get enough exercise? How extensive is the role of sports in adolescents' lives?

Exercise   Are adolescents getting enough exercise? In three recent national studies, adolescents clearly were not getting enough exercise. The first study compared adolescents' exercise patterns in 1987 and 2001 (American Sports Data, 2001). In 1987, 31 percent of 12- to 17-year-olds said that they exercised frequently, compared to only 18 percent in 2001. In the second study, physical activity declined from early to late adolescence (National Center for Health Statistics, 2000). Adolescents in grade 9 were more likely to participate in moderate or vigorous physical activity than their counterparts in grades 10 through 12. Male adolescents were far more likely to exercise than female adolescents were. In the third study, few adolescents participated in school physical education (PE) classes (Gordon-Larsen, McMurray, & Popkin, 2000). Only about 20 percent took a PE class one or more days per week. Participation in PE classes was especially low for African American and Latino adolescents.

Do U.S. adolescents exercise less than their counterparts in other countries. In a recent comparison of adolescents in 28 countries. U.S. adolescents exercised less and ate more junk food than adolescents in most countries (World Health Organization, 2000). Just two-thirds of U.S. adolescents exercised at least twice a week compared to 80 percent or more adolescents in Ireland, Austria, Germany, and the Slovak Republic. U.S. adolescents were more likely to eat fried food and less likely to eat fruits and vegetables than adolescents in most other countries studied. U.S. adolescents' eating choices were similar to those of adolescents in England.

Some health experts blame television for the poor physical condition of American adolescents. In one investigation, adolescents who watched little television were much more physically fit than those who watched heavy doses of television (Tucker, 1987). The more adolescents watch television, the more likely they are to be overweight. No one is quite sure whether this is because they spend their leisure time in front of a television set, because they eat a lot of junk food they see advertised on television, or because less physically fit youth find physical activity less reinforcing than watching television.

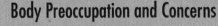

THROUGH THE EYES OF ADOLESCENTS

Body Preoccupation and Concerns

After locking the bathroom door, 12-year-old Anya carefully examines her still shower-damp body. She pokes disgustedly at her stomach. A year ago she wasn't as concerned about her body and it felt more familiar. Now the body she looks at in the mirror has new curves and hair she is not sure she likes. She feels as though she is too heavy and thinks, "Maybe I should try that diet that Becky told me about." Sighing, she pulls on her oversize sweatshirt and wonders what to do (Lerner & Olson, 1995).

What is the nature of adolescents' physical activity? What might schools possibly do to improve adolescents' physical fitness?

Some of the blame for the poor physical condition of U.S. children and adolescents falls on U.S. schools, many of which fail to provide physical education class on a daily basis. One extensive investigation of behavior in physical education classes at four different schools revealed how little vigorous exercise takes place in these classes (Parcel & others, 1987). Boys and girls moved through space only 50 percent of the time they were in the classes, and they moved continuously an average of only 2.2 minutes. In sum, not only does the adolescent's school week include inadequate physical education classes, but the majority of adolescents do not exercise vigorously even when they are in physical education classes. Further, while we hear a lot about the exercise revolution among adults, most children and adolescents report that their parents are poor role models when it comes to vigorous physical exercise (Feist & Brannon, 1989).

Does it make a difference if children and adolescents are pushed to exercise more vigorously in school? One investigation provided an affirmative answer to this question (Tuckman & Hinkle, 1988). One hundred fifty-four boys and girls were randomly assigned to either three 30-minute running programs per week or to regular attendance in physical education classes. Although the results sometimes varied by sex, for the most part those in the running program had increased cardiovascular health and showed increased creativity. For example, the running-program boys had less body fat, and the running-program girls had more creative involvement in their classrooms.

An exciting possibility is that physical exercise might provide a buffer to adolescents' stress. In one investigation of 364 females in grades 7 through 11 in Los Angeles, the negative impact of stressful events on health declined as exercise levels increased, suggesting that exercise can be a valuable resource for combating adolescents' life stresses (Brown & Siegel, 1988). In another investigation, adolescents who exercised regularly coped more effectively with stress and had more positive identities than did adolescents who engaged in little exercise (Grimes & Mattimore, 1989). And in one recent study, high school seniors who exercised frequently had higher grade point averages, used drugs less frequently, were less depressed, and got along better with their parents than their counterparts who rarely exercised (Field, Diego, & Sanders, 2001).

In the fourth century B.C., Aristotle commented that the quality of life is determined by its activities. In today's world, we know that exercise is one of the principal activities that improves the quality of life, both adolescents' and adults' (Malina, 2001).

Sports Sports play an important role in the lives of many adolescents (Kuchenbecker, 2000). Some estimates indicate that as many as 40 to 70 percent of American youths participate in various organized sports (Ferguson, 1999).

Sports can have positive and negative influences on adolescent development. Many sports activities can improve adolescents' physical well-being and health, self-confidence, motivation to excel, and ability to work with others (Cornock, Bowker, & Gadbois, 2001). In some cases, adolescents who spend considerable time in sports are less likely to engage in drugs and delinquency.

In one recent study of sports participation and health-related behaviors in more than 14,000 U.S. high school students, approximately 70 percent of the males and 53 percent of the females said that they had participated in one or more sports teams in school or nonschool settings (Pate & others, 2000). Male sports participants were more likely than nonparticipants to say they ate fruit and vegetables on the previous day and less likely to report cigarette smoking, cocaine and other illegal drug use, and trying to lose weight. Compared with female nonparticipants, female sports participants were more likely to say they ate vegetables on the previous day and less likely to report having sexual intercourse in the past three months.

The downside of the extensive participation in sports by American adolescents includes the increased high expectations by parents and coaches to win at all costs (Kuchenbecker, 2000). Researchers have found that adolescents' participation in competitive sports is linked with competition anxiety and self-centeredness (Bredemeier & Shields, 1996; Smith & Smoll, 1997). Another problem is that some adolescents spend so much time in sports that their academic skills suffer. And overuse injuries are increasing in adolescents who stretch their bodies beyond their capabilities. As they seek to become stars in their field, some adolescents increase the duration, intensity, and frequency of their training to a point that harms their bodies (Hellmich, 2000).

How might changing sleep patterns in adolescents affect their school performance?

Some of the problems that adolescents experience in sports involves coaches. Many youth coaches create a performance-oriented motivational climate focused on winning, public recognition, and performance relative to others. However, some coaches place more emphasis on mastery motivation that focuses adolescents' attention on the development of their skills and efforts to reach self-determined standards of success. Researchers have found that athletes with a mastery focus are more likely to see the benefits of practice, persist in the face of difficulty, and show more skill development over the course of a season (Roberts, Treasure, & Kavussanu, 1997).

Sleep

There has been a recent surge of interest in adolescent sleep patterns. This interest focuses on the belief that many adolescents are not getting enough sleep, that there are physiological underpinnings to adolescents' (especially older ones) desire to stay up later at night and sleep longer in the morning, and that these findings have implications for the hours that adolescents learn most effectively in school (Fukuda & Ishihara, 2001).

In one recent study, the sleep patterns of children in the second, fourth, and sixth grades were examined (Sadeh, Raviv, & Gruber, 2000). The children were evaluated with activity monitors, and the children and their parents completed sleep questionnaires and daily reports. Sixth-grade children went to sleep at night about one hour later (just after 10:30 P.M. versus just after 9:30 P.M.) and reported more daytime sleepiness than the second-grade children. Girls spent more time in sleep than boys. Also, family stress was linked with poor sleep, such as nightly wakings, in children.

Mary Carskadon and her colleagues (Acebo & others, 1999; Carskadon, Acebo, & Seifer, 2001; Carskadon & others, 1998; Carskadon & others, 1999; Wolfson & Carskadon, 1998) have conducted a number of research studies on adolescent sleep patterns. They found that adolescents would sleep an average of nine hours and 25 minutes when given the opportunity to sleep as long as they like. Most adolescents get considerably less than this nine hours of sleep, especially during the week. This creates a sleep debt, which adolescents often try to make up on the weekend. They also revealed that older adolescents are often more sleepy during the day than younger adolescents. Carskadon and her team of researchers theorized that this was not because of factors such as academic work and social pressures. Rather, their research suggests that adolescents' biological clocks undergo a hormonal phase shift as they get older. This pushes the time of wakefulness to an hour later than when they were young adolescents. The researchers found that this shift was caused by a delay in the nightly presence of the hormone melatonin, which is produced by the brain's pineal gland in preparation for the body to sleep. Melatonin is secreted at about 9:30 P.M. in younger adolescents but is produced approximately an hour later in older adolescents, which delays the onset of sleep.

Carskadon determined that early school starting times may result in grogginess and lack of attention in class and poor performance on tests. Based on this research, schools in Edina, Minnesota, made the decision to start classes at 8:30 A.M. rather than the earlier time they had been starting: 7:25 A.M. Under this later start time, there have been fewer referrals for discipline problems and the number of students who report an illness or depression has decreased. The Edina School System reports that test scores have improved for high school students, but not middle school students, which supports Carskadon's ideas about older adolescents being affected by earlier school start times than younger adolescents.

As we have just seen, changing sleep patterns in adolescence may have ramifications for how alert adolescents are in school. Next, we further explore the role of schools in adolescent health.

Health Services

Though adolescents have a greater number of acute health conditions than adults do, they use private physician services at a lower rate than any other age group does (Edelman, 1996). And adolescents often underutilize other health-care systems as well (Drotar, 2000; Klein & others, 2001; Millstein, 1993; Seiffge-Krenke, 1998). Health services are especially unlikely to meet the health needs of younger adolescents, ethnic minority adolescents, and adolescents living in poverty.

In the National Longitudinal Study of Adolescent Health, more than 12,000 adolescents were interviewed about the extent to which they needed health care but did not obtain it (Ford, Bearman, & Moody, 1999). Approximately 19 percent of the adolescents reported forgoing health care in the preceding year. Among the adolescents who especially needed health care but did not seek it were those who smoked cigarettes on a daily basis, frequently drank alcohol, and engaged in sexual intercourse.

Health Risks for Adolescents
http://www.mhhe.com/santrocka9

Among the chief barriers to better health services for adolescents are cost, poor organization, and availability of health services, as well as confidentiality of care. Also, few health-care providers receive any special training for working with adolescents. Many say that they feel unprepared to provide services such as contraceptive counseling and accurate evaluation of what constitutes abnormal behavior in adolescence (Irwin, 1993). Health-care providers might transmit to their patients their discomfort in discussing such topics as sexuality and drugs, which can lead to adolescents' unwillingness to discuss sensitive issues with them (Marcell & Millstein, 2001).

Leading Causes of Death

Medical improvements have increased the life expectancy of today's adolescents compared to their counterparts who lived early in the twentieth century. Still, life-threatening factors continue to exist in adolescents' lives.

The three leading causes of death in adolescence are accidents, homicide, and suicide (National Center for Health Statistics, 2000). More than half of all deaths in adolescents ages 10 to 19 are due to accidents, and most of those involve motor vehicles, especially for older adolescents. Risky driving habits, such as speeding, tailgating, and driving under the influence of alcohol or other drugs, might be more important causes of these accidents than lack of driving experience. In about 50 percent of the motor vehicle fatalities involving an adolescent, the driver has a blood alcohol level of 0.10 percent, twice the level needed to be "under the influence" in some states. A high rate of intoxication is also often present in adolescents who die as pedestrians or while using recreational vehicles.

Homicide also is a leading cause of death in adolescence. Homicide is especially high among African American male adolescents. They are three times more likely to be killed by guns than by natural causes (Simons, Finlay, & Yang, 1991).

Suicide accounts for 6 percent of the deaths in the 10 to 14 age group, a rate of 1.3 per 100,000 population. In the 15 to 19 age group, suicide accounts for 12 percent of deaths or 9 per 100,000 population. Since the 1950s, the adolescent suicide rate has tripled. We will discuss suicide further in chapter 14, "Adolescent Problems."

In this chapter we have discussed some important aspects of health. In later chapters, we will further explore many aspects of adolescent health. For example, we will examine many aspects of adolescent sexuality, such as unprotected sexual intercourse and sexually transmitted diseases in chapter 11, "Sexuality." We will evaluate drug abuse, violence, smoking, and eating disorders in chapter 14, "Adolescent Problems."

Since the last review, we have discussed developmental change in the brain and adolescent health. The following review should help you to reach your learning goals related to these topics.

☐ FOR YOUR REVIEW

Learning Goal 2
Know about developmental changes in the brain

- Neurons are the basic units of the nervous system and are made up of a cell body, dendrites, and an axon. So far, researchers have found that greater increases in the axon (probably because of increased myelination) take place in adolescence than in the cell body or dendrites. Synaptogenesis in the prefrontal cortex, where reasoning and self-regulation occur, continues through adolescence.
- Using magnetic resonance imaging (MRI), in one study, scientists found that between 3 to 15 years of age, rapid, distinct spurts of growth in the brain occur. In this study, from age 6 through puberty, the most growth took place in the temporal and parietal lobes, especially in areas that involve language and spatial relations. Other researchers have found that during adolescence, brain activity is more pronounced in the amygdala, which is involved in emotion, while in young adults, greater brain activity occurs in the frontal lobes, where higher reasoning takes place. Research on the development of the brain is in its infancy and the next decade is likely to see an increasing number of studies as technology in investigating the brain advances.

Learning Goal 3
Evaluate adolescent health

- Adolescence is a critical juncture in the adoption of positive health behaviors.
- A lower basal metabolism in adolescence means adolescents have to burn up more calories to maintain a healthy weight. There is concern about the eating habits of adolescents and obesity.
- Many adolescents do not get adequate exercise. Television, parents, and schools are possible contributors to the low exercise levels of adolescents. There are both positive and negative aspects of adolescents' participation in organized sports.
- Adolescents like to go to bed later and sleep later than children do. This may be linked with developmental changes in the brain. A special concern is the extent to which these changes in sleep patterns in adolescence affect academic behavior.
- Adolescents use health services far less than any other age group. There are a number of barriers to providing better health services for adolescents.
- The leading causes of death in adolescence are (1) accidents, (2) homicide, and (3) suicide.

Earlier in the chapter, we indicated that both heredity and environment are important influences on the onset of puberty. Let's now further explore the influence of heredity and environment on adolescent development.

By permission of Johnny Hart and Creators Syndicate, Inc.

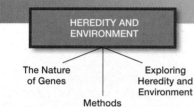

The Nature
of Genes

Methods

Exploring
Heredity and
Environment

HEREDITY AND ENVIRONMENT

As with all other species, we must have some mechanism for transmitting characteristics from one generation to the next. Each adolescent carries a genetic code inherited from her or his parents. The genetic codes of all adolescents are alike in one important way—they all contain the human genetic code. Because of the human genetic code, a fertilized human egg cannot grow into an eel, an egret, or an elephant.

The Nature of Genes

We each begin life as a single cell weighing one twenty-millionth of an ounce! This tiny piece of matter housed our entire genetic code—the information about who we would become. These instructions orchestrated growth from that single cell to an adolescent made of trillions of cells, each containing a perfect replica of the original genetic code. Physically, the hereditary code is carried by biochemical agents called genes and chromosomes. Aside from the obvious physical similarity this code produces among adolescents (such as in anatomy, brain structure, and organs), it also may account for much of our psychological sameness (or universality).

No one possesses all the characteristics that our genetic structure makes possible. A **genotype** *is a person's genetic heritage, the actual genetic material.* However, not all of this genetic material is apparent in our observed and measurable characteristics. A **phenotype** *is the way an individual's genotype is expressed in observed and measurable characteristics.* Phenotypes include physical traits, such as height, weight, eye color, and skin pigmentation, as well as psychological characteristics, such as intelligence, creativity, personality, and social tendencies. For each genotype, a range of phenotypes can be expressed. Imagine that we could identify all of the genes that would make an adolescent introverted or extraverted. Would measured introversion-extraversion be predictable from knowledge of the specific genes? The answer is no, because even if our genetic model was adequate, introversion-extraversion is a characteristic shaped by experience throughout life. For example, a parent might push an introverted child into social situations and encourage the child to become more gregarious.

Methods

Among the ways that the effects of heredity on development are studied are behavior genetics and molecular genetics.

genotype
A person's genetic heritage; the actual genetic material.

phenotype
The way an individual's genotype is expressed in observed and measurable characteristics.

Behavior Genetics   **Behavior genetics** *is the study of the degree and nature of behavior's hereditary basis.* Behavior geneticists assume that behaviors are jointly determined by the interaction of heredity and environment (Plomin & others, 1997; Wahlsten, 2000). To study heredity's influence on behavior, behavior geneticists often use either twin studies or adoption studies.

In a **twin study,** *the behavioral similarity of identical twins is compared with the behavioral similarity of fraternal twins. Identical twins* (called monozygotic twins) develop from a single fertilized egg that splits into two genetically identical replicas, each of which becomes a person. *Fraternal twins* (called dizygotic twins) develop from separate eggs and separate sperm, making them genetically no more similar than nontwin siblings. Although fraternal twins share the same womb, they are no more alike genetically than are nontwin brothers and sisters, and they may be of different sexes. By comparing groups of identical and fraternal twins, behavior geneticists capitalize on the basic knowledge that identical twins are more similar genetically than are fraternal twins (Silberg & Rutter, 1997). In one twin study, 7,000 pairs of Finnish identical and fraternal twins were compared on the personality traits of extraversion (outgoingness) and neuroticism (psychological instability) (Rose & others, 1988). On both of these personality traits, identical twins were much more similar than fraternal twins were, suggesting the role of heredity in both traits. However, several issues crop up as a result of twin studies. Adults may stress the similarities of identical twins more than those of fraternal twins, and identical twins may perceive themselves as a "set" and play together more than fraternal twins. If so, observed similarities in identical twins could be environmentally influenced.

In an **adoption study,** *investigators seek to discover whether the behavior and psychological characteristics of adopted children are more like those of their adoptive parents, who provided a home environment, or those of their biological parents, who contributed their heredity. Another form of adoption study is to compare adoptive and biological siblings.* In one investigation, the educational levels attained by biological parents were better predictors of adopted children's IQ scores than were the IQs of the children's adopted parents (Scarr & Weinberg, 1983). Because of the genetic relation between the adopted children and their biological parents, the implication is that heredity influences children's IQ scores (Moldin, 1999).

What is the nature of the twin study method?

Molecular Genetics   Studies of behavior genetics do not focus on the molecular makeup of genes. Rather behavior geneticists study the effects of heredity at a more global level by such methods as comparing the behavior of identical and fraternal twins.

Today, there is a great deal of enthusiasm about the use of molecular genetics to discover the specific locations on genes that determine an individual's susceptibility to many diseases and other aspects of health and well-being (Magee, Gordon, & Whelan, 2001; Peters & others, 2001; Sheffield, 1999).

The term *genome* is used to describe the complete set of instructions for making an organism. It contains the master blueprint for all cellular structures and activities for the life span of the organism. The human genome consists of tightly coiled threads of DNA.

The Human Genome Project, begun in the 1970s, has made stunning progress in mapping the human genome. A current goal for 2003 is to determine the sequences of the 3 billion chemical base pairs that make up human DNA (U.S. Department of Energy, 2001). In regard to adolescent development, we are likely to see efforts to identify

behavior genetics
The study of the degree and nature of behavior's hereditary basis.

twin study
A study in which the behavioral similarity of identical twins is compared with the behavioral similarity of fraternal twins.

adoption study
A study in which investigators seek to discover whether, in behavior and psychological characteristics, adopted children and adolescents are more like their adoptive parents, who provided a home environment, or their biological parents, who contributed their heredity. Another form of adoption study is to compare adoptive and biological siblings.

CHAPTER MAP

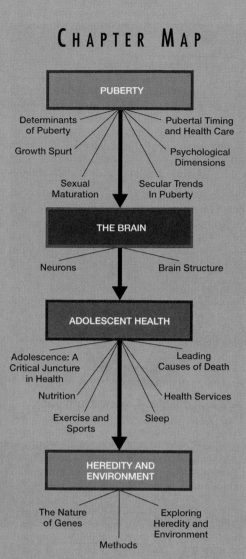

REACH YOUR LEARNING GOALS

At the beginning of the chapter, we stated four learning goals and encouraged you to review material related to these goals at three points in the chapter. This is a good time to return to these reviews and use them to guide your study and help you to reach your learning goals.

Page 87
Learning Goal 1   Understand pubertal change

Page 95
Learning Goal 2   Know about developmental changes in the brain
Learning Goal 3   Evaluate adolescent health

Page 101
Learning Goal 4   Explain heredity and environment

KEY TERMS

puberty 76
hormones 77
androgens 77
estrogens 77
menarche 79
spermarche 79
neurons 87
basal metabolism rate (BMR) 90
genotype 96
phenotype 96
behavior genetics 97

twin study 97
adoption study 97
passive genotype-environment
   correlations 98
evocative genotype-environment
   correlations 98
active (niche-picking) genotype-
   environment correlations 98
shared environmental influences 99
nonshared environmental influences 99

KEY PEOPLE

Roberta Simmons and Dale Blyth 84
Mary Carskadon 93
Sandra Scarr 98

RESOURCES FOR IMPROVING THE LIVES OF ADOLESCENTS

Journal of Adolescent Health Care

This journal includes articles about a wide range of health-related and medical issues, including reducing smoking, improving nutrition, health promotion, and physicians' and nurses' roles in reducing health-compromising behaviors of adolescents.

The Society for Adolescent Medicine

10727 White Oak Avenue
Granada Hills, CA 91344

This organization is a valuable source of information about competent physicians who specialize in treating adolescents. It maintains a list of recommended adolescent specialists across the United States.

TAKING IT TO THE NET

1. The growth spurt is accompanied by weight increases. Those whose weight increases too much are at an increased risk for negative health outcomes, including obesity, hypertension, and other health risks. One's body mass index (BMI) is a measure of the "fit" of one's weight to one's height. *Is your BMI in the "healthy" range or are you at risk for future health problems? How does your BMI relate to diet, exercise, and other measures of healthiness?*

2. Your instructor assigns a brief paper in which you are, first, to define the term "body image," including positive and negative aspects of it and, second, to devise procedures to improve an adolescent's negative body image, focusing on male body image as opposed to the

http://www.mhhe.com/santrocka9

more commonly researched and discussed female body image. *What procedures would you suggest to enhance a negative male body image?*

3. A major health concern during the adolescent years centers on the adolescent's diet. Keep track of everything you eat and drink for the next three days. *What is your daily caloric intake? Is it in the appropriate quantities recommended in the food pyramid? Are you eating healthy?*

Connect to *http://www.mhhe.com/santrocka9* to research the answers and complete these exercises. In some cases, you'll also find further instructions on this site.

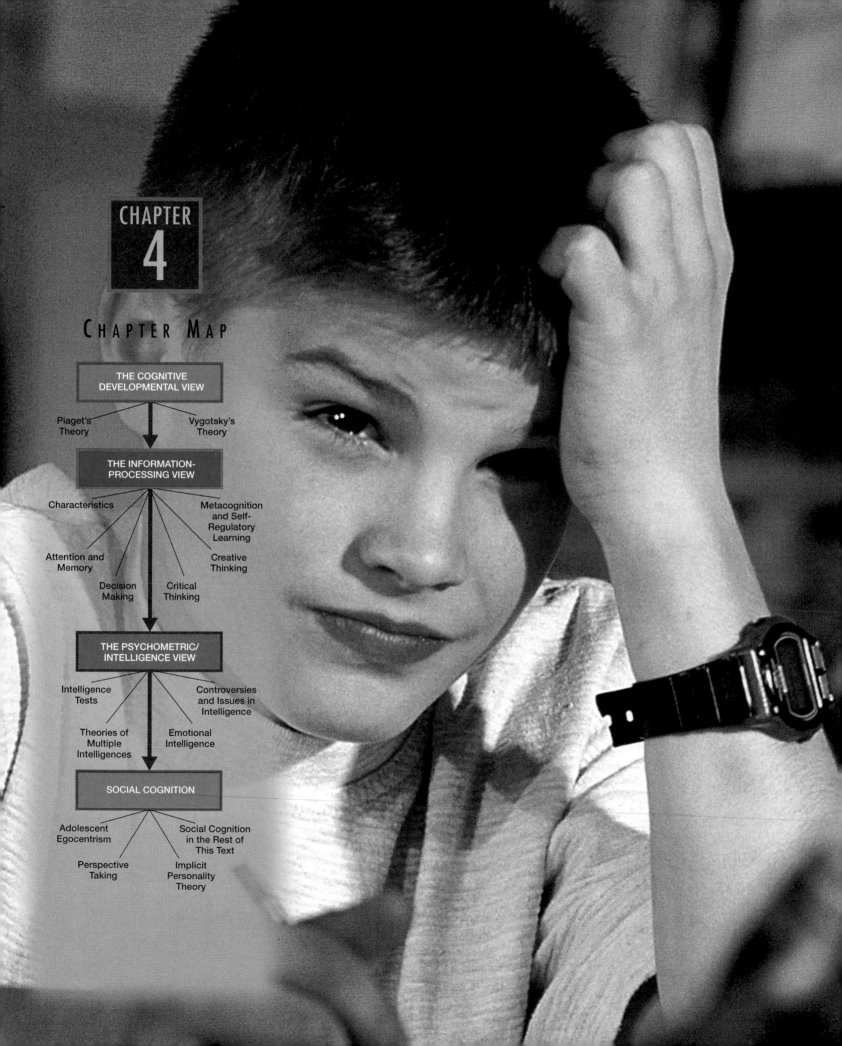

CHAPTER
4

CHAPTER MAP

THE COGNITIVE
DEVELOPMENTAL VIEW

Piaget's
Theory

Vygotsky's
Theory

THE INFORMATION-
PROCESSING VIEW

Characteristics

Metacognition
and Self-
Regulatory
Learning

Attention and
Memory

Creative
Thinking

Decision
Making

Critical
Thinking

THE PSYCHOMETRIC/
INTELLIGENCE VIEW

Intelligence
Tests

Controversies
and Issues in
Intelligence

Theories of
Multiple
Intelligences

Emotional
Intelligence

SOCIAL COGNITION

Adolescent
Egocentrism

Social Cognition
in the Rest of
This Text

Perspective
Taking

Implicit
Personality
Theory

COGNITIVE DEVELOPMENT

The thoughts of youth are long, long thoughts.
—Henry Wadsworth Longfellow
American Poet, 19th Century

■ THE DEVELOPING THOUGHTS OF ADOLESCENTS

When you were a young adolescent, what was your thinking like? Were your thinking skills as good as they are now? Could you solve difficult, abstract problems and reason logically about complex topics? Or did such skills improve in your high school years? Can you come up with any ways your thinking now is better than it was in high school?

Many young adolescents begin to think in more idealistic ways. How idealistic was your thinking when you were in middle school and high school? Did you think more about what is ideal versus what is real as an adolescent or as a child? Has your thinking gotten less idealistic now that you are in college, or do you still think a lot about an ideal world and how you might achieve it?

When we think about thinking, we usually consider it in terms of school subjects like math and English, or solving intellectual problems. But people's thoughts about social circumstances are also important. Psychologists are increasingly studying how adolescents think about social matters.

One of my most vivid memories of the adolescence of my oldest daughter, Tracy, is from when she was 12 years of age. I had accompanied her and her younger sister, Jennifer (10 at the time), to a tennis tournament. As we walked into a restaurant to have lunch, Tracy bolted for the restroom. Jennifer and I looked at each other, wondering what was wrong. Five minutes later Tracy emerged looking calmer. I asked her what had happened. Her response: "This one hair was out of place and every person in here was looking at me!"

Consider two other adolescents—Margaret and Adam. During a conversation with her girlfriend, 16-year-old Margaret says, "Did you hear about Catherine? She's pregnant. Do you think I would ever let that happen to me? Never." Thirteen-year-old Adam describes himself: "No one understands me, especially my parents. They have no idea of what I am feeling. They have never experienced the pain I'm going through." These experiences of Tracy, Margaret, and Adam represent the emergence of egocentric thought in adolescence. Later in the chapter we will explore adolescent egocentrism in greater detail.

WHEN PEOPLE THINK ABOUT CHANGES in adolescents, they often focus on the biological changes of puberty and socioemotional changes, such as independence, identity, relations with parents and peers, and so on. However, as you will see in this chapter, adolescents also undergo some impressive cognitive changes. When you have completed this chapter, you should be able to reach these learning goals:

1 Discuss Piaget's theory

2 Understand Vygotsky's theory

3 Evaluate the information-processing view

4 Explain the psychometric/intelligence view

5 Describe changes in social cognition

THE COGNITIVE
DEVELOPMENTAL VIEW

Piaget's
Theory

Vygotsky's
Theory

THE COGNITIVE DEVELOPMENTAL VIEW

In chapter 2, "The Science of Adolescent Development," we briefly examined Piaget's theory ◀▥ P. 46. Here we will explore his theory in more detail and describe another cognitive developmental theory that is receiving increased attention, that of Lev Vygotsky.

Piaget's Theory

Piaget's Theory
http://www.mhhe.com/santrocka9

Piaget had a number of things to say about adolescents' thinking being different from children's. We begin our coverage of Piaget's theory by describing its basic nature and the cognitive processes involved. Then we turn to his cognitive stages, giving special attention to concrete operational and formal operational thought.

The Nature of Piaget's Theory and Cognitive Processes Piaget's theory is the most well known, most widely discussed theory of adolescent cognitive development. Piaget stressed that adolescents are motivated to understand their world because doing so is biologically adaptive. In Piaget's view, adolescents actively construct their own cognitive worlds; information is not just poured into their minds from the environment. To make sense out of their world, adolescents organize their experiences. They separate important ideas from less important ones. They connect one idea to another. They not only organize their observations and experiences, they also adapt their thinking to include new ideas because additional information furthers understanding.

In actively constructing their world, adolescents use schemas. A **schema** *is a concept or framework that exists in an individual's mind to organize and interpret information.* Piaget's interest in schemas focused on how children and adolescents organize and make sense out of their current experiences.

Piaget (1952) said that two processes are responsible for how children and adolescents use and adapt their schemas: assimilation and accommodation.

Assimilation *occurs when individuals incorporate new information into existing knowledge.* In assimilation, the schema does not change. **Accommodation** *occurs when individuals adjust to new information.* In accommodation, the schema changes. Suppose that a 16-year-old girl wants to learn how to use a computer. Her parents buy her a computer for her birthday. She has never had the opportunity to use one. From her experience and observation, though, she realizes that software discs are inserted in a slot and a switch must be pressed to turn the computer on. Thus far she has incorporated her behavior into a conceptual framework she already had (assimilation). As she strikes several keys, she makes some errors. Soon she realizes that she needs to get someone to

schema

A concept or framework that exists in the individual's mind to organize and interpret information, in Piaget's theory.

assimilation

The incorporation of new information into existing knowledge.

accommodation

An adjustment to new information.

help her learn to use the computer efficiently or take a class on using a computer at her high school. These adjustments show her awareness of the need to alter her concept of computer use (accommodation).

Equilibration *is a mechanism in Piaget's theory that explains how children or adolescents shift from one state of thought to the next. The shift occurs as they experience cognitive conflict or a disequilibrium in trying to understand the world. Eventually, the child or adolescent resolves the conflict and reaches a balance, or equilibrium, of thought.* Piaget believed there is considerable movement between states of cognitive equilibrium and disequilibrium as assimilation and accommodation work in concert to produce cognitive change. For example, if a child believes that the amount of a liquid changes simply because the liquid is poured into a container with a different shape, she might be puzzled by such issues as where the "extra" liquid came from and whether there is actually more liquid to drink. The child will eventually resolve these puzzles as her thought becomes more advanced. In the everyday world, the child is constantly faced with such counterexamples and inconsistencies.

Stages of Cognitive Development

Piaget said that individuals develop through four main cognitive stages: sensorimotor, preoperational, concrete operational, and formal operational. Each of the stages is age related and consists of distinct ways of thinking. It is the *different* way of understanding the world that makes one stage more advanced than the other; knowing *more* information does not make the adolescent's thinking more advanced, in the Piagetian view. This is what Piaget meant when he said that the person's cognition is *qualitatively* different in one stage compared to another. We will briefly again define the first two stages in Piaget's theory, which were first introduced in chapter 2, and then explain concrete and formal operational thought.

Sensorimotor and Preoperational Thought

The **sensorimotor stage**, *which lasts from birth to about 2 years of age, is the first Piagetian stage. In this stage, infants construct an understanding of the world by coordinating sensory experiences (such as seeing and hearing) with physical, motoric actions—hence the term* sensorimotor. At the beginning of this stage, newborns have little more than reflexive patterns with which to work. By the end of the stage, 2-year-olds have complex sensorimotor patterns and are beginning to operate with primitive symbols.

The **preoperational stage**, *which lasts approximately from 2 to 7 years of age, is the second Piagetian stage. In this stage, children begin to represent the world with words, images, and drawings.* Symbolic thought goes beyond simple connections of information and action.

Concrete Operational Thought

The **concrete operational stage**, *which lasts approximately from 7 to 11 years of age, is the third Piagetian stage. In this stage, children can perform operations. Logical reasoning replaces intuitive thought as long as the reasoning can be applied to specific or concrete examples.*

Piaget said that concrete operational thought involves *operations*—mental actions that allow the individual to do mentally what was done before physically. And he said that the concrete operational thinker can engage in mental actions that are reversible. For example, the concrete operational thinker can mentally reverse liquid from one beaker to another and understand that the volume is the same even though the beakers differ in height and width. In Piaget's most famous task, a child is presented with two identical beakers, each filled with the same amount of liquid (see figure 4.1 on p. 108). Children are asked if these beakers have the same amount of liquid, and they usually say yes. Then, the liquid from one beaker is poured into a third beaker, which is taller and thinner than the first two (see figure 4.1 on p. 108). Children are then asked if the amount of liquid in the tall, thin beaker is equal to that which remains in one of the original beakers. Concrete operational thinkers answer yes and justify their answers appropriately. Preoperational thinkers (usually children under the age of 7) often answer no and justify their answer in terms of the differing height and width of the beakers. This example reveals the ability of the concrete operational thinker to decenter and

equilibration

A mechanism in Piaget's theory that explains how children or adolescents shift from one state of thought to the next. The shift occurs as they experience cognitive conflict or a disequilibrium in trying to understand the world. Eventually, the child or adolescent resolves the conflict and reaches a balance, or equilibrium.

We are born capable of learning.
—Jean-Jacques Rousseau
Swiss-Born French Philosopher,
18th Century

sensorimotor stage

Piaget's first stage of development, lasting from birth to about 2 years of age. In this stage, infants construct an understanding of the world by coordinating sensory experiences with physical, motoric actions.

preoperational stage

Piaget's second stage, which lasts approximately from 2 to 7 years of age. In this stage, children begin to represent their world with words, images, and drawings.

concrete operational stage

Piaget's third stage, which lasts approximately from 7 to 11 years of age. In this stage, children can perform operations. Logical reasoning replaces intuitive thought as long as the reasoning can be applied to specific or concrete examples.

Thinking Critically

Formal Operational Thought, Politics, and Ideology

The development of formal operational thought expands adolescents' worlds by allowing them to consider possibilities, to conduct experiments and test hypotheses, and to think about thoughts. Part of the cognitive expansion of their worlds involves constructing theories involving politics and ideology. During adolescence, for the first time individuals become adept at generating ideas about the world as it *could* be. In the realm of moral development, adolescents often quickly make a leap from how the world could be to how it *should* be. And many adolescents believe the world *should* be transformed in the direction of some utopian ideal.

Suppose an 8-year-old and a 16-year-old are watching a political convention on television. In view of where each is likely to be in terms of Piaget's stages of cognitive development, how would their perceptions of the political proceedings likely differ? What would the 8-year-old "see" and comprehend? What Piagetian changes would these differences reflect?

"and give me good abstract-reasoning ability, interpersonal skills, cultural perspective, linguistic comprehension, and a high sociodynamic potential."

is a "halving" strategy (Q: Is the picture in the right half of the array? A: No. Q: OK. Is it in the top half? And so on.). A correct halving strategy guarantees the answer to this problem in seven questions or less. In contrast, the concrete operational thinker might persist with questions that continue to test some of the same possibilities that previous questions could have eliminated. For example, they might ask whether the correct picture is in row 1 and be told that it is not, then later ask whether the picture is *x*, which is in row 1.

Thus, formal operational thinkers test their hypotheses with judiciously chosen questions and tests. Concrete operational thinkers, on the other hand, often fail to understand the relation between a hypothesis and a well-chosen test of it, stubbornly clinging to ideas that already have been discounted.

Piaget believed that formal operational thought is the best description of how adolescents think. A summary of formal operational thought's characteristics is shown in figure 4.3 on page 111. As we see next, though, formal operational thought is not a homogeneous stage of development.

Not all adolescents are full-fledged formal operational thinkers. Some developmentalists believe that formal operational thought consists of two subperiods: early and late (Broughton, 1983). In *early formal operational thought*, adolescents' increased ability to think in hypothetical ways produces unconstrained thoughts with unlimited possibilities. In this early period, formal operational thought submerges reality, and there is an excess of assimilation as the world is perceived too subjectively and idealistically. *Late formal operational thought* involves a restoration of intellectual balance. Adolescents now test out the products of their reasoning against experience, and a consolidation of formal operational thought takes place. An intellectual balance is restored, as the adolescent accommodates to the cognitive upheaval that has occurred. Late formal operational thought may appear during the middle adolescent years. In this view, assimilation of formal operational thought marks the transition to adolescence; accommodation to formal operational thought marks a later consolidation (Lapsley, 1990).

Piaget's (1952) early writings indicated that the onset and consolidation of formal operational thought are completed during early adolescence, from about 11 to 15 years of age. Later, Piaget (1972) revised his view and concluded that formal operational thought is not completely achieved until later in adolescence, between approximately 15 and 20 years of age. As we see next, many developmentalists believe that there is considerable individual variation in adolescent cognition.

Piaget's theory emphasizes universal and consistent patterns of formal operational thought. His theory does not adequately account for the unique, individual differences that characterize the cognitive development of adolescents (Overton & Byrnes, 1991). These individual variations in adolescents' cognitive development have been documented in a number of investigations (Neimark, 1982).

Some individuals in early adolescence are formal operational thinkers; others are not. A review of formal operational thought investigations revealed that only about one of every three eighth-grade students is a formal operational thinker (Strahan, 1983). Some investigators find that formal operational thought increases with age in adolescence; others do not. Many college students and adults do not think in formal operational ways either. For example, investigators have found that from 17 to 67 percent of college students think in formal operational ways (Elkind, 1961; Tomlinson-Keasey, 1972).

Many young adolescents are at the point of consolidating their concrete operational thought, using it more consistently than in childhood. At the same time, many

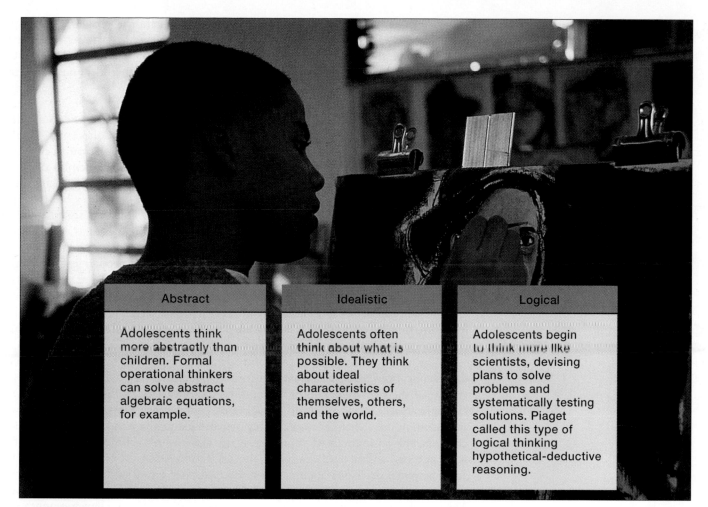

Abstract	Idealistic	Logical
Adolescents think more abstractly than children. Formal operational thinkers can solve abstract algebraic equations, for example.	Adolescents often think about what is possible. They think about ideal characteristics of themselves, others, and the world.	Adolescents begin to think more like scientists, devising plans to solve problems and systematically testing solutions. Piaget called this type of logical thinking hypothetical-deductive reasoning.

■ FIGURE 4.3
Characteristics of Formal Operational Thought

Adolescents begin to think more as scientists think, devising plans to solve problems and systematically testing solutions. Piaget gave this type of thinking the imposing name of hypothetical-deductive reasoning.

young adolescents are just beginning to think in a formal operational manner. By late adolescence, many adolescents are beginning to consolidate their formal operational thought, using it more consistently. And there often is variation across the content areas of formal operational thought, just as there is in concrete operational thought in childhood. A 14-year-old adolescent might reason at the formal operational level when analyzing algebraic equations but not do so with verbal problem solving or when reasoning about interpersonal relations.

Formal operational thought is more likely to be used in areas in which adolescents have the most experience and knowledge. Children and adolescents gradually build up elaborate knowledge through extensive experience and practice in various sports, games, hobbies, and school subjects, such as math, English, and science. The development of expertise in different domains of life may make possible high-level, developmentally mature-looking thought. In some instances, the sophisticated reasoning of formal operational thought might be responsible. In other instances, however, the thought might be largely due to the accumulation of knowledge that allows more automatic,

■ THROUGH THE EYES OF ADOLESCENTS

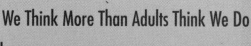

We Think More Than Adults Think We Do

"I don't think adults understand how much kids think today. We just don't take something at face value. We want to understand why things are the way they are and the reasons behind things. We want it to be a better world and we are thinking all of the time how to make it that way. When we get to be adults, we will make the world better."

—Jason, Age 15
Dallas, Texas

memory-based processes to function. Some developmentalists wonder if the acquisition of knowledge could account for all cognitive growth. Most, however, argue that *both* cognitive changes in such areas as concrete and formal operational thought *and* the development of expertise through experience are at work in understanding the adolescent's cognitive world.

Piaget's Theory and Adolescent Education

Piaget's theory has been widely applied to education, although more extensively with children than with adolescents. Piaget was not an educator and never pretended to be. But he did provide a sound conceptual framework from which to view educational problems. What principles of Piaget's theory of cognitive development can be applied to education? David Elkind (1976) described two.

First, the foremost issue in education is *communication*. In Piaget's theory, the adolescent's mind is not a blank slate. To the contrary, the adolescent has a host of ideas about the physical and natural world. Adolescents come to school with their own ideas about space, time, causality, quantity, and number. Educators need to learn to comprehend what adolescents are saying and to respond to their ideas. Second, adolescents are, by nature, knowing creatures. The best way to nurture this motivation for knowledge is to allow adolescents to spontaneously interact with the environment. Educators need to ensure that they do not dull adolescents' eagerness to know by providing an overly rigid curriculum that disrupts adolescents' rhythm and pace of learning.

Why have applications to adolescent education lagged behind applications to children's education? Adolescents who are formal operational thinkers are at a level similar to that of their teachers and of the authors of textbooks. In Piaget's model, it is no longer necessary to pay attention to qualitative changes in cognition. Also, the structure of education itself changes considerably between elementary and secondary levels. For children, the basic focus of education is the classroom. Children might be involved with, at most, several teachers during the day. In secondary schools, the focus shifts to subject-matter divisions of curriculum. Each teacher sees a student for 45 to 60 minutes a day in connection with one content area (English, history, math, for example). Thus, both teachers and texts can become more focused on the development of curriculum than on the developmental characteristics of students. And when teachers *are* concerned about students' developmental characteristics in adolescence, they pay more attention to social-personality dimensions than to cognitive dimensions.

One main argument that has emerged from the application of Piaget's theory to education is that instruction may too often be at the formal operational level, even though the majority of adolescents are not actually formal operational thinkers. That is, the instruction might be too formal and too abstract. Possibly, it should be less formal and more concrete. Researchers have found that adolescents construct a view of the world on the basis of observations and experiences and that educators should take this into account when developing a curriculum for adolescents (Linn, 1991).

Evaluating Piaget's Theory

What were Piaget's main contributions? Has his theory withstood the test of time?

Contributions   Piaget is a giant in the field of developmental psychology. We owe to him the present field of cognitive development and a long list of masterful concepts of enduring power and fascination: assimilation, accommodation, conservation, hypothetical-deductive reasoning, and others. We also owe to him the current vision of children as active, constructive thinkers (Vidal, 2000).

Piaget also was a genius when it came to observing children. His careful observations showed us inventive ways to discover how children act on and adapt to their world. Piaget showed us some important things to look for in cognitive development, such as the shift from preoperational to concrete operational thinking. He also showed us how children need to make their experiences fit their schemas (cognitive frameworks) yet simultaneously adapt their schemas to experience. Piaget also revealed how cognitive change is likely to occur if the context is structured to allow gradual movement to the next-higher level. And we owe him the current belief that a concept does not emerge all of a sudden, full-blown, but instead develops through a series of partial accomplishments that lead to increasingly comprehensive understanding (Haith & Benson, 1998).

Criticisms   Piaget's theory has not gone unchallenged. Questions are raised about these areas:

• *Estimates of children's competence.* Some cognitive abilities emerge earlier than Piaget thought. For example, some aspects of object permanence emerge earlier in infancy than he believed. Even 2-year-olds are nonegocentric in some contexts. When they realize that another person will not see an object, they investigate whether the person is blindfolded or looking in a different direction. Conservation of number has been demonstrated as early as age 3, although Piaget thought it did not emerge until 7. Young children are not as uniformly "pre-" this and "pre-" that (precausal, preoperational) as Piaget thought.

Other cognitive abilities can emerge later than Piaget thought. Many adolescents still think in concrete operational ways or are just beginning to master formal operations. Even many adults are not formal operational thinkers. In sum, recent theoretical revisions highlight more cognitive competencies of infants and young children and more cognitive shortcomings of adolescents and adults (Flavell, Miller, & Miller, 2001; Wertsch, 2000).

• *Stages.* Piaget conceived of stages as unitary structures of thought. Thus, his theory assumes developmental synchrony: various aspects of a stage should emerge at the same time. However, some concrete operational concepts do not appear in synchrony. For example, children do not learn to conserve at the same time as they learn to cross-classify. Thus, most contemporary developmentalists agree that children's cognitive development is not as stagelike as Piaget thought (Brainerd, 2002; Kuhn, 2000a).

• *Training children to reason at a higher level.* Some children who are at one cognitive stage (such as preoperational) can be trained to reason at a higher cognitive stage (such as concrete operational). This poses a problem for Piaget's theory. Piaget argued that such training is only superficial and ineffective, unless the child is at a maturational transition point between the stages (Gelman & Williams, 1998).

• *Culture and education.* Culture and education exert stronger influences on development than Piaget envisioned. The age at which individuals acquire conservation skills is associated to some extent with the degree to which their culture provides relevant practice (Cole, 1997). And in many developing countries, formal operational thought is rare. Shortly, you will read about Lev Vygotsky's theory of cognitive development in which culture and education are given more prominent roles than in Piaget's theory.

Piaget, shown sitting on a bench, was a genius at observing children. By carefully observing and interviewing children, Piaget constructed his comprehensive theory of children's cognitive development. *What are some other contributions, as well as criticisms, of Piaget's theory?*

One group of cognitive developmentalists believe that Piaget's theory needs to be modified. These **neo-Piagetians** *argue that Piaget got some things right, but that his theory needs considerable revision. In their revision of Piaget, they give more emphasis to how children process information through attention, memory, and strategies and to more precise explanations of cognitive changes.* They especially believe that a more accurate vision of children's and adolescents' thinking requires more knowledge of strategies, how fast and automatically information is processed, the particular cognitive task involved, and dividing cognitive problems into smaller, more precise steps.

The leading proponent of the neo-Piagetian view is Canadian developmental psychologist Robbie Case (1992, 1998, 2000). He accepts Piaget's four main stages of cognitive development but believes that a more precise description of changes within each

neo-Piagetians

Theorists who argue that Piaget got some things right but that his theory needs considerable revision. In their revision, they give more emphasis to information processing that involves attention, memory, and strategies; they also seek to provide more precise explanations of cognitive changes.

stage needs to be carried out. Case also argues that children's and adolescents' ability to process information more efficiently is linked to their brain growth and memory development. He especially cites the increasing ability to hold information in working memory (a workbench for memory similar to short-term memory) and manipulate it more effectively as critical to understanding cognitive development.

Is There a Fifth, Postformal Stage?

As we saw earlier in the chapter, Piaget did not believe there is a fifth, postformal stage. He argued that formal operational thought is the highest *qualitative* stage of thought and that it is entered in early adolescence. However, some theorists argue that Piaget was wrong about formal operations being the most advanced stage of thought. They believe that young adults can enter a fifth, postformal stage.

postformal thought

A form of thought, proposed as a fifth stage, that is qualitatively different from Piaget's formal operational thought. It involves understanding that the correct answer to a problem can require reflective thinking, that the correct answer can vary from one situation to another, and that the search for truth is often an ongoing, never-ending process.

Postformal thought *is qualitatively different from Piaget's formal operational thought. Postformal thought involves understanding that the correct answer to a problem requires reflective thinking and can vary from one situation to another, and that the search for truth is often an ongoing, never-ending process.* Also part of the fifth stage is the belief that solutions to problems need to be realistic and that emotion and subjective factors can influence thinking (Kitchener & King, 1981). Researchers have found that young adults are more likely to engage in this postformal thinking than adolescents are (Commons & others, 1989).

As young adults engage in more reflective judgment when solving problems, they might think deeply about many aspects of politics, their career and work, relationships, and other areas of life (Labouvie-Vief & Diehl, 1999). They might understand that what might be the best solution to a problem at work (with a co-worker or boss) might not be the best solution at home (with a romantic partner). Many young adults also become more skeptical about there being a single truth and often are not willing to accept an answer as final. They also often recognize that thinking can't just be abstract but rather has to be realistic and pragmatic. And many young adults understand that emotions can play a role in thinking—for example, that one likely thinks more clearly in a calm, collected state than in an angry, highly aroused state.

How strong is the research evidence for a fifth, postformal stage of cognitive development? The fifth stage is controversial, and some critics argue that the research evidence has yet to be provided to document it as clearly a qualitatively more advanced stage than formal operational thought.

William Perry (1970, 1999) especially believes that changes in reflective and relativistic thinking take place as individuals make the transition from adolescence to adulthood, a time referred to as emerging adulthood. He said that younger adolescents tend to view the world in terms of polarities—right/wrong, we/they, good/bad. As adolescents make the transition to adulthood, they gradually move away from this type of absolute thinking. This change occurs as they become aware of the diverse opinions and multiple perspectives of others.

Perry said that college is a pivotal time for the change from absolute to more relativistic thinking. Indeed, researchers have found that individuals who go to college think in more relativistic ways than those who do not attend college (King & Kitchener, 1994). This likely occurs because of the exposure to instructors and peers with views that are quite different from one's own.

Vygotsky's Theory

We introduced Vygotsky's theory in chapter 2, "The Science of Adolescent Development." Here we expand on those ideas ◀▥ P. 47.

Vygotsky's (1962) theory has stimulated considerable interest in the view that knowledge is *situated* and *collaborative* (Greeno, Collins, & Resnick, 1996; Rogoff, 1998)—that knowledge is distributed among people and environments, which include objects, artifacts, tools, books, and the communities in which people live. This suggests that knowing can best be advanced through interaction with others in cooperative activities (Glassman, 2001; Gojdamaschko, 1999; Kozulin, 2000; Tudge & Scrimsher, 2002).

One of Vygotsky's most important concepts is the **zone of proximal development (ZPD),** *which refers to the range of tasks that are too difficult for an individual to master alone, but that can be mastered with the guidance and assistance of adults or more-skilled peers.* Thus, the lower level of the ZPD is the level of problem solving reached by the adolescent working independently. The upper limit is the level of additional responsibility the adolescent can accept with the assistance of an able instructor (see figure 4.4). Vygotsky's emphasis on the ZPD underscored his belief in the importance of social influences on cognitive development.

In Vygotsky's approach, formal schooling is but one cultural agent that determines adolescents' growth (Keating, 1990). Parents, peers, the community, and the technological orientation of the culture are other forces that influence adolescents' thinking. For example, the attitudes toward intellectual competence that adolescents encounter through relationships with their parents and peers affect their motivation for acquiring knowledge. So do the attitudes of teachers and other adults in the community. Media influences, especially through the development of television and the computer, play increasingly important roles in the cognitive socialization of adolescents. For example, does television train adolescents to become passive learners and detract significantly from their intellectual pursuit? We will consider television's role in adolescent development in chapter 8.

The cognitive socialization of adolescents can be improved through the development of more cognitively stimulating environments and additional focus on the role of social factors in cognitive growth (Brown, Metz, & Campione, 1996). Approaches that take into account adolescents' self-confidence, achievement expectations, and sense of purpose are likely to be just as effective as, or even more effective than, more narrow cognitive approaches in shaping adolescents' cognitive growth. For example, a knowledge of physics could be of limited use to inner-city youth with severely limited prospects of employment (Keating, 1990).

Exploring Some Contemporary Concepts A number of contemporary concepts are compatible with Vygotsky's theory. These include the concepts of scaffolding, cognitive apprenticeship, tutoring, cooperative learning, and reciprocal teaching.

Scaffolding *Scaffolding* refers to changing the level of support over the course of a teaching session: a more-skilled person (teacher or more-advanced peer of the adolescent) adjusts the amount of guidance to fit the adolescent's current level of performance. When the task the adolescent is learning is new, direct instruction might be used. As the adolescent's competence increases, less guidance is provided. Think of scaffolding in learning as like the scaffolding used to build a bridge—it is used for support when needed, but is adjusted or removed as the project unfolds.

Cognitive Apprenticeship Barbara Rogoff (1990, 1998) believes that an important aspect of learning is *cognitive apprenticeship,* in which an expert stretches and supports the novice's understanding of and use of the culture's skills. The term *apprenticeship* underscores the importance of activity in learning and highlights the situated nature of learning. In a cognitive apprenticeship, adults often model strategies for adolescents then support their efforts at doing the task. Finally, they encourage adolescents to work independently.

zone of proximal development (ZPD)
Vygotsky's concept that refers to the range of tasks that are too difficult for an individual to master alone, but that can be mastered with the guidance or assistance of adults or more-skilled peers.

Lev Vygotsky: Revolutionary Scientist
Vygotsky Links
http://www.mhhe.com/santrocka9

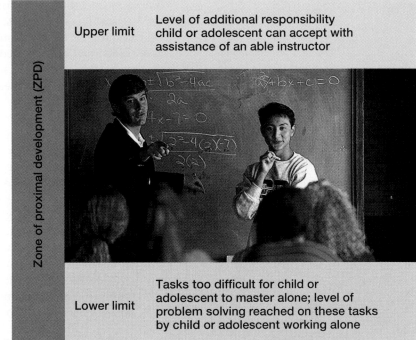

■ FIGURE 4.4
Vygotsky's Zone of Proximal Development (ZPD)

Vygotsky's zone of proximal development has a lower limit and an upper limit. Tasks in the ZPD are too difficult for the child or adolescent to perform alone. They require assistance from an adult or a more-skilled youth. As children and adolescents experience the verbal instruction or demonstration, they organize the information in their existing mental structures so they can eventually perform the skill or task alone.

Scaffolding
Cognitive Apprenticeship
Peer Tutoring
http://www.mhhe.com/santrocka9

A key aspect of a cognitive apprenticeship is the expert's evaluation of when the learner is ready to take the next step with support from the expert. In one study of secondary school science and math students, experts used the timing of the students' participation in discourse to infer student understanding of the points of the lesson; the experts provided pauses to allow students to take responsibility for an idea by anticipating or completing the experts' ideas (Fox, 1993). Experts also used information regarding the length of each response opportunity students passed up and what the students were doing during the passed-up opportunity (such as calculating or expressing a blank stare). When students passed up two or three opportunities, experts continued with an explanation. If no evidence of understanding occurred during the explanation, the expert repeated or reformulated it. The experts also used "hint" questions to get students unstuck and observed the looks on their faces and how they responded to questions for discerning their understanding.

Tutoring   Tutoring involves a cognitive apprenticeship between an expert and a novice. Tutoring can take place between an adult and an adolescent or between a more-skilled adolescent and a less-skilled adolescent. Fellow students can be effective tutors. Cross-age tutoring usually works better than same-age tutoring. Researchers have found that peer tutoring often benefits students' achievement (Mathes & others, 1998). And tutoring can benefit the tutor as well as the tutee, especially when the older tutor is a low-achieving student. Teaching something to someone else is one of the best ways to learn.

Cooperative Learning
Schools for Thought
http://www.mhhe.com/santrocka9

Cooperative Learning   *Cooperative learning* involves students working in small groups to help each other learn. Cooperative learning groups vary in size, although a typical group will have about four students. Researchers have found that cooperative learning can be an effective strategy for improving achievement, especially when these two conditions are met (Slavin, 1995): (1) group rewards are generated (these help group members see that it is in their best interest to help each other learn), and (2) individuals are held accountable (that is, some method of evaluating an individual's contribution, such as an individual quiz, is used). Cooperative learning helps promote interdependence and connection with other students. In chapter 7, "Schools," we will further examine the concept of cooperative learning.

Reciprocal Teaching   *Reciprocal teaching* involves students taking turns leading a small-group discussion. Reciprocal teaching also can involve an adult and an adolescent. As in scaffolding, the teacher gradually assumes a less active role, letting the student assume more initiative. This technique has been widely used to help students learn to read more effectively. For example, Ann Brown and Annemarie Palincsar (1984) used reciprocal teaching to improve students' abilities to enact certain strategies to improve their reading comprehension. In this teacher-scaffolded instruction, teachers worked with students to help them *generate questions* about the text they had read, *clarify* what they did not understand, *summarize* the text, and *make predictions*.

Ann Brown's most recent efforts focused on transforming schools into communities of thinking and learning. Her ideas have much in common with Vygotsky's emphasis on learning as a collaborative process.

Comparing Piaget and Vygotsky   Awareness of Vygotsky's theory came later than awareness of Piaget's, so it has not yet been thoroughly evaluated. However, Vygotsky's theory has been embraced by many teachers and successfully applied to education. His view of the importance of sociocultural influences on development fits with the current belief in the importance of contextual factors in learning (Greenfield, 2000). However, criticisms of his theory have emerged; for example, it has been argued that he overemphasized the role of language in thinking.

Vygotsky's and Piaget's theories are constructivist. *Constructivism* emphasizes that individuals actively construct knowledge and understanding. In the constructivist view, information is not directly given to children and adolescents and

THROUGH THE EYES OF PSYCHOLOGISTS

Barbara Rogoff
University of California–Santa Cruz

"Cognitive development occurs as new generations collaborate with older generations in varying forms of interpersonal engagement and institutional practices."

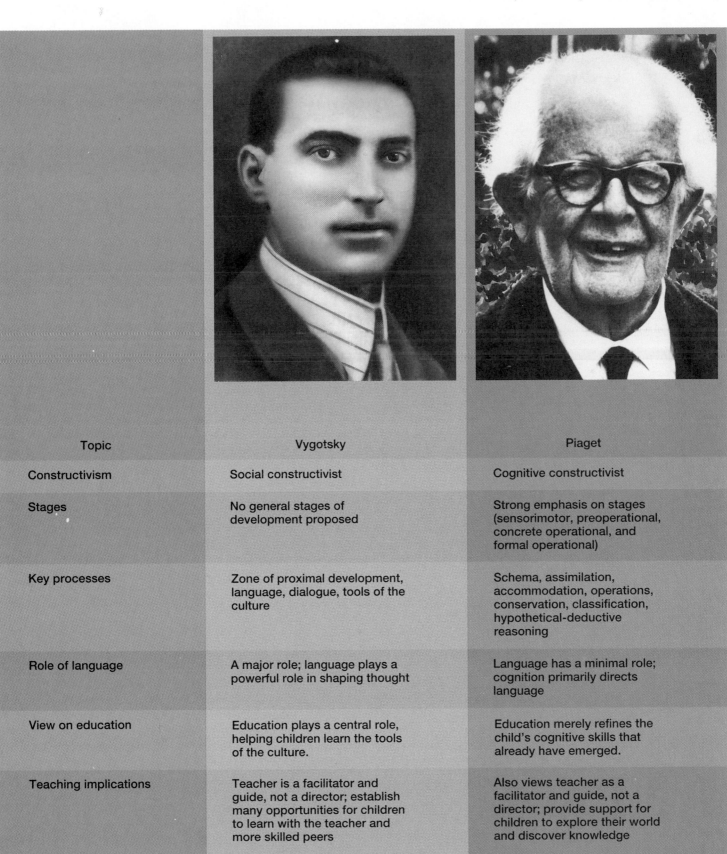

Topic	Vygotsky	Piaget
Constructivism	Social constructivist	Cognitive constructivist
Stages	No general stages of development proposed	Strong emphasis on stages (sensorimotor, preoperational, concrete operational, and formal operational)
Key processes	Zone of proximal development, language, dialogue, tools of the culture	Schema, assimilation, accommodation, operations, conservation, classification, hypothetical-deductive reasoning
Role of language	A major role; language plays a powerful role in shaping thought	Language has a minimal role; cognition primarily directs language
View on education	Education plays a central role, helping children learn the tools of the culture.	Education merely refines the child's cognitive skills that already have emerged.
Teaching implications	Teacher is a facilitator and guide, not a director; establish many opportunities for children to learn with the teacher and more skilled peers	Also views teacher as a facilitator and guide, not a director; provide support for children to explore their world and discover knowledge

■ FIGURE 4.5
Comparison of Vygotsky's and Piaget's Theories

poured into their minds. Rather, they are encouraged to explore their world, discover knowledge, and think critically (Perkins, 1999).

Distinctions can be drawn between cognitive and social constructivist approaches. In a *cognitive constructivist approach,* emphasis is on the individual's cognitive construction of knowledge and understanding. Piaget's theory is cognitive constructivist. In a *social constructivist approach,* emphasis is on collaboration with others to produce knowledge and understanding. Vygotsky's theory is social constructivist.

In Piaget's and Vygotsky's theories, teachers serve as facilitators and guides rather than directors and molders of learning. Figure 4.5 on page 117 provides a comparison of Piaget's and Vygotsky's theories.

At this point we have studied a number of ideas about Piaget's and Vygotsky's theories. This review should help you to reach your learning goals related to these topics.

☐ FOR YOUR REVIEW

Learning Goal 1
Discuss Piaget's theory

- Piaget's widely acclaimed theory stresses adaptation, schemas, assimilation, accommodation, and equilibration.
- Piaget said that individuals develop through four cognitive stages: sensorimotor, preoperational, concrete operational, and formal operational. Formal operational thought, which Piaget believed appears from 11 to 15 years of age, is characterized by abstract, idealistic, and hypothetical-deductive thinking. Some experts argue that formal operational thought has two phases: early and late. Individual variation in adolescent cognition is extensive. Many young adolescents are still consolidating their concrete operational thought or are early formal operational thinkers rather than full-fledged ones.
- Although Piaget was not an educator, his constructivist ideas have been applied to education.
- In terms of Piaget's contributions, we owe to him the entire field of cognitive development and a masterful list of concepts. He also was a genius at observing children. Criticisms of Piaget's theory focus on estimates of competence, stages, training to reason at higher stages, and the role of culture and education. Neo-Piagetians have proposed some substantial changes in Piaget's theory.
- Piaget did not believe there is a fifth, postformal stage of thought. However, some theorists argue that this stage is entered by many young adults. Perry believed that emerging adulthood is a time when individuals think more reflectively and relativistically, especially if they go to college.

Learning Goal 2
Understand Vygotsky's theory

- Vygotsky's view stimulated considerable interest in the idea that knowledge is situated and collaborative. One of his important concepts is the zone of proximal development, which involves guidance by more-skilled peers and adults. Vygotsky argued that learning the skills of the culture is a key aspect of development.
- Some contemporary concepts linked with Vygotsky's theory include scaffolding, cognitive apprenticeship, tutoring, cooperative learning, and reciprocal teaching.
- Piaget's and Vygotsky's views are both constructivist—Piaget's being cognitive constructivist, Vygotsky's social constructivist. In both views, teachers should be facilitators, not directors, of learning.

Now that we have discussed the cognitive developmental views of Piaget and Vygotsky, we will turn our attention to another major framework for understanding adolescent cognition: information processing.

THE INFORMATION-PROCESSING VIEW

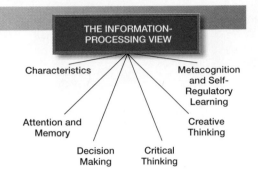

In chapter 2, "The Science of Adolescent Development," we briefly described the information-processing view ◄IIII P. 48. We indicated that information processing includes how information gets into adolescents' minds, how it is stored, and how it is retrieved to think about and solve problems.

Information processing is both a framework for thinking about adolescent development and a facet of that development. As a framework, the information-processing view includes certain ideas about how adolescents' minds work and the best methods for studying this (Logan, 2000). As a facet of development, different aspects of information processing change as children make the transition through adolescence to adulthood. For example, changes in attention and memory are essentially changes in the way individuals process information. In our exploration of information processing, we will discuss developmental changes in attention and memory, as well as other cognitive processes, but first let's examine some basic characteristics of the information-processing approach.

Characteristics

Robert Siegler (1998) described three main characteristics of the information-processing approach:

- *Thinking.* In Siegler's view, thinking is information processing. In this regard, Siegler provides a broad perspective on thinking. He says that when adolescents perceive, encode, represent, and store information from the world, they are engaging in thinking. Siegler believes that thinking is highly flexible, which allows individuals to adapt and adjust to many changes in circumstances, task requirements, and goals. However, the human's remarkable thinking abilities have some constraints. Individuals can attend to only a limited amount of information at one point in time, and they are constrained by how fast they can process information.
- *Change mechanisms.* Siegler (2000) argues that the information-processing approach should focus on the role of mechanisms of change in development. He believes that four main mechanisms—encoding, automatization, strategy construction, and generalization—work together to create changes in children's and adolescents' cognitive skills. *Encoding* is the process by which information gets into memory. Siegler states that a key aspect of solving problems is encoding the relevant information and ignoring the irrelevant parts. Because it often takes time and effort to construct new strategies, children and adolescents must practice them in order to eventually execute them automatically and maximize their effectiveness. The term *automaticity* refers to the ability to process information with little or no effort. With age and experience, information processing becomes increasingly automatic on many tasks, allowing children and adolescents to detect connections among ideas and events that they otherwise would miss. An able 12-year-old zips through a practice list of multiplication problems with little conscious effort, and a 16-year-old picks up the newspaper and quickly scans the entertainment section for the location and time of a movie. In both cases, the information processing of these adolescents is more automatic and less effortful than that of children.

Recall that earlier in the chapter we described Robbie Case's neo-Piagetian view. Case's view includes an emphasis on changes in the way that adolescents process information differently than children. His view includes an aspect of information processing emphasized by Siegler: automaticity. In Case's (1992, 1998, 2000) view adolescents have more cognitive resources available to them because of automaticity, increased information-processing capacity, and more familiarity with a range of content knowledge. These advances in information processing reduce the load on cognitive systems, allowing adolescents to hold in mind several dimensions of a topic or a problem simultaneously. In contrast, children are more prone to focus on only one dimension.

Strategies
http://www.mhhe.com/santrocka9

The third and fourth change mechanisms proposed by Siegler are strategy construction and generalization. *Strategy construction* involves the discovery of a new procedure for processing information. Siegler says that adolescents need to encode key information about a problem and coordinate the information with relevant prior knowledge to solve the problem. To fully benefit from a newly constructed strategy, adolescents need to *generalize* it, or apply it to other problems.

• *Self-modification.* The contemporary information-processing approach argues, as does Piaget's theory of cognitive development, that adolescents play an active role in their development. They use knowledge and strategies that they have learned in previous circumstances to adapt their responses to a new learning situation. In this manner, adolescents build newer and more sophisticated responses from prior knowledge and strategies.

Attention and Memory

Although the bulk of research on information processing has been conducted with children and adults, the information-processing perspective is important in understanding adolescent cognition. As we saw in the example of the adolescent solving an algebraic equation, attention and memory are two important cognitive processes.

Attention   *Pay attention* is a phrase children and adolescents hear all of the time. Just what is *attention? Attention* is the concentration and focusing of mental effort. Attention also is both selective and shifting. For example, when adolescents take a test, they must attend to it. This implies that they have the ability to focus their mental effort on certain stimuli (the test questions) while excluding other stimuli, an important aspect of attention called *selectivity.* When selective attention fails adolescents, they have difficulty ignoring information that is irrelevant to their interest or goals. For example, if a television set is blaring while the adolescent is studying, the adolescent could have difficulty concentrating.

Not only is attention selective, but it is also *shiftable.* If a teacher asks students to pay attention to a certain question and they do so, their behavior indicates that they can shift the focus of their mental effort from one stimulus to another. If the telephone rings while the adolescent is studying, the adolescent may shift attention from studying to the telephone. An external stimulus is not necessary to shift attention. At any moment, adolescents can shift their attention from one topic to another, virtually at will. They might think about the last time they went to a play, then think about an upcoming musical recital, and so on.

In one investigation, 12-year-olds were markedly better than 8-year-olds and slightly worse than 20-year-olds at allocating their attention in a situation involving two tasks (Manis, Keating, & Morrison, 1980). Adolescents might have more resources available (through increased processing speed, capacity, and automaticity), or they might be more skilled at directing these resources.

Memory   There are few moments when adolescents' lives are not steeped in memory. Memory is at work with each step adolescents take, each thought they think, and each word they utter. *Memory* is the retention of information over time. It is central to mental life and to information processing. To successfully learn and reason, adolescents need to hold on to information and to retrieve the information they have tucked away. Three important memory systems are short-term memory, working memory, and long-term memory.

Short-Term Memory   *Short-term memory* is a limited-capacity memory system in which information is retained for as long as 30 seconds, unless the information is rehearsed, in which case it can be retained longer. A common way to assess short-term memory is to present a list of items to remember, which is often referred to as a memory span task. If you have taken an IQ test, you probably were asked to remember a string of numbers or words. You simply

What changes in attention characterize adolescence?

hear a short list of stimuli—usually digits—presented at a rapid pace (one per second, for example). Then you are asked to repeat the digits back. Using the memory span task, researchers have found that short-term memory increases extensively in early childhood and continues to increase in older children and adolescents, but at a slower pace. For example, in one investigation, memory span increased by 1½ digits between the ages of 7 and 13 (Dempster, 1981). Keep in mind, though, memory span's individual differences, which is why IQ and various aptitude tests are used.

How might short-term memory be used in problem solving? In a series of experiments, Robert Sternberg and his colleagues (Sternberg, 1977; Sternberg & Nigro, 1980; Sternberg & Rifkin, 1979) attempted to answer this question by giving third-grade, sixth-grade, ninth-grade, and college students analogies to solve. The main differences occurred between the younger (third- and sixth-grade) and older (ninth-grade and college) students. The older students were more likely to complete the information processing required to solve the analogy task. The children, by contrast, often stopped their processing of information before they had considered all of the necessary steps required to solve the problems. Sternberg believes that information processing was incomplete because the children's short-term memory was overloaded. Solving problems such as analogies requires individuals to make continued comparisons between newly encoded information and previously coded information. Sternberg argues that adolescents probably have more storage space in short-term memory, which results in fewer errors on problems like analogies.

In addition to more storage space, are there other reasons adolescents might perform better on memory span tasks and in solving analogies? Though many other factors could be involved, information-processing psychologists believe that changes in the speed and efficiency of information processing are important, especially the speed with which information can be identified.

Working Memory

An increasing number of psychologists believe that the way short-term memory has been historically described is too passive and does not do justice to the amount of cognitive work that is done over the short term in memory (Kail & Hall, 2001; Murdock, 1999). They prefer the concept of working memory to describe how memory works on a short-term basis (Sussman, 2001; Waters & Caplan, 2001). British psychologist Alan Baddeley (1992, 2000) proposed the concept of *working memory,* which is a kind of "mental workbench" where information is manipulated and assembled to help make decisions, solve problems, and comprehend written and spoken language.

In one recent study across the life span, the performances of individuals from 6 to 57 years of age were examined on both verbal and visuospatial working memory tasks (Swanson, 1999). The two verbal tasks were auditory digit sequence (the ability to remember numerical information embedded in a short sentence, such as "Now suppose somebody wanted to go to the supermarket at 8651 Elm Street") and semantic association (the ability to organize words into abstract categories). In the semantic association task, the participant was presented with a series of words and then asked to remember how they go together (such as shirt, saw, pants, hammer, shoes, and nails).

The two visuospatial tasks used in this study involved mapping/directions and a visual matrix. In the mapping/directions task, the participant was shown a street map in which the lines connected to a number of dots illustrating the direction the bicycle (child/young adolescent) or car (adult) would go to get through the city. The dots represented stoplights and the lines the direction of the vehicle. After briefly looking at the map, participants were asked to draw the directions and dots on a blank map. In the visual matrix task, participants were asked to remember visual sequences within a matrix that involved a series of dots. After looking at the visual matrix for five seconds, it was removed and the participants were asked questions about the location of the dots.

As shown in figure 4.6 on page 122, there was a substantial increase in the working memory of individuals from 8 through 24 years of age on all four tasks. Thus, it is likely that the adolescent years are an important developmental time frame for improvement

I come into the fields and spacious palaces of my memory, where are treasures of countless images of things of every manner.
—St. Augustine
Christian Church Father, 5th Century

Memory Links
http://www.mhhe.com/santrocka9

■ FIGURE 4.6
Developmental Changes in Working Memory

Note: The scores shown here are the means for each age group and the age also represents a mean age. Higher scores reflect superior working memory performance.

		Verbal		Visuospatial	
		Semantic Association	Digit/ Sentence	Mapping/ Directions	Visual Matrix
Age	8	1.33	1.75	3.13	1.67
	10	1.70	2.34	3.60	2.06
	13	1.86	2.94	4.09	2.51
	16	2.24	2.98	3.92	2.68
	24	2.60	3.71	4.64	3.47

Task

Highest Working Memory Performance

3.02	3.97	4.90	3.47
(age 45)	(age 35)	(age 35)	(age 24)

in working memory and that working memory continues to improve through the transition to adulthood and beyond.

Long-Term Memory   *Long-term memory* is a relatively permanent memory system that holds huge amounts of information for a long period of time. Long-term memory increases substantially in the middle and late childhood years and likely continues to improve during adolescence, although this has not been well documented by researchers. If anything at all is known about long-term memory, it is that it depends on the learning activities engaged in when learning and remembering information (Pressley & Schneider, 1997; Siegler, 1996). Most learning activities fit under the category of *strategies,* activities under the learner's conscious control. They sometimes are also called control processes. There are many of these activities, but one of the most important is organization, the tendency to group or arrange items into categories. We will have more to say about strategies shortly.

Attention and memory are important dimensions of information processing, but other dimensions also are important. Once adolescents attend to information and retain it, they can use the information to engage in a number of cognitive activities, such as making decisions, thinking critically, and thinking creatively. Let's begin our exploration of these cognitive activities by examining what is involved in decision making.

Decision Making

Adolescence is a time of increased decision making—about the future, which friends to choose, whether to go to college, which person to date, whether to have sex, whether to buy a car, and so on (Byrnes, 1997; Galotti & Kozberg, 1996; Parker & Fischhoff, 2002). How competent are adolescents at making decisions? In some reviews, older adolescents are described as more competent than younger adolescents, who, in turn, are more competent than children (Keating, 1990). Compared to children, young adolescents are more likely to generate options, to examine a situation from a variety of perspectives, to anticipate the consequences of decisions, and to consider the credibility of sources.

One study documents that older adolescents are better at decision making than younger adolescents are (Lewis, 1981). Eighth-, tenth-, and twelfth-grade students were presented with dilemmas involving the choice of a medical procedure. The oldest students were most likely to spontaneously mention a variety of risks, to recommend consultation with an outside specialist, and to anticipate future consequences. For example, when asked a question about whether to have cosmetic surgery, a twelfth-grader said that different aspects of the situation need to be examined along with its effects on the individual's future, especially relationships with other people. In contrast, an eighth-grader presented a more limited view, commenting on the surgery's effects on getting turned down for a date, the money involved, and being teased by peers.

In sum, older adolescents often make better decisions than do younger adolescents, who, in turn, make better decisions than children do. But the decision-making skills of older adolescents are far from perfect, as are those of adults (Klaczynski, 1997). Indeed, some researchers have recently found that adolescents and adults do not differ in their decision-making skills (Quadrel, Fischoff, & Davis, 1993).

Being able to make competent decisions does not guarantee that one will make them in everyday life, where breadth of experience often comes into play (Jacobs & Potenza, 1990; Keating, 1990). For example, driver-training courses improve adolescents' cognitive and motor skills to levels equal to, or sometimes superior to, those of adults. However, driver training has not been effective in reducing adolescents' high rate of traffic accidents (Potvin, Champagne, & Laberge-Nadeau, 1988). An important research agenda is to study the ways adolescents make decisions in practical situations.

Adolescents need more opportunities to practice and discuss realistic decision making (Jones, Rasmussen, & Moffitt, 1997). Many real-world decisions occur in an atmosphere of stress that includes such factors as time constraints and emotional involvement. One strategy for improving adolescent decision making about real-world choices involving such matters as sex, drugs, and daredevil driving is for schools to provide more opportunities for adolescents to engage in role-playing and group problem solving related to such circumstances.

Another strategy is for parents to involve their adolescents in appropriate decision-making activities. In one study of more than 900 young adolescents and a subsample of their parents, adolescents were more likely to participate in family decision making when they perceived themselves as in control of what happens to them and if they thought that their input would have some bearing on the outcome of the decision-making process (Liprie, 1993).

Critical Thinking

Closely related to making competent decisions is engaging in critical thinking, a current buzzword in education and psychology (Brooks & Brooks, 1999; Halonen, 1995) ◀▥ P. 28. **Critical thinking** *involves thinking reflectively and productively and evaluating the evidence.* In a recent study of fifth-, eighth-, and eleventh-graders, critical thinking increased with age but still only occurred in 43 percent of even the eleventh-graders, and many adolescents showed self-serving biases in their reasoning (Klaczynski & Narasimham, 1998).

Adolescence is an important transitional period in the development of critical thinking (Keating, 1990). Among the cognitive changes that allow improved critical thinking in adolescence are:

- Increased speed, automaticity, and capacity of information processing, which free cognitive resources for other purposes
- More breadth of content knowledge in a variety of domains
- Increased ability to construct new combinations of knowledge
- A greater range and more spontaneous use of strategies or procedures for applying or obtaining knowledge, such as planning, considering alternatives, and cognitive monitoring

Although adolescence is an important period in the development of critical-thinking skills, if a solid basis of fundamental skills (such as literacy and math skills) is

THROUGH THE EYES OF PSYCHOLOGISTS

Daniel Keating
University of Toronto

"In any consideration of adolescent cognition, it is important to recognize the wide variability in performance among adolescents."

critical thinking
Thinking reflectively and productively and evaluating the evidence.

Exploring Critical Thinking
Critical Thinking Resources
Odyssey of the Mind
http://www.mhhe.com/santrocka9

CAREERS IN ADOLESCENT DEVELOPMENT

Laura Bickford
Secondary School Teacher

Laura Bickford teaches English and journalism in grades 9 to 12 and she is Chair of the English Department at Nordhoff High School in Ojai, California.

Laura especially believes it is important to encourage students to think. Indeed, she says that "the call to teach is the call to teach students how to think." She believes teachers need to show students the value in asking their own questions, in having discussions, and in engaging in stimulating intellectual conversations. Laura says that she also encourages students to engage in metacognitive strategies (knowing about knowing). For example, she asks students to comment on their learning after particular pieces of projects have been completed. She requires students to keep reading logs so they can observe their own thinking as it happens.

Laura Bickford, working with students writing papers.

The Jasper Project
Teresa Amabile's Research
http://www.mhhe.com/santrocka9

creativity
The ability to think in novel and unusual ways and come up with unique solutions to problems.

convergent thinking
A pattern of thinking in which individuals produce one correct answer; characteristic of the items on conventional intelligence tests; coined by Guilford.

divergent thinking
A pattern of thinking in which individuals produce many answers to the same question; more characteristic of creativity than convergent thinking; coined by Guilford.

not developed during childhood, such critical-thinking skills are unlikely to mature in adolescence. For the subset of adolescents who lack such fundamental skills, potential gains in adolescent thinking are not likely.

Considerable interest has recently developed in teaching critical thinking in schools. Cognitive psychologist Robert J. Sternberg (1985) believes that most school programs that teach critical thinking are flawed. He thinks that schools focus too much on formal reasoning tasks and not enough on the critical-thinking skills needed in everyday life. Among the critical-thinking skills that Sternberg believes adolescents need in everyday life are these: recognizing that problems exist, defining problems more clearly, handling problems with no single right answer or any clear criteria for the point at which the problem is solved (such as selecting a rewarding career), making decisions on issues of personal relevance (such as deciding to have a risky operation), obtaining information, thinking in groups, and developing long-term approaches to long-term problems.

One educational program that embodies Sternberg's recommendations for increased critical thinking in schools is the *Jasper Project,* twelve videodisc-based adventures that focus on solving real-world math problems. The Jasper Project is the brainchild of the Cognition and Technology Group at Vanderbilt (1997). Figure 4.7 on page 125 shows one of the Jasper adventures. For students in grades 5 and up, Jasper helps them make connections with other disciplines including science, history, and social studies. Jasper's creators think that students need to be exposed to authentic, real-world problems that occur in everyday life. As students work together over several class periods, they have numerous opportunities to communicate about math, share their problem-solving strategies, and get feedback from others that refines their thinking. Jasper videodiscs for science also have been created.

For many years, the major debate in teaching critical thinking has been whether critical-thinking skills should be taught as general entities or in the context of specific subject matter instruction (math, English, or science, for example). A number of experts on thinking believe the evidence has come down on the side of teaching critical thinking embedded in a rich subject matter (Kuhn, 1999, 2000a).

Today, another debate regarding critical thinking has emerged. On the one side are traditionalists who see critical thinking as a set of mental competencies that reside in adolescents' heads. On the other side are advocates of a situated-cognition approach to critical thinking who regard intellectual skills as social entities that are exercised and shared within a community (Resnick & Nelson-Gall, 1997; Rogoff, 1998). This ongoing debate has not yet been resolved.

Creative Thinking

Creativity *is the ability to think in novel ways and come up with unique solutions to problems.* Thus, intelligence, which we will discuss shortly, and creativity are not the same thing. This was recognized by J. P. Guilford (1967), who distinguished between **convergent thinking,** *which produces one correct answer and is characteristic of the kind of thinking required on a conventional intelligence test,* and **divergent thinking,** *which produces many answers to the same question and is more characteristic of creativity.* For example, a typical item on a conventional intelligence test is "How many quarters will you get in return for 60 dimes?" In contrast, the following questions have many possible answers: "What image comes to mind when you hear the phrase *sitting alone in a dark room?*" or "Can you think of some unique uses for a paper clip?"

Are intelligence and creativity related? Although most creative adolescents are quite intelligent, the reverse is not necessarily true. Many highly intelligent adolescents are not very creative.

An important goal is to help adolescents become more creative (Csikszentmihalyi, 2000). Here are some good strategies for accomplishing this goal:

- *Have adolescents engage in brainstorming and come up with as many meaningful ideas as possible.* Brainstorming is a technique in which individuals are encouraged to come up with creative ideas in a group, play off each other's ideas, and say practically whatever comes to mind about a particular topic. Whether in a group or on an individual basis, a good creativity strategy is to generate as many new ideas possible. The famous twentieth-century Spanish artist Pablo Picasso produced more than 20,000 works of art. Not all of them were masterpieces. The more ideas adolescents produce, the better are their chance of creating something unique (Rickards, 1999).
- *Provide adolescents with environments that stimulate creativity.* Some settings nourish creativity, others depress it. People who encourage adolescents' creativity rely on adolescents' natural curiosity. Science and discovery museums offer rich opportunities for the stimulation of adolescents' creative thinking.
- *Don't overcontrol.* Telling adolescents exactly how to do things leaves them feeling that any originality is a mistake and any exploration is a waste of time (Amabile, 1993). Letting adolescents select their interests and supporting their inclinations is less likely to destroy their natural curiosity than dictating which activities they should pursue (Conti & Amabile, 1999; Runco, 2000).
- *Encourage internal motivation.* Excessive use of prizes, such as money, can stifle creativity by undermining the intrinsic pleasure adolescents derive from creative activities. Creative adolescents' motivation is the satisfaction generated by the work itself.
- *Foster flexible and playful thinking.* Creative thinkers are flexible and play with ideas and problems—which gives rise to a paradox: Although creativity takes effort, the effort goes more smoothly if adolescents take it lightly. In a way, humor can grease the wheels of creativity (Goleman, Kaufmann, & Ray, 1993). When adolescents are joking around, they are more likely to consider unusual solutions to problems (O'Quin & Dirks, 1999).
- *Introduce adolescents to creative people.* Poet Richard Lewis (1997) visits classrooms in New York City. He brings with him only the glassy spectrum that is encased in a circular glass case. He lifts it above his head so that every student can see its colored charm, asking "Who can see something playing inside?" Then he asks students to write about what they see. One middle school student named Snigdha wrote that she sees the rainbow rising and the sun sleeping with the stars. She also wrote that she sees the rain dropping on the ground, stems breaking, apples falling from trees, and the wind blowing the leaves.
- *Talk with adolescents about creative people or have them read about them.* Mihaly Csikszentmihalyi (pronounced ME-high CHICK-sent-me-high-ee) (1995) interviewed 90 leading figures in the sciences, government, business, and education about their creativity. One such individual was Mark Strand, a U.S. poet laureate, who said that his most creative moments come when he loses a sense of time and becomes totally absorbed in what he is doing. He commented that the absorbed state comes and goes; he can't stay in it for an

"Blueprint for Success"   **Christina and Marcus,** two students from Trenton, visit an architectural firm on Career Day. While learning about the work of architects, Christina and Marcus hear about a vacant lot being donated in their neighborhood for a playground. This is exciting news because there is no place in their downtown neighborhood for children to play. Recently, several students have been hurt playing in the street. The challenge is for students to help Christina and Marcus design a playground and ballfield for the lot.

■ FIGURE 4.7
A Problem-Solving Adventure in the Jasper Project

 Harvard Project Zero
Csikszentmihalyi's Ideas
http://www.mhhe.com/santrocka9

"What do you mean 'What is it?' It's the spontaneous, unfettered expression of a young mind not yet bound by the restraints of narrative or pictorial representation."

metacognition
Cognition about cognition, or "knowing about knowing."

entire day. When Strand gets an intriguing idea, he focuses intensely on it and transforms it into a visual image.

We have discussed some important aspects of the way adolescents process information, but we still need to explore adolescents' monitoring of their information processing and self-regulatory learning strategies.

Metacognition and Self-Regulatory Learning

What is metacognition? How can adolescents develop better information-processing and self-regulatory learning strategies?

What Is Metacognition?   Earlier in the chapter when we discussed Piaget's theory, we indicated that adolescents increase their thinking about thinking. Today, cognitive psychologists define **metacognition** *as cognition about cognition, or "knowing about knowing"* (Flavell, 1999; Flavell, Miller, & Miller, 2002).

Metacognitive skills have been taught to students to help them solve math problems (Cardelle-Elawar, 1992). In each of thirty daily lessons involving math story problems, a teacher guided low-achieving students in learning to recognize when they did not know the meaning of a word, did not have all of the necessary information to solve a problem, did not know how to subdivide the problem into specific steps, or did not know how to carry out a computation. After the thirty daily lessons, the students who were given the metacognitive training had better math achievement and attitudes toward math.

One expert on thinking, Deanna Kuhn (2000b), believes that metacognition should be a stronger focus of efforts to help individuals become better critical thinkers, especially at the middle school and high school levels. She distinguishes between first-order cognitive skills that enable adolescents to know about the world (such skills have been the main focus of critical thinking programs) and second-order cognitive skills—*meta-knowing skills*—that entail knowing about one's own (and others') knowing.

Exploring Strategies and the Self-Regulation of Strategies   In the view of Michael Pressley (1983; McCormick & Pressley, 1997; Pressley & Roehrig, 2002), the key to education is helping students learn a rich repertoire of strategies that result in solutions to problems. Good thinkers routinely use strategies and effective planning to solve problems. Good thinkers also know when and where to use strategies (they have metacognitive knowledge about strategies). Understanding when and where to use strategies often results from the learner's monitoring of the learning situation.

Pressley argues that when students are given instruction about effective strategies that are new to them, they often can apply these strategies on their own. However, some strategies are not effective for young children. For example, young children cannot competently use mental imagery. Pressley emphasizes that students benefit when the teacher models the appropriate strategy and overtly verbalizes the steps in the strategy. Then, students subsequently practice the strategy. Their practice of the strategy is guided and supported by the teacher's feedback until the students can effectively execute the strategy autonomously. When instructing students about employing the strategy, it also is a good idea to explain to them how using the strategy will benefit them.

Having practice in the new strategy usually is not enough for students to continue to use the strategy and transfer it to new situations. For effective maintenance and transfer, encourage students to monitor the effectiveness of the new strategy relative to their use of old strategies by comparing their performance on tests and other assessments. Pressley says that it is not enough to say "Try it, you will like it"; you need to say "Try it and compare."

Learning how to use strategies effectively usually takes time and requires guidance and support from the teacher. With practice, strategies are executed faster and more competently. "Practice" means using the effective strategy over and over again until it is automatically performed. For learners to execute the strategies effectively, they need to have the strategies in long-term memory, and extensive practice makes this possible. Learners also need to be motivated to use the strategies.

Do children and adolescents use one strategy or multiple strategies in memory and problem solving? They often use more than one strategy (Schneider & Bjorklund, 1998; Siegler, 1998). Most children and adolescents benefit from generating a variety of alternative strategies and experimenting with different approaches to a problem, discovering what works well, when, and where (Schneider & Bjorklund, 1998).

Self-Regulatory Learning

Self-regulatory learning *consists of the self-generation and self-monitoring of thoughts, feelings, and behaviors to reach a goal.* These goals might be academic (improving comprehension while reading, becoming a more organized writer, learning how to do multiplication, asking relevant questions) or they might be socioemotional (controlling one's anger, getting along better with peers). What are some of the characteristics of self-regulated learners? Self-regulatory learners (Winne, 1995, 1997; Winne & Perry, 2000):

• Set goals for extending their knowledge and sustaining their motivation
• Are aware of their emotional makeup and have strategies for managing their emotions
• Periodically monitor their progress toward a goal
• Fine-tune or revise their strategies based on the progress they are making
• Evaluate obstacles that arise and make the necessary adaptations

Researchers have found that most high-achieving students are self-regulatory learners (Paris & Paris, 2001; Pressley, 1995; Rudolph & others, 2001; Schunk & Zimmerman, 1994; Zimmerman, 2000, 2002). For example, compared with low-achieving students, high-achieving students set more specific learning goals, use more strategies to learn, self-monitor their learning more, and more systematically evaluate their progress toward a goal (Schnuk & Ertmer, 2000).

Teachers, tutors, mentors, counselors, and parents can help students become self-regulatory learners. Barry Zimmerman, Sebastian Bonner, and Robert Kovach (1996) developed a model of turning low-self-regulatory students into students who engaged in these multistep strategies: (1) self-evaluation and monitoring, (2) goal setting and strategic planning, (3) putting a plan into action and monitoring it, and (4) monitoring outcomes and refining strategies (see figure 4.8).

They describe a seventh-grade student who is doing poorly in history and apply their self-regulatory model to her situation. In step 1, she self-evaluates her studying and test preparation by keeping a detailed record of them. The teacher gives her some guidelines for keeping these records. After several weeks, the student turns in the records and traces her poor test performance to low comprehension of difficult reading material.

In step 2, the student sets a goal, in this case of improving reading comprehension, and plans how to achieve the goal. The teacher assists her in breaking down the goal into component parts, such as locating main ideas and setting specific goals for understanding a series of paragraphs in her textbook. The teacher also provides the student with strategies, such as focusing initially on the first sentence of each paragraph and then scanning the others as a means of identifying main ideas. Another support the teacher might offer the student is adult or peer tutoring in reading comprehension if it is available.

In step 3, the student puts the plan into action and begins to monitor her progress. Initially she

self-regulatory learning
The self-generation and self-monitoring of thoughts, feelings, and behaviors to reach a goal.

Self-Regulatory Learning
http://www.mhhe.com/santrocka9

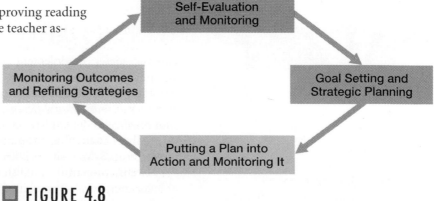

◻ FIGURE 4.8
A Model of Self-Regulatory Learning

might need help from the teacher or tutor in identifying main ideas in the reading. This feedback can help her monitor her reading comprehension more effectively on her own.

In step 4, the student monitors her improvement in reading comprehension by evaluating whether it has had any impact on her learning outcomes. Most importantly: Has her improvement in reading comprehension led to better performance on history tests?

Since the last review, we have examined a number of ideas about the information-processing view. These questions should help you to reach your learning goals related to this topic.

☐ FOR YOUR REVIEW

Learning Goal 3
Evaluate the information-processing view

- Siegler states that the information-processing view emphasizes thinking, change mechanisms (encoding, automaticity, strategy construction, and generalization), and self-modification.
- Adolescents typically have better attentional skills than children do. They also have better short-term memory, working memory, and long-term memory than children.
- Adolescence is a time of increased decision making. Older adolescents make better decisions than younger adolescents, who in turn are better at this than children are. Being able to make competent decisions, however, does not mean they actually will be made in everyday life, where breadth of experience comes into play.
- Critical thinking involves thinking reflectively, productively, and evaluating the evidence. Adolescence is an important transitional period in critical thinking because of such cognitive changes as increased speed, automaticity, and capacity of information processing; more breadth of content knowledge; increased ability to construct new combinations of knowledge; and a greater range and spontaneous use of strategies. Debates about critical thinking involve whether it should be taught in a general way or tied to specific subject matter and whether it resides in adolescents' heads or involves situated cognition.
- Thinking creatively is the ability to think in novel and unusual ways and come up with unique solutions to problems. Guilford distinguished between convergent and divergent thinking. A number of strategies, including brainstorming, can be used to stimulate creative thinking.
- Metacognition is cognition about cognition, or knowing about knowing. In Pressley's view, the key to education is helping students learn a rich repertoire of strategies that results in solutions to problems. Kuhn argues that metacognition is the key to developing critical-thinking skills. Self-regulatory learning consists of the self-generation and self-monitoring of thoughts, feelings, and behaviors to reach a goal. Most high-achieving students are self-regulatory learners.

So far in this chapter we have explored two major approaches to adolescent cognition: cognitive developmental and information processing. Next, we will explore a third major approach: psychometric/intelligence.

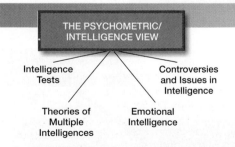

psychometric/intelligence view
A view that emphasizes the importance of individual differences in intelligence; many advocates of this view also argue that intelligence should be assessed with intelligence tests.

THE PSYCHOMETRIC/INTELLIGENCE VIEW

The two views of adolescent cognition that we have discussed so far—cognitive developmental and information processing—do not emphasize IQ tests or individual variations in intelligence. The **psychometric/intelligence view** *does emphasize the importance of individual differences in intelligence, and many advocates of this view argue that intelligence should be assessed with intelligence tests.* An increasing issue in the field of intelligence involves pinning down what the components of intelligence really are (Embretson & McCollom, 2000).

Twentieth-century English novelist Aldous Huxley said that children are remarkable for their curiosity and intelligence. What did Huxley mean when he used the word *intelligence*? Intelligence is one of our most prized possessions, yet even the most intelligent people have not been able to agree on what intelligence is. Unlike height, weight, and age, intelligence cannot be directly measured. You can't peer into a student's head and observe the intelligence going on inside. We only can evaluate a student's intelligence *indirectly* by studying the intelligent acts that it generates. For the most part, we have relied on written intelligence tests to provide an estimate of a student's intelligence (Aiken, 2003; Kaufman, 2000a).

Some experts describe intelligence as including verbal ability and problem-solving skills. Others describe it as the ability to adapt to and learn from life's everyday experiences. Combining these ideas we can arrive at a fairly traditional definition of **intelligence** *as problem-solving skills and the ability to adapt to and learn from life's everyday experiences.* But even this broad definition doesn't satisfy everyone. As you will see shortly, some theorists propose that musical skills should be considered part of intelligence. And a definition of intelligence based on a theory like Vygotsky's would have to include the ability to use the tools of the culture with help from more-skilled individuals. Because intelligence is such an abstract, broad concept, it is not surprising that there are so many different possible definitions of it.

intelligence

Mental ability related to problem-solving skills, and the ability to adapt to and learn from life's everyday experiences; not everyone agrees on what constitutes intelligence.

Intelligence Tests

Robert J. Sternberg recalls being terrified of taking IQ tests as a child. He says that he literally froze when the time came to take such tests. Even as an adult, Sternberg feels stung by humiliation when he recalls being in the sixth grade and taking an IQ test with fifth-graders. Sternberg eventually overcame his anxieties about IQ tests. Not only did he begin to perform better on them, but at age 13 he devised his own IQ test and began using it to assess classmates—that is, until the school principal found out and scolded him. Sternberg became so fascinated by intelligence that he made its study one of his lifelong pursuits. Later in this chapter we will discuss his theory of intelligence. To begin, though, let's go back in time to examine the first valid intelligence test.

The Binet Tests   In 1904 the French Ministry of Education asked psychologist Alfred Binet to devise a method of identifying children who were unable to learn in school. School officials wanted to reduce crowding by placing in special schools students who did not benefit from regular classroom teaching. Binet and his student Theophile Simon developed an intelligence test to meet this request. The test is called the 1905 Scale. It consisted of 30 questions, ranging from the ability to touch one's ear to the ability to draw designs from memory and define abstract concepts.

Mental Measurements Yearbook
Alfred Binet
http://www.mhhe.com/santrocka9

Binet developed the concept of **mental age (MA),** *an individual's level of mental development relative to others.* Not much later, in 1912, William Stern created the concept of **intelligent quotient (IQ),** *which refers to a person's mental age divided by chronological age (CA), multiplied by 100. That is, IQ = MA/CA × 100.*

If mental age is the same as chronological age, then the person's IQ is 100. If mental age is above chronological age, then IQ is more than 100. If mental age is below chronological age, then IQ is less than 100. Scores noticeably above 100 are considered above-average. Scores noticeably below 100 are labeled below-average. For example, a 16-year-old with a mental age of 20 would have an IQ of 125, while a 16-year-old child with a mental age of 12 would have an IQ of 75.

mental age (MA)

An individual's level of mental development relative to others; a concept developed by Binet.

intelligent quotient (IQ)

A person's tested mental age divided by chronological age, multiplied by 100.

The Binet test has been revised many times to incorporate advances in the understanding of intelligence and intelligence testing (Naglieri, 2000). These revisions are called the Stanford-Binet tests (because the revisions were made at Stanford University). By administering the test to large numbers of people of different ages from different backgrounds, researchers have found that scores on a Stanford-Binet test approximate a normal distribution (see figure 4.9 on p. 130). A **normal distribution** *is symmetrical, with a majority of the scores falling in the middle of the possible range of scores and few scores appearing toward the extremes of the range.*

The current Stanford-Binet is administered individually to people from the age of 2 through the adult years. It includes a variety of items, some of which require verbal responses and others of which require nonverbal responses. For example, items that reflect a typical 6-year-old's level of performance on the test include the verbal ability to define at least six words, such as *orange* and *envelope,* as well as the nonverbal ability

normal distribution

A symmetrical distribution of values or scores, with a majority of scores falling in the middle of the possible range of scores and few scores appearing toward the extremes of the range; a distribution that yields what is called a "bell-shaped curve."

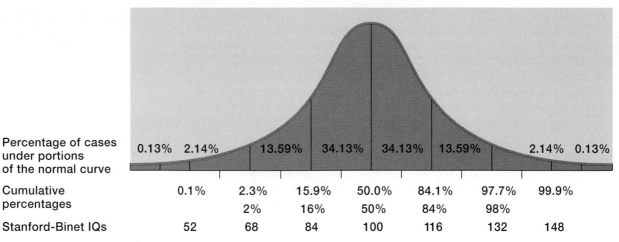

Percentage of cases under portions of the normal curve	0.13%	2.14%	13.59%	34.13%	34.13%	13.59%	2.14%	0.13%	
Cumulative percentages		0.1%	2.3%	15.9%	50.0%	84.1%	97.7%	99.9%	
			2%	16%	50%	84%	98%		
Stanford-Binet IQs		52	68	84	100	116	132	148	

■ FIGURE 4.9
The Normal Curve and Stanford-Binet IQ Scores

The distribution of IQ scores approximates a normal curve. Most of the population falls in the middle range of scores. Notice that extremely high and extremely low scores are very rare. Slightly more than two-thirds of the scores fall between 84 and 116. Only about 1 in 50 individuals has an IQ of more than 132 and only about 1 in 50 individuals has an IQ of less than 68.

to trace a path through a maze. Items that reflect an average adult's level of performance include defining such words as *disproportionate* and *regard,* explaining a proverb, and comparing idleness and laziness.

The fourth edition of the Stanford-Binet was published in 1985. One important addition in this version was the analysis of the individual's responses in terms of four functions: verbal reasoning, quantitative reasoning, abstract/visual reasoning, and short-term memory. A general composite score is still obtained to reflect overall intelligence. The Stanford-Binet continues to be one of the tests most widely used to assess a student's intelligence.

The Wechsler Scales   Another set of tests widely used to assess students' intelligence is the Wechsler scales, developed by David Wechsler (Kaufman, 2000b). They include the Wechsler Preschool and Primary Scale of Intelligence–Revised (WPPSI-R) to test children 4 to 6½ years of age; the Wechsler Intelligence Scale for Children–Revised (WISC-R) for children and adolescents 6 to 16 years of age; and the Wechsler Adult Intelligence Scale–Revised (WAIS-R).

In addition to an overall IQ, the Wechsler scales also yield verbal and performance IQs. Verbal IQ is based on six verbal subscales, performance IQ on five performance subscales (Naglieri, 2000). This allows the examiner to quickly see patterns of strengths and weaknesses in different areas of the student's intelligence. Samples of WAIS-R subscales are shown in figure 4.10 on page 131.

Theories of Multiple Intelligences

Is it more appropriate to think of an adolescent's intelligence as a general ability or as a number of specific abilities?

Early Views   Binet and Stern both focused on a concept of general intelligence, which Stern called IQ. Wechsler believed it was possible and important to describe both a person's general intelligence and more specific verbal and performance intelligences. He was building on the ideas of Charles Spearman (1927), who said that people have both a general intelligence, which he called *g,* and specific types of intelligence, which he called *s.* As early as the 1930s, L. L. Thurstone (1938) said people have seven of these specific abilities, which he called primary mental abilities: verbal comprehension, number ability, word fluency, spatial visualization, associative memory, reasoning,

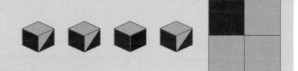

VERBAL SUBSCALES

SIMILARITIES
An individual must think logically and abstractly to answer a number of questions about how things might be similar.

For example, "In what ways are boats and trains the same?"

PERFORMANCE SUBSCALES

BLOCK DESIGN
An individual must assemble a set of multicolored blocks to match designs that the examiner shows. Visual-motor coordination, perceptual organization, and the ability to visualize spatially are assessed.

For example, "Use the four blocks on the left to make the pattern at the right."

Remember that the Wechsler includes 11 subscales, 6 verbal and 5 nonverbal. Two of the subscales are shown here.

◻ FIGURE 4.10
Sample Subscales of the Wechsler Adult Intelligence Scale–Revised

Remember that the Wechsler includes 11 subscales, 6 verbal and 5 nonverbal. Two of the subscales are shown here.

and perceptual speed. More recently, the search for specific types of intelligence has heated up.

Sternberg's Triarchic Theory   Robert J. Sternberg (1986) developed the **triarchic theory of intelligence,** *which states that intelligence comes in three forms: analytical, creative, and practical.*

Analytical intelligence involves the ability to analyze, judge, evaluate, compare, and contrast. Creative intelligence consists of the ability to create, design, invent, originate, and imagine. Practical intelligence focuses on the ability to use, apply, implement, and put into practice (Wagner, 2000). Consider these three students:

- Ann scores high on traditional intelligence tests, such as the Stanford-Binet, and is a star analytical thinker.
- Todd does not have the best tests scores but has an insightful and creative mind.
- Art is street-smart and has learned to deal in practical ways with his world although his scores on traditional intelligence tests are low.

Some students are equally high in all three areas; others do well in one or two.

Sternberg (1997, 1999, 2000; Sternberg, Torff, & Grigorenko, 1998) says that students with different triarchic patterns "look different" in school. Students with high analytic ability tend to be favored in conventional schooling. They often do well in direct-instruction classes in which the teacher lectures and students are given objective tests. They often are considered to be "smart" students who get good grades, show up in high-level tracks, do well on traditional tests of intelligence and the SAT, and later get admitted to competitive colleges.

Students who are high in creative intelligence often are not on the top rung of their class. Sternberg says that many teachers have expectations about how assignments should be done, and that creatively intelligent students might not conform to these. Instead of giving conformist answers, they give unique answers, for which they sometimes are reprimanded or marked down. Most teachers do not want to discourage

triarchic theory of intelligence
Sternberg's view that intelligence comes in three main forms: analytical, creative, and practical.

Sternberg's Theory
http://www.mhhe.com/santrocka9

"You're wise, but you lack tree smarts."

creativity, but Sternberg believes that too often a teacher's desire to improve students' knowledge inhibits creative thinking.

Like students high in creative intelligence, students who are high in practical intelligence often do not relate well to the demands of school. However, these students often do well outside the classroom. They might have excellent social skills and good common sense. As adults, they sometimes become successful managers, entrepreneurs, or politicians, despite undistinguished school records.

Sternberg believes that few tasks are purely analytic, creative, or practical. Most require some combination of these skills. For example, when students write a book report, they might (1) analyze the book's main themes, (2) generate new ideas about how the book might have been written better, and (3) think about how the book's themes can be applied to people's lives.

He believes that in teaching it is important to balance instruction related to the three types of intelligence. That is, students should be given opportunities to learn through analytical, creative, and practical thinking, in addition to conventional strategies that focus on simply "learning" and remembering a body of information. You might be wondering whether there is a Sternberg triarchic intelligence test available. As yet, there isn't.

Gardner's Eight Frames of Mind

Howard Gardner (1983, 1993, 2002) believes there are eight types of intelligence. They are described here, along with examples of the types of individuals in which they are reflected as strengths (Campbell, Campbell, & Dickinson, 1999):

- *Verbal skills:* the ability to think in words and to use language to express meaning (authors, journalists, speakers)
- *Mathematical skills:* the ability to carry out mathematical operations (scientists, engineers, accountants)
- *Spatial skills:* the ability to think in three-dimensional ways (architects, artists, sailors)
- *Bodily-kinesthetic skills:* the ability to manipulate objects and be physically skilled (surgeons, craftspeople, dancers, athletes)
- *Musical skills:* possessing a sensitivity to pitch, melody, rhythm, and tone (composers, musicians, and sensitive listeners)
- *Interpersonal skills:* ability to understand and effectively interact with others (successful teachers, mental health professionals)
- *Intrapersonal skills:* ability to understand oneself and effectively direct one's life (theologians, psychologists)
- *Naturalist skills:* ability to observe patterns in nature and understand natural and human-made systems (farmers, botanists, ecologists, landscapers)

Gardner says that the different forms of intelligence can be destroyed by brain damage, that each involves unique cognitive skills, and that each shows up in unique ways in both the gifted and idiot savants (individuals with mental retardation who have an exceptional talent in a particular domain, such as drawing, music, or computing).

Evaluating the Multiple-Intelligences Approaches

Sternberg's and Gardner's approaches have much to offer. They have stimulated broader thinking about what makes up adolescents' competencies. And they have motivated educators to develop programs that instruct students in multiple domains (Torff, 2000). These approaches also have contributed to the interest in assessing intelligence in innovative ways that go beyond conventional standardized and paper-and-pencil memory tasks.

Some critics say that classifying musical skills as a main type of intelligence is off base. Why not also classify other skill domains as types of intelligence? For

An Interview with Howard Gardner
Multiple-Intelligences Links
http://www.mhhe.com/santrocka9

Social Cognition

Social cognition refers to how in
world—the people they watch
groups in which they participa
Developmentalists have recently
lescents reason about social ma
ment focused primarily on co
numbers, words, time, and the
adolescents reason about their s
discussion of social cognition fo
personality theory.

Adolescent Egocentrism

Adolescent egocentrism *refers*
is reflected in their belief that oth
in their sense of personal unique.

David Elkind (1976) believe
types of social thinking—imagi
ence involves attention-getting
stage." Tracy's comments and b
chapter, reflect the imaginary au
as aware of a small spot on his
bated. Another adolescent, an e
that all eyes are riveted on her
"on stage" in early adolescence, b
the audience.

According to Elkind, the *p*
egocentrism involving an adol
cents' sense of personal unique
understand how they really feel
that her mother cannot possibl
her boyfriend broke up with her
of personal uniqueness, adoles
that is filled with fantasy, imm
removed from reality. Personal
diaries.

Developmentalists have in
trism in recent years. The resear
nents of egocentrism really are
why egocentric thought emerg
centrism in adolescent proble
believes that adolescent egocen
ational thought. Others, howev
not entirely a cognitive phenom
inary audience is due both to th
operational thought) and the a
ticipate the reactions of others i
tive taking) (Lapsley & Murphy

Perspective Taking

Perspective taking is the ability t
and understand his or her thoug
proposed a developmental th

example, there are outstanding chess players, prizefighters, writers, politicians, physicians, lawyers, ministers, and poets, yet we do not refer to chess intelligence, prizefighter intelligence, and so on. Other critics say that the research has not yet been conducted to support the thesis that Sternberg's three intelligences and Gardner's eight intelligences are the best ways to categorize intelligence.

Emotional Intelligence

Both Sternberg's and Gardner's views include categories of social intelligence. In Sternberg's theory the category is called "practical intelligence" and in Gardner's theory the categories are "insights about self" and "insights about others." However, the greatest interest in recent years in the social aspects of intelligence has focused on the concept of emotional intelligence. **Emotional intelligence** *was proposed in 1990 as a form of social intelligence that involves the ability to monitor one's own and others' feelings and emotions, to discriminate among them, and to use this information to guide one's thinking and action* (Salovy & Mayer, 1990). However, the main interest in emotional intelligence was ushered in with the publication of Daniel Goleman's (1995) book, *Emotional Intelligence*. Goleman believes that when it comes to predicting an adolescent's competence, IQ as measured by standardized intelligence tests matters less than emotional intelligence. In Goleman's view, emotional intelligence involves these four main areas:

- *Developing emotional self-awareness* (such as the ability to separate feelings from actions)
- *Managing emotions* (such as being able to control anger)
- *Reading emotions* (such as taking the perspectives of others)
- *Handling relationships* (such as the ability to solve relationship problems)

One private school in San Francisco, the Nueva School, has a class in self science that is closely related to the concept of emotional intelligence. The subject in self science is feelings—the adolescent's own and those involved in relationships. Teachers speak to such emotional issues as hurt over being left out, envy, and disagreements that can disrupt relationships. These are some of the topics in a fifth-grade self-science class at the Nueva School:

- Having self-awareness (in the sense of recognizing feelings and building a vocabulary for them; seeing links between thoughts, feelings, and reactions)
- Knowing if thoughts or feelings are governing a decision
- Seeing the consequences of alternative choices
- Applying these insights to decisions about such issues as drugs, smoking, and sex
- Managing emotions; learning to handle anxieties, anger, and sadness
- Taking responsibility for decisions and actions, such as following through on commitments
- Understanding that empathy, understanding others' feelings, and respecting differences in how people feel about things are key aspects of getting along in the social world
- Recognizing the importance of relationships and learning how to be a good listener and question asker; learning how to cooperate, resolve conflicts, and negotiate

Names for these classes range from "Social Development" to "Life Skills" to "Social and Emotional Learning." Their common goal is raise every child's and adolescent's emotional competence as part of regular education rather than focus on emotional skills as only something to be taught remedially to those who are faltering and identified as "troubled."

Measures of emotional intelligence have been and are being developed, but as yet none has reached the point of wide acceptance (Goleman, 1995; Rockhill & Greener, 1999; Salovy & Woolery, 2000). Especially lacking is research on the predictive validity of these measures (Mayer, Caruso, & Salovy, 2000).

emotional intelligence
A form of social intelligence that involves the ability to monitor one's own and others' feelings and emotions, to discriminate among them, and to use this information to guide one's thinking and action.

Since the last review, we have
you to reach your learning goa

☐ FOR YOUR

Learning Goal 4
Explain the psychometric
intelligence view

So far in this chapter we have
information processing, and p
cognition: how adolescents th

THE CONTEXTS OF ADOLESCENT DEVELOPMENT

◻

Man is a knot, a web, a mesh into which relationships are tied.
—Antoine de Saint-Exupery
French Novelist and Aviator, 20th Century

Adolescent development takes place in social contexts, which provide the setting and sociohistorical, cultural backdrop for physical, cognitive, and socioemotional growth. This third section consists of four chapters: chapter 5, "Families"; chapter 6, "Peers"; chapter 7, "Schools"; and chapter 8, "Culture."

CHAPTER 5

CHAPTER MAP

THE NATURE OF FAMILY PROCESSES

Family Interactions

Cognition and Emotion

The Developmental Construction of Relationships

Maturation

Sociocultural and Historical Changes

PARENT-ADOLESCENT RELATIONSHIPS

Parents as Managers

Autonomy and Attachment

Parenting Techniques

Parent-Adolescent Conflict

SIBLING RELATIONSHIPS

Sibling Roles

Birth Order

Developmental Changes

THE CHANGING FAMILY IN A CHANGING SOCIETY

Effects of Divorce

Gender and Parenting

Stepfamilies

Culture and Ethnicity

Working Parents

SOCIAL POLICY AND FAMILIES

■ VARIATIONS IN ADOLESCENTS' PERCEPTIONS OF PARENTS

FAMILIES

■

My mother and I depend on each other. However, if something separated us, I think I could still get along O.K. I know that my mother continues to have an important influence on me. Sometimes she gets on my nerves, but I still basically like her, and respect her, a lot. We have our arguments, and I don't always get my way, but she is willing to listen to me.

It is not enough for parents to understand children. They must accord children the privilege of understanding them.
—Milton Saperstein
American Author, 20th Century

—Amy, age 16

You go from a point at which your parents are responsible for you to a point at which you want a lot more independence. Finally, you are more independent, and you feel like you have to be more responsible for yourself; otherwise you are not going to do very well in this world. It's important for parents to still be there to support you, but at some point, you've got to look in the mirror and say, "I can do it myself."

—John, age 18

I don't get along very well with my parents. They try to dictate how I dress, who I date, how much I study, what I do on weekends, and how much time I spend talking on the phone. They are big intruders in my life. Why won't they let me make my own decisions? I'm mature enough to handle these things. When they jump down my throat at every little thing I do, it makes me mad and I say things to them I probably shouldn't. They just don't understand me very well.

—Ed, age 17

My father never seems to have any time to spend with me. He is gone a lot on business, and when he comes home, he is either too tired to do anything or plops down and watches TV and doesn't want to be bothered. He thinks I don't work hard enough and don't have values that were as solid as his generation. It is a very distant relationship. I actually spend more time talking to my mom than to him. I guess I should work a little harder in school than I do, but I still don't think he has the right to say such negative things to me. I like my mom a lot better because I think she is a much nicer person.

—Tom, age 15

We have our arguments and our differences, and there are moments when I get very angry with my parents, but most of the time they are like heated discussions. I have to say what I think because I don't think they are always right. Most of the time when there is an argument, we can discuss the problem and eventually find a course that we all can live with. Not every time, though, because there are some occasions when things just remain unresolved. Even when we have an unresolved conflict, I still would have to say that I get along pretty good with my parents.

—Ann, age 16

Old model		New model	
Autonomy, detachment from parents; parent and peer worlds are isolated	Intense, stressful conflict throughout adolescence; parent-adolescent relationships are filled with storm and stress on virtually a daily basis	Attachment and autonomy; parents are important support systems and attachment figures; adolescent-parent and adolescent-peer worlds have some important connections	Moderate parent-adolescent conflict common and can serve a positive developmental function; conflict greater in early adolescence, especially during the apex of puberty

◼ FIGURE 5.3
The Old and New Models of Parent-Adolescent Relationships

Reengaging Families with Adolescents
http://www.mhhe.com/santrocka9

conflict is intense and stressful throughout adolescence. The new model emphasizes that parents serve as important attachment figures, resources, and support systems as adolescents explore a wider, more complex social world. The new model also emphasizes that, in the majority of families, parent-adolescent conflict is moderate rather than severe and that everyday negotiations and minor disputes are normal, serving the positive developmental function of promoting independence and identity (see figure 5.3).

So far in this chapter we have examined the nature of family processes and parent-adolescent relationships. In addition to parent-adolescent relationships, there is another aspect to the family worlds of most adolescents—sibling relationships—which we discuss next.

SIBLING RELATIONSHIPS

SIBLING RELATIONSHIPS

Sibling Roles   Birth Order

Developmental Changes

Sandra describes to her mother what happened in a conflict with her sister:

> We had just come home from the ball game. I sat down on the sofa next to the light so I could read. Sally (the sister) said, "Get up. I was sitting there first. I just got up for a second to get a drink." I told her I was not going to get up and that I didn't see her name on the chair. I got mad and started pushing her—her drink spilled all over her. Then she got really mad; she shoved me against the wall, hitting and clawing at me. I managed to grab a handful of hair.

At this point, Sally comes into the room and begins to tell her side of the story. Sandra interrupts, "Mother, you always take her side." Sound familiar? How much does conflict characterize sibling relations? As we examine the roles siblings play in social development, you will discover that conflict is a common dimension of sibling relationships but that siblings also play many other roles in social development.

Sibling Roles

More than 80 percent of American adolescents have one or more siblings—that is, sisters and brothers. As anyone who has had a sibling knows, the conflict experienced by Sally and Sandra in their relationship with each other is a common interaction style of siblings. However, conflict is only one of the many dimensions of sibling relations. Adolescent sibling relations include helping, sharing, teaching, fighting, and playing, and adolescent siblings can act as emotional supports, rivals, and communication partners (Zukow-Goldring, 2002). In a recent study, positive sibling relationships in adolescence contributed to a sense of emotional and school-related support (Seginer, 1998).

In some instances, siblings can be stronger socializing influences on the adolescent than parents are (Teti, 2002). Someone close in age to the adolescent—such as a sibling—might be able to understand the adolescent's problems and communicate more effectively than parents can. In dealing with peers, coping with difficult teachers, and discussing taboo subjects (such as sex), siblings might be more influential in socializing adolescents than parents are. In one recent study, both younger and older adolescent siblings viewed older siblings as sources of social support for social and scholastic activities (Tucker, McHale, & Crouter, 2001). Furthermore, in one study, children showed more consistent behavior when interacting with siblings and more varied behavior when interacting with parents (Baskett & Johnson, 1982). In this study, children interacted in much more aggressive ways with their siblings than with their parents. In another study, adolescents reported a higher degree of conflict with their siblings than with anyone else (Buhrmester & Furman, 1990).

Developmental Changes

Although adolescent sibling relations reveal a high level of conflict in comparison to adolescents' relationships with other social agents (parents, peers, teachers, and romantic partners, for example), there is evidence that sibling conflict is actually lower in adolescence than in childhood. In a recent study, the lessened sibling conflict during adolescence was due partly to a dropoff in the amount of time siblings spent playing and talking with each other during adolescence (Buhrmester & Furman, 1990). The decline also reflected a basic transformation in the power structure of sibling relationships that seems to occur in adolescence. In childhood, there is an asymmetry of power, with older siblings frequently playing the role of "boss" or caregiver. This asymmetry of power often produces conflicts when one sibling tries to force the other to comply with his or her demands. As younger siblings grow older and their maturity level "catches up" to older siblings', the power asymmetry decreases. As siblings move through adolescence, most learn how to relate to each other on a more equal footing and, in doing so, come to resolve more of their differences than in childhood. Nonetheless, as we said earlier, sibling conflict in adolescence is still reasonably high.

THROUGH THE EYES OF ADOLESCENTS

Dealing with My Sister

"Like a lot of brothers and sisters, my sister and I have our fights. Sometimes when I talk to her, it is like talking to a brick! Her favorite thing to do is to storm off and slam the door when she gets mad at me. After a while, I cool off. When I calm down, I realize fighting with your sister is crazy. I go to my sister and apologize. It's a lot better to cool off and apologize than to keep on fighting and make things worse."

—Cynthia, Age 11

More than 80 percent of us have one or more siblings. *What are some developmental changes in siblings?*

Birth Order

Birth order has been of special interest to sibling researchers, who want to identify the characteristics associated with being born into a particular slot in a family. Firstborns have been described as more adult oriented, helpful, conforming, anxious, and self-controlled, and less aggressive than their siblings. Parental demands and high standards established for firstborns may result in firstborns realizing higher academic and professional achievements than their siblings (Furman & Lanthier, 2002). For example, firstborns are overrepresented in *Who's Who* and among Rhodes Scholars. However, some of the same pressures placed on firstborns for high achievement can be the reason firstborns also have more guilt, anxiety, difficulty in coping with stressful situations, and higher admission to guidance clinics.

Birth order also plays a role in siblings' relationships with each other (Vandell, Minnett, & Santrock, 1987). Older siblings invariably take on the dominant role in sibling interaction, and older siblings report feeling more resentful that parents give preferential treatment to younger siblings.

What are later-borns like? Characterizing later-borns is difficult because they can occupy so many different sibling positions. For example, a later-born might be the second-born male in a family of two siblings or a third-born female in a family of four siblings. In two-child families, the profile of the later-born child is related to the sex of his or her sibling. For example, a boy with an older sister is more likely to develop "feminine" interests than a boy with an older brother. Overall, later-borns usually enjoy better relations with peers than firstborns. Last-borns, who are often described as the "baby" in the family even after they have outgrown infancy, run the risk of becoming overly dependent. Middle-borns tend to be more diplomatic, often performing the role of negotiator in times of dispute (Sutton-Smith, 1982).

The popular conception of the only child is of a "spoiled brat" with such undesirable characteristics as dependency, lack of self-control, and self-centered behavior. But research presents a more positive portrayal of the only child, who often is achievement oriented and displays a desirable personality, especially in comparison to later-borns and children from large families (Thomas, Coffman, & Kipp, 1993).

So far our consideration of birth-order effects suggest that birth order might be a strong predictor of adolescent behavior. However, an increasing number of family researchers believe that birth order has been overdramatized and overemphasized. The critics argue that, when all of the factors that influence adolescent behavior are considered, birth order itself shows limited ability to predict adolescent behavior. Consider just sibling relationships alone. They vary not only in birth order, but also in number of siblings, age of siblings, age spacing of siblings, and sex of siblings. For example, in one recent study male sibling pairs had a less-positive relationship (less caring, less intimate, and lower conflict resolution) than male/female or female/female sibling pairs (Cole & Kerns, 2001).

Consider also the temperament of siblings. Researchers have found that siblings' temperamental traits (such as "easy" and "difficult"), as well as differential treatment of siblings by parents, influence how siblings get along (Brody, Stoneman, & Burke, 1987). Siblings with "easy" temperaments who are treated in relatively equal ways by parents tend to get along with each other the best, whereas siblings with "difficult" temperaments, or siblings whose parents gave one sibling preferential treatment, get along the worst.

Beyond temperament and differential treatment of siblings by parents, think about some of the other important factors in adolescents' lives that influence their behavior beyond birth order. They include heredity, models of competency or incompetency that parents present to adolescents on a daily basis, peer influences, school influences, socioeconomic factors, sociohistorical factors, cultural variations, and so on. When someone says firstborns are always like this, but last-borns are always like that, you now know that they are making overly simplistic statements that do not adequately take into account the complexity of influences on an adolescent's behavior. Keep in mind,

Big sisters are the crab grass in the lawn of life.
—Charles Schultz
American Cartoonist, 20th Century

though, that, although birth order itself may not be a good predictor of adolescent behavior, sibling relationships and interaction are important dimensions of family processes in adolescence.

Since the last review, you have studied many aspects of parent-adolescent relationships and sibling relationships. This review should help you to reach your learning goals related to this topic.

☐ FOR YOUR REVIEW

Learning Goal 2
Discuss parent-adolescent relationships

- An increasing trend is to conceptualize parents as managers of adolescents' lives.
- Authoritarian, authoritative, neglectful, and indulgent are four main parenting styles. Authoritative parenting is associated with socially competent adolescent behavior more than the other styles.
- Conflict with parents does increase in early adolescence, but such conflict is usually moderate and can serve a positive developmental function of increasing independence and identity exploration. The generation gap is exaggerated, although in as many as 20 percent of families parent-adolescent conflict is too high and is linked with adolescent problems.
- Many parents have a difficult time handling the adolescent's push for autonomy. Autonomy is a complex concept with many referents. Developmental transitions in autonomy include the onset of early adolescence and the time when individuals leave home and go to college. A special concern about autonomy involves runaways. The wise parent relinquishes control in areas where the adolescent makes mature decisions and retains more control in areas where the adolescent makes immature decisions. Adolescents do not simply move away into a world isolated from parents. Attachment to parents in adolescence increases the probability that an adolescent will be socially competent and explore a widening social world in a healthy way. Increasingly, researchers classify attachment in adolescence into one secure category (secure-autonomous) and three insecure categories (dismissing/avoidant, preoccupied/ambivalent, and unresolved/disorganized).

Learning Goal 3
Know about sibling relationships

- Sibling relationships often involve more conflict than relationships with other individuals. However, adolescents also share many positive moments with siblings through emotional support and social communication.
- Although sibling conflict in adolescence is reasonably high, it is usually less than in childhood.
- Birth order has been of special interest and differences between firstborns and later-borns have been reported. The only child often is more socially competent than the stereotype "spoiled child" suggests. An increasing number of family researchers believe that birth-order effects have been overdramatized and that other factors are more important in predicting the adolescent's behavior.

So far in this chapter we have examined the nature of family processes, parent-adolescent relationships, and sibling relationships. Next, we will explore the changing family in a changing society.

THE CHANGING FAMILY IN A CHANGING SOCIETY

More adolescents are growing up in a greater variety of family structures than ever before in history (Hernandez, 1997). Many mothers spend the greater part of their day away from their children. More than one of every two mothers with a child under the age of 5, and more than two of every three with a child from 6 to 17 years of age, is in the labor force. The number of adolescents growing up in single-parent families is staggering. The United States has the highest percentage of single-parent families, compared to virtually all other countries (see figure 5.4 on p. 170). Also, by age 18, approximately one-fourth of all American children will have lived a portion of their lives in a stepfamily.

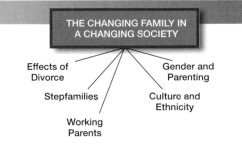

THE CHANGING FAMILY IN A CHANGING SOCIETY

Effects of Divorce

Stepfamilies

Working Parents

Gender and Parenting

Culture and Ethnicity

CHAPTER 6

CHAPTER MAP

THE NATURE OF PEER RELATIONS

- Peer Group Functions
- Family-Peer Linkages
- Peer Conformity
- Peer Statuses
- Bullying
- Conglomerate Strategies for Improving Social Skills
- Emotional Regulation in Peer Relations
- Social Cognition

FRIENDSHIP

- Its Importance
- Sullivan's Ideas
- Mixed-Age Friendships
- Intimacy and Similarity

ADOLESCENT GROUPS

- Group Function and Formation
- Children Groups and Adolescent Groups
- Youth Organizations
- Cliques and Crowds
- Ethnic and Cultural Variations

DATING AND ROMANTIC RELATIONSHIPS

- Functions of Dating
- Types of Dating and Developmental Changes
- Culture and Dating
- Romantic Love and Its Construction
- Emotion and Romantic Relationships
- Male and Female Dating Scripts

YOUNG ADOLESCENT GIRLS' FRIENDS AND RELATIONAL WORLDS

Lynn Brown and Carol Gilligan (1992) conducted in-depth interviews of 100 girls 10 to 13 years of age who were making the transition to the relational worlds of adolescence. They listened to what these girls were saying about how important friends were to them. The girls were very curious about the human world they lived

A man's growth is seen in the successive choirs of his friends.
—Ralph Waldo Emerson, 1841
American Poet and Essayist, 19th Century

in and kept track of what was happening to the peers and friends in their world. The girls spoke about the pleasure they derived from the intimacy and fun of human connection, and about the potential for hurt in relationships. They especially highlighted the importance of clique formation in their lives.

One girl, Noura, says that she learned about what it feels like to be the person that everyone doesn't like and that it was very painful. Another girl, Gail, reflected on her life over the last year and says that she is now getting along better with people, probably because she is better at understanding how they think and at accepting them. A number of the girls talked about "whitewashing" in the adolescent relational world. That is, many girls say nice and kind things to be polite but often don't really mean them. They know the benefits of being perceived as the perfect, happy girl, at least on the surface. Suspecting that people prefer the "perfect girl," they experiment with her image and the happiness she might bring. The perfectly nice girl seems to gain popularity with other girls, and as many girls strive to become her, jealousies and rivalries break out. Cliques can provide emotional support for girls who are striving to be perfect but know they are not. One girl, Victoria, commented that some girls like her, who weren't very popular, nonetheless were accepted into a "club" with three other girls. She now feels that when she is sad or depressed she can count on the "club" for support. Though they were "leftovers" and did not get into the most popular cliques, these four girls say they know they are liked and it feels great.

Another girl, Judy, at age 13, spoke about her interest in romantic relationships. She says that although she and her girlfriends are only 13, they want to have romantic relationships. She covers her bodily desires and sexual feelings with romantic ideals. She describes a girl who goes out with guys and goes farther than most girls would and says the girl's behavior is "disgusting." Rather than sex, Judy says she is looking for a really good relationship with a guy.

■ FROM NO MORE "WHAT IF" QUESTIONS TO AUTHORS' WEEK

SCHOOLS

■

Some schools for adolescents are ineffective, others effective, as revealed in these excerpts (Lipsitz, 1984):

The whole art of teaching is only the art of awakening the natural curiosity of young minds.
—Anatole France,
French Novelist, 20th Century

> A teacher in a social studies class squelches several imaginative questions, exclaiming, "You're always asking 'what if' questions. Stop asking 'what if.'" When a visitor asks who will become president if the president-elect dies before the electoral college meets, the teacher explodes, "You're as bad as they are! That's another 'what if' question!"

> A teacher drills students for a seemingly endless amount of time on prime numbers. After the lesson, not one student can say why it is important to learn prime numbers.

> A visitor asks a teacher if hers is an eighth-grade class. "It's called eighth grade," the teacher answers harshly, "but we know it's really kindergarten, right class?"

> In a predominantly Latino school, only the one adult hired as a bilingual teacher speaks Spanish.

> In a biracial school, the principal and the guidance counselor cite test scores with pride. They are asked if the difference between the test scores of African American and white students is narrowing: "Oh, that's an interesting question!" says the guidance counselor with surprise. The principal agrees. It has never been asked by or of them before.

The preceding vignettes are from middle schools where life seems to be difficult and unhappy for students. By contrast, consider these circumstances in effective middle schools (Lipsitz, 1984):

> Everything is peaceful. There are open cubbies instead of locked lockers. There is no theft. Students walk quietly in the corridors. "Why?" they are asked. "So as not to disturb the media center," they answer, which is self-evident to them, but not the visitor. . . . When asked, "Do you like this school?" [They] answer, "No, we don't like it. We love it!"

> When asked how the school feels, one student answered, "It feels smart. We're smart. Look at our test scores." Comments from one of the parents of a student at the school are revealing: "My child would have been a dropout. In elementary school, his teacher said to me, 'That child isn't going to give you anything but heartaches.' He had perfect attendance here. He didn't want to miss a day. Summer vacation was too long and boring. He got here and someone cared for him."

> The humane environment that encourages teachers' growth is translated by the teachers into a humane environment that encourages students' growth. The school feels cold when one first enters. It has the institutional feeling of any large school building with metal lockers and impersonal halls. Then one opens the door to a team area, and it is filled with energy, movement, productivity, doing. There is a lot of informal relating among students and between students and teachers. Visible from one vantage point are students working on written projects, putting the last touches on posters, watching a film, and working independently from reading kits. . . . Most know what they are doing, can say why it is important, and go back to work immediately after being interrupted.

> Authors' Week is a special activity built into the school's curriculum that entices students to consider themselves in relation to the rich variety of making and doing in peoples' lives. Based on student interest, availability, and diversity, authors are invited to discuss their craft. Students sign up to meet with individual authors. They must have read one individual book by the author. Students prepare questions for their sessions with the authors. Sometimes, an author stays several days to work with a group of students on his or her manuscript.

CAREERS IN ADOLESCENT DEVELOPMENT

Jimmy Furlow
Secondary School Teacher

Ninth-grade history teacher Jimmy Furlow believes that students learn best when they have to teach others. He has groups of students summarize textbook sections and put them on transparencies to help the entire class prepare for a test. Furlow lost both legs in Vietnam but he rarely stays in one place, moving his wheelchair around the room, communicating with students at eye level. When the class completes their discussion of all the points on the overhead, Furlow edits their work to demonstrate concise, clear writing and help students zero in on an important point (Marklein, 1998).

Ninth-grade history teacher Jimmy Furlow converses with a student in his class.

Parent Involvement in Schools
http://www.mhhe.com/santrocka9

priority in improving education (Chira, 1993). In an analysis of 16,000 students, the students were more likely to get A's and less likely to repeat a grade or be expelled if both parents were highly involved in their schooling (National Center for Education Statistics, 1997).

One example of a successful school-family partnership involves the New York City School System and the Children's Aid Society, which provide school-based programs for 1,200 adolescents and their families (Carnegie Council on Adolescent Development, 1995). The participating school's family resource center is open from 8:30 A.M. to 8:30 P.M. Staffed by social workers, parents, and other volunteers, the center houses adult education, drug-abuse prevention, and other activities. Because many of the families who send adolescents to the school are of Dominican origin, the school offers English-as-a-second-language classes for parents, 400 of whom recently were enrolled.

Joyce Epstein (1990, 1996; Epstein & Sanders, 2002) has provided a framework for understanding how parental involvement in adolescents' schooling can be improved. First, *families have a basic obligation to provide for the safety and health of their adolescents.* Many parents are not knowledgeable about the normal age-appropriate changes that characterize adolescents. School-family programs can help to educate parents about the normal course of adolescent development. Schools also can offer programs about health issues in adolescence, including sexually transmitted diseases, depression, drugs, delinquency, and eating disorders. Schools also can help parents find safe places for their adolescents to spend time away from home. Schools are community buildings that could be used as program sites by youth organizations and social service agencies.

Second, *schools have a basic obligation to communicate with families about school programs and the individual progress of their adolescents.* Teachers and parents rarely get to know each other in the secondary school years. Programs are needed to facilitate more direct and personalized parent-teacher communication. Parents also need to receive better information about curricular choices that may be related to eventual career choices. This is especially important with regard to females and ethnic minority students enrolling in science and math courses.

Third, *parents' involvement at school needs to be increased.* Parents and other family members may be able to assist teachers in the classroom in a variety of ways, such as tutoring, teaching special skills, and providing clerical or supervisory assistance. Such involvement is especially important in inner-city schools.

Fourth, *parent involvement in the adolescent's learning activities at home needs to be encouraged.* Secondary schools often raise a concern about parents' expertise and ability in helping their adolescents with homework. Given this concern, schools could provide parents with supplementary educational training so that parents can be more helpful and confident in their ability. "Family Math" and "Family Computers" are examples of programs that have been developed by some secondary schools to increase parent involvement in adolescent learning.

Fifth, *parents need to be increasingly involved in decision making at school.* Parent-teacher associations are the most common way for parents to be involved in school decision making. In some school districts, school improvement teams consisting of school staff and parents have been formed to address specific concerns.

Sixth, *collaboration and exchange with community organizations need to be encouraged.* Agencies and businesses can join with schools to improve adolescents'

RESOURCES FOR LIVES OF ADOLES

Adolescence in the 1990s

(1993) edited by Ruby Takanishi
New York: Teachers College Press

A number of experts on adolescence discuss the risk a
for adolescents in today's world. Many chapters focus
the quality of schooling for adolescents.

Council for Exceptional Children (CEC)

1920 Association Drive
Reston, VA 22091
703–620–3660

The CEC maintains an information center on the ed
dren and adolescents who are exceptional and publis
a wide variety of topics.

National Dropout Prevention Center

205 Martin Street
Clemson University
Clemson, SC 29634
803–656–2599

The center operates as a clearinghouse for informati
dropout prevention and at-risk youth and publishes
Dropout Prevention Newsletter.

TAKING IT TO T

1. The dramatic increase in the n
tions for Ritalin due to the la
diagnosis of ADD and ADHD has sparked co
versy, particularly among parents. *What are th
rounding the use of Ritalin?*

2. Much has been made of means of altering
student/teacher ratios, and providing special p
groups of students as means of enhancing the
ence. *As a future parent, what types of educati
career-planning opportunities would you want
gifted child?*

females. Thus, a better effort needs t
and involve the Latina's family more

American anthropologist John
view that ethnic minority students a
ucational system. He believes that s
Latino students, have inferior educa
ministrators who have low academ
stereotypes of ethnic minority grou
nantly Latino areas of Miami, Lati
American students as having more b
rated the same students as having (Z

Like Ogbu, Margaret Beale Spen
of institutional racism permeates ma
ers, acting out of misguided liberali
Such teachers prematurely accept a l
stituting warmth and affection for hig

Here are some strategies for imp
dents (Santrock, 2001):

- *Turn the class into a jigsaw.* Wher
  of Texas at Austin, the Austin Sch
  the increasing racial tension in th
  cept of the **jigsaw classroom,** w.
  are placed in a cooperative group
  project to reach a common goal. Are
  the technique as being like a grou
  ent pieces of a jigsaw puzzle.

  How might this work? Consi
  American, some Latino, and some
  groups focuses on the life of Jose
  groups of six students each, with
  ethnic composition and achievem
  vided into six parts, with each pa
  The parts might be paragraphs fro
  family came to the United States, P
  students in each group are given a
  members teach their parts to the g
  dependence and cooperation in re
- *Encourage students to have positive*
  tact alone does not do the job of i
  example, busing ethnic minority st
  versa, has not reduced prejudice o
  Shapiro, 1983). What matters is wh
  school. Especially beneficial in imp
  ferent ethnicities to share with one
  strategies, interests, and other per
  people more as individuals than as
- *Encourage students to engage in pers*
  students see other's perspective can
  dents "step into the shoes" of stude
  is like to be treated in fair or unfair
- *Help students to think critically and*
  are involved. Students who learn to
  relations are likely to decrease their
  who think in narrow ways are more
  intelligent includes understanding t
  tening to what others are saying, an

educational experiences. Business personnel can especially provide insights into careers and the world of work. Some schools have formed partnerships with businesses, which provide some financial backing for special projects.

In summary, the collaborative relationship between parents and schools has usually decreased as children move into the adolescent years. Yet parent involvement might be just as important in the adolescent's schooling as in the child's schooling. For example, Epstein (1996) created a program designed to increase parents' involvement in the education of their middle school students and it had positive effects on the students' school performance. It is to be hoped that the future will bring much greater family/school/community collaboration in the adolescent years (Eccles & Harold, 1993).

We have discussed a number of ideas about schools, classrooms, teachers, and parents. Next, we will explore the roles of socioeconomic status and ethnicity in schools.

SOCIOECONOMIC STATUS AND ETHNICITY IN SCHOOLS

Adolescents from low-income, ethnic minority backgrounds often have more difficulties in school than their middle-socioeconomic status, White counterparts. Why? Critics argue that schools have not done a good job of educating low-income, ethnic minority students to overcome the barriers to their achievement (Scott-Jones, 1995). Let's examine the roles of socioeconomic status (SES) and ethnicity in schools.

Socioeconomic Status

Adolescents in poverty often face problems at home and at school that present barriers to their learning (McLoyd, 2000; Spring, 2002). At home, they might have parents who don't set high educational standards for them, who are incapable of helping them read or with their homework, and who don't have enough money to pay for educational materials and experiences such as books and trips to zoos and museums. They might experience malnutrition and live in areas where crime and violence are a way of life.

The schools that adolescents from impoverished backgrounds attend often have fewer resources than schools in higher-SES neighborhoods (Shade, Kelly, & Oberg, 1997). Schools in low-SES areas are more likely to have a higher percentage of students with lower achievement test scores, lower graduation rates, and fewer students going to college. They also are more likely to have young teachers with less experience than schools in higher-SES neighborhoods. In some instances, though, federal aid has provided a context for improved learning in schools located in low-income areas. Schools in low-SES areas are more likely to encourage rote learning, whereas schools in higher-SES areas are more likely to work with adolescents to improve their thinking skills (Spring, 1998). In sum, far too many schools in low-SES neighborhoods provide students with environments that are not conducive to effective learning and the schools' buildings and classrooms often are old, crumbling, and poorly maintained.

Jonathan Kozol (1991) vividly described some of these problems adolescents in poverty face in their neighborhood and at school in *Savage Inequalities.* Following are some of his observations in East St. Louis, Illinois, an inner-city area that is 98 percent African American and has no obstetric services, no regular trash collection, and few jobs. Nearly one-third of the families live on less than $7,500 a year, and

SOCIOECONOMIC STATUS
AND ETHNICITY IN SCHOOLS

Socioeconomic   Ethnicity
Status

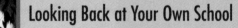
Poverty and Learning
Interview with Jonathan Kozol
http://www.mhhe.com/santrocka9

THINKING CRITICALLY

Looking Back at Your Own School

Think back on your own secondary school experiences. How diverse were your classmates in terms of

- ethnic or religious background?
- socioeconomic background?
- place of birth?

How diverse were your teachers in these respects? How sensitive were they to ethnic and cultural diversity?

In your experience, how fairly did the curriculum and the general educational programs of the school address the histories, traditions, and other needs of different groups in your schools? Were some groups favored over others?

What problems arose that reflected ethnic, religious, or socioeconomic differences?

If you had been a teacher back then instead of a student, are there things you would have wanted to change about your school to produce more social harmony and meet unmet needs related to diversity? What would you have tried to change?

Dr. Henry Gaskins began an after-scho[...]
ethnic minority students in 1983 in W[...]
hours every weeknight and all day Satu[...]
one-on-one assistance from Gaskins a[...]
volunteers, and academically talented [...]
afford it contribute five dollars to cove[...]
supplies. In addition to tutoring in spe[...]
home-based academy helps students to[...]
to commit to a desire to succeed. Many[...]
from families in which the parents are [...]
and either cannot or are not motivated [...]
adolescents achieve in school. In additi[...]
prepares students to qualify for scholar[...]
entrance exams. Gaskins was recently a[...]
Volunteer Action Award at the White H[...]

CHAPTER MAP

```
THE NATURE OF
ADOLESCENTS' SCHOOLING

Approaches                Schools' Changing
to Educating              Social Developmental
Students                  Contexts

TRANSITIONS
IN SCHOOLING

Transition to             High School
Middle or Junior          Dropouts and
High School               Noncollege Youth

What Makes                Transition from
a Successful              High School
Middle School?            to College

SCHOOLS, CLASSROOMS,
TEACHERS, AND PARENTS

Size and Climate          Teachers
of Schools                and Parents

Person-Environment
Fit and Aptitude-
Treatment Interaction

SOCIOECONOMIC STATUS
AND ETHNICITY IN SCHOOLS

Socioeconomic             Ethnicity
Status

ADOLESCENTS WHO
ARE EXCEPTIONAL

Who Are                   Adolescents Who
Adolescents with          Are Gifted
Disabilities?

Learning Disabilities     Educational
                          Issues Involving
                          Adolescents with
                          Disabilities

Attention Deficit
Hyperactivity Disorder
```

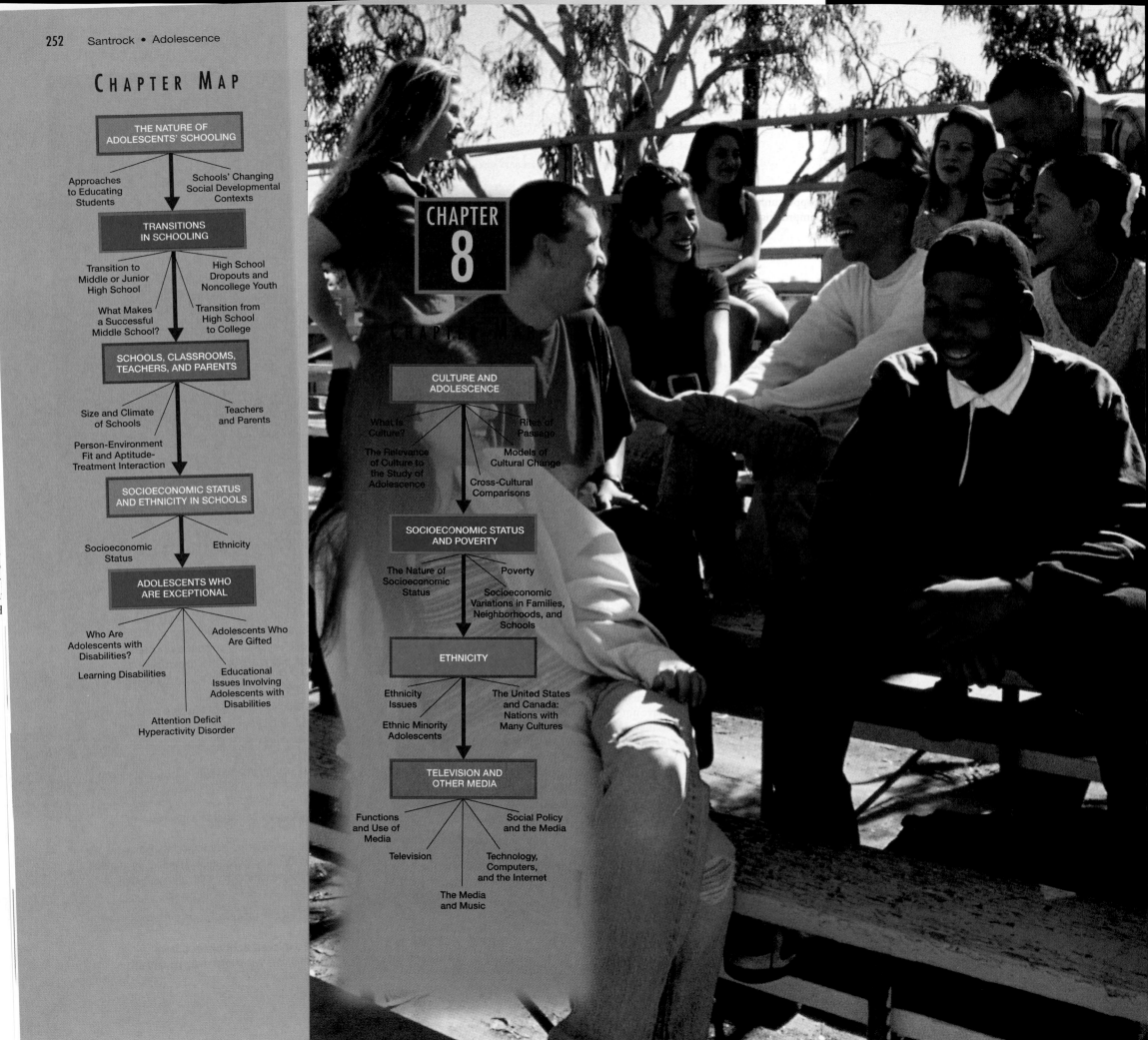

CHAPTER 8

CHAPTER MAP

```
CULTURE AND
ADOLESCENCE

What Is                   Rites of
Culture?                  Passage

The Relevance             Models of
of Culture to             Cultural Change
the Study of
Adolescence               Cross-Cultural
                          Comparisons

SOCIOECONOMIC STATUS
AND POVERTY

The Nature of             Poverty
Socioeconomic
Status                    Socioeconomic
                          Variations in Families,
                          Neighborhoods, and
                          Schools

ETHNICITY

Ethnicity                 The United States
Issues                    and Canada:
                          Nations with
Ethnic Minority           Many Cultures
Adolescents

TELEVISION AND
OTHER MEDIA

Functions                 Social Policy
and Use of                and the Media
Media

Television                Technology,
                          Computers,
                          and the Internet

The Media
and Music
```

DATING PROBLEMS OF A 16-YEAR-OLD JAPANESE AMERICAN GIRL AND SCHOOL PROBLEMS OF A 17-YEAR-OLD CHINESE AMERICAN BOY

Sonya, a 16-year-old Japanese girl, was upset over her family's reaction to her White American boyfriend. Her parents refused to meet him and more than once threatened to disown her. Her older brothers also reacted angrily to Sonya's dating a White American, warning that they were going to beat him up. Her parents were also disturbed that Sonya's grades, above average in middle school, were beginning to drop.

Generational issues contributed to the conflict between Sonya and her family (Nagata, 1989). Her parents had experienced strong sanctions against dating Whites when they were growing up and were legally prevented from marrying anyone but a Japanese. As Sonya's older brothers were growing up, they valued ethnic pride and solidarity. The brothers saw her dating a White as "selling out" her own ethnic group. Sonya's and her family members' cultural values obviously differ.

Michael, a 17-year-old Chinese American high school student, was referred to an outpatient adolescent crisis center by the school counselor for depression and suicidal tendencies (Huang & Ying, 1989). Michael was failing several subjects and was repeatedly absent or late for school. Michael's parents were successful professionals who told the therapist that there was nothing wrong with them or with Michael's younger brother and sister, so what, they wondered, was wrong with Michael! What was wrong was that the parents expected all of their children to become doctors. They were frustrated and angered by Michael's school failures, especially since he was the firstborn son, who in Chinese families is expected to achieve the highest standards of all siblings.

The therapist underscored the importance of the parents' putting less pressure for achievement on Michael and gradually introduced more realistic expectations for Michael (who was not interested in becoming a doctor and did not have the necessary academic record anyway). The therapist supported Michael's desire not to become a doctor and empathized with the pressure he had experienced from his parents. As Michael's school attendance improved, his parents noted his improved attitude toward school and supported a continuation of therapy. Michael's case illustrates how expectations that Asian American youth will be "whiz kids" can become destructive.

Sonya's and Michael's circumstances underscore the importance of culture in understanding adolescent development.

CULTURE

■

Consider the flowers of a garden: Though differing in kind, color, form, and shape, yet, inasmuch as they are refreshed by the waters of one spring, revived by the breath of one wind, invigorated by the rays of one sun, this diversity increases their charm and adds to their beauty. . . . How unpleasing to the eye if all the flowers and plants, the leaves and blossoms, the fruits, the branches, and the trees of that garden were all of the same shape and color! Diversity of hues, form, and shape enriches and adorns the garden and heightens its effect.

—'Abdu'l Baha
Persian Baha'i Religious Leader, 19th/20th Century

Culture has a powerful impact on people's lives. In Xinjian, China, a woman prepares for horseback courtship. Her suitor must chase her, kiss her, and evade her riding crop—all on the gallop. A new marriage law took effect in China in 1981. The law sets a minimum age for marriage—22 years for males, 20 years for females. Late marriage and late childbirth are critical aspects of China's effort to control population growth.

Cross-Cultural Comparisons

Cross-Cultural Comparisons
http://www.mhhe.com/santrocka9

cross-cultural studies
Studies that compare a culture with one or more other cultures. Such studies provide information about the degree to which adolescent development is similar, or universal, across cultures or about the degree to which it is culture-specific.

Early in the twentieth century, overgeneralizations about the universal aspects of adolescents were made based on data and experience in a single culture—the middle-socioeconomic-status culture of the United States (Havighurst, 1976). For example, it was believed that adolescents everywhere went through a period of "storm and stress" characterized by self-doubt and conflict. However, as we saw in chapter 1, when Margaret Mead visited the island of Samoa, she found that the adolescents of the Samoan culture were not experiencing much stress ◀◀ P. 7.

Cross-cultural studies *involve the comparison of a culture with one or more other cultures, which provides information about the degree to which adolescent development is similar, or universal, across cultures, or the degree to which it is culture-specific.* The study of adolescence has emerged in the context of Western industrialized society, with the practical needs and social norms of this culture dominating thinking about adolescents. Consequently, the development of adolescents in Western cultures has evolved as the norm for all adolescents of the human species, regardless of economic and cultural circumstances. This narrow viewpoint can produce erroneous conclusions about the nature of adolescents (Berry, 2000; Goldstein, 2000; Miller, 2001). To develop a more global, cosmopolitan perspective on adolescents, we will consider adolescents' achievement behavior and sexuality in different cultures, as well as rites of passage.

Achievement   The United States is an achievement-oriented culture, and U.S. adolescents are more achievement oriented than the adolescents in many other countries. Many American parents socialize their adolescents to be achievement oriented and

Cross-cultural studies involve the comparison of a culture with one or more other cultures. Shown here is a 14-year-old !Kung girl who has added flowers to her beadwork during the brief rainy season in the Kalahari desert in Botswana, Africa. Delinquency and violence occur much less frequently in the peaceful !Kung culture than in most other cultures around the world.

independent. In one investigation of 104 societies, parents in industrialized countries like the United States placed a higher value on socializing adolescents for achievement and independence than did parents in nonindustrialized countries like Kenya, who placed a higher value on obedience and responsibility (Bacon, Child, & Barry, 1963).

Anglo-American adolescents are more achievement oriented than Mexican and Mexican American adolescents are. For example, in one study, Anglo-American adolescents were more competitive and less cooperative than their Mexican and Mexican American counterparts (Kagan & Madsen, 1972). In this study, Anglo-Americans were more likely to discount the gains of other students when they could not reach the goals themselves. In other investigations, Anglo-American youth were more individual centered, while Mexican youth were more family centered (Holtzmann, 1982). Some developmentalists believe that the American culture is too achievement oriented for rearing mentally healthy adolescents (Elkind, 1981).

Although Anglo-American adolescents are more achievement oriented than adolescents in many other cultures, they are not as achievement oriented as many Japanese, Chinese, and Asian American adolescents. For example, as a group, Asian American adolescents demonstrate exceptional achievement patterns (Stevenson, 1995). Asian American adolescents exceed the national average for high school and college graduates. Eighty-six percent of Asian Americans, compared to 64 percent of White Americans, are in some higher-education program two years after high school graduation. Clearly, education and achievement are highly valued by many Asian American youth. More about Asian American youth appears later in this chapter and in chapter 13, where we discuss achievement.

CHAPTER MAP

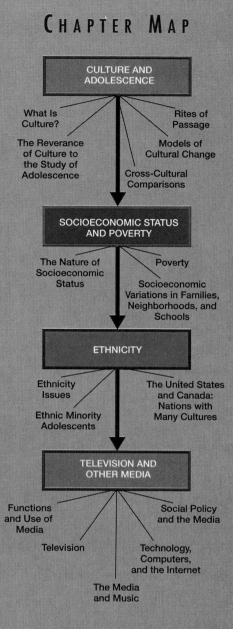

REACH YOUR LEARNING GOALS

At the beginning of this chapter we stated six learning goals and encouraged you to review material related to these goals at four points in the chapter. This is a good time to return to these reviews and use them to guide your study and help you to reach your learning goals:

Page 263

Learning Goal 1   Understand culture and adolescent development

Page 268

Learning Goal 2   Discuss socioeconomic status and adolescence

Learning Goal 3   Describe the role of poverty in adolescent development

Page 277

Learning Goal 4   Evaluate issues related to ethnicity

Learning Goal 5   Know about ethnic minority adolescents

Page 285

Learning Goal 6   Discuss television and other media influences

KEY TERMS

culture 256
socioeconomic status (SES) 257
ethnicity 257
ethnocentrism 257
cross-cultural studies 258
assimilation 260
acculturation 260
alternation model 261

multicultural model 261
rites of passage 261
feminization of poverty 266
prejudice 271
Chicano 274
Internet 282
e-mail 283

KEY PEOPLE

Richard Brislin 256
Carola Suárez-Orozco 270
Stanley Sue 271
James Jones 271
Vonnie McLoyd 273
Sandra Calvert 285

RESOURCES FOR IMPROVING THE LIVES OF ADOLESCENTS

The Adolescent & Young Adult Fact Book

(1991) by Janet Simons, Belva Finlay, and
Alice Yang
Washington, DC: Children's Defense Fund

This book is filled with valuable charts that describe the roles that poverty and ethnicity play in adolescent development.

Advocates for Youth Media Project

3733 Motor Avenue, Suite 204
Los Angeles, CA 90034
310–559–5700

This project promotes responsible portrayals of sexuality in the entertainment media. The project members work with media professionals by sponsoring informational events and offering free consultation services to writers, producers, and other media personnel.

Canadian Ethnocultural Council/Conseil Ethnoculturel du Canada

251 Laurier Avenue West, Suite 110
Ottawa, Ontario K1P 5J6
613–230–3867

CEC's objective is to secure equality of opportunity, of rights, and of dignity for ethnocultural minorities and all other Canadians.

Children's Journey Through the Information Age

(1999) by Sandra Calvert
New York: McGraw-Hill

This is an excellent, contemporary treatment of many dimensions of the information age, such as television and computers.

Cybereducator

(1999) by Joan Bissell, Anna Manring, and Veronica Roland

A guide to using the Internet for K–12 education.

Quantum Opportunity Program

1415 North Broad Street
Philadelphia, PA 19122
215–236–4500

This is a year-round youth development program funded by the Ford Foundation. It has demonstrated that intervening in the lives of 13-year-old African Americans from poverty backgrounds can significantly improve their prospects.

Studying Ethnic Minority Adolescents

(1998) by Vonnie McLoyd & Laurence Steinberg (Eds.)
Mahwah, NJ: Erlbaum

An excellent resource book for learning about the best methods for studying ethnic minority adolescents.

Understanding Culture's Influence on Behavior

(1993) by Richard Brislin
Fort Worth, TX: Harcourt Brace

This is an excellent book on culture's role in behavior and development.

TAKING IT TO THE NET   http://www.mhhe.com/santrocka9

1. Adolescents who come from severe poverty, who experience parental divorce, who are the subjects of discrimination, and who attend very poor schools are at risk for various psychological and behavioral disorders. Yet, it is not at all inevitable that those who are at risk will experience poor development. *How do they develop the resilience that insulates them from the negative environmental conditions?*

2. Rites of passage mark important developmental milestones. Some are more formal, for example, a religious ceremony, and others are less formal, for example, entrance into sexual behavior. *How might you use the concept of rites of passage to explain various aspects of ado-*

lescent behavior (for example, body piercing, tattooing) to high school teachers?

3. The multicultural model of cultural change promotes a pluralistic approach to meeting common needs. *As a student in higher education, how would you explain the role of education, and particularly multicultural education, in achieving this form of cultural change?*

Connect to *http://www.mhhe.com/santrocka9* to research the answers and complete these exercises. In some cases, you'll also find further instructions on this site.

SOCIAL, EMOTIONAL, AND PERSONALITY DEVELOPMENT

◻

He who would learn to fly one day must learn to stand and walk and climb and dance: one cannot fly into flying.
—Friedrich Nietzsche
German Philosopher, 19th Century

So far, we have studied the biological, cognitive, and social contexts of adolescent development. In this section, we will examine the adolescent's social, emotional, and personality development. Section 4 consists of five chapters: chapter 9, "The Self and Identity"; chapter 10, "Gender"; chapter 11, "Sexuality"; chapter 12, "Moral Development, Values, and Religion"; and chapter 13, "Achievement, Careers, and Work."

CHAPTER
9

CHAPTER MAP

THE SELF

Self-Understanding

Self-Esteem and Self-Concept

IDENTITY

Erikson's Ideas on Identity

Gender and Identity Development

The Four Statuses of Identity

Cultural and Ethnic Aspects of Identity

Developmental Changes

Family Influences on Identity

IDENTITY AND INTIMACY

Intimacy

Loneliness

THE SELF AND IDENTITY

■

■ A 15-YEAR-OLD GIRL'S SELF-DESCRIPTION

How do adolescents describe themselves? How would you have described yourself when you were 15 years old? What features would you have emphasized? The following is a self-portrait of one 15-year-old girl:

> What am I like as a person? Complicated! I'm sensitive, friendly, outgoing, popular, and tolerant, though I can also be shy, self-conscious, and even obnoxious. Obnoxious! I'd *like* to be friendly and tolerant all of the time. That's the kind of person I *want* to be, and I'm disappointed when I'm not. I'm responsible, even studious now and then, but on the other hand, I'm a goof-off, too, because if you're too studious, you won't be popular. I don't usually do that well at school. I'm a pretty cheerful person, especially with my friends, where I can even get rowdy. At home I'm more likely to be anxious around my parents. They expect me to get all A's. It's not fair! I worry about how I probably *should* get better grades. But I'd be mortified in the eyes of my friends. So I'm usually pretty stressed-out at home, or sarcastic, since my parents are always on my case. But I really don't understand how I can switch so fast. I mean, how can I be cheerful one minute, anxious the next, and then be sarcastic? Which one is the *real* me? Sometimes, I feel phony, especially around boys. Say I think some guy might be interested in asking me out. I try to act different, like Madonna. I'll be flirtatious and fun-loving. And then everybody, I mean *everybody* else is looking at me like they think I'm totally weird. Then I get self-conscious and embarrassed and become radically introverted, and I don't know who I really am! Am I just trying to impress them or what? But I don't really care what they think anyway. I don't *want* to care, that is. I just want to know what my close friends think. I can be my true self with my close friends. I can't be my real self with my parents. They don't understand me. What do *they* know about what it's like to be a teenager? They still treat me like I'm still a kid. At least at school people treat you more like you're an adult. That gets confusing, though. I mean, which am I, a kid or an adult? It's scary, too, because I don't have any idea what I want to be when I grow up. I mean, I have lots of *ideas.* My friend Sheryl and I talk about whether we'll be flight attendants, or teachers, or nurses, veterinarians, maybe mothers, or actresses. I know I *don't* want to be a waitress or a secretary. But how do you decide all of this? I really don't know. I mean, I think about it a lot, but I can't resolve it. There are days when I wish I could just become immune to myself. (Harter, 1990b, pp. 352–353)

> "Who are you?" said the Caterpillar. Alice replied, rather shyly, "I—I hardly know, Sir, just at present—at least I know who I was when I got up this morning, but I must have changed several times since then."
>
> —Lewis Carroll
> *English Writer, 19th Century*

CHAPTER 10

CHAPTER MAP

WHAT IS GENDER?

BIOLOGICAL, SOCIAL, AND COGNITIVE INFLUENCES ON GENDER

Biological Influences

Cognitive Influences

Social Influences

GENDER STEREOTYPES, SIMILARITIES, AND DIFFERENCES

Gender Stereotyping

Gender in Context

Gender Similarities and Differences

Gender Controversy

GENDER-ROLE CLASSIFICATION

Traditional Gender Roles

Gender-Role Transcendence

Androgyny

Traditional Masculinity and Problem Behaviors in Adolescent Males

DEVELOPMENTAL CHANGES AND JUNCTURES

Early Adolescence and Gender Intensification

Is Early Adolescence a Critical Juncture for Females?

■ TOMORROW'S GENDER WORLDS OF TODAY'S ADOLESCENTS

GENDER

■

It is fatal to be man or woman pure and simple; one must be woman-manly or man-womanly.

—Virginia Woolf
English Novelist, 20th Century

Controversy characterizes today's females and males. Females increasingly struggle to gain influence and change the worlds of business, politics, and relationships with males. The changes are far from complete, but social reformers hope that a generation from now the struggles of the last decades of the twentieth century will have generated more freedom, influence, and flexibility for females (Denmark, Rabinowitz, & Sechzer, 2000; Lopez, 2001). Possibly in the next generation, when today's adolescents become tomorrow's adults, such issues as equal pay, child care, abortion, rape, and domestic violence will no longer be discussed as "women's issues" but, rather, as economic issues, family issues, and ethical issues—reflecting the equal concern of females *and* males. Possibly one of today's adolescent females will become the head of a large corporation several decades from now and the appointment will not make headlines by virtue of her gender. Half the presidential candidates may be women and nobody will notice.

What would it take for today's adolescent females to get from here to there? The choices are not simple ones. When Barbara Bush celebrated motherhood and wifely virtues in a commencement address at Wellesley College, she stimulated a national debate among the young on what it means to be a successful woman. The debate was further fueled by TV anchorwoman Connie Chung's announcement that she would abandon the fast track at CBS in a final drive to become a mother at age 44. At the same time, male role models are also in flux. Wall Street star Peter Lynch, the head of Fidelity Investment's leading mutual fund, resigned to have more time with his family and to pursue humanitarian projects (Gibbs, 1990). In 1993, both Chung and Lynch returned to work.

When asked to sketch their futures, many of today's youth say they want good careers, good marriages, and two or three children, but they don't want their children to be raised by strangers (Spade & Reese, 1991). Idealistic? Maybe. Some will reach these goals; some will make other choices as they move from adolescence into adulthood, and then through the adult years. Some of today's adolescents will choose to remain single as they move into adulthood and pursue their career goals; others will become married but not have children; and yet others will balance the demands of family and work. In a word, not all of today's females have the same goals; neither do all of today's males. What is important is to develop a society free of barriers and discrimination, one that allows females and males to freely choose, to meet their expectations, and to realize their potential.

Alice Eagly's Research
http://www.mhhe.com/santrocka9

social cognitive theory of gender

This theory emphasizes that children's and adolescents' gender development occurs through observation and imitation of gender behavior, and through rewards and punishments they experience for gender-appropriate and -inappropriate behavior.

In the contemporary view of evolutionary psychology, because men competed with other men for access to women, men's evolved dispositions favor violence, competition, and risk taking. Women in turn developed a preference for long-term mates who could support a family. As a consequence, men strived to acquire more resources than other men in order to attract women, and women developed preferences for successful, ambitious men who could provide these resources.

Critics of the evolutionary psychology view argue that humans have the decision-making ability to change their gender behavior and therefore are not locked into the evolutionary past. They also stress that the extensive cross-cultural variation in sex differences and mate preferences provides stronger evidence for a social influence view of gender differences than for an evolutionary view. Next, we will explore what some of these social influences are.

Social Influences

Many social scientists, such as Alice Eagly (1997, 2000, 2001), locate the cause of psychological sex differences not in biologically evolved dispositions but in the contrasting positions and social roles of women and men. In contemporary American society and in most cultures around the world, women have less power and status than men and control fewer resources. Women perform more domestic work than men and spend fewer hours in paid employment. Although most women are in the workforce, they receive lower pay than men and are thinly represented in the highest levels of organizations. Thus, from the perspective of social influences, gender hierarchy and sexual division of labor are important causes of sex-differentiated behavior. As women adapted to roles with less power and less status in society, they showed more cooperative, less dominant profiles than men.

Parental Influences   Parents, by action and example, influence their children's and adolescents' gender development. During the transition from childhood to adolescence, parents allow boys more independence than girls, and concern about girls' sexual vulnerability may cause parents to monitor their behavior more closely and ensure that they are chaperoned. Families with young adolescent daughters indicate that they experience more intense conflict about sex, choice of friends, and curfews than do families with young adolescent sons (Papini & Sebby, 1988). When parents place severe restrictions on their adolescent sons, it is disruptive to their sons' development (Baumrind, 1991).

Parents often have different expectations for their adolescent sons and daughters, especially in such academic areas as math and science. For example, many parents believe that math is more important for their sons' futures than for their daughters', and their beliefs influence the value adolescents place on math achievement (Eccles, 1987). More about gender and achievement appears later in this chapter.

Social cognitive theory has been especially important in understanding social influences on gender ◀▯▯▯ P. 50. The **social cognitive theory of gender** *emphasizes that children's and adolescents' gender development occurs through observation and imitation of gender behavior, and through rewards and punishments they experience for gender-appropriate and -inappropriate behavior.* By observing parents and other adults, as well as peers, at home, at school, in the neighborhood, and in the media, adolescents are exposed to a myriad of models who display masculine and feminine behavior. And parents often use rewards and punishments to teach their daughters to be feminine ("Karen, that dress you are wearing makes you look so pretty.") and their sons to be masculine ("Bobby, you were so aggressive in that game. Way to go!").

One major change in the gender-role models adolescents have been exposed to in recent years is the increasing number of working mothers. Most adolescents today have a mother who is employed at least part-time. Although maternal employment is not specific to adolescence, it does influence gender-role development, and its influence likely depends on the age of the child or adolescent involved. Young adolescents may be especially attuned to understanding adult roles, so their mothers' role choices may be important influences on their concepts and attitudes about women's roles (Huston & Alvarez, 1990). Adolescents with working mothers have less-stereotyped concepts of female roles (and sometimes male roles as well) than do adolescents whose mothers are full-time homemakers. They also have more positive attitudes about nontraditional roles for women. Daughters of employed mothers have higher educational and occupational aspirations than do daughters of homemakers (Hoffman, 1989, 2000). Thus, working mothers often serve as models who combine traditional feminine home roles with less traditional activities away from home.

Peers   Parents provide the earliest discrimination of gender behavior, but before long, peers join in the societal process of responding to and modeling masculine and feminine behavior. In middle and late childhood, children show a clear preference for being with and liking same-sex peers (Maccoby, 1996, 1998). After extensive observations of elementary school playgrounds, two researchers characterized the play settings as "gender school," pointing out that boys teach one another the required masculine behavior and reinforce it, and that girls also teach one another the required feminine behavior and reinforce it (Luria & Herzog, 1985).

In earlier chapters, we learned that adolescents spend increasing amounts of time with peers ◀|||| P. 186. In adolescence, peer approval or disapproval is a powerful influence on gender attitudes and behavior. Peers can socialize gender behavior partly by accepting or rejecting others on the basis of their gender-related attributes. Deviance from sex-typed norms often leads to low peer acceptance, but within a broad range of normal behavior it is not clear that conformity to sex-typed personality attributes is a good predictor of peer acceptance (Huston & Alvarez, 1990).

School and Teacher Influences   In certain ways, both girls and boys might receive an education that is not fair (Sadker & Sadker, 1994). For example:

- Girls' learning problems are not identified as often as boys' are.
- Boys are given the lion's share of attention in schools.
- Girls start school testing higher than boys in every academic subject, yet they graduate from high school scoring lower than boys do on the SAT exam.
- Pressure to achieve is more likely to be heaped on boys than on girls.

Consider this research study (Sadker & Sadker, 1986). Observers were trained to collect data in more than 100 fourth-, sixth-, and eighth-grade classrooms. At all three grade levels, male students were involved in more interactions with teachers than female students were, and male students were given more attention than their female counterparts were. Male students were also given more remediation, more criticism, and more praise than female students. Further, girls with strong math abilities are given lower-quality instruction than their male counterparts are (Eccles, 1993).

Myra Sadker and David Sadker (1994, 2003), who have been studying gender discrimination in schools for more than two decades, believe that many educators are unaware of the subtle ways in which gender infiltrates the school's environment. Their hope is that sexism can be eradicated in the nation's schools.

A special concern is that most middle and junior high schools consist of independent, masculine learning environments, which appear better suited to the learning style of the average adolescent boy than to that of the average adolescent girl (Huston & Alvarez, 1990). Compared to elementary schools, middle and junior high schools provide a more impersonal environment, which meshes better with the autonomous

A special concern is that, because they are more impersonal and encourage independence more than elementary schools do, most middle and junior high schools are better suited to the learning styles of males.

CHAPTER MAP

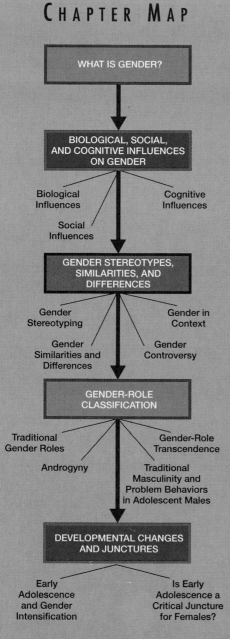

REACH YOUR LEARNING GOALS

At the beginning of the chapter we stated seven learning goals and encouraged you to review material related to these goals at four points in the chapter. This is a good time to return to these reviews. Use them to guide your study and help you to reach your learning goals.

Page 324

Learning Goal 1   Know what is meant by gender

Learning Goal 2   Explain biological, social, and cognitive influences on gender

Page 330

Learning Goal 3   Describe gender stereotypes, similarities, and differences

Learning Goal 4   Discuss gender controversy and gender in context

Page 336

Learning Goal 5   Evaluate traditional gender roles and androgyny

Learning Goal 6   Understand possible problems with masculinity and explain gender-role transcendence

Page 339

Learning Goal 7   Describe developmental changes and junctures

KEY TERMS

gender 318
gender role 318
social cognitive theory of gender 320
cognitive developmental theory
    of gender 323
schema 324
gender schema 324
gender schema theory 324

gender stereotypes 325
sexism 326
rapport talk 328
report talk 328
androgyny 331
gender-role transcendence 335
gender intensification hypothesis 336

KEY PEOPLE

Sigmund Freud 319
Erik Erikson 319
Alice Eagly 320
Myra Sadker and David Sadker 321
Lawrence Kohlberg 323
Eleanor Maccoby 327
Carol Jacklin 327

Janet Shibley Hyde 328
Deborah Tannen 328
David Buss 329
Sandra Bem 332
Joseph Pleck 334
Carol Gilligan 337

RESOURCES FOR IMPROVING THE LIVES OF ADOLESCENTS

Beyond Appearance

(1999) by Norine Johnson, Michael Roberts, and Judith Worrell (Eds.)
Washington, DC: American Psychological Association

In this book you can read about many aspects of girls' development in adolescence.

The Mismeasure of Woman

(1992) by Carol Tavris
New York: Simon & Schuster

This is an excellent book on gender stereotyping, similarities and differences between the sexes, and how females should be measured by their own standards, not males'.

A New Psychology of Men

(1995) by Ronald Levant and William Pollack
New York: Basic Books

This edited volume includes chapters by leading authorities in men's issues and gender roles related to the male's development. The contributors detail how some male problems are unfortunate by-products of the current way males are socialized.

The Two Sexes

(1998) by Eleanor Maccoby
Cambridge, MA: Harvard University Press

In this book you can explore how gender differences emerge in children's groups.

YMCA

101 North Wacker Drive
Chicago, IL 60606

The YMCA provides a number of programs for teenage boys. A number of personal health and sports programs are available.

You Just Don't Understand

(1990) by Deborah Tannen
New York: Ballantine

This is a book about how women and men communicate—or, all too often, miscommunicate—with each other.

YWCA

726 Broadway
New York, NY 10003

The YWCA promotes health, sports participation, and fitness for women and girls. Its programs include instruction in health, teen pregnancy prevention, family life education, self-esteem enhancement, parenting, and nutrition.

TAKING IT TO THE NET

1. Gender roles influence how we perceive ourselves and others, our desires and goals, and our personalities. But they also impact on the everyday lives of adults in very basic and fundamental ways. *What might the issues of balancing home and career be and how are they similar and different for males and females?*

2. Great changes have occurred in gender roles since the 1970s, particularly in the lives of women. But have these changes impacted on the nature and quality of married life? *How do you view the relation*

http://www.mhhe.com/santrocka9

between gender roles and marriage? How might your spouse view that relationship?

3. Gender differences in humans in part reflect physical/biological differences. *How might other disciplines such as biology inform your understanding of how these physical differences came into play?*

Connect to *http://www.mhhe.com/santrocka9* to research the answers and complete these exercises. In some cases, you'll also find further instructions on this site.

CHAPTER
11

CHAPTER MAP

EXPLORING ADOLESCENT
SEXUALITY

A Normal Aspect
of Adolescent
Development

Sexual Attitudes
and Behavior

ADOLESCENT SEXUAL
PROBLEMS

Adolescent
Pregnancy

Forcible Sexual
Behavior and
Sexual Harassment

Sexually Transmitted
Diseases

SEXUAL KNOWLEDGE
AND SEX EDUCATION

Sexual Knowledge

Sex Education
in the Schools

Sources of
Sex Information

SEXUAL WELL-BEING,
SOCIAL POLICY, AND
ADOLESCENTS

Sexual
Well-Being
and Developmental
Transitions

Social Policy and
Adolescent Sexuality

■ The Mysteries and Curosities of Adolescent Sexuality

I am 16 years old, and I really like this one girl. She wants to be a virgin until she marries. We went out last night, and she let me go pretty far, but not all the way. I know she really likes me, too, but she always stops me when things start getting hot and heavy. It is getting hard for me to handle. She doesn't know it, but I'm a virgin, too. I feel I am ready to have sex. I have to admit I think about having sex with other girls, too. Maybe I should be dating other girls.

—Frank C.

I'm 14 years old. I have a lot of sexy thoughts. Sometimes, just before I drift off to sleep at night, I think about this hunk who is 16 years old and plays on the football team. He is so gorgeous, and I can feel him holding me in his arms and kissing and hugging me. When I'm walking down the hall between classes at school, I sometimes start daydreaming about guys I have met and wonder what it would be like to have sex with them. Last year I had this crush on the men's track coach. I'm on the girls' track team, so I saw him a lot during the year. He hardly knew I thought about him the way I did, although I tried to flirt with him several times.

—Amy S.

Is it weird to be a 17-year-old guy and still be a virgin? Sometimes, I feel like the only 17-year-old male on the planet who has not had sex. I feel like I am missing out on something great, or at least that's what I hear. I'm pretty religious, and I sometimes feel guilty when I think about sex. The thought runs through my mind that maybe it is best to wait until I'm married or at least until I have a long-term relationship that matters a lot to me.

—Tom B.

I'm 15 years old, and I had sex for the first time recently. I had all of these expectations about how great it was going to be. He didn't have much experience either. We were both pretty scared about the whole thing. It was all over in a hurry. My first thought was, "Is that all there is?" It was a very disappointing experience.

—Claire T.

I've felt differently than most boys for a long time and I had my first crush on another boy when I was 13. I'm 16 years old now and I'm finally starting to come to grips with the fact that I am gay. I haven't told my parents yet. I don't know if they will be able to handle it. I'm still a little confused by all of this. I know I will have to "come out" at some point.

—Jason R.

SEXUALITY
■

If we listen to boys and girls at the very moment they seem most pimply, awkward, and disagreeable, we can penetrate a mystery most of us once felt heavily within us, and have now forgotten. This mystery is the very process of creation of man and woman.

—Colin McInnes
Contemporary Scottish Author

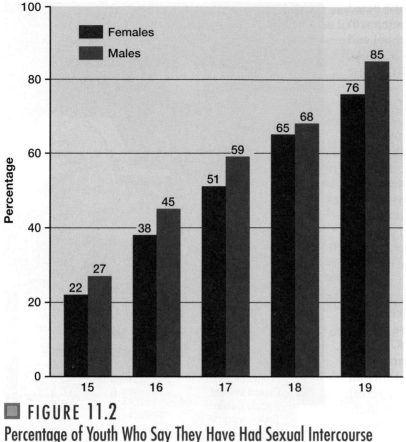

FIGURE 11.2
Percentage of Youth Who Say They Have Had Sexual Intercourse at Various Ages

sexual script
A stereotyped pattern of role prescriptions for how individuals should behave sexually. Females and males have been socialized to follow different sexual scripts.

SEXUAL TIMETABLE	WHITE	AFRICAN AMERICAN	LATINO	ASIAN AMERICAN
Kiss	14.3	13.9	14.5	15.7
French kiss	15.0	14.0	15.3	16.2
Touch breast	15.6	14.5	15.5	16.9
Touch penis	16.1	15.0	16.2	17.8
Touch vagina	16.1	14.6	15.9	17.1
Sexual intercourse	16.9	15.5	16.5	18.0
Oral sex	17.1	16.9	17.1	18.3

FIGURE 11.3
Sexual Timetables of White, African American, Latino, and Asian American Adolescents

in developing countries. However, in the United States, the overwhelming majority of 15- to 19-year-old females are unmarried.

Adolescent Female and Male Sexual Scripts As adolescents explore their sexual identities, they are guided by sexual scripts. A **sexual script** *is a stereotyped pattern of role prescriptions for how individuals should sexually behave. Females and males have been socialized to follow different sexual scripts.* Differences in female and male sexual scripting can cause problems and confusions for adolescents as they work out their sexual identities. Female adolescents learn to link sexual intercourse with love (Michael & others, 1994). They often rationalize their sexual behavior by telling themselves that they were swept away by the passion of the moment. A number of studies have found that adolescent females are more likely than their male counterparts to report being in love as the main reason they are sexually active (Cassell, 1984). Other reasons that females give for being sexually active include giving in to male pressure, gambling that sex is a way to get a boyfriend, curiosity, and sexual desire unrelated to loving and caring.

The majority of adolescent sexual experiences involve the male making sexual advances, and it is up to the female to set the limits on the male's sexual overtures (Goodchilds & Zellman, 1984). Adolescent boys experience considerable peer pressure to have sexual intercourse. As one adolescent remarked, "I feel a lot of pressure from my buddies to go for the score." I vividly remember the raunchy conversation that filled our basketball locker room in junior high school. By the end of the ninth grade, I was sure that I was the only virgin left on the 15-member team, but I wasn't about to acknowledge that to my teammates.

One study found that adolescent boys expected to have sex, put pressure on girls to have sex with them, but said that they do not force girls to have sex with them (Crump & others, 1996). And in a national survey, 12- to 18-year-olds said these are "often a reason" teenagers have sex (Kaiser Family Foundation, 1996):

- A boy or girl is pressuring them (61 percent of girls, 23 percent of boys)
- They think they are ready (59 percent of boys, 51 percent of girls)
- They want to be loved (45 percent of girls, 28 percent of boys)
- They don't want people to tease them for being a virgin (43 percent of boys, 38 percent of girls)

Risk Factors for Sexual Problems Most adolescents become sexually active at some point during adolescence. Many adolescents are at risk for sexual problems and other problems when they have sexual intercourse before 16 years of age. Adolescents who have sex before they are 16 are often ineffective users of contraceptives and are at risk for adolescent pregnancy and sexually transmitted diseases. Early sexual activity is also linked with other at-risk behaviors such as excessive drinking, drug use, delinquency, and school-related problems (Rosenbaum & Kandel, 1990).

In one recent longitudinal study, sexual involvement by girls in early adolescence was linked with their lower

What is the nature of adolescent sexual scripts?

self-esteem, greater depression, greater sexual activity, and lower grades in the high school years (Buhrmester, 2001). Early sexual involvement by boys was related to greater substance abuse and sexual activity in the high school years.

Risk factors for sexual problems in adolescence include contextual factors such as socioeconomic status (SES) and family/parenting circumstances. In one recent review, living in a dangerous and/or a low-income neighborhood were at-risk factors for adolescent pregnancy (Miller, Benson, & Galbraith, 2001). Also in this review, these aspects of parenting were linked with reduced risk of adolescent pregnancy: parent/adolescent closeness or connectedness, parental supervision or regulation of adolescents' activities, and parental values against intercourse or unprotected intercourse in adolescence (Miller, Benson, and Galbraith, 2001). Further, having older sexually active siblings or pregnant/parenting teenage sisters place adolescents at an elevated risk of adolescent pregnancy (Miller, Benson, & Galbraith, 2001).

Now that we have considered a number of ideas about heterosexual attitudes and behaviors in adolescence, we will turn our attention to homosexual attitudes and behaviors.

Homosexual Attitudes and Behavior   Most individuals think that heterosexual behavior and homosexual behavior are distinct patterns that can be easily defined. In fact, however, preference for a sexual partner of the same or opposite sex is not always a fixed decision, made once in life and adhered to forever. For example, it is not unusual for an individual, especially a male, to engage in homosexual experimentation in adolescence, but not engage in homosexual behavior as an adult. And some individuals engage in heterosexual behavior during adolescence, then turn to homosexual behavior as adults.

A Continuum of Heterosexuality and Homosexuality   Until the end of the nineteenth century, it was generally believed that people were either heterosexual or homosexual. Today, it is

The Kinsey Institute
Sexuality Research Information Service
http://www.mhhe.com/santrocka9

THROUGH THE EYES OF ADOLESCENTS

Struggling with a Sexual Decision

Elizabeth is an adolescent girl who is reflecting on her struggle with whether to have sex with a guy she is in love with. She says it is not a question of whether she loves him or not. She does love him, but she still doesn't know if it is right or wrong to have sex with him. He wants her to have sex, but she knows her parents don't. With her friends, some say yes others say no. So Elizabeth is confused. After a few days of contemplation, in a moment of honesty, she admits that she is not his special love. This finally tilts the answer to not having sex with him. She realizes that if the relationship falls through, she will look back and regret it if she does have sex. In the end, Elizabeth decided not to have sex with him.

Elizabeth's reflections reveal her struggle to understand what is right and what is wrong, whether to have sex or not. In her circumstance, the fact that in a moment of honesty she admitted that she was not his special love made a big difference in her decision.

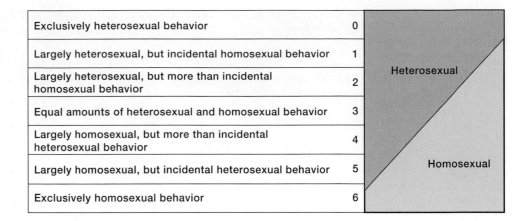

Exclusively heterosexual behavior	0
Largely heterosexual, but incidental homosexual behavior	1
Largely heterosexual, but more than incidental homosexual behavior	2
Equal amounts of heterosexual and homosexual behavior	3
Largely homosexual, but more than incidental heterosexual behavior	4
Largely homosexual, but incidental heterosexual behavior	5
Exclusively homosexual behavior	6

☐ FIGURE 11.4
The Continuum of Sexual Orientation

The continuum ranges from exclusive heterosexuality, which Kinsey and associates (1948) rated as 0, to exclusive homosexuality (6). People who are about equally attracted to both sexes (ratings 2 to 4) are bisexual.

bisexual
A person who is attracted to people of both sexes.

The International Lesbian and Gay Association
National Gay and Lesbian Task Force
Supporting Gay and Lesbian Rights
Lesbian and Gay Issues
http://www.mhhe.com/santrocka9

more acceptable to view sexual orientation as a continuum from exclusive heterosexuality to exclusive homosexuality. Pioneering this view were Alfred Kinsey and his associates (1948), who described sexual orientation as a continuum on a six-point scale, with 0 signifying exclusive heterosexuality and 6 indicating exclusive homosexuality (see figure 11.4). Some individuals are **bisexual,** *being sexually attracted to people of both sexes.* In Kinsey's research, approximately 1 percent of individuals reported being bisexual (1.2 percent of males and 0.7 percent of females) and between 2 to 5 percent of individuals reported being homosexual (4.7 percent of males and 1.8 percent of females). In one national survey, only 2.3 percent of males said they have had same-sex experience and only 1.1 percent said they are exclusively gay (Alan Guttmacher Institute, 1995). And in another national study, the percentage of individuals who reported being active homosexuals was much lower (2.7 percent of males and 1.3 percent of females) than the ofttimes reported 10 percent (Michael & others, 1994).

Causes of Homosexuality   Why are some individuals homosexual and others heterosexual? Speculation about this question has been extensive, but no firm answers are available. Homosexual and heterosexual males and females have similar physiological responses during sexual arousal and seem to be aroused by the same types of tactile stimulation. Investigators find no differences between homosexuals and heterosexuals for a wide range of attitudes, behaviors, and adjustments (Bell, Weinberg, & Mammersmith, 1981; Savin-Williams, 1995). Both the American Psychiatric Association and the American Psychological Association recognized that homosexuality is not a form of mental illness and discontinued classification of homosexuality as a disorder in the 1970s.

Recently researchers have explored the possible biological basis of homosexuality (D'Augelli, 2000; Herek, 2000). In this regard, we will evaluate hormone, brain, and twin studies regarding homosexual orientation. The results of hormone studies have been inconsistent. Indeed, if male homosexuals are given male sexual hormones (androgens), their sexual orientation does not change; their sexual desire merely increases. A very early critical period might influence sexual orientation. In the second to fifth months after conception, exposure of the fetus to hormone levels characteristic of females might cause the individual (female or male) to become attracted to males (Ellis & Ames, 1987). If this critical-period hypothesis turns out to be correct, it would explain why clinicians have found that sexual orientation is difficult, if not impossible, to modify (Meyer-Bahlburg & others, 1995).

With regard to anatomical structures, neuroscientist Simon LeVay (1991) found that an area of the hypothalamus that governs sexual behavior is twice as large (about the size of a grain of sand) in heterosexual men as in homosexual men. The area is about the same size in homosexual men as in heterosexual women. Critics of LeVay's work point out that many of the homosexuals in the study had AIDS and their brains could have been altered by the disease.

One study investigated homosexual orientation in pairs of twins (Whitman, Diamond, & Martin, 1993). The researchers began with a group of homosexuals, each of whom had a twin sibling, and investigated the sexual orientation of the siblings. The siblings who were a monozygotic twin of a homosexual came from the same fertilized egg as the homosexual and thus were genetically identical to the homosexual. Of these, almost two-thirds had a homosexual orientation. The siblings who were a dizygotic twin of a homosexual came from a different fertilized egg than the homosexual and thus were genetically no more similar to the homosexual than a nontwin sibling would be. Of these, less than one-third had a homosexual orientation. The authors interpret their results as supporting a biological interpretation of homosexuality. However, not all of the monozygotic twins had a homosexual orientation, so clearly environmental factors were involved in at least those cases.

An individual's sexual orientation—heterosexual, homosexual, or bisexual—is most likely determined by a combination of genetic, hormonal, cognitive, and environmental factors (Strickland, 1995). Most experts on homosexuality believe that no one factor alone causes homosexuality and that the relative weight of each factor may vary from one individual to the next. In effect, no one knows exactly what causes an individual to be homosexual. Scientists have a clearer picture of what does not cause homosexuality. For example, children raised by gay or lesbian parents or couples are no more likely to be homosexual than are children raised by heterosexual parents (Patterson, 1995). There also is no evidence that male homosexuality is caused by a dominant mother or a weak father, or that female homosexuality is caused by girls' choosing male role models.

Gay or Lesbian Identity in Adolescence   Although the development of gay or lesbian identity has been widely studied in adults, few researchers have investigated the gay or lesbian identity (often referred to as the coming-out process) in adolescents (Flowers & Buston, 2001). In one study of gay male adolescents, coming out was conceptualized in three stages: sensitization; awareness with confusion, denial, guilt, and shame; and acceptance (Newman & Muzzonigro, 1993). The majority of the gay adolescents said they felt different from other boys as children. The average age at having their first crush on another boy was 12.7 years, and the average age at realizing they were gay was 12.5 years. Most of the boys said they felt confused when they first became aware that they were gay. About half of the boys said they initially tried to deny their identity as a gay.

Reactions to homosexual self-recognition range from relief and happiness ("Now I understand and I feel better") to anxiety, depression, and suicidal thoughts ("I can't let anybody know; I've got to kill myself"). Gay adolescents often develop a number of defenses against self-recognition and labeling. The defenses include these (Savin-Williams & Rodriguez, 1993):

"I guess I was drunk."
"It was just a phase I was going through."
"I've heard that all guys do it once."
"I just love her and not all girls."
"I was lonely."
"I was just curious."

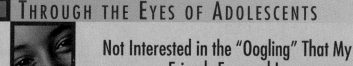

THROUGH THE EYES OF ADOLESCENTS

Not Interested in the "Oogling" That My Friends Engaged In

"In middle school I was very involved with the drama club. My singing voice is a cross between Elvis and Roger Rabbit, but I was always on stage in the school musicals. I was an attention 'addict.' . . . I was very charismatic and self-confident until the subject of sex was brought up. I just couldn't participate in the 'oogling' that my friends engaged in. I didn't find Danissa and her chest as inviting as everyone else did. John's conquest of Cindy wasn't the least bit interesting to me, particularly because I didn't have the sex drive to engage in these behaviors myself. When I did develop this drive, I guess in the eighth grade, I found myself equally disinterested in Danissa and her chest. Instead, I found myself very interested in Tony and his sharp features and muscular build."

—Gay Adolescent Male

CHAPTER MAP

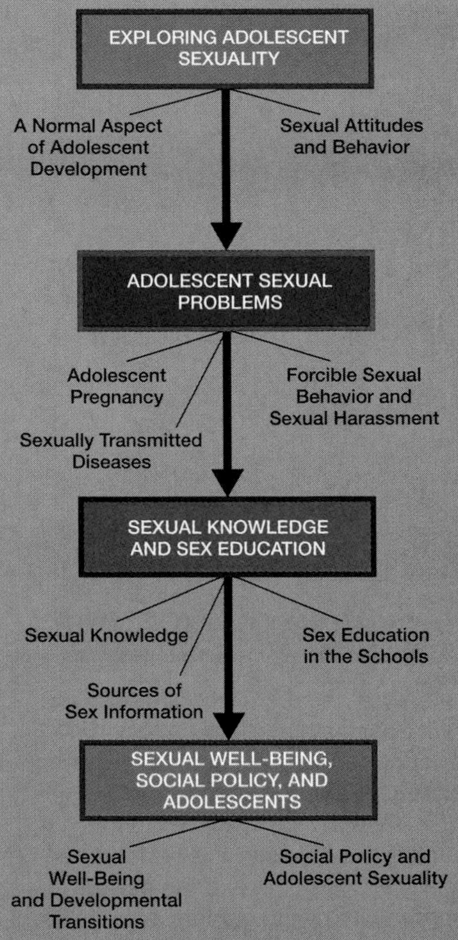

EXPLORING ADOLESCENT
SEXUALITY

A Normal Aspect
of Adolescent
Development

Sexual Attitudes
and Behavior

ADOLESCENT SEXUAL
PROBLEMS

Adolescent
Pregnancy

Forcible Sexual
Behavior and
Sexual Harassment

Sexually Transmitted
Diseases

SEXUAL KNOWLEDGE
AND SEX EDUCATION

Sexual Knowledge

Sex Education
in the Schools

Sources of
Sex Information

SEXUAL WELL-BEING,
SOCIAL POLICY, AND
ADOLESCENTS

Sexual
Well-Being
and Developmental
Transitions

Social Policy and
Adolescent Sexuality

REACH YOUR LEARNING GOALS

At the beginning of the chapter we stated nine learning goals and encouraged you to review material related to these goals at five points in the chapter. This is a good time to return to these reviews. Use them to guide your study and help you to reach your learning goals.

Page 348

Learning Goal 1   Understand that sexuality is a normal aspect of adolescence

Page 356

Learning Goal 2   Know about adolescent heterosexual attitudes and behavior
Learning Goal 3   Describe adolescent homosexual attitudes and behavior
Learning Goal 4   Discuss self-stimulation and evaluate contraceptive use

Page 362

Learning Goal 5   Know about adolescent pregnancy

Page 368

Learning Goal 6   Describe sexually transmitted diseases
Learning Goal 7   Explain forcible sexual behavior and sexual harassment

Page 375

Learning Goal 8   Evaluate sexual knowledge and sex education
Learning Goal 9   Explore sexual well-being, social policy, and adolescents

KEY TERMS

sexual script 350
bisexual 352
sexually transmitted diseases (STDs) 363
gonorrhea 363
syphilis 363
chlamydia 363

genital herpes 364
AIDS 364
rape 367
date, or acquaintance, rape 367
quid pro quo sexual harassment 368
hostile environment sexual harassment 368

KEY PEOPLE

Shirley Feldman 345
Alfred Kinsey 352
Simon LeVay 353
Richard Savin-Williams 354
June Reinisch 369
Jeanne Brooks-Gunn 373

RESOURCES FOR IMPROVING THE LIVES OF ADOLESCENTS

AIDS Hotline

National AIDS Information Clearinghouse
P.O. Box 6003
Rockville, MD 20850
800–342–AIDS; 800–344–SIDA (Spanish);
800–AIDS–TTY (Deaf)

The people answering the hotline will respond to any questions children, youth, or adults have about HIV infection or AIDS. Pamphlets and other materials on AIDS are available.

Alan Guttmacher Institute

111 Fifth Avenue
New York, NY 10003
212–254–5656

The Alan Guttmacher Institute is an especially good resource for information about adolescent sexuality. The Institute publishes a well-respected journal, *Family Planning Perspectives,* which includes articles on many dimensions of sexuality, such as adolescent pregnancy, statistics on sexual behavior and attitudes, and sexually transmitted diseases.

Boys and Sex

(1991) by Wardell Pomeroy
New York: Delacorte Press

This book was written for adolescent boys and stresses the responsibility that comes with sexual maturity.

Girls and Sex

(1991) by Wardell Pomeroy
New York: Delacorte Press

The author poses a number of questions that young girls often ask about sex and then answers them. Many myths that young girls hear about sex are also demystified.

Mom, Dad, I'm Gay

(2001) by Ritch Savin-Williams
Washington, DC: American Psychological Association

Leading researcher on adolescent homosexual relationships, Ritch Savin-Williams examines how gay and lesbian adolescents develop their sexual identity.

National Sexually Transmitted Diseases Hotline

800–227–8922

This hotline provides information about a wide variety of sexually transmitted diseases.

Sex Information and Education Council of the United States (SIECUS)

130 West 42nd Street
New York, NY 10036
212–819–9770

This organization serves as an information clearinghouse about sex education. The group's objective is to promote the concept of human sexuality as an integration of physical, intellectual, emotional, and social dimensions.

TAKING IT TO THE NET   http://www.mhhe.com/santrocka9

1. Adolescence is a time when we not only are learning about sexuality but also are dealing with emerging sexuality and learning sexual scripts. Your instructor assigns a paper in which you are to evaluate the importance of sexual scripts in the change, or not, of gender roles. *What information will you include?*

2. While home for vacation you notice that your younger sister says that she wants to break up with her boyfriend but she fears he will hurt himself or someone else. She seems to feel guilty about wanting to break up because she seems to be the only person who loves and understands him. You begin to wonder if she might be in an abusive relationship. *What are the signs of an abusive dating relationship?*

3. Do you or any of your friends know a teenage father? *How does he cope with being a father? What special needs might he have in becoming a responsible father?*

Connect to *http://www.mhhe.com/santrocka9* to research the answers and complete these exercises. In some cases, you'll also find further instructions on this site.

CHAPTER
12

CHAPTER MAP

```
┌─────────────────────┐
│  WHAT IS MORAL      │
│  DEVELOPMENT?       │
└─────────────────────┘
          │
          ▼
┌─────────────────────┐
│   MORAL THOUGHT     │
└─────────────────────┘
```

Piaget's Ideas
and Cognitive
Disequilibrium
Theory

Reasoning in
Different Social
Cognitive Domains

Kohlberg's Ideas
on Moral Development

Kohlberg's
Critics

```
┌─────────────────────┐
│   MORAL BEHAVIOR    │
└─────────────────────┘
```

Basic Processes

Altruism

Social Cognitive
Theory of Moral
Development

```
┌─────────────────────┐
│   MORAL FEELINGS    │
└─────────────────────┘
```

Psychoanalytic
Theory

The Contemporary
Perspective

Child-Rearing
Techniques

Empathy

```
┌─────────────────────┐
│  MORAL EDUCATION    │
└─────────────────────┘
```

The Hidden
Curriculum

Service
Learning

Character
Education

Cognitive
Moral Education

Values
Clarification

```
┌─────────────────────┐
│  VALUES, RELIGION,  │
│  AND CULTS          │
└─────────────────────┘
```

Values

Cults

Religion

MORAL DEVELOPMENT, VALUES, AND RELIGION

THE MORALS OF A HIGH SCHOOL NEWSPAPER

Fred, a senior in high school, wanted to publish a mimeographed newspaper for students so that he could express many of his opinions. He wanted to speak out against some of the school's rules, like the rule forbidding boys to have long hair.

Before Fred started his newspaper, he asked his principal for permission. The principal said that it would be all right if, before every publication, Fred would turn over all his articles for the principal's approval. Fred agreed and turned in several articles for approval. The principal approved all of them, and Fred published two issues of the paper in the next two weeks.

But the principal had not expected that Fred's newspaper would receive so much attention. Students were so excited about the paper that they began to organize protests against the hair regulation and the other school rules. Angry parents objected to Fred's opinions. They phoned the principal, telling him that the newspaper was unpatriotic and should not be published. As a result of the rising excitement, the principal ordered Fred to stop publishing. He gave as a reason that Fred's activities were disruptive to the operation of the school. (Rest, 1986, p.194)

It is one of the beautiful compensations of this life that no one can sincerely try to help another without helping himself.
—Charles Dudley Warner
American Essayist, 19th Century

The preceding story about Fred and his newspaper raises a number of questions related to adolescents' moral development:

Should the principal have stopped the newspaper?

When the welfare of the school is threatened, does the principal have the right to give orders to students?

Does the principal have the freedom of speech to say no in this case?

When the principal stopped the newspaper, was he preventing full discussion of an important problem?

Is Fred actually being loyal to his school and patriotic to his country?

What effect would stopping the newspaper have on the students' education in critical thinking and judgments?

Was Fred in any way violating the rights of others in publishing his own opinions?

What moral dilemmas might crop up for adolescents who are responsible for the school newspaper?

CHAPTER LEARNING GOALS

THIS CHAPTER IS ABOUT ADOLESCENTS' moral development, values, and religion. These topics have to do with right and wrong, what matters to people, and what people should do in their interactions and relationships with others. By the time you have completed this chapter, you should be able to reach these learning goals:

1 Know what moral development is

2 Explain moral thought

3 Discuss moral behavior

4 Understand moral feelings

5 Describe moral education

6 Evaluate values in adolescence

7 Discuss religion in adolescence

8 Know about cults

WHAT IS MORAL
DEVELOPMENT?

WHAT IS MORAL DEVELOPMENT?

Moral development is one of the oldest topics of interest to those who are curious about human nature. Today, most people have strong opinions about acceptable and unacceptable behavior, ethical and unethical behavior, and ways in which acceptable and ethical behaviors are to be fostered in adolescents.

moral development
Thoughts, feelings, and behaviors regarding standards of right and wrong.

Moral development *involves thoughts, feelings, and behaviors regarding standards of right and wrong.* Moral development has an *intrapersonal* dimension (a person's basic values and sense of self) and an *interpersonal* dimension (a focus on what people should do in their interactions with other people) (Walker, 1996; Walker & Pitts, 1998). The intrapersonal dimension regulates a person's activities when she or he is not engaged in social interaction. The interpersonal dimension regulates people's social interactions and arbitrates conflict. Let's now further explore some basic ideas about moral thoughts, feelings, and behaviors.

First, how do adolescents *reason* or *think* about rules for ethical conduct? For example, an adolescent can be presented with a story in which someone has a conflict about whether or not to cheat in a particular situation, such as taking an exam in school. The adolescent is asked to decide what is appropriate for the character to do and why. This was the strategy used in the section regarding Fred's newspaper. The focus is placed on the reasoning adolescents use to justify their moral decisions.

Second, how do adolescents actually *behave* in moral circumstances? For example, with regard to cheating, the emphasis is on observing adolescents' cheating and the environmental circumstances that produced and maintain the cheating. Adolescents might be observed through a one-way mirror as they are taking an exam. The observer might note whether they take out "cheat" notes, look at another student's answers, and so on.

Third, how do adolescents *feel* about moral matters? In the example of cheating, do the adolescents feel enough guilt to resist temptation? If adolescents do cheat, do feelings of guilt after the transgression keep them from cheating the next time they face temptation? The remainder of this discussion of moral development focuses on these three facets—thought, behavior, and feelings. Keep in mind that although we have separated moral development into three components—thought, behavior, and feelings—the components often are interrelated. For example, if the focus is on the individual's behavior, it is still important to evaluate the person's intentions (moral thought). And emotions accompany moral reasoning and can distort moral reasoning.

MORAL THOUGHT

How do adolescents think about standards of right and wrong? Piaget had some thoughts about this question. So did Lawrence Kohlberg.

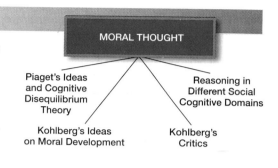

Piaget's Ideas and Cognitive Disequilibrium Theory

Interest in how children and adolescents think about moral issues was stimulated by Piaget (1932), who extensively observed and interviewed children from the ages of 4 to 12. Piaget watched children play marbles to learn how they used and thought about the game's rules. He also asked children questions about ethical issues—theft, lies, punishment, and justice, for example. Piaget concluded that children think in two distinct ways about morality, depending on their developmental maturity. **Heteronomous morality** *is the first stage of moral development in Piaget's theory, occurring at 4 to 7 years of age. Justice and rules are conceived of as unchangeable properties of the world, removed from the control of people.* **Autonomous morality,** *the second stage of moral development in Piaget's theory, is displayed by older children (about 10 years of age and older). The child becomes aware that rules and laws are created by people, and that, in judging an action, one should consider the actor's intentions as well as the consequences.* Children 7 to 10 years of age are in a transition between the two stages, evidencing some features of both.

A heteronomous thinker judges the rightness or goodness of behavior by considering the consequences of the behavior, not the intentions of the actor. For example, the heteronomous thinker says that breaking twelve cups accidentally is worse than breaking one cup intentionally while trying to steal a cookie. For the moral autonomist, the reverse is true. The actor's intentions assume paramount importance. The heteronomous thinker also believes that rules are unchangeable and are handed down by all-powerful authorities. When Piaget suggested to a group of young children that new rules be introduced into the game of marbles, they resisted. By contrast, older children—moral autonomists—accept change and recognize that rules are merely convenient, social agreed-upon conventions, subject to change by consensus.

According to Piaget, the heteronomous thinker also believes in **immanent justice,** *the idea that, if a rule is broken, punishment will be meted out immediately.* The young child somehow believes that the violation is connected automatically to the punishment. Thus, young children often look around worriedly after committing a transgression, expecting inevitable punishment. Immanent justice also implies that if something unfortunate happens to someone, it must be because the person had transgressed earlier. Older children, who are moral autonomists, recognize that punishment is socially mediated and occurs only if a relevant person witnesses the wrongdoing and that, even then, punishment is not inevitable.

Piaget argued that, as children develop, they become more sophisticated in thinking about social matters, especially about the possibilities and conditions of cooperation. Piaget believed that this social understanding comes about through the mutual give-and-take of peer relations. In the peer group, where others have power and status similar to the child's, plans are negotiated and coordinated, and disagreements are reasoned about and eventually settled. Parent-child relations, in which parents have the power and children do not, are less likely to advance moral reasoning, because rules are often handed down in an authoritarian way.

As discussed in earlier chapters, Piaget believed that adolescents usually become formal operational thinkers ◀▪▪▪ P. 108. Thus, they no longer are tied to immediate and concrete phenomena but are more logical, abstract, and deductive reasoners. Formal operational thinkers frequently compare the real to the ideal; create contrary-to-fact propositions; are cognitively capable of relating the distant past to the present;

heteronomous morality

The first stage of moral development in Piaget's theory, occurring at 4 to 7 years of age. Justice and rules are conceived of as unchangeable properties of the world, removed from the control of people.

autonomous morality

The second stage of moral development in Piaget's theory, displayed by older children (about 10 years of age and older). The child becomes aware that rules and laws are created by people and that, in judging an action, one should consider the actor's intentions as well as the consequences.

immanent justice

Piaget's concept that if a rule is broken, punishment will be meted out immediately.

CHAPTER
13

CHAPTER MAP

ACHIEVEMENT

The Importance
of Adolescence
in Achievement

Motivating
Hard-to-Reach,
Low-Achieving
Adolescents

Achievement
Processes

Ethnicity
and Culture

CAREER DEVELOPMENT

Theories of Career
Development

Social Contexts

Cognitive
Factors

WORK

Sociohistorical
Context of
Adolescent
Work

Work/Career-
Based Learning

Advantages
and Disadvantages
of Part-Time Work
in Adolescence

The
Transition
from School
to Work

KIM-CHI AND THUY

Kim-Chi Trinh was only 9 years old in Vietnam when her father used his savings to buy passage for her on a fishing boat. It was a costly and risky sacrifice for the family, who placed Kim-Chi on the small boat, among strangers, in the hope that she eventually would reach the United States, where she would get a good education and enjoy a better life.

They can because they think they can.
—Virgil
Roman Poet, 1st Century B.C.

Kim made it to the United States and coped with a succession of three foster families. When she graduated from high school in San Diego in 1988, she had a straight-A average and a number of college scholarship offers. When asked why she excels in school, Kim-Chi says that she has to do well because she owes it to her parents, who are still in Vietnam.

Kim-Chi is one of a wave of bright, highly motivated Asians who are immigrating to America. Asian Americans are the fastest-growing ethnic minority group in the United States—two out of five immigrants are now Asian. Although Asian Americans make up only 2.4 percent of the U.S. population, they constitute 17 percent of the undergraduates at Harvard, 18 percent at MIT, 27 percent at the University of California at Berkeley, and a staggering 35 percent at the University of California at Irvine.

Not all Asian American youth do this well, however. Poorly educated Vietnamese, Cambodian, and Hmong refugee youth are especially at risk for school-related problems. Many refugee children's histories are replete with losses and trauma. Thuy, a 12-year-old Vietnamese girl, has been in the United States for two years and resides with her father in a small apartment with a cousin's family of five in the inner city of a West Coast metropolitan area (Huang, 1989). While trying to escape from Saigon, the family became separated, and the wife and two younger children remained in Vietnam. Thuy's father has had an especially difficult time adjusting to the United States, struggling with English classes and being unable to maintain several jobs as a waiter. When Thuy received a letter from her mother saying that her 5-year-old brother had died, Thuy's schoolwork began to deteriorate, and she showed marked signs of depression—lack of energy, loss of appetite, withdrawal from peer relations, and a general feeling of hopelessness. At the insistence of the school, she and her father went to the child and adolescent unit of a community mental health center. It took the therapist a long time to establish credibility with Thuy and her father, but eventually they began to trust the therapist as a good listener who had competent advice about how to handle different experiences in the new country. The therapist also contacted Thuy's teacher, who said that Thuy had been involved in several interethnic skirmishes at school. With the assistance of the mental health clinic, the school initiated interethnic student panels to address cultural differences and discuss reasons for ethnic hostility. Thuy was selected to participate in these panels. Her father became involved in the community mutual assistance association, and Thuy's academic performance began to improve.

CHAPTER MAP

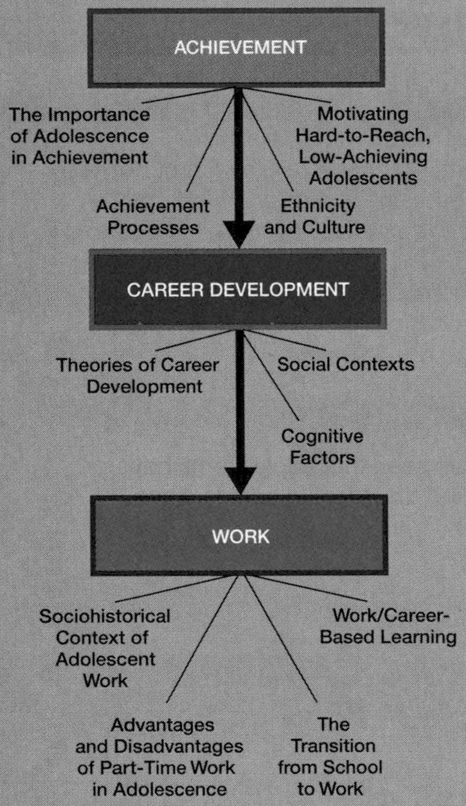

```
        ┌─────────────────────────┐
        │      ACHIEVEMENT        │
        └─────────────────────────┘
   The Importance          Motivating
   of Adolescence          Hard-to-Reach,
   in Achievement          Low-Achieving
                           Adolescents
       Achievement         Ethnicity
       Processes           and Culture

        ┌─────────────────────────┐
        │    CAREER DEVELOPMENT   │
        └─────────────────────────┘
   Theories of Career      Social Contexts
   Development
                           Cognitive
                           Factors

        ┌─────────────────────────┐
        │          WORK           │
        └─────────────────────────┘
   Sociohistorical         Work/Career-
   Context of              Based Learning
   Adolescent
   Work
       Advantages          The
       and Disadvantages   Transition
       of Part-Time Work   from School
       in Adolescence      to Work
```

REACH YOUR LEARNING GOALS

At the beginning of the chapter we stated six learning goals and reviewed material related to these goals at four points in the chapter. This is a good time to return to these reviews. Use them to guide your study and help you to reach your learning goals.

Page 414

Learning Goal 1   Explain why adolescence is a critical juncture in achievement

Learning Goal 2   Discuss achievement processes

Page 419

Learning Goal 3   Describe the roles of ethnicity and culture in achievement

Learning Goal 4   Understand how to motivate hard-to-reach, low-achieving adolescents

Page 427

Learning Goal 5   Know about career development

Page 432

Learning Goal 6   Discuss the role of work in adolescence

KEY TERMS

extrinsic motivation 409
intrinsic motivation 409
flow 409
attribution theory 410
mastery orientation 411
helpless orientation 412
performance orientation 412

self-efficacy 412
anxiety 414
failure syndrome 417
self-handicapping strategies 419
developmental career choice theory 420
career self-concept theory 420
personality type theory 421

KEY PEOPLE

Mihaly Csikszentmihalyi 409
Bernard Weiner 410
Carol Dweck 411
Albert Bandura 412
Dale Schunk 412
Sandra Graham 415
Harold Stevenson 416
Martin Covington 419

Eli Ginzberg 420
Donald Super 420
John Holland 421
David Elkind 423
Anna Roe 424
Ellen Greenberger
    and Laurence Steinberg 428

RESOURCES FOR IMPROVING THE LIVES OF ADOLESCENTS

All Grown Up & No Place to Go: Teenagers in Crisis

(1984) by David Elkind
Reading, MA: Addison-Wesley

Elkind believes that raising teenagers in today's world is more difficult than ever. He argues that teenagers are expected to confront adult challenges too early in their development.

Becoming Adult

(2000) by Mihaly Csikszentmihalyi and Barbara Schneider
New York: Basic Books

This report of a longitudinal study provides valuable information about the ways that work during adolescence influences developmental pathways into adulthood.

Motivating Students to Learn

(1998) by Jere Brophy
New York: McGraw-Hill

An excellent book on motivating students in the classroom.

Motivation for Achievement

(1999) by M. Kay Alderman
Mahwah, NJ: Erlbaum

This book explores contemporary ideas about motivating adolescents.

National Youth Employment Coalition

1501 Broadway, Room 111
New York, NY 10036
212–840–1801

This organization promotes youth employment.

Through Mentors

202–393–0512

Mentors are recruited from corporations, government agencies, universities, and professional firms. Their goal is to provide every youth in the District of Columbia with a mentor through high school. To learn how to become involved in a mentoring program or to start such a program, call the number listed here. Also, the National One-to-One Partnership Kit guides businesses in establishing mentoring programs (call 202–338–3844).

What Color Is Your Parachute?

(2000) by Richard Bolles
Berkeley, CA: Ten Speed Press

What Color Is Your Parachute? is an extremely popular book on job hunting.

What Kids Need to Succeed

by Peter Benson, Judy Galbraith, and Pamela Espeland
Minneapolis: Search Institute

This easy-to-read book presents commonsense ideas for parents, educators, and youth workers that can help youth succeed.

TAKING IT TO THE NET

http://www.mhhe.com/santrocka9

1. There are a number of career tests that are used as an aid in helping people select potential careers. *If you took several, would you get the same recommendations? How well did they do for you? What cautions would you advise friends taking such tests to keep in mind?*

2. One of your concerns as an undergraduate member of the College Curriculum Committee is making education relevant to the world of work that you and the other students will be entering. *How would you suggest the curriculum be structured in order to maximize its relevance to the world of work?*

3. The study of motivation is an important component of explaining human behavior. *How might the study of needs, attribution theory, and other aspects of motivation be important to the study of personality?*

Connect to *http://www.mhhe.com/santrocka9* to research the answers and complete these exercises. In some cases, you'll also find further instructions on this site.

ADOLESCENT PROBLEMS

□

There is no easy path leading out of life, and few are the easy ones that lie within it.
—Walter Savage Landor
English Poet, 19th Century

Modern life is stressful and leaves its psychological scars on too many adolescents, who, unable to cope effectively, never reach their human potential. The need is not only to find better treatments for adolescents with problems, but to find ways to encourage adolescents to adopt healthier lifestyles, which can prevent problems from occurring in the first place. This section consists of one chapter (14), "Adolescent Problems."

CHAPTER
14

CHAPTER MAP

EXPLORING ADOLESCENT
PROBLEMS

Biological
Factors

Psychological
Factors

Sociocultural
Factors

The Biopsychosocial
Approach

Resilience

Characteristics
of Adolescent
Problems

The Developmental
Psychopathology
Approach

PROBLEMS AND
DISORDERS

Drugs and
Alcohol

Juvenile
Delinquency

Eating
Disorders

Depression
and Suicide

INTERRELATION OF
PROBLEMS AND PREVENTION/
INTERVENTION

ADOLESCENT PROBLEMS

ANNIE AND ARNIE

Some mornings, Annie, a 15-year-old cheerleader, was too drunk to go to school. Other days, she would stop for a couple of beers or a screwdriver on the way to school. She was tall and blonde and good-looking, and no one who sold her liquor, even at 8:00 A.M., questioned her age. She got her money from baby-sitting and what her mother gave her to buy lunch. Finally, Annie was kicked off the cheerleading squad for missing practice so often. Soon she and several of her peers were drinking almost every morning. Sometimes, they skipped school and went to the woods to drink. Annie's whole life began to revolve around her drinking. It went on for two years, and, during the last summer, anytime she saw anybody she was drunk. After a while, her parents began to detect Annie's problem. But even when they punished her, she did not stop drinking. Finally, Annie started dating a boy she really liked and who would not put up with her drinking. She agreed to go to Alcoholics Anonymous and has just successfully completed treatment. She has stopped drinking for four consecutive months now, and continued abstinence is the goal.

Arnie is 13 years old. He has a history of committing thefts and physical assaults. The first theft occurred when Arnie was 8—he stole a cassette player from an electronics store. The first physical assault took place a year later, when he shoved his 7-year old brother up against the wall, bloodied his face, and then threatened to kill him with a butcher knife. Recently, the thefts and physical assaults have increased. In the last week, he stole a television set and struck his mother repeatedly and threatened to kill her. He also broke some neighborhood streetlights and threatened youths with a wrench and a hammer. Arnie's father left home when Arnie was 3 years old. Until the father left, his parents argued extensively, and his father often beat up his mother. Arnie's mother indicates that, when Arnie was younger, she was able to control him, but in the last several years she has not been able to enforce any sanctions on his antisocial behavior. Arnie's volatility and dangerous behavior have resulted in the recommendation that he be placed in a group home with other juvenile delinquents.

They cannot scare me with their empty spaces.
Between stars—on stars where no human race is.
I have it in me so much nearer home. To scare
myself with my own desert places.

—Robert Frost
American Poet, 20th Century

EXPLORING ADOLESCENT PROBLEMS

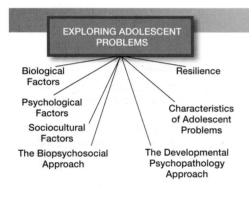

Let's explore what might cause adolescent problems, several approaches to understanding these causes, and the characteristics of adolescent problems.

Biological Factors

In the biological approach, adolescent problems are believed to be caused by a malfunctioning of the adolescent's body. Today, scientists who adopt a biological approach often focus on the brain and genetic factors as causes of adolescent problems. In the biological approach, drug therapy is frequently used to treat problems. For example, if an adolescent is depressed, in the biological approach, an antidepressant drug might be prescribed.

Psychological Factors

Among the psychological factors that have been proposed as causing adolescent problems are distorted thoughts, emotional turmoil, inappropriate learning, and troubled relationships. Two of the theoretical perspectives that we discussed in chapter 2, "The Science of Adolescent Development," address why adolescents might develop problems. Recall that psychoanalytic theorists attribute problems to stressful early experiences with parents. Also remember that behavioral and social cognitive theorists believe that adolescent problems are a consequence of social experiences with others.

Family and peer influences are especially believed to be important contributors to adolescent problems. For example, when we discuss substance abuse as well as juvenile delinquency, you will see that relationships with parents and peers are linked with these adolescent problems.

Sociocultural Factors

The psychological problems that adolescents develop appear in most cultures. However, the frequency and intensity of the problems vary across cultures with the variations being linked to social, economic, technological, and religious aspects of the cultures (Draguns, 1990; Tanaka-Matsumi, 2001).

Sociocultural factors that influence the development of adolescent problems include socioeconomic status and neighborhood quality (Brown & Adler, 1998). For example, poverty is a factor in the occurrence of delinquency.

The Biopsychosocial Approach

Some experts argue that all three factors—biological, psychological, and sociocultural—may be involved in determining whether an adolescent develops problems or not. Thus, if an adolescent engages in substance abuse it may be due to a combination of biological (heredity or brain processes), psychological (emotional turmoil or relationship difficulties), and sociocultural (poverty) factors. The combination of all three approaches is called the *biopsychosocial* approach.

American Psychiatric Association
Internet Mental Health
Mental Health Net
http://www.mhhe.com/santrocka9

The Developmental Psychopathology Approach

The field of **developmental psychopathology** *focuses on describing and exploring the developmental pathways of problems.* Many researchers in this field seek to establish links between early precursors of a problem (such as risk factors and early experiences) and outcomes (such as delinquency or depression) (Egeland, Pianta, & Ogawa, 1996; Egeland, Warren, & Aquilar, 2001; Harper, 2000; Popper, Ross, & Jennings, 2000). A developmental pathway describes continuities and transformations in factors that influence outcomes (Chang & Gjerde, 2000; Kremen & Block, 2000).

Adolescent problems can be categorized as internalizing or externalizing. **Internalizing problems** *occur when individuals turn their problems inward. Examples of internalizing disorders include anxiety and depression.* **Externalizing problems** *occur when problems are turned outward. An example of an externalizing problem is juvenile delinquency.* Links have been established between patterns of problems in childhood and outcomes in adulthood. In one study, males with internalizing patterns (such as anxiety and depression) in the elementary school years were likely to have similar forms of problems at age 21, but they did not have an increased risk of externalizing problems as young adults (Quinton, Rutter, & Gulliver, 1990). Similarly, the presence of an externalizing pattern (such as aggression or antisocial behavior) in childhood elevated risk for antisocial problems at age 21. For females in the same study, early internalizing and externalizing patterns both predicted internalizing problems at age 21.

Alan Sroufe and his colleagues (1999) have found that anxiety problems in adolescence are linked with anxious/resistant attachment in infancy, and that conduct problems in adolescence are related to avoidant attachment in infancy. Sroufe believes that a combination of early supportive care (attachment security) and early peer competence help to buffer adolescents from developing problems. In another recent developmental psychopathology study, Ann Masten and her colleagues (in press) followed 205 children for 10 years from childhood into adolescence. They found that good intellectual functioning and parenting served protective roles in keeping adolescents from engaging in antisocial behaviors. Later in this chapter, we will further explore such factors in our discussion of resilient adolescents.

developmental psychopathology

The area of psychology that focuses on describing and exploring the developmental pathways of problems.

internalizing problems

Occur when individuals turn problems inward. Examples include anxiety and depression.

externalizing problems

Occur when individuals turn problems outward. An example is juvenile delinquency.

Characteristics of Adolescent Problems

The spectrum of adolescent problems is wide. The problems vary in their severity and in how common they are for girls versus boys and for different socioeconomic groups. Some adolescent problems are short-lived; others can persist over many years. One 13-year-old adolescent might show a pattern of acting-out behavior that is disruptive to his classroom. As a 14-year-old, he might be assertive and aggressive, but no longer disruptive. Another 13-year-old might show a similar pattern of acting-out behavior. At age 16, she might have been arrested for numerous juvenile offenses and still be a disruptive influence in the classroom.

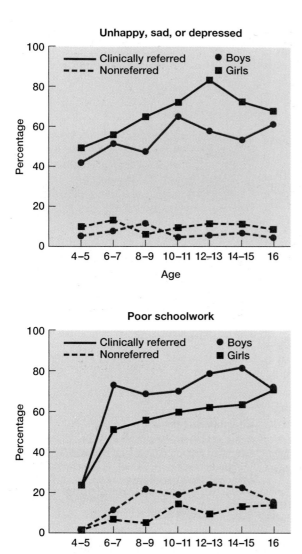

Unhappy, sad, or depressed

Poor schoolwork

■ FIGURE 14.1
The Two Items Most Likely to Differentiate Clinically Referred and Nonreferred Children and Adolescents

Developmental Assets
http://www.mhhe.com/santrocka9

Some problems are more likely to appear at one developmental level than at another. For example, fears are more common in early childhood, many school-related problems surface for the first time in middle and late childhood, and drug-related problems become more common in adolescence (Achenbach & Edelbrock, 1981). In one study, depression, truancy, and drug abuse were more common among older adolescents, while arguing, fighting, and being too loud were more common among younger adolescents (Edelbrock, 1989).

In the large-scale investigation by Thomas Achenbach and Craig Edelbrock (1981), adolescents from a lower-SES background were more likely to have problems than those from a middle-SES background. Most of the problems reported for adolescents from a lower-SES background were undercontrolled, externalizing behaviors—destroying others' things and fighting, for example. These behaviors also were more characteristic of boys than girls. The problems of middle-SES adolescents and girls were more likely to be overcontrolled and internalizing—anxiety or depression, for example.

The behavioral problems most likely to cause adolescents to be referred to a clinic for mental health treatment were feelings of unhappiness, sadness, or depression, and poor school performance (see figure 14.1). Difficulties in school achievement, whether secondary to other kinds of problems or primary problems in themselves, account for many referrals of adolescents.

In another investigation, Achenbach and his colleagues (1991) studied the problems and competencies of 2,600 children and adolescents 4 to 16 years old assessed at intake into mental health services and 2,600 demographically matched nonreferred children and adolescents. Lower-socioeconomic-status children and adolescents had more problems and fewer competencies than did their higher-socioeconomic-status counterparts. Children and adolescents had more problems when they had fewer related adults in their homes, had biological parents who were unmarried in their homes, had parents who were separated or divorced, lived in families who received public assistance, and lived in households in which family members had received mental health services. Children and adolescents who had more externalized problems came from families in which parents were unmarried, separated, or divorced, as well as from families receiving public assistance.

Many studies have shown that factors such as poverty, ineffective parenting, and mental disorders in parents *predict* adolescent problems. Predictors of problems are called *risk factors.* Risk factor means that there is an elevated probability of a problem outcome in groups of people who have that factor. Children with many risk factors are said to have a "high risk" for problems in childhood and adolescence, but not every one of these children will develop problems.

The Search Institute in Minneapolis has prescribed 40 developmental assets that they believe adolescents need to achieve positive outcomes in their lives (Benson, 1997). Half of these assets are external, half internal. The 20 *external* assets include support (such as family and neighborhood), empowerment (such as adults in the community valuing youth and youth being given useful community roles), boundaries and expectations (such as the family setting clear rules and consequences and monitoring the adolescent's whereabouts as well as positive peer influence), and constructive use of time (such as engaging in creative activities three or more times a week and participating three or more hours a week in organized youth programs). The 20 *internal* assets include commitment to learning (such as motivation to achieve in school and doing at least one hour of homework on school days), positive (values helping others and demonstrating integrity), social competencies (such as knowing how to plan and make decisions, and having interpersonal competencies like empathy and friendship skills), and positive identity (such as having a sense of control over life and high self-esteem). In research conducted by the Search Institute, adolescents with more assets reported engaging in fewer risk-taking behaviors, such as alcohol and tobacco use, sexual intercourse, and violence. For example, in one survey of more than 12,000 ninth- to twelfth-graders, 53 percent of the students with 0 to 10 assets reported using alcohol three or more times in the past month or getting drunk more than once in the past two weeks, compared to only 16 percent of the students with 21 to 30 assets or 4 percent of the students with 31 to 40 assets.

Resilience

Even when children and adolescents are faced with adverse conditions, such as poverty, are there characteristics that help buffer and make them resilient to developmental outcomes? Some children and adolescents do triumph over life's adversities (Garmezy, 1993; Luthar, Cicchetti, & Becker, 2000; Markstrom & Tryon, 1997; Taylor & Wong, 2000). Ann Masten (Masten & Coatsworth, 1998; Willis & others, 2001) analyzed the research literature on resilience and concluded that a number of individual factors (such as good intellectual functioning), family factors (close relationship to a caring parent figure), and extrafamilial factors (bonds to prosocial adults outside the family) characterize resilient children and adolescents (see figure 14.2).

Norman Garmezy (1993) described a setting in a Harlem neighborhood of New York City to illustrate resilience: In the foyer of the walkup apartment building is a large frame on a wall in the entranceway. It displays the photographs of children who live in the apartment building, with a written request that if anyone sees any of the children endangered on the street, they bring them back to the apartment house. Garmezy commented that this is an excellent example of adult competence and concern for the safety and well-being of children.

Source	Characteristic
Individual	Good intellectual functioning Appealing, sociable, easygoing disposition Self-efficacy, self-confidence, high self-esteem Talents Faith
Family	Close relationship to caring parent figure Authoritative parenting: warmth, structure, high expectations Socioeconomic advantages Connections to extended supportive family networks
Extrafamilial context	Bonds to prosocial adults outside the family Connections to prosocial organizations Attending effective schools

☐ FIGURE 14.2
Characteristics of Resilient Children and Adolescents

Developing Resilience in Urban Youth
http://www.mhhe.com/santrocka9

At this point we have discussed a number of ideas about abnormality. This review should help you to reach your learning goals related to this topic.

☐ FOR YOUR REVIEW

Learning Goal 1
Know about the nature of adolescent problems

- Biological, psychological, and sociocultural factors have been proposed as causes of adolescent problems. In the biopsychosocial approach, all three factors—biological, psychological, and sociocultural—are emphasized.
- In the developmental psychopathology approach, the emphasis is on describing and exploring developmental pathways of problems.
- The spectrum of adolescent problems is wide, varying in severity, developmental level, sex, and socioeconomic status. One way of classifying problems is as internalizing or externalizing. Middle-SES adolescents and females have more internalizing problems, low-SES adolescents and males have more externalizing problems.
- Adolescents who have a number of external and internal assets have fewer problems than their counterparts with few external and internal assets.
- Three sets of characteristics are reflected in the lives of children and adolescents who show resilience in the face of adversity and disadvantage: (1) cognitive skills and positive responsiveness from others; (2) families marked by warmth, cohesion, and the presence of a caring adult; and (3) some source of external support.

Now that we have examined the basic nature of abnormality, let's turn our attention to specific problems in adolescence.

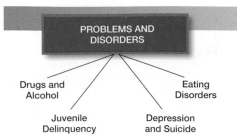

PROBLEMS AND DISORDERS

Drugs and Alcohol

Juvenile Delinquency

Eating Disorders

Depression and Suicide

PROBLEMS AND DISORDERS

What are some of the major problems and disorders in adolescence? They include drugs and alcohol, juvenile delinquency, school-related problems, sexual problems, depression and suicide, and eating disorders. We discussed school-related and sexual problems in earlier chapters. Here we will examine the other problems, beginning with drugs and alcohol.

Drugs and Alcohol

Why do adolescents take drugs? How pervasive is adolescent drug use in the United States? What are the nature and effects of various drugs taken by adolescents? What factors contribute to adolescent drug use? These are among the questions we now evaluate.

Why Do Adolescents Take Drugs?   During one phase of his medical career, Sigmund Freud experimented with therapeutic uses of cocaine. He was searching for possible medical applications, such as a painkiller for eye surgery. He soon found that the drug induced ecstasy. He even wrote to his fiancée and told her how just a small dose of cocaine produced lofty, wonderful sensations. As it became apparent that some people become psychologically addicted to cocaine, and after several died from overdoses, Freud quit using the drug.

Since the beginning of history, humans have searched for substances that would sustain and protect them and also act on the nervous system to produce pleasurable sensations. Individuals are attracted to drugs because drugs help them to adapt to an ever-changing environment. Smoking, drinking, and taking drugs reduce tension and frustration, relieve boredom and fatigue, and in some cases help adolescents to escape the harsh realities of their world. Drugs provide pleasure by giving inner peace, joy, relaxation, kaleidoscopic perceptions, surges of exhilaration, or prolonged heightened sensation. They may help some adolescents to get along better in their world. For example, amphetamines might help the adolescent to stay awake to study for an exam.

Why do adolescents take drugs?

Drugs also satisfy adolescents' curiosity—some adolescents take drugs because they are intrigued by sensational accounts of drugs in the media, while others may listen to a popular song and wonder if the drugs described can provide them with unique, profound experiences. Drugs are taken for social reasons also, allowing adolescents to feel more comfortable and to enjoy the company of others.

But the use of drugs for personal gratification and temporary adaptation carries a very high price tag: drug dependence, personal and social disorganization, and a predisposition to serious and sometimes fatal diseases (Gullotta, Adams, & Montemayor, 1995; Ksir, 2000). Thus, what is intended as adaptive behavior is maladaptive in the long run. For example, prolonged cigarette smoking, in which the active drug is nicotine, is one of the most serious yet preventable health problems. Smoking has been described by some experts as "suicide in slow motion."

As adolescents continue to take a drug, their bodies develop **tolerance,** *which means that a greater amount of the drug is needed to produce the same effect.* The first time someone takes 5 milligrams of Valium, for example, the drug will make them feel very relaxed. But after taking the pill every day for six months, 10 milligrams might be needed to achieve the same calming effect.

Physical dependence *is the physical need for a drug that is accompanied by unpleasant withdrawal symptoms when the drug is discontinued.* **Psychological dependence** *is the strong desire and craving to repeat the use of a drug because of various emotional reasons, such as a feeling of well-being and reduction of stress.* Both physical and psychological dependence mean that the drug is playing a powerful role in the adolescent's life.

Trends in Overall Drug Use

The 1960s and 1970s were a time of marked increases in the use of illicit drugs. During the social and political unrest of those years, many youth turned to marijuana, stimulants, and hallucinogens. Increases in adolescent alcohol consumption during this period also were noted (Robinson & Greene, 1988). More precise data about drug use by adolescents have been collected in recent years.

Each year since 1975, Lloyd Johnston, Patrick O'Malley, and Gerald Bachman, working at the Institute of Social Research at the University of Michigan, have carefully monitored the drug use of America's high school seniors in a wide range of public and private high schools. Since 1991, they also have surveyed drug use by eighth- and tenth-graders. The University of Michigan study is called the Monitoring the Future Study.

The use of drugs among U.S. secondary school students declined in the 1980s but began to increase in the early 1990s (Johnston, O'Malley, & Bachman, 2001). In 2001, adolescents' use of any illicit was below the peaks attained in 1997 (Johnston, O'Malley, & Bachman, 2001). Figure 14.3 on page 446 shows the overall trends in drug use by high school seniors since 1975.

Nonetheless, even with the recent leveling off in use, the United States still has the highest rate of adolescent drug use of any industrialized nation. Also, the University of Michigan survey likely underestimates the percentage of adolescents who take drugs because it does not include high school dropouts, who have a higher rate of drug use than do students who are still in school. Johnston, O'Malley, and Bachman (1999) believe that "generational forgetting" contributed to the rise of adolescent drug use in the 1990s, with adolescents' beliefs about the dangers of drugs eroding considerably. Let's now consider separately a number of drugs that are used by adolescents.

Alcohol

To learn more about the role of alcohol in adolescents' lives, we examine how alcohol influences behavior and brain activity, the use and abuse of alcohol by adolescents, and risk factors in adolescents' alcohol abuse.

Effects of Alcohol on Adolescents' Behavior and Brain Activity

Alcohol is an extremely potent drug. It acts on the body as a depressant and slows down the brain's activities. If used in sufficient quantities, it will damage or even kill biological tissues, including muscle and brain cells. The mental and behavioral effects of alcohol include reduced inhibition and impaired judgment. Initially, adolescents feel more talkative and more confident

National Clearinghouse for Alcohol and Drug Information National Institute of Drug Abuse Drug Abuse and Adolescents
http://www.mhhe.com/santrocka9

tolerance

The condition in which a greater amount of a drug is needed to produce the same effect as a smaller amount used to produce.

physical dependence

Physical need for a drug that is accompanied by unpleasant withdrawal symptoms when the drug is discontinued.

psychological dependence

Strong desire and craving to repeat the use of a drug for various emotional reasons, such as a feeling of well-being and reduction of distress.

Monitoring the Future Study
http://www.mhhe.com/santrocka9

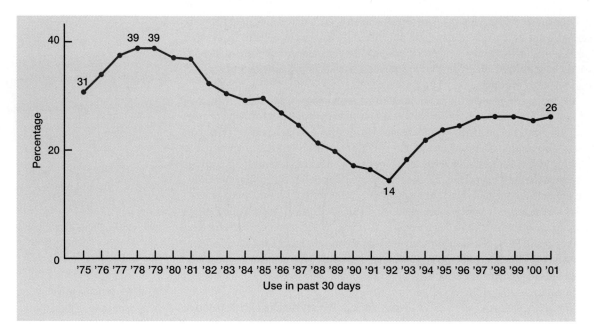

■ FIGURE 14.3
Trends in Drug Use by U.S. High School Seniors

This graph shows the percentage of high school seniors who say they have taken an illicit drug in the past 30 days. Notice the increased use in the last half of the 1970s, the decrease in the 1980s, and the increase in much of the 1990s.

Source: Johnston, O'Malley, & Bachman (2001).

Alcohol is a good preservative for everything but brains.

—Mary Pettibone Poole
American Author, 20th Century

when they use alcohol. However, skilled performances, such as driving, become impaired, and as more alcohol is ingested, intellectual functioning, behavioral control, and judgment become less efficient. Eventually, the drinker becomes drowsy and falls asleep. With extreme intoxication, the drinker may lapse into a coma. Each of these behavioral effects varies according to how the adolescent's body metabolizes alcohol, the individual's body weight, the amount of alcohol ingested, and whether previous drinking has led to tolerance.

Alcohol is the drug most widely used by U.S. adolescents. It has produced many enjoyable moments and many sad ones as well. Alcoholism is the third leading killer in the United States. Each year, approximately 25,000 individuals are killed, and 1.5 million injured, by drunk drivers. In 65 percent of the aggressive male acts against females, the offender has been under the influence of alcohol (Goodman & others, 1986). In numerous instances of drunk driving and assaults on females, the offenders have been adolescents. More than 13 million individuals are classified as alcoholics, many of whom established their drinking habits during adolescence.

In recent research, heavy, regular drinking in adolescence was linked with impairment to the brain:

- Brain scans of adolescents who abuse alcohol revealed damage to the hippocampus, a region of the brain especially involved in learning and memory. In one study, 24 adolescents and young adults with serious drinking problems were compared with similar-aged individuals without drinking problems (De Bellis & others, 2000). Brain scans revealed that the hippocampus of the heavy drinkers was 10 percent smaller than their peers, which is a substantial difference.
- Brain scans of females who drank heavily as adolescents but had quit as young adults were compared with young adult females who did not drink heavily as adolescents (Tapert & others, 2001). Images of their brains were taken while they completed a memory task in which they had to remember the location of an object on a screen. Compared with young women who were not heavy drinkers in adolescence, the adolescent drinkers had considerably more trouble remembering the

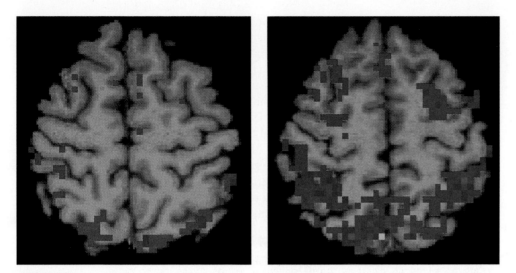

■ FIGURE 14.4
Brain Images of a Young Woman Who Abused Alcohol as an Adolescent and One Who Did Not

The brain image (MRI scan) on the left is the brain of the young woman who abused alcohol as an adolescent. The lack of color indicates sluggish brain activity. In contrast, the brain scan on the right of a young woman who did not abuse alcohol as an adolescent reveals more color, suggesting greater brain activity.

location of the object on the screen and the images of their brains revealed sluggish activity. Figure 14.4 shows the differences in the brains of two 20-year-old women, one who abused alcohol as an adolescent and one who did not.

More research needs to be carried out before definitive conclusions are reached about heavy alcohol use in adolescence and impairment to the brain. However, these recent studies suggest that there may be a harmful link.

Adolescent Alcohol Use and Abuse   Alcohol use remains very high among adolescents and has dropped only slightly in the last several years (Johnston, O'Malley, & Bachman, 2001). Monthly prevalence among high school seniors was 72 percent in 1980 but declined to 50 percent in 2001. Binge drinking (defined in the University of Michigan surveys as having five or more drinks in a row in the last two weeks) fell from 41 percent to 33 percent in 2001. A consistent sex difference occurs in binge drinking, with males engaging in this more than females. In 1997, 39 percent of male high school seniors said they had been drunk in the last two weeks, compared to 29 percent of their female counterparts.

Risk Factors in Adolescents' Alcohol Abuse   Among the risk factors in adolescents' abuse of alcohol are heredity, family influences, peer relations, personality characteristics, and the college transition. There is increasing evidence of a genetic predisposition to alcoholism, although it is important to remember that both genetic and environmental factors are involved (Moos, Finney, & Cronkite, 1990).

Adolescent alcohol use is related to parent and peer relations. Adolescents who drink heavily often come from unhappy homes in which there is a great deal of tension, have parents who give them little nurturance, are insecurely attached to their parents, have parents who use poor family management practices (low monitoring, unclear expectations, few rewards for positive behavior), and have parents who sanction alcohol use (Barnes, Farrell, & Banerjee, 1995: Peterson & others, 1994).

The peer group is especially important in adolescent alcohol abuse (Dielman & others, 1992). In one study, exposure to peer use and misuse of alcohol, along with susceptibility to peer pressure, were strong predictors of adolescent alcohol abuse

National Institute on Alcohol Abuse and Alcoholism
Exploring Alcohol Abuse
Research on Alcohol Abuse
http://www.mhhe.com/santrocka9

(Dielman, Shope, & Butchart, 1990). Whether adolescents have older, same-age, or younger peers as friends is also related to alcohol and drug abuse in adolescence. In one study, adolescents who took drugs were more likely to have older friends than were their counterparts who did not take drugs (Blyth, Durant, & Moosbrugger, 1985).

In another study, the Friendly PEERsuasion program reduced the incidence of drinking among girls who already drank and delayed the onset of drinking among girls who had not drunk previously (Girls, Inc., 1993). This program also improved the girls' resistance skills; the participants indicated that they were less likely than nonpartici-pants to stay in a drinking situation. The PEERsuasion program consists of fourteen one-hour sessions that include enjoyable, interactive activities related to using drugs. Adolescents are taught healthy ways to manage stress, detect media and peer pressure to use drugs, and practice skills for making responsible decisions about drug use. Then the girls serve as peer leaders to plan and implement substance-abuse prevention activities for 6- to 10-year-olds.

In one recent study of more than 3,000 eleventh-grade students, peer pressure was strongly related to alcohol use (Borden, Donnermeyer, & Scheer, 2001). Also in this study, participation in school-based and non-school-based activities was related to lower incidence of drug use and getting drunk less in the past year.

In another recent study, three types of tenth-grade adolescent drinkers were found: (1) those involved in problem behaviors at high rates; (2) highly anxious adolescents who report that they have performance anxiety; and (3) popular, well-functioning adolescents (these included crowds such as "jocks" and "brains" (Barber, Eccles, & Stone, 2001). Later, as they were making the transition to adulthood, the "jocks" and "criminals" showed the highest rates of being in substance abuse rehabilitation programs. Thus, associating with certain crowds in adolescence is linked with drinking behavior in adolescence and alcohol problems in the transition to adulthood.

Is there a personality profile that also might provide information about adolescents at risk for alcohol abuse? Alcohol researcher Robert Cloninger (1991) found that three traits present as early as 10 years of age are associated with alcoholism at the age of 28: (1) easily bored, needing constant activity and challenge; (2) driven to avoid negative consequences of actions; and (3) craving immediate external reward for effort. Cloninger advises parents who notice these traits in their children and young adolescents to ensure that their children have a structured, challenging environment and to provide them with considerable support.

A strong family support system is clearly an important preventive strategy in reducing alcohol abuse by adolescents (Waldron, Brody, & Slesnick, 2001). Are there others? Would raising the minimum drinking age have an effect? In one investigation, raising the minimum drinking age did lower the frequency of automobile crashes involving adolescents, but raising the drinking age alone did not reduce alcohol abuse (Wagennar, 1983). Another effort to reduce alcohol abuse involved a school-based program in which adolescents discussed alcohol-related issues with peers (Wodarski & Hoffman, 1984). At a one-year follow-up, students in the intervention schools reported less alcohol abuse and had discouraged each other's drinking more often than had students in other schools who had not been involved in the peer discussion of alcohol-related issues. Efforts to help the adolescent with a drinking problem vary enormously. Therapy may include working with other family members, peer-group discussion sessions, and specific behavioral techniques. Unfortunately, there has been little interest in identifying different types of adolescent alcohol abusers and then attempting to match treatment programs to the particular problems of the adolescent drinker. Most efforts simply assume that adolescents with drinking problems are a homogeneous group, and do not take into account the varying developmental patterns and social histories of different adolescents. Some adolescents with drinking problems may be helped more through family therapy, others through peer counseling, and yet others through intensive behavioral strategies, depending on the type of drinking problem and the social agents who have the most influence on the adolescent (Maguin, Zucker, & Fitzgerald, 1995).

In one recent study, binge-drinking trajectories from early adolescence to emerging adulthood were studied (Chassin, Pitts, & Prost, 2001). Individuals who were binge drinkers at 18 to 23 years of age often began drinking early and heavily, had parents who had alcohol problems, associated with peers who drank heavily, took other drugs, and engaged in antisocial behavior. These risk factors for binge drinking in emerging adulthood were assessed when the individuals were 13 years of age.

The transition from high school to college may be a critical transition in alcohol abuse (Schulenberg & Maggs, in press; Schulenberg & others, 2001). The large majority of older adolescents and youth who drink recognize that drinking is common among people their age and is largely acceptable, even expected by their peers. They also may perceive some social and coping benefits from alcohol use and even occasional heavy drinking. They also often diminish their drinking as they move further into the early adulthood years.

What kinds of problems are associated with binge drinking in college?

Heavy binge drinking can take a toll on college students. In a recent national survey of drinking patterns on college campuses, almost half of the binge drinkers reported problems that included missed classes, injuries, troubles with police, and unprotected sex (see figure 14.5) (Wechsler & others, 1994, 2000). Binge-drinking college students were 11 times more likely to fall behind in school, 10 times more likely to drive after drinking, and twice as likely to have unprotected sex than college students who did not binge drink.

While most youth drink long before they go to college, there often is an increase in heavy drinking during the first two years of college (Schulenberg, 1999; Schulenberg & Maggs, in press). For youth who do not go to college, there actually is a decline in drinking after high school (Schulenberg, 1999; Schulenberg & others, 2000). Chronic binge drinking for college students is more common for males than females and for students living away from home, especially males living at fraternity houses (Schulenberg, 1999). Clearly, it is important for colleges to recognize how critical the transition

THE TROUBLES THAT "FREQUENT BINGE DRINKERS" CREATE FOR...

Themselves[1] (% of those surveyed who admitted having had the problem)		and Others[2] (% of those surveyed who had been affected)	
Missed a class	61	Had study or sleep interrupted	68
Forgot where they were or what they did	54	Had to care for drunken student	54
Engaged in unplanned sex	41	Been insulted or humiliated	34
Got hurt	23	Experienced unwanted sexual advances	26
Had unprotected sex	22	Had serious argument	20
Damaged property	22	Had property damaged	15
Got into trouble with campus or local police	11	Been pushed or assaulted	13
Had five or more alcohol-related problems in school year	47	Had at least one of above problems	87

◼ FIGURE 14.5
The Hazardous Consequences of Binge Drinking in College

[1]Frequent binge drinkers were defined as those who had had at least four or five drinks at one time on at least three occasions in the previous two weeks.
[2]These figures are from colleges where at least 50% of students are binge drinkers.

from high school to college is and to develop programs that reduce binge drinking (Santrock & Halonen, 2002; Schulenberg & others, 2001).

Many young people decrease their use of alcohol as they move into adult roles, such as taking a permanent job, marriage or cohabitation, and parenthood (Schulenberg & Maggs, in press).

hallucinogens

Drugs that alter an individual's perceptual experiences and produce hallucinations; also called psychedelic or mind-altering drugs.

Hallucinogens   **Hallucinogens** *are drugs that modify an individual's perceptual experiences and produce hallucinations. Hallucinogens are called psychedelic (mind-altering) drugs.* First, we discuss LSD, which has powerful hallucinogenic properties, and then marijuana, a milder hallucinogen.

LSD   *LSD,* lysergic acid diethylamide, is a hallucinogen that, even in low doses, produces striking perceptual changes. Objects glow and change shape. Colors become kaleidoscopic. Fabulous images unfold as users close their eyes. Sometimes the images are pleasurable, sometimes unpleasant or frightening. In one drug trip, an LSD user might experience a cascade of beautiful colors and wonderful scenes; in another drug trip, the images might be frightening and grotesque. LSD's effects on the body may include dizziness, nausea, and tremors. Emotional and cognitive effects may include rapid mood swings or impaired attention and memory.

LSD's popularity in the 1960s and 1970s was followed by a reduction in use by the mid 1970s as its unpredictable effects become publicized. However, adolescents' use of LSD increased in the 1990s (Johnston, O'Malley, & Bachman, 2001). In 1985, 1.8 percent of U.S. high school seniors reported LSD use the last 30 days; in 1994, this increased to 4.0 percent but then declined to 2.3 percent in 2001.

LSD
Marijuana
http://www.mhhe.com/santrocka9

Marijuana   *Marijuana,* a milder hallucinogen than LSD, comes from the hemp plant Cannabis sativa, which originated in Central Asia but is now grown in most parts of the world. Marijuana is made of the hemp plant's dry leaves; its dried resin is known as hashish. The active ingredient in marijuana is THC, which stands for the chemical delta-9-tetrahydrocannabinol. This ingredient does not resemble the chemicals of other psychedelic drugs. Because marijuana is metabolized slowly, its effects may be present over the course of several days.

The physical effects of marijuana include increases in pulse rate and blood pressure, reddening of the eyes, coughing, and dryness of the mouth. Psychological effects include a mixture of excitatory, depressive, and hallucinatory characteristics, making the drug difficult to classify. The drug can produce spontaneous and unrelated ideas; perceptions of time and place can be distorted; verbal behavior may increase or cease to occur at all; and sensitivity to sounds and colors might increase. Marijuana also can impair attention and memory, which suggests that smoking marijuana is not conducive to optimal school performance. When marijuana is used daily in heavy amounts, it also can impair the human reproductive system and may be involved in some birth defects.

stimulants

Drugs that increase the activity of the central nervous system.

Marijuana use by adolescents decreased in the 1980s. For example, in 1979, 37 percent of high school seniors said they had used marijuana in the last month, but in 1992 that figure had dropped to 12 percent. Figure 14.6 shows the increase in marijuana use by eighth-, tenth-, and twelfth-graders in the United States in the 1990s, although this use has started to level off. In one analysis, the increased use of marijuana in the 1990s was not related to such factors as religious commitment or grades but was linked with increased approval of using the drug and decreased perception that the drug is harmful (Johnston, O'Malley, & Bachman, 1999).

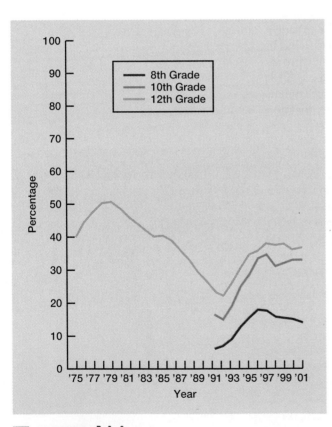

■ **FIGURE 14.6**
Trends in Marijuana Use by U.S. Eighth-, Tenth-, and Twelfth-Graders: Use in the Past Year

Note the increase in marijuana use in the last half of the 1970s, the decreased use in the 1980s, and the increased use in the 1990s.

Stimulants   **Stimulants** *are drugs that increase the activity of the central nervous system.* The most widely used stimulants are caffeine, nicotine, amphetamines, and cocaine. Stimulants increase heart rate, breathing, and temperature but decrease appetite. Stimulants increase energy, decrease feelings of fatigue, and lift mood and self-confidence. After the effects wear off, though, the user often becomes tired, irritable, and depressed, and may experience headaches. Stimulants can be physically addictive.

Cigarette Smoking Cigarette smoking (in which the active drug is nicotine) is one of the most serious yet preventable health problems. Smoking is likely to begin in grades 7 through 9, although sizable portions of youth are still establishing regular smoking habits during high school and college. Since the national surveys by Johnston, O'Malley, and Bachman began in 1975, cigarettes have been the substance most frequently used on a daily basis by high school seniors.

Smoking often begins in early adolescence. The peer group especially plays an important role in smoking (McRee & Gebelt, 2001). In one recent study, the risk of current smoking was linked with peer networks in which at least half of the members smoked, one or two best friends smoked, and smoking was common in the school (Alexander & others, 2001).

The good news is that cigarette smoking is decreasing among adolescents. In the national survey by the Institute of Social Research, the percentage of high school seniors who are current cigarette smokers continued to decline in 2001 (Johnston, O'Malley, & Bachman, 2001). Cigarette smoking peaked in 1997 among high school seniors and since then has been gradually declining. Among high school seniors, a decline from 36.5 percent in 1997 to 29.5 percent in 2001 occurred regarding smoking one or more cigarettes in the past 30 days. Among eighth- and tenth-graders, the decline was even greater. However, despite these recent improvements, approximately one-third of America's youth are active smokers at the end of their high school years.

The devastating effects of early smoking were brought home in a recent research study, which found that smoking in the adolescent years causes permanent genetic changes in the lungs and forever increases the risk of lung cancer, even if the smoker quits (Weincke & others, 1999). Such damage was much less likely among smokers in the study who started in their twenties. One of the remarkable findings in the study was that the early age of onset of smoking was more important in predicting genetic damage than how much the individuals smoked.

In two recent studies, cigarette smoking in adolescence was linked with emotional problems. In the first study, more than 15,000 adolescents were tracked for one year to assess the possible link between cigarette smoking and depression (Goodman & Capitman, 2000). Those who began smoking during the one-year duration of the study were four times more likely to become depressed at the end of that year. In the second study, more than 600 adolescents (average age 16) were followed into their early adulthood years (average age 22) to discover possible connections between cigarette smoking in adolescence and the prevalence of mental disorders in early adulthood (Johnson & others, 2000). Those who smoked heavily as adolescents were far more likely to have anxiety disorders as adults.

**Cigarette Smoking and Cancer
National Cancer Institute
Cigarette Brands and
Adolescents
Addicted to Nicotine
Effective Prevention Programs
for Tobacco Use**
http://www.mhhe.com/santrocka9

Cigarettes are readily available to these underage youth. Of the eighth-graders, most of whom are 13 to 14 years of age, three-fourths said that they can get cigarettes fairly easily if they want them. By the tenth grade, more than 90 percent say they can buy cigarettes easily.

In another study smoking initiation rates increased rapidly after 10 years of age and peaked at 13 to 14 years of age (Escobedo & others, 1993). Students who began smoking at 12 years of age or younger were more likely to be regular and heavy smokers than were students who began at older ages. Students who had participated in interscholastic sports were less likely to be regular and heavy smokers than were their counterparts who were not sports participants. In another study, adolescents whose parents smoked were more likely to be smokers themselves than were adolescents whose parents did not smoke (Kandel & Wu, 1995). Maternal smoking was more strongly related to smoking by young adolescents (especially girls) than paternal smoking was.

"I'll tell you one thing. As soon as I'm thirteen I'm gonna stop!"

Reprinted by permission of Tribune Media Services.

Traditional school health programs have often succeeded in educating adolescents about the long-term health consequences of smoking but have had little effect on adolescent smoking behavior. That is, adolescent smokers know as much about the health risks of smoking as do nonadolescent smokers, but this knowledge has had little impact on reducing their smoking behavior (Miller & Slap, 1989). The need for effective intervention has prompted investigators to focus on those factors that place young adolescents at high risk for future smoking, especially social pressures from peers, family members, and the media (Copeland, Heim, & Rome, 2001; Kulig & others, 2001).

A number of researchers have developed strategies for interrupting behavioral patterns that lead to smoking (Bruess & Richardson, 1992; Perry, Kelder, & Komro, 1993). In one investigation, high school students were recruited to help seventh-grade students resist peer pressure to smoke (McAlister & others, 1980). The high school students encouraged the younger adolescents to resist the influence of high-powered ads suggesting that liberated women smoke by saying, "She is not really liberated if she is hooked on tobacco." The students also engaged in role-playing exercises called "chicken." In these situations, the high school students called the younger adolescents "chicken" for not trying a cigarette. The seventh-graders practiced resistance to the peer pressure by saying, "I'd be a real chicken if I smoked just to impress you." Following several sessions, the students in the smoking prevention group were 50 percent less likely to begin smoking compared to a group of seventh-grade students in a neighboring junior high school, even though the parents of both groups of students had the same smoking rate.

One comprehensive health approach that includes an attempt to curb cigarette smoking by adolescents was developed by clinical psychologist Cheryl Perry and her colleagues (1988). Three programs were developed based on peer group norms, healthy role models, and social skills training. Elected peer leaders were trained as instructors. In seventh grade, adolescents were offered "Keep It Clean," a six-session course emphasizing the negative effects of smoking. In eighth grade, students were involved in "Health Olympics," an approach that included exchanging greeting cards on smoking and health with peers in other countries. In ninth grade, students participated in "Shifting Gears," which included six sessions focused on social skills. In the social skills program, students critiqued media messages and created their own positive health videotapes. At the same time as the school intervention, a community-wide smoking cessation program, as well as a diet and health awareness campaign, were initiated. After five years, students who were involved in the smoking and health program were much less likely to smoke cigarettes, use marijuana, or drink alcohol than their counterparts who were not involved in the program.

Cocaine   *Cocaine* is a stimulant that comes from the coca plant, native to Bolivia and Peru. For many years, Bolivians and Peruvians chewed on the plant to increase their stamina. Today, cocaine is either snorted or injected in the form of crystals or powder. The effect is a rush of euphoric feelings, which eventually wear off, followed by depressive feelings, lethargy, insomnia, and irritability. Cocaine can have a number of damaging effects on the body, resulting in heart attacks, strokes, and brain seizures.

How many adolescents use cocaine? Use of cocaine in the last 30 days by high school seniors dropped from a peak of 6.7 percent in 1985 to 2.1 percent in 2001 (Johnston, O'Malley, & Bachman, 2001). A growing percentage of high school students are reaching the conclusion that cocaine use entails considerable unpredictable risk. Still, the percentage of adolescents who have used cocaine is precariously high. About 1 of every 13 high school seniors has tried cocaine at least once.

A troublesome part of the cocaine story rests in the dangerous shift in how it is administered, due in large part to the advent of crack cocaine—an inexpensive, purified,

Cocaine
http://www.mhhe.com/santrocka9

smokable form of the drug. Crack use is especially heavy among non-college-bound youth in urban settings.

Amphetamines

Amphetamines are widely prescribed stimulants, sometimes appearing in the form of diet pills. They are called "pep pills" and "uppers." Amphetamine use among high school seniors has decreased significantly. Use of amphetamines in the last 30 days by high school seniors declined from 10.7 percent in 1982 to 5.6 percent in 2001. However, use of over-the-counter stay-awake pills, which usually contain caffeine as their active ingredient, has sharply increased. Use of over-the-counter diet pills has decreased in recent years, although 40 percent of females have tried using diet pills by the time they graduate from high school.

Ecstasy

Ecstasy, the street name for the synthetic drug MDMA, has stimulant and hallucinogenic effects. Its chemical structure is similar to methamphetamines. It usually comes in a pill form. Tolerance builds up rapidly so users may take three or four pills at a time. Ecstasy produces euphoric feelings and heightened sensations (especially touch and sight). The drug is popular at raves, where youth dance all night long with light sticks and other visual enhancements. Users often become hyperactive and sleepless. Ecstasy use can lead to dangerous increases in blood pressure, as well as stroke or a heart attack (Johnston, O'Malley, & Bachman, 2000). Repeated Ecstasy use may damage the areas of the brain that involve the regulation of mood, sexual response, sleep, and pain sensitivity.

There is a special concern about Ecstasy use by adolescents. In the national study conducted by the Institute of Social Research at the University of Michigan, the percentage of twelfth-graders who had used Ecstasy in the last year increased from 5.6 percent in 1998 to 9.2 percent in 2001 (Johnston, O'Malley, & Bachman, 2001). Similar increases in Ecstasy use, although at lower percentages, also occurred for eighth- and tenth-graders.

Depressants

Depressants *are drugs that slow down the central nervous system, bodily functions, and behavior.* Medically, depressants have been used to reduce anxiety and to induce sleep. Among the most widely used depressants are alcohol, which we discussed earlier, barbiturates, and tranquilizers. Though used less frequently, the opiates are especially dangerous depressants.

Barbiturates, such as Nembutal and Seconal, are depressant drugs that induce sleep or reduce anxiety. *Tranquilizers,* such as Valium and Xanax, are depressant drugs that reduce anxiety and induce relaxation. They can produce symptoms of withdrawal when an individual stops taking them. Since the initial surveys, begun in 1975, of drug use by high school seniors, use of depressants has decreased. For example, use of barbiturates at least every 30 days in 1975 was 4.7 percent; in 2001, it was only 2.8 percent. Over the same time period, tranquilizer use also decreased, from 4.1 percent to 3.0 percent, for 30-day prevalence.

CAREERS IN ADOLESCENT DEVELOPMENT

Cheryl Perry
Epidemiologist, School of Public Health

Cheryl Perry is a professor of epidemiology in the School of Public Health at the University of Minnesota. She obtained her undergraduate degree in math from UCLA, a master's degree in education from the University of California at Davis, and a Ph.D. in education from Stanford.

Cheryl teaches courses in the prevention of high-risk behavior among adolescents and conducts a number of research studies. These currently include a cancer prevention program in the St. Paul, Minnesota, schools, a program to reduce alcohol use among U.S. adolescents, and a 30-school study of cardiovascular health in New Delhi, India.

Cheryl has received numerous awards for her outstanding contributions to understanding adolescent health and reducing at-risk adolescent behavior. She has served on the Board of Directors of the American School Health Association and as a scientific editor on the U.S. Surgeon General's Report on preventing tobacco use in young adolescents.

Cheryl Perry

depressants
Drugs that slow the central nervous system, bodily functions, and behavior.

Opiates, which consist of opium and its derivatives, depress the activity of the central nervous system. They are commonly known as narcotics. Many drugs have been produced from the opium poppy, among them morphine and heroin (which is converted to morphine when it enters the brain). For several hours after taking an opiate, an individual feels euphoria, pain relief, and an increased appetite for food and sex; however, the opiates are among the most physically addictive drugs. The body soon craves more heroin and experiences very painful withdrawal unless more is taken.

The rates of heroin use among adolescents are quite low, but they have risen significantly for grades 8, 10, and 12 in the 1990s (Johnston, O'Malley, & Bachman, 2001). In 2001, 0.4 percent of high school seniors said they had used heroin the last 30 days. A positive note occurred in the University of Michigan's recent surveys—more students perceived heroin as dangerous than in surveys conducted in the early to mid 1990s. Perceived dangerousness is usually a precursor to a drop in a drug's use.

At this point, we have discussed a number of depressants, stimulants, and hallucinogens. Their medical uses, duration of effects, overdose symptoms, health risks, physical addiction risk, and psychological dependence risk are summarized in figure 14.7 on page 455.

anabolic steroids

Drugs derived from the male sex hormone, testosterone. They promote muscle growth and lean body mass.

Anabolic Steroids
http://www.mhhe.com/santrocka9

Anabolic Steroids

Anabolic steroids *are drugs derived from the male sex hormone, testosterone. They promote muscle growth and increase lean body mass.* Anabolic steroids have medical uses, but they increasingly have been abused by some athletes and others who hope to improve their performance and physical attractiveness. Nonmedical uses of these drugs carry a number of physical and psychological health risks (National Clearinghouse for Alcohol and Drug Information, 1999).

Both males and females who take large doses of anabolic steroids usually experience changes in sexual characteristics. In males, this can involve a shrinking of the testicles, reduced sperm count, impotence, premature baldness, enlargement of the prostate gland, breast enlargement, and difficulty or pain in urinating. In females, their use can trigger severe acne on the face and body, a weakening of tendons (which can result in rupturing or tearing), reduction in HDL (the "good" cholesterol), and high blood pressure. Psychological effects in both males and females can involve irritability, uncontrollable bursts of anger, severe mood swings (which can lead to depression when individuals stop using the steroids), impaired judgment stemming from feelings of invincibility, and paranoid jealousy.

In the University of Michigan study (Johnston, O'Malley, & Bachman, 2001), 1.6 percent of eighth-graders, 2.1 percent of tenth-graders, and 2.4 percent of twelfth-graders said they had used anabolic steroids in the last year. In one recent study conducted in Sweden, use of anabolic steroids by high school students was linked with strength training, tobacco use, heavy alcohol consumption, and truancy (Kindlundh & others, 1999).

Factors in Adolescent Drug Abuse

Earlier, we discussed the factors that place adolescents at risk for alcohol abuse. Researchers also have examined the factors that are related to drug use in adolescence, especially the roles of development, parents, peers, and schools (Hops, 2002; Petraitis, Flay, & Miller, 1995).

Most adolescents become drug users at some point in their development, whether their use is limited to alcohol, caffeine, and cigarettes, or extended to marijuana, cocaine, and hard drugs. A special concern involves adolescents using drugs as a way of coping with stress, which can interfere with the development of competent coping skills and responsible decision making. Researchers have found that drug use in childhood or early adolescence has more detrimental long-term effects on the development of responsible, competent behavior than drug use that occurs in late adolescence (Newcomb & Bentler, 1989). When they use drugs to cope with stress, young adolescents often enter adult roles of marriage and work prematurely without adequate socioemotional growth and experience greater failure in adult roles.

How early are adolescents beginning drug use? National samples of eighth- and ninth-grade students were included in the Institute for Social Research survey of drug

3. Teacher train
   based progra
   riculum is in
   prepared teac
   and resource:

4. Social skills
   skills and re
   promising of
   However, the
   ing programs
   they are as
   others are no

5. Peer-led pro
   teacher-led
   when older st
   role models
   middle schoo

6. Most of the s
   programs dir
   risk adolescer

7. The most effe
   vention effort
   nesses, youth

The basic phil
programs have to b
Ann Pentz (1994),
used local media,
substance-abuse cu
and after four year
adolescents in the
the program was n

Since the last revie
your learning goals

☐ F O R

Learning Goa
Discuss drugs :

DRUG CLASSIFICATION	MEDICAL USES	SHORT-TERM EFFECTS	OVERDOSE	HEALTH RISKS	RISK OF PHYSICAL/ PSYCHOLOGICAL DEPENDENCE
Depressants					
Alcohol	Pain relief	Relaxation, depressed brain activity, slowed behavior, reduced inhibitions	Disorientation, loss of consciousness, even death at high blood-alcohol levels	Accidents, brain damage, liver disease, heart disease, ulcers, birth defects	Physical: moderate; psychological: moderate
Barbiturates	Sleeping pill	Relaxation, sleep	Breathing difficulty, coma, possible death	Accidents, coma, possible death	Physical and psychological moderate to high
Tranquilizers	Anxiety reduction	Relaxation, slowed behavior	Breathing difficulty, coma, possible death	Accidents, coma, possible death	Physical: low to moderate; psychological: moderate to high
Opiates (narcotics)	Pain relief	Euphoric feelings, drowsiness, nausea	Convulsions, coma, possible death	Accidents, infectious diseases such as AIDS (when the drug is injected)	Physical: high; psychological: moderate to high
Stimulants					
Amphetamines	Weight control	Increased alertness, excitability; decreased fatigue, irritability	Extreme irritability, feelings of persecution, convulsions	Insomnia, hypertension, malnutrition, possible death	Physical: possible; psychological: moderate to high
Cocaine	Local anesthetic	Increased alertness, excitability, euphoric feelings; decreased fatigue, irritability	Extreme irritability, feelings of persecution, convulsions, cardiac arrest, possible death	Insomnia, hypertension, malnutrition, possible death	Physical: possible; psychological: moderate (oral) to very high (injected or smoked)
Hallucinogens					
LSD	None	Strong hallucinations, distorted time perception	Severe mental disturbance, loss of contact with reality	Accidents	Physical: none; psychological: low
Marijuana	Treatment of the eye disorder glaucoma	Euphoric feelings, relaxation, mild hallucinations, time distortion, attention and memory impairment	Fatigue, disoriented behavior	Accidents, respiratory disease	Physical: very low; psychological: moderate

▣ **FIGURE 14.7**

Psychoactive Drugs: Depressants, Stimulants, and Hallucinogens

use for the first time in 1991 (Johnston, O'Malley, & Bachman, 1992). Early on in the increase in drug use in the United States (late 1960s, early 1970s), drug use was much higher among college students than among high school students, who in turn had much higher rates of drug use than did middle or junior high school students. However, today the rates for college and high school students are similar, and the rates for

*"Just tell me wh
to take*

Now that we have examined drug and alcohol use by adolescents, let's turn our attention to another major adolescent problem: juvenile delinquency.

Juvenile Delinquency

Thirteen-year-old Arnie, in the section that opened this chapter, has a history of thefts and physical assaults. Arnie is a juvenile delinquent. What is a juvenile delinquent? What are the antecedents of delinquency? What types of interventions have been used to prevent or reduce delinquency?

What Is Juvenile Delinquency?   The term **juvenile delinquency** *refers to a broad range of behaviors, from socially unacceptable behavior (such as acting out in school) to status offenses (such as running away) to criminal acts (such as burglary).* For legal purposes, a distinction is made between index offenses and status offenses. **Index offenses** *are criminal acts, whether they are committed by juveniles or adults. They include such acts as robbery, aggravated assault, rape, and homicide.* **Status offenses,** *such as running away, truancy, underage drinking, sexual promiscuity, and uncontrollability, are less serious acts. They are performed by youth under a specified age, which classifies them as juvenile offenses.* States often differ in the age used to classify an individual as a juvenile or an adult. Approximately three-fourths of the states have established age 18 as a maximum for defining juveniles. Two states use age 19 as the cutoff, seven states use age 17, and four states use age 16. Thus, running away from home at age 17 may be an offense in some states but not others.

One issue in juvenile justice is whether an adolescent who commits a crime should be tried as an adult (Cassel & Bernstein, 2001). One study found that trying adolescent offenders as adults increased rather than reduced their crime rate (Myers, 1999). The study evaluated more than 500 violent youths in Pennsylvania, which has adopted a "get tough" policy. Although these 500 offenders had been given harsher punishment than a comparison group retained in juvenile court, they were more likely to be rearrested—and rearrested more quickly—for new offenses once they were returned to the community. This suggests that the price of short-term public safety attained by prosecuting juveniles as adults might increase long-term criminal offenses.

In one analysis, it was proposed that individuals 12 and under should not be evaluated under adult criminal laws but that those 17 and older should be (Steinberg & Cauffman, 1999). It was recommended that individuals 13 to 16 years of age be given some type of individualized assessment in terms of whether to be tried in a juvenile court or an adult criminal court. This framework argues strongly against court placement based solely on the nature of an offense and takes into account the offender's developmental maturity.

In addition to the legal classifications of index offenses and status offenses, many of the behaviors considered delinquent are included in widely used classifications of abnormal behavior. **Conduct disorder** *is the psychiatric diagnostic category used when multiple behaviors occur over a six-month period. These behaviors include truancy, running away, fire setting, cruelty to animals, breaking and entering, excessive fighting, and others. When three or more of these behaviors co-occur before the age of 15 and the child or adolescent is considered unmanageable or out of control, the clinical diagnosis is conduct disorder.*

In sum, most children or adolescents at one time or another act out or do things that are destructive or troublesome for themselves or others. If these behaviors occur

juvenile delinquency
A broad range of child and adolescent behaviors, including socially unacceptable behavior, status offenses, and criminal acts.

index offenses
Whether they are committed by juveniles or adults, these are criminal acts, such as robbery, rape, and homicide.

status offenses
Performed by youths under a specified age, these are juvenile offenses that are not as serious as index offenses. These offenses may include such acts as drinking under age, truancy, and sexual promiscuity.

Office of Juvenile Justice and Delinquency Prevention
Justice Information Center
Preventing Crime
http://www.mhhe.com/santrocka9

**Drug-Abus
Center for
Preventio
Drug-Abus
http://www

conduct disorder
The psychiatric diagnostic category for the occurrence of multiple delinquent activities over a six-month period. These behaviors include truancy, running away, fire setting, cruelty to animals, breaking and entering, and excessive fighting.

often in childhood or early adolescence, psychiatrists diagnose them as conduct disorders. If these behaviors result in illegal acts by juveniles, society labels them as *delinquents.*

In the Pittsburgh Youth Study, a longitudinal study that focused on more than 1,500 inner-city boys, three developmental pathways to delinquency were (Loeber & others, 1998).

- *Authority conflict.* Youth on this pathway showed stubbornness prior to age 12, then moved on to defiance and avoidance of authority.
- *Covert.* This pathway included minor covert acts, such as lying, followed by property damage and moderately serious delinquency, then serious delinquency.
- *Overt.* This pathway included minor aggression followed by fighting and violence.

How many adolescents are arrested each year for committing juvenile delinquency offenses? In 1997, law enforcement agencies made an estimated 2.8 million arrests of individuals under the age of 18 in the United States (Office of Juvenile Justice and Prevention, 1998). This represents about 10 percent of adolescents 10 to 18 years of age in the United States. Note that this figure reflects only adolescents who have been arrested and does not include those who committed offenses but were not apprehended.

Recent U.S. government statistics reveal that 8 of 10 cases of juvenile delinquency involve males (Snyder & Sickmund, 1999). Although males are still far more likely to engage in juvenile delinquency, there has been a greater percentage increase in female than male juvenile delinquents in the last two decades (Hoyt & Scherer, 1998). For both male and female delinquents, rates for property offenses are higher than rates for other offenses (such as toward persons, drug offenses, and public order offenses).

Antecedents of Juvenile Delinquency

Predictors of delinquency include identity (negative identity), self-control (low degree), age (early initiation), sex (male), expectations for education (low expectations, little commitment), school grades (low achievement in early grades), peer influence (heavy influence, low resistance), socioeconomic status (low), family influence (lack of monitoring, low support, and ineffective discipline), and neighborhood quality (urban, high crime, high mobility). A summary of these antecedents of delinquency is presented in figure 14.8 on page 460.

National Youth Gang Center
http://www.mhhe.com/santrocka9

Let's look in more detail at several of these factors that are related to delinquency. Erik Erikson (1968) believes that adolescents whose development has restricted them from acceptable social roles or made them feel that they cannot measure up to the demands placed on them might choose a negative identity. Adolescents with a negative identity may find support for their delinquent image among peers, reinforcing the negative identity. For Erikson, delinquency is an attempt to establish an identity, although it is a negative identity.

Although delinquency is less exclusively a lower-SES phenomenon than it was in the past, some characteristics of lower-SES culture might promote delinquency P. 263. The norms of many low-SES peer groups and gangs are antisocial, or counterproductive to the goals and norms of society at large. Getting into and staying out of trouble are prominent features of life for some adolescents in low-SES neighborhoods. Adolescents from low-SES backgrounds might sense that they can gain attention and status by performing antisocial actions. Being "tough" and "masculine" are high-status traits for low-SES boys, and these traits are often measured by the adolescent's success in performing and getting away with delinquent acts.

The nature of a community can contribute to delinquency (Farrington, 2000; Tolan, Guerra, & Kendall, 1995). A community with a high crime rate allows adolescents to observe many models who engage in criminal activities and might be rewarded for their criminal accomplishments. Such communities often are characterized by poverty, unemployment, and feelings of alienation. The quality of schools, funding for education, and organized neighborhood activities are other community factors that might be related to delinquency. Are there caring adults in the schools and neighborhood who can convince adolescents with

THROUGH THE EYES OF PSYCHOLOGISTS

Gerald Patterson
University of Oregon

"Common parenting weaknesses in the families of antisocial boys include a lack of supervision, poor disciplining skills, limited problem-solving abilities, and a tendency to be uncommunicative with sons."

Antecedent	Association with delinquency	Description
Identity	Negative identity	Erikson believes delinquency occurs because the adolescent fails to resolve a role identity.
Self-control	Low degree	Some children and adolescents fail to acquire the essential controls that others have acquired during the process of growing up.
Age	Early initiation	Early appearance of antisocial behavior is associated with serious offenses later in adolescence. However, not every child who acts out becomes a delinquent.
Sex	Males	Boys engage in more antisocial behavior than girls do, although girls are more likely to run away. Boys engage in more violent acts.
Expectations for education and school grades	Low expectations and low grades	Adolescents who become delinquents often have low educational expectations and low grades. Their verbal abilities are often weak.
Family influences	Monitoring (low), support (low), discipline (ineffective)	Delinquents often come from families in which parents rarely monitor their adolescents, provide them with little support, and ineffectively discipline them.
Peer influences	Heavy influence, low resistance	Having delinquent peers greatly increases the risk of becoming delinquent.
Socioeconomic status	Low	Serious offenses are committed more frequently by lower-class males.
Neighborhood quality	Urban, high crime, high mobility	Communities often breed crime. Living in a high-crime area, which also is characterized by poverty and dense living conditions, increases the probability that a child will become a delinquent. These communities often have grossly inadequate schools.

■ FIGURE 14.8
The Antecedents of Juvenile Delinquency
After John W. Santrock. Copyright © The McGraw-Hill Companies.

delinquent tendencies that education is the best route to success? When family support becomes inadequate, then such community supports take on added importance in preventing delinquency.

Family support systems are also associated with delinquency (Henry, Tolan, & Gorman-Smith, 2001). Parents of delinquents are less skilled in discouraging antisocial behavior and in encouraging skilled behavior than are parents of nondelinquents. Parental monitoring of adolescents is especially important in determining whether an adolescent becomes a delinquent (Patterson, DeBarsyhe, & Ramsey, 1989; Pettit & others, 2001). "It's 10 P.M.; do you know where your children are?" seems to be an important question for parents to answer affirmatively. Family discord and inconsistent and inappropriate discipline are also associated with delinquency.

An increasing number of studies have found that siblings can have a strong influence on delinquency (Conger & Reuter, 1996; Lyons & others, 1995). In one recent study, high levels of hostile sibling relationships and older sibling delinquency were linked with younger sibling delinquency in both brother and sister pairs (Slomkowksi & others, 2001).

Peer relations also play an important role in delinquency. Having delinquent peers increases the risk of becoming delinquent (Henry, Tolan, & Gorman-Smith, 2001).

A current special concern in low-income areas is escalating gang violence.

Violence and Youth   An increasing concern is the high rate of adolescent violence (Price, 2001; Tolan, 2001; Weist & Cooley-Quille, 2001). In a recent school year, 57 percent of elementary and secondary school principals reported that one or more incidents of crime or violence occurred in their school and were reported to law enforcement officials (National Center for Education Statistics, 1998). Ten percent of all public schools experience one or more serious violent crimes (murder, rape, physical attack or fight with a weapon, robbery) each year (National Center for Education Statistics, 1998). Physical attacks or fights with a weapon lead the list of reported crimes. Each year more than 6,000 students are expelled for bringing firearms or explosives to school.

In a recent study, 17 percent of high school students reported carrying a gun or other weapon in the past 30 days (National Center for Health Statistics, 2000). In this same study, a smaller percentage (7 percent) reported bringing a gun or other weapon onto school property. Not all violence-related behaviors involve weapons. In this study 44 percent of male and 27 percent of female high school students said that they were involved in one or more physical fights.

In the late 1990s, a series of school shootings gained national attention. In April 1999, two Columbine High School (in Littleton, Colorado) students, Eric Harris (18) and Dylan Klebold (17) shot and killed 12 students and a teacher, wounded 23 others, and then killed themselves. In May 1998, slightly built Kip Kinkel strode into a cafeteria at Thurston High School in Springfield, Oregon, and opened fire on his fellow students, murdering two and injuring many others. Later that day, police went to Kip's home and found his parents lying dead on the floor, also victims of Kip's violence.

In 2001, 15-year-old Charles Andrew "Andy" Williams fired shots at Santana High School in Santee, California, that killed two classmates and injured 13 others. According to students at the school, Andy was a victim of bullying at the school and had joked

Oregon Social Learning Center
Center for the Prevention of School Violence
School-Based Violence Prevention in Canada
A Guide for Safe Schools
School Shootings
http://www.mhhe.com/santrocka9

Andrew "Andy" Williams, escorted by police after being arrested for killing two classmates and injuring 13 others at Santana High School. *What factors might contribute to youth murders?*

Violence and Gangs
Prevention of Youth Violence
Lost Boys
http://www.mhhe.com/santrocka9

the previous weekend of his violent plans, but no one took him seriously after he later said he was just kidding.

Is there any way that psychologists can predict whether a youth will turn violent? It's a complex task but they have pieced together some clues (Cowley, 1998). The violent youth are overwhelmingly male and many are driven by feelings of powerlessness. Violence seems to infuse these youth with a sense of power.

Small-town shooting sprees attract attention, but youth violence is far greater in poverty-infested areas of inner cities. Urban poverty fosters powerlessness and the rage that goes with it. Living in poverty is frustrating and many inner-city neighborhoods provide almost daily opportunities to observe violence. Many urban youth who live in poverty also lack adequate parent involvement and supervision.

James Garbarino (1999, 2001) says there is a lot of ignoring that goes on in these kinds of situations. Parents often don't want to acknowledge what might be a very upsetting reality. Harris and Klebold were members of the Trenchcoat Mafia clique of Columbine outcasts. The two even had made a video for a school video class the previous fall that depicted them walking down the halls at the school and shooting other students. Allegations were made that a year earlier the Sheriff's Department had been given information that Harris had bragged openly on the Internet that he and Klebold had built four bombs. Kip Kinkel had an obsession with guns and explosives, a history of abusing animals, and a nasty temper when crossed. When police examined his room, they found two pipe bombs, three larger bombs, and bomb-making recipes that Kip had downloaded from the Internet. Clearly, some signs were presented in these students' lives to suggest some serious problems, but it is still very difficult to predict whether youth like these will actually act on their anger and sense of powerlessness to commit murder.

Garbarino (1999, 2001) has interviewed a number of youth killers. He concludes that nobody really knows precisely why a tiny minority of youth kill but that it might be a lack of a spiritual center. In the youth killers he interviewed, Garbarino often found a spiritual or emotional emptiness in which the youth sought meaning in the dark side of life.

The following factors often are present in at-risk youths and seem to propel them toward violent acts (Walker, 1998):

- Early involvement with drugs and alcohol
- Easy access to weapons, especially handguns
- Association with antisocial, deviant peer groups
- Pervasive exposure to violence in the media

Many at-risk youths are also easily provoked to rage, reacting aggressively to real or imagined slights and acting on them, sometimes with tragic consequences. They might misjudge the motives and intentions of others toward them because of the hostility and agitation they carry (Coie & Dodge, 1998). Consequently, they frequently engage in hostile confrontations with peers and teachers. It is not unusual to find the anger-prone youth issuing threats of bodily harm to others.

In one recent study based on data collected in the National Longitudinal Study of Adolescent Health, secure attachment to parents, living in an intact family, and attending church services with parents were linked with lower incidences of engaging in violent behavior in seventh- through twelfth-graders (Franke, 2000).

These are some of the Oregon Social Learning Center's recommendations for reducing youth violence (Walker, 1998):

- *Recommit to raising children safely and effectively.* This includes engaging in parenting practices that have been shown to produce healthy, well-adjusted children. Such practices include consistent, fair discipline that is not harsh or severely punitive, careful monitoring and supervision, positive family management techniques, involvement in the child's daily life, daily debriefings about the child's experiences, and teaching problem-solving strategies.
- *Make prevention a reality.* Too often lip service is given to prevention strategies without investing in them at the necessary levels to make them effective.
- *Give more support to schools, which are struggling to educate a population that includes many at-risk children.*
- *Forge effective partnerships among families, schools, social service systems, churches, and other agencies to create the socializing experiences that will provide all youth with the opportunity to develop in positive ways.*

David and Roger Johnson (1995) believe it is important to go beyond violence prevention to include conflict resolution training in schools. Violence does need to be prevented in schools, but many violence prevention programs haven't worked because they are poorly targeted (too general and not focused on the relatively small group of students who need them the most), provide materials but don't focus on program implementation (too often they assume that a few hours will "fix" students who engage in violent behavior), and are unrealistic about the strength of social factors that produce violent behavior (schools alone can't solve all of our nation's social problems, such as decaying neighborhoods, lack of parental support, and so on).

Two approaches to conflict resolution programs are the cadre approach and the total student body approach. In the *cadre approach*, a small number of students are trained to serve as peer mediators for the entire school. Johnson and Johnson do not believe this approach is as effective as the *total student body approach*, in which every student learns how to manage conflicts constructively by negotiating agreements and mediating schoolmates' conflicts. A disadvantage of the total student body approach is the time and commitment required from school personnel to implement it. However, the more students there are who are trained in conflict resolution, the more likely it is that conflicts will be constructively managed.

One example of the total student body approach was developed by Johnson and Johnson (1991). Their Teaching Students to Be Peacemakers program involves both negotiation and mediation strategies. The steps students learn in negotiation are to (1) define what they want, (2) describe their feelings, (3) explain the reasons underlying the wants and feelings, (4) take the perspective of the other student to see the conflict from both sides, (5) generate at least three optional agreements that benefit both parties, and (6) come to an agreement about the best course of action.

CAREERS IN ADOLESCENT DEVELOPMENT

Rodney Hammond
Health Psychologist

When Rodney Hammond went to college at the University of Illinois in Champaign-Urbana, he had not decided on a major. To help finance his education, he took a part-time job in a child development research program sponsored by the psychology department. In this job, he observed inner-city children in contexts designed to improve their learning. He saw firsthand the contributions psychology can make and knew then that he wanted to be a psychologist.

Rodney Hammond went on to obtain a doctorate in school and community psychology with a focus on children's development. Today, he is Director of Violence Prevention at the National Center for Injury Prevention and Control in Atlanta. Rodney calls himself a "health psychologist," although when he went to graduate school, training for that profession did not exist as it does now. He and his associates teach at-risk youth how to use social skills to manage conflict effectively and to recognize situations that could become violent. They have shown in their research that with this intervention many youth are less likely to become juvenile delinquents. Hammond's message to undergraduates: "If you are interested in people and problem solving, psychology is a great way to combine the two."

Rodney Hammond, talking with an adolescent about strategies for coping with stress and avoiding risk-taking behaviors.

The steps students learn in mediation are to (1) stop the hostilities, (2) ensure that the disputants are committed to the mediation, (3) facilitate negotiations between the disputants, and (4) formalize the agreement.

When students have completed negotiation and mediation training, the school or teacher implements the Peacemakers program by choosing two student mediators for each day. Being a mediator helps students learn how to negotiate and resolve conflicts. Evaluations of the Peacemakers program have been positive, with participants showing more constructive conflict resolution than nonparticipants (Johnson & Johnson, 1995).

Since the last review, we have discussed a number of ideas about juvenile delinquency. This review should help you to reach your learning goals related to this topic.

□ FOR YOUR REVIEW

Learning Goal 3
Evaluate juvenile delinquency

- Juvenile delinquency consists of a broad range of behaviors, from socially undesirable behavior to status offenses. For legal purposes, a distinction is made between index and status offenses. Conduct disorder is a psychiatric category often used to describe delinquent-type behaviors.
- Predictors of juvenile delinquency include a negative identity, low self-control, early initiation of delinquency, weak educational orientation, heavy peer influence, low parental monitoring, ineffective discipline, and living in a high-crime, urban area.
- The high rate of violence among youth is an increasing concern. Ten percent of public schools experience one or more serious violent incidents each year.
- A number of strategies have been proposed for reducing youth violence, including conflict resolution training.

So far in our coverage of adolescent problems, we have focused on drugs, alcohol, and juvenile delinquency. Next, we will explore depression and suicide.

Depression and Suicide

As mentioned earlier in the chapter, one of the most frequent characteristics of adolescents referred for psychological treatment is sadness or depression, especially among girls. In this section, we discuss the nature of adolescent depression and adolescent suicide.

Depression   An adolescent who says "I'm depressed" or "I'm so down" may be describing a mood that lasts only a few hours or a much longer lasting mental disorder. In **major depressive disorder,** *an individual experiences a major depressive episode and depressed characteristics, such as lethargy and hopelessness, for at least two weeks or longer and daily functioning becomes impaired.* According to the *DSM-IV* classification of mental disorders (American Psychiatric Association, 1994), nine symptoms define a major depressive episode and to be classified as having major depressive disorder, at least five of these much be present during a two-week period:

1. Depressed mood most of the day
2. Reduced interest or pleasure in all or most activities
3. Significant weight loss or gain, or significant decrease or interest in appetite
4. Trouble sleeping or sleeping too much
5. Psychomotor agitation or retardation
6. Fatigue or loss of energy
7. Feeling worthless or guilty in an excessive or inappropriate manner
8. Problems in thinking, concentrating, or making decisions
9. Recurrent thoughts of death and suicide

major depressive disorder

The diagnosis when an individual experiences a major depressive episode and depressed characteristics, such as lethargy and depression, for two weeks or longer and daily functioning becomes impaired.

In adolescence, pervasive depressive symptoms might be manifested in such ways as tending to dress in black clothes, writing poetry with morbid themes, or a preoccupation with music that has depressive themes. Sleep problems can appear as all-night television watching, difficulty in getting up for school, or sleeping during the day. Lack of interest in usually pleasurable activities may show up as withdrawal from friends or staying alone in the bedroom most of the time. A lack of motivation and energy level can show up in missed classes. Boredom might be a result of feeling depressed. Adolescent depression also can occur in conjunction with conduct disorder, substance abuse, or an eating disorder.

How serious a problem is depression in adolescence? Surveys have found that approximately one-third of adolescents who go to a mental health clinic suffer from depression (Fleming, Boyle, & Offord, 1993). Depression is more common in the adolescent years than the elementary school years (Compas & Grant, 1993). By about age 15, adolescent females have a rate of depression that is twice that of adolescent males. Some of the reasons for this sex difference that have been proposed are these:

Depression is more likely to occur in adolescence than in childhood and more likely to characterize female adolescents than male adolescents. *Why might female adolescents be more likely to develop depression than adolescent males?*

- Females tend to ruminate in their depressed mood and amplify it.
- Females' self-images, especially their body images, are more negative than males.
- Females face more discrimination than males do.
- Hormonal changes alter vulnerability to depression in adolescence, especially among girls.
- Puberty occurs earlier for girls than boys and as a result girls experience a piling up of changes and life experiences in the middle school years, which can increase depression.

Mental health professionals believe that depression often goes undiagnosed in adolescence. Why is depression often not detected in adolescence? Normal adolescents often show mood swings, ruminate in introspective ways, express boredom with life, and indicate a sense of hopelessness. These behaviors might simply be transitory and not reflect a mental disorder but rather normal adolescent behaviors and thoughts.

Follow-up studies of depressed adolescents indicate that the symptoms of depression experienced in adolescence predict similar problems in adulthood (Garber & others, 1988). This means that adolescent depression needs to be taken seriously. It does not just automatically go away. Rather, adolescents who are diagnosed as having depression are more likely to experience the problem on a continuing basis in adulthood than are adolescents not diagnosed as having depression. In one recent longitudinal study, transient problems in adolescence were related to situation specific factors (such as negative peer events), whereas chronic problems were defined by individual characteristics, such as internalizing behaviors (Brooks-Gunn & Graber, 1995).

Other family factors are involved in adolescent depression (Sheeber, Hops, & Davis, 2001). Having a depressed parent is a risk factor for depression in childhood and adolescence (Windle & Dumenci, 1998). Parents who are emotionally unavailable, immersed in marital conflict, and have economic problems may set the stage for the emergence of depression in their adolescent children (Marmorstein & Shiner, 1996; Sheeber & others, 1997).

Poor peer relationships also are associated with adolescent depression. Not having a close relationship with a best friend, having less contact with friends, and peer rejection increase depressive tendencies in adolescents (Vernberg, 1990).

The experience of difficult changes or challenges is associated with depressive symptoms in adolescence (Compas & Grant, 1993). Parental divorce increases depressive symptoms in adolescents. Also, when adolescents go through puberty at the same time as they move from elementary school to middle or junior high school, they report

Exploring Adolescent Depression
Pathways to Adolescent Depression
Information for Adolescents About Depression
Depression Research
http://www.mhhe.com/santrocka9

being depressed more than do adolescents who go through puberty after the school transition (Petersen, Sarigiani, & Kennedy, 1991).

Depression has been treated with drug therapy and psychotherapy techniques (Beckham, 2000). Antidepressant drugs reduce the symptoms of depression in about 60 to 70 percent of cases, often taking about two to four weeks to improve mood. Cognitive therapy also has been effective in treating depression (Beck, 1993; Hollon, 2000).

Suicide   Suicidal behavior is rare in childhood but escalates in early adolescence. Suicide is the third leading cause of death today among adolescents 13 through 19 years of age in the United States (National Center for Health Statistics, 2000). Although the incidence of suicide in adolescence has increased in recent decades, it is still a relatively rare event in adolescence. In 1998, 4,135 individuals from 15 through 24 years of age committed suicide in the United States, or approximately 11 of every 100,000 individuals in this age grouping (National Vital Statistics Reports, 2001).

Far more adolescents contemplate suicide or attempt suicide unsuccessfully. In a recent national study, one-fifth of high school students said they had seriously considered or attempted suicide in the last 12 months (National Center for Health Statistics, 2000). Less than 3 percent reported a suicide attempt that resulted in an injury, poisoning, or drug overdose that had been treated by a doctor. In this study, female adolescents were more likely to consider suicide than male adolescents. From the ninth through twelfth grades, females increasingly contemplated suicide, but this trend was not found in adolescent males. Adolescent males were more likely to actually commit suicide than adolescent females because they are more likely to use more lethal means, such as a gun, while adolescent females are more likely to cut their wrists or take an overdose of sleeping pills, which is less likely to result in death.

Why do adolescents attempt suicide? There is no simple answer to this important question. It is helpful to think of suicide in terms of proximal and distal factors. Proximal, or immediate, factors can trigger a suicide attempt. Highly stressful circumstances, such as the loss of a boyfriend or girlfriend, poor grades at school, or an unwanted pregnancy, can trigger a suicide attempt. Drugs may play a proximal risk for suicide and this risk may have increased in recent years (National Center for Health Statistics, 2000).

Distal, or earlier, experiences often are involved in suicide attempts as well. A longstanding history of family instability and unhappiness may be present (Reinherz & others, 1994). Just as a lack of affection and emotional support, high control, and pressure for achievement by parents during childhood are related to adolescent depression, such combinations of family experiences are also likely to show up as distal factors in suicide attempts. The adolescent might also lack supportive friendships. In a study of suicide among gifted women, previous suicide attempts, anxiety, conspicuous instability in work and in relationships, depression, or alcoholism also were present in the women's lives (Tomlinson-Keasey, Warren, & Elliot, 1986). These factors are similar to those found to predict suicide among gifted men.

In one recent study, family connectedness was linked with a lower incidence of suicide attempts by adolescents (Borowsky, Ireland, & Resnick, 2001). In this study, drug use and having a friend who committed suicide were related to a higher incidence of adolescent suicide attempts.

Just as genetic factors are associated with depression, they are also associated with suicide. The closer the genetic relationship a person has to someone who has committed suicide, the more likely that person is to commit suicide.

What is the psychological profile of the suicidal adolescent like? Most youth who commit suicide have a history of problems. Suicidal adolescents often have depressive symptoms (Gadpaille, 1996). Although not all depressed adolescents are suicidal, depression is the most frequently cited factor associated with adolescent suicide. A sense of hopelessness, low self-esteem, and high self-blame are also associated with adolescent suicide (Harter & Marold, 1992).

In some instances, suicides in adolescence occur in clusters. That is, when one adolescent commits suicide, other adolescents who find out about this also commit suicide.

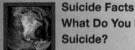

Suicide Facts
What Do You Know About Suicide?
Suicide and Homicide
Research on Suicidal Behavior
Eating Disorders
http://www.mhhe.com/santrocka9

Such "copycat" suicides raise the issue of whether suicides should be reported in the media because if so they might plant the idea of committing suicide in other adolescents' minds.

Figure 14.9 provides valuable information about what to do and what not to do when you suspect someone is likely to commit suicide.

Eating Disorders

Eating disorders have become increasing problems in adolescence. Here are some research findings regarding adolescent eating disorders:

- Girls who felt negatively about their bodies in early adolescence were more likely to develop eating disorders two years later than their counterparts who did not feel negatively about their bodies (Attie & Brooks-Gunn, 1989).
- Girls who had positive relationships with both parents had healthier eating habits than girls who had negative relationships with one or both parents (Swarr & Richards, 1996). Negative parent-adolescent relationships were linked with increased dieting in adolescent girls over a one-year period (Archibald, Graber, & Brooks-Gunn, 1999).
- Girls who were both sexually active with their boyfriends and in pubertal transition were the most likely to be dieting or engaging in disordered eating patterns (Caufmann, 1994).
- Girls who were making a lot of effort to look like same-sex figures in the media were more likely than their peers to become very concerned with their weight (Field & others, 2001).
- Many adolescent girls have a strong desire to weigh less (Graber & Brooks-Gunn, 2001).

Let's now examine different types of eating disorders in adolescence, beginning with obesity.

Obesity   In a recent national survey, 14 percent of 12- to 19-year-olds in the United States were overweight (National Center for Health Statistics, 2000). Being overweight was determined by body mass index (BMI), which is computed by a formula that takes into account height and weight. Only adolescents at or above the 95th percentile of BMI were included in the overweight category. This represents a significant increase in obesity over past years (see figure 14.10 on p. 468).

Eating patterns established in childhood and adolescence are highly associated with obesity in adulthood. For example, 80 percent of obese adolescents become obese adults. Many obese adolescents feel that everything would be great in their lives if they only could lose weight. A typical example is Debby, who at 17 has been obese since she was 12. She came from a middle-SES family and her parents pressured her to lose weight, repeatedly sending her to weight reduction centers and physicians. One summer Debby was sent to a diet camp, where she went from 200 to 150 pounds. On returning home, she was terribly disappointed when her parents pressured her to lose more. With increased tension and parental preoccupation with her weight, she gave up her dieting efforts and her weight rose rapidly. Debby isolated herself and continued her preoccupation with food. Later, clinical help was sought and fortunately Debby was able to work through her hostility toward her parents and understand her self-destructive behavior. Eventually she gained a sense of self-control and became willing to reduce her weight for herself, not for her peers or her parents.

There have been few cross-cultural comparisons of obesity in childhood and adolescence. However, in one recent study, U.S. children and adolescents (6 to 18 years of age) were four times more likely to be classified as obese than their counterparts in

What to do

1. Ask direct, straightforward questions in a calm manner: "Are you thinking about hurting yourself?"

2. Assess the seriousness of the suicidal intent by asking questions about feelings, important relationships, who else the person has talked with, and the amount of thought given to the means to be used. If a gun, pills, a rope, or other means has been obtained and a precise plan developed, clearly the situation is dangerous. Stay with the person until help arrives.

3. Be a good listener and be very supportive without being falsely reassuring.

4. Try to persuade the person to obtain professional help and assist him or her in getting this help.

What not to do

1. Do not ignore the warning signs.

2. Do not refuse to talk about suicide if a person approaches you about it.

3. Do not react with humor, disapproval, or repulsion.

4. Do not give false reassurances by saying such things as "Everything is going to be OK." Also do not give out simple answers or platitudes, such as "You have everything to be thankful for."

5. Do not abandon the individual after the crisis has passed or after professional help has commenced.

▣ FIGURE 14.9
What to Do and What Not to Do When You Suspect Someone Is Likely to Attempt Suicide

Bulimia nervosa typically begins in late adolescence or early adulthood. About 90 percent of the cases are women. Approximately 1 to 2 percent of women are estimated to develop bulimia nervosa (Gotesdam & Agras, 1995). Many women who develop bulimia nervosa were somewhat overweight before the onset of the disorder and the binge eating often began during an episode of dieting. As with anorexia nervosa, about 70 percent of individuals who develop bulimia nervosa eventually recover from the disorder (Keel & others, 1999).

Since the last review, we have discussed a number of ideas about depression, suicide, and eating disorders. This review should help you to reach your learning goals related to these topics.

☐ FOR YOUR REVIEW

Learning Goal 4
Describe depression and suicide

- Adolescents have a higher rate of depression than children do. Female adolescents are far more likely to develop depression than adolescent males are. Adolescents who develop depression are more likely than nondepressed adolescents to have depression as adults. Treatment of depression has involved both drug therapy and psychotherapy.
- The U.S. adolescent suicide rate has tripled since the 1950s. Both proximal and distal factors likely are involved in suicide.

Learning Goal 5
Understand eating disorders

- Studies suggest an increasing percentage of U.S. adolescents are obese. Both hereditary and environmental factors are involved in obesity.
- Anorexia nervosa is an eating disorder that involves the relentless pursuit of thinness through starvation. Anorexia nervosa primarily afflicts non-Latino White, middle- and upper-SES females.
- Bulimia nervosa is an eating disorder in which the individual consistently follows a binge-and-purge pattern.

So far in this chapter, we have examined the nature of abnormality and a number of adolescent problems and disorders. Next, we will explore the multiple problems that characterize many at-risk adolescents.

INTERRELATION OF
PROBLEMS AND PREVENTION/
INTERVENTION

INTERRELATION OF PROBLEMS AND PREVENTION/INTERVENTION

The adolescents most at risk have more than one problem. Researchers are increasingly finding that problem behaviors in adolescence are interrelated (Santelli & others, 2001; Tubman, Windle, and Windle, 1996). For example, heavy substance abuse is related to early sexual activity, lower grades, dropping out of school, and delinquency. Early initiation of sexual activity is associated with the use of cigarettes and alcohol, use of marijuana and other illicit drugs, lower grades, dropping out of school, and delinquency. Delinquency is related to early sexual activity, early pregnancy, substance abuse, and dropping out of school. As many as 10 percent of the adolescent population in the United States have serious multiple-problem behaviors (adolescents who have dropped out of school, or are behind in their grade level, are users of heavy drugs, regularly use cigarettes and marijuana, and are sexually active but do not use contraception). Many, but not all, of these very high-risk youth "do it all." Another 15 percent of adolescents participate in many of these same behaviors but with slightly lower frequency and less deleterious consequences. These high-risk youth often engage in two- or three-problem behaviors (Dryfoos, 1990).

In addition to understanding that many adolescents engage in multiple-problem behaviors, it also is important to develop programs that reduce adolescent problems. In a review of the programs that have been successful in preventing or reducing adolescent problems, adolescent researcher Joy Dryfoos (1990) described the common

Prevention Research
http://www.mhhe.com/santrocka9

components of these successful programs. The common components include these:

1. *Intensive individualized attention.* In successful programs, high-risk children are attached to a responsible adult who gives the child attention and deals with the child's specific needs. This theme occurred in a number of different programs. In a successful substance-abuse program, a student assistance counselor was available full-time for individual counseling and referral for treatment.

2. *Community-wide multiagency collaborative approaches.* The basic philosophy of community-wide programs is that a number of different programs and services have to be in place. In one successful substance-abuse program, a community-wide health promotion campaign was implemented that used local media and community education in concert with a substance-abuse curriculum in the schools.

3. *Early identification and intervention.* Reaching children and their families before children develop problems, or at the beginning of their problems, is a successful strategy (Botvin, 1999; Hill & others, 1999).

One preschool program serves as an excellent model for the prevention of delinquency, pregnancy, substance abuse, and dropping out of school. Operated by the High Scope Foundation in Ypsilanti, Michigan, the Perry Preschool has had a long-term positive impact on its students. This enrichment program, directed by David Weikart, services disadvantaged African American children. They attend a high-quality two-year preschool program and receive weekly home visits from program personnel. Based on official police records, by age 19 individuals who had attended the Perry Preschool program were less likely to have been arrested and reported fewer adult offenses than a control group. The Perry Preschool students also were less likely to drop out of school, and teachers rated their social behavior as more competent than that of a control group who did not receive the enriched preschool experience.

■ THINKING CRITICALLY

Why Might a Course of Risk Taking in Adolescence Likely Have More Serious Consequences Today Than in the Past?

The world is a dangerous place for too many of America's teenagers, especially those from low-SES families, neighborhoods, and schools. Many adolescents are resilient and cope with the challenges of adolescence without too many setbacks, but other adolescents struggle unsuccessfully to find jobs, are written off as losses by their schools, become pregnant before they are ready to become parents, or risk their health through drug abuse. Adolescents in virtually every era have been risk takers, testing limits and making shortsighted judgments. But why are the consequences of choosing a course of risk taking possibly more serious today than they have ever been?

Since the last review, we have discussed a number of ideas about the interrelation of problems and prevention/intervention. This review should help you to reach your learning goals related to these topics.

☐ FOR YOUR REVIEW

Learning Goal 6
Discuss the interrelation of problems and prevention/intervention

- Researchers increasingly are finding that problem behaviors in adolescence are interrelated.
- In Dryfoos' analysis, these were the common components of successful prevention/intervention programs: (1) extensive individual attention, (2) community-wide intervention, and (3) early identification.

In this, the final chapter in the book, we have examined a number of ideas about problems and disorders. To conclude the book, following this chapter is an Epilogue that is designed to encourage you to think about some of the main themes we have discussed throughout the book and to consider what adolescents' lives will be like in the future.

CHAPTER MAP

```
┌─────────────────────────────┐
│  EXPLORING ADOLESCENT       │
│  PROBLEMS                   │
└─────────────────────────────┘
```

Biological Factors

Resilience

Psychological Factors

Characteristics of Adolescent Problems

Sociocultural Factors

The Biopsychosocial Approach

The Developmental Psychopathology Approach

```
┌─────────────────────────────┐
│  PROBLEMS AND               │
│  DISORDERS                  │
└─────────────────────────────┘
```

Drugs and Alcohol

Eating Disorders

Juvenile Delinquency

Depression and Suicide

```
┌─────────────────────────────┐
│  INTERRELATION OF           │
│  PROBLEMS AND PREVENTION/   │
│  INTERVENTION               │
└─────────────────────────────┘
```

REACH YOUR LEARNING GOALS

At the beginning of the chapter we stated six learning goals and reviewed material related to these goals at five points in the chapter. This is a good time to return to these reviews. Use them as a guide for your study and to help you reach your learning goals.

Page 443

Learning Goal 1   Know about the nature of adolescent problems

Page 457

Learning Goal 2   Discuss drugs and alcohol

Page 464

Learning Goal 3   Evaluate juvenile delinquency

Page 470

Learning Goal 4   Describe depression and suicide
Learning Goal 5   Understand eating disorders

Page 471

Learning Goal 6   Discuss the interrelation of problems and prevention/intervention

KEY TERMS

developmental psychopathology 441
internalizing problems 441
externalizing problems 441
tolerance 445
physical dependence 445
psychological dependence 445
hallucinogens 450
stimulants 450
depressants 453

anabolic steroids 454
juvenile delinquency 458
index offenses 458
status offenses 458
conduct disorder 458
major depressive disorder 464
anorexia nervosa 468
bulimia nervosa 469

KEY PEOPLE

Thomas Achenbach and
   Craig Edelbrock 442
Norman Garmezy 443
Lloyd Johnston, Patrick O'Malley,
   and Gerald Bachman 445
Joy Dryfoos 456
James Garbarino 462
David and Roger Johnson 463

RESOURCES FOR IMPROVING THE LIVES OF ADOLESCENTS

Adolescents at Risk

(1990) by Joy Dryfoos
New York: Oxford University Press

This is an excellent book on adolescent problems.

American Anorexia/Bulimia Association

133 Cedar Lane
Teaneck, NJ 07666
201–836–1800

This organization provides information, referrals, and publications related to anorexia nervosa and bulimia.

Developmental Psychopathology

(1999) by Suniya Luthar, Jacob Burack, Dante Cicchetti, and John Weisz (Eds.)
New York: Cambridge University Press

This volume presents up-to-date explorations of many aspects of developmental psychopathology by leading experts.

Lost Boys

(1999) by James Garbarino
New York: Free Press

This book explores why some youth are violent and kill.

National Adolescent Suicide Hotline

800–621–4000

This hotline can be used 24 hours a day by teenagers contemplating suicide, as well as by their parents.

National Clearinghouse for Alcohol Information

P.O. Box 2345
1776 East Jefferson Street
Rockville, MD 20852
301–468–2600

This clearinghouse provides information about a wide variety of issues related to drinking problems, including adolescent drinking.

Violence Prevention for Young Adolescents

(1991) by Renee Wilson-Brewer, Stu Cohen, Lydia O'Donnell, and Irene Goodman
Carnegie Council on Adolescent Development
2400 N Street, NW
Washington, DC 20037
202–429–7979

This paper provides an overview of violence prevention programs. Eleven different programs are outlined, including several designed to curb gang violence.

TAKING IT TO THE NET

http://www.mhhe.com/santrocka9

1. Depression is one example of a mood disorder. *How common are mood disorders in adolescents? What are other examples of mood disorders, and how do the symptoms differ from "normal" behavior?*

2. Obesity is the major eating disorder. A common stereotype is that obese people simply eat too much and that they easily could achieve normal weight if they just watched how and what they ate. *If one of your friends expressed this view, how would you counter it?*

3. Think of an important stressful event or situation in which you found yourself sometime during the past three months. *What did you do; how did you deal with the stressor? Is that how you generally cope?* Take the coping test and find out.

Connect to *http://www.mhhe.com/santrocka9* to research the answers and complete these exercises. In some cases, you'll also find further instructions on this site.

EPILOGUE

ADOLESCENTS: THE FUTURE OF SOCIETY

In the end the power behind development is life.

—ERIK ERIKSON, *AMERICAN PSYCHOANALYST, 20TH CENTURY*

At the beginning of the twenty-first century, the well-being of adolescents is one of our most important concerns. We all cherish the future of adolescents, for they are the future of any society. Adolescents who do not reach their full potential, who are destined to make fewer contributions to society than society needs, and who do not take their place as productive adults diminish that society's future. In this epilogue, we will revisit a number of important themes and issues in adolescent development and then present a montage of thoughts that convey the beauty, power, and complexity of adolescents' development.

Our journey through adolescence has been long and complex, and you have read about many facets of adolescents' lives. This is a good time to stand back and ask yourself what you have learned. What theories, studies, and ideas struck you as more important than others? What did you learn about your own development as an adolescent? Did anything you learned stimulate you to rethink how adolescents develop? How did you develop into the person you are today?

Themes and Issues in Adolescent Development

As we look back across the chapters of *Adolescence*, some common themes and issues emerge. Let's explore what some of the most important themes and issues are.

The Storm-and-Stress View of Adolescence Has Been Overdramatized

Growing up has never been easy. However, adolescence is not best viewed as a time of rebellion, crisis, pathology, and deviance. A far more accurate vision of adolescence describes it as a time of evaluation, of decision making, of commitment, and of carving out a place in the world. Most problems of today's youth are not with the youth themselves. What adolescents need is access to a range of legitimate opportunities and long-term support from adults who deeply care about them.

In matters of taste and manners, the youth of every generation have seemed radical, unnerving, and different from adults—different in how they look, how they behave, the music they enjoy, their hairstyles, and the clothing they choose. But it is an enormous error to confuse the adolescent's enthusiasm for trying on new identities and enjoying moderate amounts of outrageous behavior with hostility toward parental and societal standards. Acting out and boundary testing are time-honored ways in which adolescents move toward accepting, rather than rejecting, parental values.

Although adolescence has been portrayed too negatively for too long, many adolescents today are at risk for not reaching their full potential. They do experience far too much storm and stress. This discussion underscores an important point about adolescents: They are not a homogeneous group. Different portrayals of adolescence emerge, depending on the particular group of adolescents being described.

We Need to Dramatically Reduce the Number of Adolescents at Risk for Not Reaching Their Potential

Although we emphasized that the majority of adolescents navigate the long journey of adolescence successfully, far too many adolescents in America are not reaching their potential because they are not being adequately reared by caregivers, not being adequately instructed in school, and not being adequately supported by society. Adolescents who do not reach their full potential and do not grow up to make competent contributions to their world invariably have not been given adequate individual attention and support as they were growing up. Adolescents need parents who love them; monitor their development; are sensitive to their needs; have a sound understanding of their own, as well as their adolescents', development; and help to steer them away from health-compromising behaviors.

We also need schools that place a greater emphasis on a curriculum that is developmentally appropriate and pays closer attention to adolescent health and well-being. This needs to be accomplished at all levels of education, but especially in the middle school and junior high school years. And we need to give more attention to our nation's social policy, especially in terms of ways to break the poverty cycle that enshrouds more than 25 percent of adolescents in the United States. Our nation's political values need to reflect greater concern for the inadequate conditions in which far too many adolescents live. To reduce the number of adolescents at risk for not reaching their full potential, community-wide agency cooperation and integration, as

THE JOURNEY OF ADOLESCENCE

We have come to the end of this book. I hope you can now look back and say that you learned a lot about adolescents, not only other adolescents but yourself as an adolescent and how your adolescent years contributed to who you are today. The insightful words of philosopher Søren Kierkegaard capture the importance of looking backward to understand ourselves: "Life is lived forward, but understood backwards." I also hope that those of you who become the parents of adolescents or work with adolescents in some capacity—whether as teacher, counselor, or community leader—feel that you now have a better grasp of what adolescence is all about. I leave you with the following montage of thoughts and images that convey the power, complexity, and beauty of adolescence in the human life span:

In no order of things is adolescence the time of simple life. Adolescents feel like they can last forever, think they know everything, and are quite sure about it. They clothe themselves with rainbows and go brave as the zodiac, flashing from one end of the world to the other both in mind and body. In many ways, today's adolescents are privileged, wielding unprecedented economic power. At the same time, they move through a seemingly endless preparation for life. They try on one face after another, seeking to find a face of their own. In their most pimply and awkward moments, they become acquainted with sex. They play furiously at "adult games" but are confined to a society of their own peers. They want their parents to understand them and hope that their parents will accord them the privilege of understanding them. Their generation of young people is the fragile cable by which the best and the worst of their parents' generation is transmitted to the present. In the end, there are only two lasting gifts parents can leave youth—one is roots, the other is wings.

John W. Santrock

Damon, W. (2000). Moral de
A. Kazdin (Ed.), *Encyclop*
Washington, DC, and Ne
Psychological Association
Press.

Damon, W., & Hart, D. (1988
childhood and adolescence
University Press.

Dannhausen-Brun, C.A., Sh
C.A. (1997, April). *Challe*
Teen moms and public poli
the meeting of the Society
Development, Washington

Darling, C.A., Kallen, D.J., &
Sex in transition, 1900–19
and Adolescence, 13, 385–3

Darroch, J.E., Landry, D.J., &
Changing emphases in sex
U.S. public secondary scho
Family Planning Perspectiv

Davidson, J. (2000). Giftedness
Encyclopedia of psychology.
New York: American Psych
and Oxford University Pre

Davis, L., & Stewart, R. (1997,
capacity for working with le
and transgender youth. Pap
conference on Working wit
Pittsburgh.

Davis, S.S., & Davis, D.A. (198
Moroccan town. New Bruns
University Press.

Davison, G.C. (2000). Case stu
(Ed.), *Encyclopedia of psych*
DC, & New York: American
Association and Oxford Un

Davison, G.C., & Neale, J.M. (2
psychology (8th ed.). New Yo

Day, R.D. (2002). *Introduction*
Mahwah, NJ: Erlbaum.

Day, S., Markiewitcz, D., Doyle
Ducharme, J. (2001, April).
mother, father, and best frien
quality of adolescent romant
presented at the meeting of
Research in Child Developn

De Bellis, M.D., Clark, D.B., Be
P.H., Boring, A.M., Hall, J.,
Keshaan, M.S. (2000). Hipp
adolescent-onset alcohol use
Journal of Psychiatry, 157, 73

De Bellis, M.D., Keshavan, M.S.
Frustaci, K., Masalehdan, A
(2001). Sex differences in bra
during childhood and adole:
Cortex, 11, 552–557.

de Munich Keizer, S.M., & Mul,
pubertal development in Eu
Reproduction Update, 7, 287–

deCharms, R. (1984). Motivatio
educational settings. In R. A
(Eds.), *Research on motivatio*
(Vol. 1). Orlando: Academic

Deci, E., & Ryan, R. (1994). Pror
determined education. *Scand*
Educational Research, 38, 3–1

GLOSSARY

A

accommodation an adjustment to new information. 106

acculturation cultural change that results from continuous, firsthand contact between two distinctive cultural groups. 260

active (niche-picking) genotype-environment correlations correlations that occur when adolescents seek out environments they find compatible and stimulating. 98

adolescence the developmental period of transition from childhood to early adulthood; it involves biological, cognitive, and socioemotional changes. 19

adolescent egocentrism the heightened self-consciousness of adolescents, which is reflected in their belief that others are as interested in them as they themselves are and in their sense of personal uniqueness. 137

adolescent generalization gap Adelson's concept of widespread generalizations about adolescents based on information about a limited, highly visible group of adolescents. 12

adolescents who are gifted adolescents who have above-average intelligence (usually defined as an IQ of 130 or higher) and/or superior talent in some domain, such as art, music, or mathematics. 249

adoption study a study in which investigators seek to discover whether, in behavior and psychological characteristics, adopted children and adolescents are more like their adoptive parents, who provided a home environment, or their biological parents, who contributed their heredity. Another form of adoption study is to compare adoptive and biological siblings. 97

affectionate love also called companionate love, this love occurs when an individual desires to have another person near and has a deep, caring affection for that person. 213

AIDS acquired immune deficiency syndrome, a primarily sexually transmitted disease caused by the HIV virus, which destroys the body's immune system. 364

alternation model this model assumes that it is possible for an individual to know and understand two different cultures. It also assumes that individuals can alter their behavior to fit a particular social context. 261

altruism unselfish interest in helping another person. 390

anabolic steroids drugs derived from the male sex hormone, testosterone. They promote muscle growth and lean body mass. 454

androgens the main class of male sex hormones. 77

androgyny the presence of a high degree of desirable feminine and masculine characteristics in the same individual. 331

anorexia nervosa an eating disorder that involves the relentless pursuit of thinness through starvation. 468

anticonformity this occurs when individuals react counter to a group's expectations and deliberately move away from the actions or beliefs the group advocates. 190

anxiety a vague, highly unpleasant feeling of fear and apprehension. 414

aptitude-treatment interaction (ATI) this interaction stresses the importance of both the attitudes and the characteristics of the adolescent, such as academic potential or personality traits, and the treatments or experiences, such as the educational techniques, that the adolescent receives. Aptitude refers to such characteristics as the academic potential and personality characteristics on which students differ; treatment refers to educational techniques, such as structured versus flexible classrooms. 238

assimilation (culture) the absorption of ethnic minority groups into the dominant group, which often means the loss of some or virtually all of the behavior and values of the ethnic minority group. 260

assimilation (Piaget) the incorporation of new information into existing knowledge. 106

attention deficit hyperactivity disorder (ADHD) children and adolescents with ADHD show one or more of the following characteristics over a period of time: inattention, hyperactivity, and impulsivity. 247

attribution theory states that in their effort to make sense out of their own behavior or performance, individuals are motivated to discover the underlying causes. 410

authoritarian parenting this is a restrictive, punitive style in which the parent exhorts the adolescent to follow the parent's directions and to respect work and effort. Firm limits and controls are placed on the adolescent, and little verbal exchange is allowed. This style is associated with adolescents' socially incompetent behavior. 157

authoritarian strategy of classroom management this teaching strategy is restrictive and punitive. The focus is mainly on keeping order in the classroom rather than on instruction and learning. 237

authoritative parenting this style encourages adolescents to be independent but still places limits and controls on their actions. Extensive verbal give-and-take is allowed, and parents are warm and nurturant toward the adolescent. This style is associated with adolescents' socially competent behavior. 158

authoritative strategy of classroom management this teaching strategy encourages students to be independent thinkers and doers, but still involves effective monitoring. Authoritative teachers engage students in considerable verbal give-and-take and show a caring attitude toward them. However, they still declare limits when necessary. 237

autonomous morality the second stage of moral development in Piaget's theory, displayed by older children (about 10 years of age and older). The child becomes aware that rules and laws are created by people and that, in judging an action, one should consider the actor's intentions as well as the consequences. 381

B

back-to-basics movement this philosophy stresses that the function of schools should be the rigorous training of intellectual skills through such subjects as English, mathematics, and science. 221

basal metabolism rate (BMR) the minimum amount of energy an individual uses in a resting state is the BMR. 90

behavior genetics the study of the degree and nature of behavior's hereditary basis. 97

behavioral and social cognitive theories theories that emphasize the importance of studying environmental experiences and observable behavior. Social cognitive theorists emphasize person/cognitive factors in development. 49

biological processes physical changes in an individual's body. 18

bisexual a person who is attracted to people of both sexes. 352

boundary ambiguity the uncertainty in stepfamilies about who is in or out of the family and who is performing or responsible for certain tasks in the family system. 173

bulimia nervosa in this eating disorder, the individual consistently follows a binge-and-purge eating pattern. 469

C

care perspective the moral perspective of Carol Gilligan, which views people in terms of their connectedness with others and emphasizes interpersonal communication, relationships with others, and concern for others. 387

career self-concept theory Super's theory that individuals' self-concept plays a central role in career choice and that in adolescence individuals first construct a career self-concept. 420

case study an in-depth look at an individual. 61

Connolly, J., Furman, W., &
The role of peers in the
heterosexual romantic re
adolescence. *Child Deve*

Connolly, J., & Goldberg, A
relationships in adolesce
and peers in their emerg
In W. Furman, B.B. Brov
(Eds.), *The development*
in adolescence. New York
Press.

Connolly, J., & Stevens, V. (
cliques, and young adoles
involvement. Paper prese
the Society for Research
Albuquerque.

Connors, L.J., & Epstein, J.L
school partnerships. In N
Children and parenting (
Erlbaum.

Conti, K., & Amabile, T. (19
creativity. In M.A. Runcc
Encyclopedia of creativity
Press.

Cook, T.D., Hunt, H.D., & M
April). *Comer's school de*
Chicago: A theory-based
presented at the meeting
Research in Child Devel

Cooper, C.R. (in press). *The*
Cultural perspectives on a
New York: Oxford Unive

Cooper, C.R., & Ayers-Lopez
peer systems in early add
of the role of relationship
Journal of Early Adolescer

Cooper, C.R., Cooper, R.G., J
Chavira, G. (2001). *Bridg*
How African American an
academic outreach progra
pathways to college. Unpu
University of California a

Cooper, C.R., & Denner, J. (1
linking culture and psych
community-specific proc
Psychology, 49, 559–584.

Cooper, C.R., & Grotevant, H
Individuality and connect
adolescents' self and relati
presented at the meeting
Research in Child Develo

Cooper, C.R., Jackson, J.F., A
Dunbar, N. (1995). Bridg
worlds: African American
academic outreach progra
R.G. Garcia-Ramos (Eds.
changing students. Santa E
California Linguistic Min
Institute.

Cooper, M.L., Shaver, P.R., &
Attachment styles, emotic
adjustment in adolescenc
and Social Psychology, 74,

Coopersmith, S. (1967). *The*
esteem. San Francisco: W.

Gottfried, A.E., Fleming, J.S., & Gottfried, A.W.
(2001). Continuity of academic intrinsic
motivation from childhood through late
adolescence: A longitudinal study. *Journal of*
Educational Psychology, 93.

Gottfried, A.E., Gottfried, A.W., & Bathurst, K.
(2002). Maternal and dual-earner employment
status and parenting. In M. Bornstein (Ed.),
Handbook of parenting (2nd ed., Vol. 2).
Mahwah, NJ: Erlbaum.

Gottlieb, G. (2000). Nature and nurture theories. In
A. Kazdin (Ed.), *Encyclopedia of psychology.*
Washington, DC, & New York: American
Psychological Association and Oxford University
Press.

Gottlieb, G., Wahlsten, D., & Lickliter, R. (1998).
The significance of biology for human
development: A developmental psychobiological
systems view. In W. Damon (Ed.), *Handbook of*
child psychology (5th ed., Vol. 1). New York:
Wiley.

Gottman, J.M., & Levenson, R.W. (1985). A valid
procedure for obtaining self-report of affect in
marital interaction. *Journal of Consulting and*
Clinical Psychology, 53, 156–160.

Gottman, J.M., & Parker, J.G. (Eds.). (1987).
Conversations with friends. New York:
Cambridge University Press.

Graber, J.A., Britto, P.R., & Brooks-Gunn, J. (1999).
What's love got to do with it? Adolescents' and
young adults' beliefs about sexual and romantic
relationships. In W. Furman, C. Feiring, & B.B.
Brown (Eds.), *Contemporary perspectives on*
adolescent relationships. New York: Cambridge
University Press.

Graber, J.A., & Brooks-Gunn, J. (2001).
Co-occurring eating and depressive problems: An
8-year study of adolescent girls. Unpublished
manuscript, Center for Children and Families,
Columbia University.

Graber, J.A., & Brooks-Gunn, J. (in press).
Expectations for and precursors of leaving home
in young women. In J.A. Graber & J.S. Dubas
(Eds.), *Leaving home.* San Francisco: Jossey-Bass.

Graber, J.A., & Brooks-Gunn, J. (in press). In G.M.
Wingood & R.J. Diclemente (Eds.), *Women's*
sexual and reproductive health: Social,
psychological, and public health perspectives. New
York: Plenum.

Graber, J.A., Brooks-Gunn, J., & Galen, B.R. (1999).
Betwixt and between: Sexuality in the context of
adolescent transitions. In R. Jessor (Ed.), *New*
perspectives on adolescent risk behavior. New
York: Cambridge University Press.

Graber, J.A., Brooks-Gunn, J., & Petersen, A.C.
(1996). Adolescent transitions in context. In J.A.
Graber, J. Brooks-Gunn, & A.C. Petersen (Eds.),
Transitions through adolescence: Interpersonal
domains and contexts. Mahwah, NJ: Erlbaum.

Graham, J.H., & Beller, A.H. (2002). Non-resident
fathers and their children: Child support and
visitation from an economic perspective. In C.S.
Tamis-LeMonda & N. Cabrera (Eds.), *The*
handbook of father involvement. Mahwah, NJ:
Erlbaum.

Graham, S. (1986, August). *Can attribution theory*
tell us something about motivation in blacks?
Paper presented at the meeting of the American
Psychological Association, Washington, DC.

Graham, S. (1990). Motivation in Afro-Americans.
In G.L. Berry & J.K. Asamen (Eds.), *Black*
students: Psychosocial issues and academic
achievement. Newbury Park, CA: Sage.

Graham, S. (1992). Most of the subjects were white
and middle class. *American Psychologist, 47,*
629–637.

Graham, S. & Taylor, A.Z. (2001). Ethnicity, gender,
and the development of achievement values. In
A. Wigfield, & J.S. Eccles (Eds.), *Development of*
achievement motivation. San Diego: Academic
Press.

Graham, S., & Weiner, B. (1996). Theories and
principles of motivation. In D.C. Berliner & R.C.
Calfee (Eds.), *Handbook of educational*
psychology. New York: Macmillan.

Greenberg, B.S. (1988). *Mass media and adolescents:*
A review of research reported from 1980–1987.
Manuscript prepared for the Carnegie Council
on Adolescent Development.

Greenberg, B.S., Stanley, C., Siemicki, M.,
Heeter, C., Soderman, A., & Linsangan, R.
(1986). *Sex content on soaps and prime-time*
television series most viewed by adolescents.
Project CAST Report /ns/2. East Lansing:
Michigan State Department of
Telecommunication.

Greenberger, E., & Chu, C. (1996). Perceived family
relationships and depressed mood in early
adolescence: A comparison of European and
Asian Americans. *Developmental Psychology, 32,*
707–716.

Greenberger, E., & Steinberg, L. (1981). *Project for*
the study of adolescent work: Final report. Report
prepared for the National Institute of Education,
U.S. Department of Education, Washington, DC.

Greenberger, E., & Steinberg, L. (1986). *When*
teenagers work: The psychological social costs of
adolescent employment. New York: Basic Books.

Greene, B. (1988, May). The children's hour. *Esquire*
Magazine, pp. 47–49.

Greenfield, P.M. (2000). Culture and development.
In A. Kazdin (Ed.), *Encyclopedia of psychology.*
Washington, DC, & New York: American
Psychological Association and Oxford University
Press.

Greenfield, P.M. (2002, April). *The role of cultural*
values in adolescent peer conflict. Paper presented
at the meeting of the Society for Research on
Adolescence, New Orleans.

Greeno, J.G., Collins, A.M., & Resnick, L.B. (1996).
Cognition and learning. In D.C. Berliner & R.C.
Chafee (Eds.), *Handbook of educational*
psychology. New York: Macmillan.

Greenough, W.T. (1997, April 21). Commentary in
article, "Politics of biology." *U.S. News & World*
Report, p. 79.

Greenough, W.T. (2000). Brain development. In
A. Kazdin (Ed.), *Encyclopedia of psychology.*
Washington, DC, & New York: American
Psychological Association and Oxford University
Press.

Greenough, W.T., & Black, J.R. (1992). Induction of
brain structure by experience: Substrates for
cognitive development. In M.R. Gunnar & C.A.
Nelson (Eds.), *Minnesota Symposia on Child*
Psychology: Vol. 24. Developmental behavioral
neuroscience (pp. 155–200). Hillsdale, NJ:
Erlbaum.

Greenough, W.T., Wallace, C.S., Alcantara, A.A.,
Anderson, B.J., Hawrylak, R.B., Sirevaag, A.M.,
Weiler, I.J., & Withers, G.S. (1997, August). *The*
development of the brain. Paper presented at the
meeting of the American Psychological
Association, Chicago.

Grigorenko, E.L. (2000). Heritability and
intelligence. In R.J. Sternberg (Ed.), *Handbook of*
intelligence. New York: Cambridge University
Press.

Grimes, B., & Mattimore, K. (1989, April). *The*
effects of stress and exercise on identity formation
in adolescence. Paper presented at the biennial
meeting of the Society for Research in Child
Development, Kansas City.

Grizenko, N. (1998). Protective factors in
development of psychopathology. In H.S.
Friedman (Ed.), *Encyclopedia of mental health*
(Vol. 3). San Diego: Academic Press.

Grotevant, H.D. (1996). Unpublished review of J.W.
Santrock's *Adolescence,* 7th ed. (Dubuque, IA:
Brown & Benchmark).

Grotevant, H.D. (1998). Adolescent development in
family contexts. In W. Damon (Ed.), *Handbook*
of child psychology (5th ed., Vol. 3). New York:
Wiley.

Grotevant, H.D., & Cooper, C.R. (1985). Patterns of
interaction in family relationships and the
development of identity exploration in
adolescence. *Child Development, 56,* 415–428.

Grotevant, H.D., & Cooper, C.R. (1998).
Individuality and connectedness in adolescent
development: Review and prospects for research
on identity, relationships, and context. In E. Skoe
& A. von der Lippe (Eds.), *Personality*
development in adolescence: A cross-national and
life-span perspective. London: Routledge.

Grotevant, H.D., & Durrett, M.E. (1980).
Occupational knowledge and career
development in adolescence. *Journal of*
Vocational Behavior, 17, 171–182.

Grumbach, M.M., & Styne, D.M. (1992). Puberty:
Ontogeny, neuroendocrinology, physiology, and
disorders. In J.D. Wilson & P.W. Foster (Eds.),
Williams textbook of endocrinology.
(pp. 1139–1231). Philadelphia: W.B. Saunders.

Guilford, J.P. (1967). *The structure of intellect.* New
York: McGraw-Hill.

Gullotta, T.P., Adams, G.R., & Montemayor, R.
(Eds.). (1995). *Substance misuse in adolescence.*
Newbury Park, CA: Sage.

Gur, R.C., Mozley, L.H., Mozley, P.D., Resnick, S.M.,
Karp, J.S., Alavi, A., Arnold, S.E., & Gur, R.E.
(1995). Sex differences in regional cerebral
glucose metabolism during a resting state.
Science, 267, 528–531.

Gutman, L.M. (2002, April). *The role of stage-*
environment fit from early adolescence to young
adulthood. Paper presented at the meeting of the
Society for Research on Adolescence, New
Orleans.

Guttentag, M., & Bray, H. (1976). *Undoing sex stereotypes: Research and resources for educators.* New York: McGraw-Hill.

Guyer, B. (2000). *ADHD.* Boston: Allyn & Bacon.

H

Haas, A. (1979). *Teenage sexuality: A survey of teenage sexual behavior.* New York: Macmillan.

Hahn, A. (1987, December). Reaching out to America's dropouts: What to do? *Phi Delta Kappan,* pp. 256–263.

Haidt, J.D. (1997, April). *Cultural and class variations in the domain of morality and the morality of conventions.* Paper presented at the meeting of the Society for Research in Child Development, Washington, DC.

Haith, M.M., & Benson, J.B. (1998). Infant cognition. In W. Damon (Ed.), *Handbook of child psychology* (5th ed., Vol. 2). New York: Wiley.

Hall, G.S. (1904). *Adolescence* (Vols. 1 & 2). Englewood Cliffs, NJ: Prentice Hall.

Hall, W. (1998, February 24). I.Q. scores are up, and psychologists wonder why. *Wall Street Journal,* pp. B11–12.

Hallahan, D.P., & Kaufman, J.M. (2003). *Exceptional learners* (9th ed.). Boston: Allyn & Bacon.

Halonen, J. (1995). Demystifying critical thinking. *Teaching of Psychology, 22,* 75–81.

Halonen, J.A., & Santrock, J.W. (1999). *Psychology: Contexts and applications* (3rd ed.). New York: McGraw-Hill.

Halpern, D.F. (1996). *Thinking critically about critical thinking.* Mahwah, NJ: Erlbaum.

Hamburg, D.A. (1997). Meeting the essential requirements for healthy adolescent development in a transforming world. In R. Takanishi & D. Hamburg (Eds.), *Preparing adolescents for the 21st century.* New York: Cambridge University Press.

Hansen, D. (1996, March). *Adolescent employment and psychosocial outcomes: A comparison of two employment contexts.* Paper presented at the meeting of the Society for Research on Adolescence, Boston.

Hardman, M.L., Drew, C.J., & Egan, M.W. (2002). *Human exceptionality* (7th Ed.). Boston: Allyn & Bacon.

Hare, B.R., & Castenell, L.A. (1985). No place to run, no place to hide: Comparative status and future prospects of Black boys. In M.B. Spencer, G.K. Brookins, & W.R. Allen (Eds.), *Beginnings: The social and affective development of Black children.* Hillsdale, NJ: Erlbaum.

Hare-Muston, R., & Marecek, J. (1988). The meaning of difference: Gender theory, postmodernism, and psychology. *American Psychologist, 43,* 455–464.

Harkness, S., & Super, C.M. (1995). Culture and parenting. In M.H. Bornstein (Ed.), *Children and parenting* (Vol. 2). Hillsdale, NJ: Erlbaum.

Harkness, S., & Super, S.M. (2002). Culture and parenting. In M. Bornstein (Ed.), *Handbook of parenting* (2nd ed., Vol. 2). Mahwah, NJ: Erlbaum.

Harper, D.C. (2000). Developmental disorders. In A. Kazdin (Ed.), *Encyclopedia of psychology.* Washington, DC, and New York: American Psychological Association and Oxford University Press.

Harper, M.S., Welsch, D., & Woody, T. (2002, April). *Silencing the self: Depressive symptoms and loss of self in adolescent romantic relationships.* Paper presented at the meeting of the Society for Research on Adolescence, New Orleans.

Harris, J.R. (1998). *The nurture assumption.* New York: Free Press.

Hart, D. (1996). Unpublished review of J.W. Santrock's *Child development,* 8th ed. (Dubuque, IA: Brown & Benchmark).

Hart, D., & Fegley, S. (1995). Prosocial behavior and caring in adolescence: Relations to self-understanding and social judgment. *Child Development, 66,* 1346–1359.

Harter, S. (1986). Processes underlying the construction, maintenance, and enhancement of the self-concept of children. In J. Suls & A. Greenwald (Eds.), *Psychological perspective on the self* (Vol. 3). Hillsdale, NJ: Erlbaum.

Harter, S. (1987). The determinants and mediational role of global self-worth in children. In N. Eisenberg (Ed.), *Contemporary issues in developmental psychology.* New York: Wiley.

Harter, S. (1989a). Causes, correlates, and the functional role of global self-worth: A life-span perspective. In J. Kolligian & R. Sternberg (Eds.), *Perceptions of competence and incompetence across the life span.* New Haven, CT: Yale University Press.

Harter, S. (1989b). *Self-perception profile for adolescents.* Denver: University of Denver, Department of Psychology.

Harter, S. (1990a). Processes underlying adolescent self-concept formation. In R. Montemayor, G.R. Adams, & T.P. Gullotta (Eds.), *From childhood to adolescence: A transitional period?* Newbury Park, CA: Sage.

Harter, S. (1990b). Self and identity development. In S.S. Feldman & G.R. Elliott (Eds.), *At the threshold: The developing adolescent.* Cambridge, MA: Harvard University Press.

Harter, S. (1998). The development of self-representations. In W. Damon (Ed.), *Handbook of child psychology* (5th ed., Vol. 3). New York: Wiley.

Harter, S. (1999). *The construction of the self.* New York: Guilford.

Harter, S., & Lee, L. (1989). *Manifestations of true and false selves in adolescence.* Paper presented at the meeting of the Society for Research in Child Development, Kansas City.

Harter, S., & Marold, D.B. (1992). Psychosocial risk factors contributing to adolescent suicide ideation. In G. Noam & S. Borst (Eds.), *Child and adolescent suicide.* San Francisco: Jossey-Bass.

Harter, S., & Monsour, A. (1992). Developmental analysis of conflict caused by opposing attributes in the adolescent self-portrait. *Developmental Psychology, 28,* 251–260.

Harter, S., Waters, P., & Whitesell, N. (1996, March). *False self behavior and lack of voice among adolescent males and females.* Paper presented at the meeting of the Society for Research on Adolescence, Boston.

Harter, S., & Whitesell, N. (2002, April). *Global and relational features of the fluctuating and stable self among adolescents.* Paper presented at the meeting of the Society for Research on Adolescence, New Orleans.

Hartshorne, H., & May, M.S. (1928–1930). *Moral studies in the nature of character: Studies in deceit* (Vol. 1); *Studies in self-control* (Vol. 2); *Studies in the organization of character* (Vol. 3). New York: Macmillan.

Hartup, W.W. (1983). Peer relations. In P.H. Mussen (Ed.), *Handbook of child psychology* (4th ed., Vol. 4). New York: Wiley.

Hartup, W.W. (1996). The company they keep: Friendships and their developmental significance. *Child Development, 67,* 1–13.

Hartup, W.W. (1999, April). *Peer relations and the growth of the individual child.* Paper presented at the meeting of the Society for Research in Child Development, Albuquerque.

Hartup, W.W., & Collins, A. (2000) Middle childhood: Socialization and social contexts. In A. Kazdin (Ed.), *Encyclopedia of psychology.* Washington, DC, & New York: American Psychological Association and Oxford University Press.

Hauser, S.T., & Bowlds, M.K. (1990). Stress, coping, and adaptation. In S.S. Feldman & G.R. Elliott (Eds.), *At the threshold: The developing adolescent.* Cambridge, MA: Harvard University Press.

Hauser, S.T., Powers, S.I., Noam, G.G., Jacobson, A.M., Weisse, B., & Follansbee, D.J. (1984). Familial contexts of adolescent ego development. *Child Development, 55,* 195–213.

Havighurst, R.J. (1976). A cross-cultural view. In J.F. Adams (Ed.), *Understanding adolescence.* Boston: Allyn & Bacon.

Havighurst, R.J. (1987). Adolescent culture and subculture. In V.B. Van Hasselt & M. Hersen (Eds.), *Handbook of adolescent psychology.* New York: Pergamon.

Hawkins, J.A., & Berndt, T.J. (1985, April). *Adjustment following the transition to junior high school.* Paper presented at the biennial meeting of the Society for Research in Child Development, Toronto.

Hayes, C. (Ed.). (1987). *Risking the future: Adolescent sexuality, pregnancy, and childbearing* (Vol. 1). Washington, DC: National Academy Press.

Hayes, S.C. (2000). Applied behavior analysis. In A. Kazdin (Ed.), *Encyclopedia of psychology.* Washington, DC, & New York: American Psychological Association and Oxford University Press.

Haynie, D.L., Nansel, T., Eitel, P., Crump, A.D., Saylor, K., Yu, K., & Simons-Morton, B. (2001). Bullies, victims, and bully/victims: Distinct groups of at-risk youth. *Journal of Early Adolescence, 21,* 29–49.

Heath, S.B. (1983). *Ways with words.* Cambridge, England: Cambridge University Press.

Heath, S.B. (1997, April 21). *Language and work: Learning and identity development of older children in community settings* (George Miller Committee Lecture), University of Illinois.

Heath, S.B. (1999). Dimensions of language development: Lessons from older children. In A.S. Masten (Ed.), *Cultural processes in child development: The Minnesota symposium on child psychology* (Vol. 29). Mahwah, NJ: Erlbaum.

Heath, S.B., & McLaughlin, M.W. (Eds.). (1993). *Identity and inner-city youth: Beyond ethnicity and gender.* New York: Teachers College Press.

Hechinger, J. (1992). *Fateful choices.* New York: Hill & Wang.

Hecht, M.L., Jackson, R.L., & Ribeau, S.A. (2002). *African American communication* (2nd Ed.). Mahwah, NJ: Erlbaum.

Hellmich, N. (2000, November 7). Kids' bodies break down at play. *USA Today,* p. 1D.

Helms, J.E. (1996). *Where do we go from here? Affirmative action: Who benefits?* Washington, DC: American Psychological Association.

Helms, J.E. (Ed.). (1990). *Black and white racial identity: Theory, research, and practice.* Westport, CT: Greenwood Press.

Helson, R., Elliot, T., & Leigh, J. (1989). Adolescent antecedents of women's work patterns. In D. Stern & D. Eichorn (Eds.), *Adolescence and work.* Hillsdale, NJ: Erlbaum.

Henderson, K.A., & Zivian, M.T. (1995, March). *The development of gender differences in adolescent body image.* Paper presented at the meeting of the Society for Research in Child Development, Indianapolis.

Henderson, V.L., & Dweck, C.S. (1990). Motivation and achievement. In S.S. Feldman & G.R. Elliott (Eds.), *At the threshold: The developing adolescent.* Cambridge, MA: Harvard University Press.

Hendry, J. (1999). *Social anthropology.* New York: Macmillan.

Henry, D.B., Tolan, P.H., & Gorman-Smith, D. (2001). Longitudinal family and peer group effects on violence and nonviolent delinquency. *Journal of Clinical Child Psychology, 30,* 172–186.

Herek, G. (2000). Homosexuality. In A. Kazdin (Ed.), *Encyclopedia of psychology.* Washington, DC, and New York: American Psychological Association and Oxford University Press.

Hernandez, D.J. (1997). Child development and the social demography of childhood. *Child Development, 68,* 149–169.

Herpertz-Dahlmann, B., Muller, B., Herpertz, S., Heussen, N., Hebebrand, J., & Remschmidt, H. (2001). Prospective 10-year follow up in adolescent anorexia nervosa—course, outcome, psychiatric comorbidity, and psychosocial adaptation. *Journal of Child Psychology and Psychiatry, 42,* 603–612.

Herrnstein, R.J., & Murray, C. (1994). *The bell curve: Intelligence and class structure in modern life.* New York: Free Press.

Hertzog, N.B. (1998, Jan/Feb). Gifted education specialist. *Teaching Exceptional Children,* pp. 39–43.

Hess, L., Lonky, E., & Roodin, P.A. (1985, April). *The relationship of moral reasoning and ego strength to cheating behavior.* Paper presented at the meeting of the Society for Research in Child Development, Toronto.

Hetherington, E.M. (1972). Effects of father-absence on personality development in adolescent daughters. *Developmental Psychology, 7,* 313–326.

Hetherington, E.M. (1977). *My heart belongs to daddy: A study of the remarriages of daughters of divorcees and widows.* Unpublished manuscript, University of Virginia.

Hetherington, E.M. (1989). Coping with family transitions: Winners, losers, and survivors. *Child Development, 60,* 1–14.

Hetherington, E.M. (1995, March). *The changing American family and the well-being of children.* Paper presented at the meeting of the Society for Research in Child Development, Indianapolis.

Hetherington, E.M. (1999). *Should we stay together for the sake of the children?* Unpublished manuscript, Dept. of Psychology, University of Virginia, Charlottesville.

Hetherington, E.M. (2000). Divorce. In A. Kazdin (Ed.), *Encyclopedia of psychology.* Washington, DC, and New York: American Psychological Association and Oxford University Press.

Hetherington, E.M., Bridges, M., & Insabella, G.M. (1998). What matters? What does not? Five perspectives on the association between marital transitions and children's adjustment. *American Psychologist, 53,* 167–184.

Hetherington, E.M., & Clingempeel, W.G. (1992). Coping with marital transitions: A family systems perspective. *Monographs of the Society for Research in Child Development, 57,* (2–3, Serial No. 227).

Hetherington, E.M., Cox, M., & Cox, R. (1982). Effects of divorce on children and parents. In M.E. Lamb (Ed.), *Nontraditional families.* Hillsdale, NJ: Erlbaum.

Hetherington, E.M., Henderson, S.H., Reiss, D., & others. (1999). Adolescent siblings in stepfamilies: Family functioning and adolescent adjustment. *Monographs of the Society for Research in Child Development, 64* (No. 4).

Hetherington, E.M., & Jodl, K.M. (1994). Stepfamilies as settings for child development. In A. Booth & J. Dunn (Eds.), *Stepfamilies: Who benefits? Who does not?* Hillsdale, NJ: Erlbaum.

Hetherington, E.M., & Kelly, J. (2002). *For better or for worse: Divorce reconsidered.* New York: Norton.

Hetherington, E.M., Reiss, D., & Plomin, R. (1994). *Separate social worlds of siblings: Impact of nonshared environment on development.* Mahwah, NJ: Erlbaum.

Hetherington, E.M., & Stanley-Hagan, M. (2002). Parenting in divorced and remarried families. In M. Bornstein (Ed.), *Handbook of parenting* (2nd ed., Vol. 3). Mahwah, NJ: Erlbaum.

Heward, W.L. (2000). *Exceptional children* (6th ed.). Upper Saddle River, NJ: Merrill.

Hicks, R., & Connolly, J.A. (1995, March). *Peer relations and loneliness in adolescence: The interactive effects of social self-concept, close friends, and peer networks.* Paper presented at the meeting of the Society for Research in Child Development, Indianapolis.

Higgins, A., Power, C., & Kohlberg, L. (1983, April). *Moral atmosphere and moral judgment.* Paper presented at the biennial meeting of the Society for Research in Child Development, Detroit.

Hightower, E. (1990). Adolescent interpersonal and familial precursors of positive mental health at midlife. *Journal of Youth and Adolescence, 19,* 257–275.

Hill, J.P., & Holmbeck, G.N. (1986). Attachment and autonomy during adolescence. *Annals of Child Development, 3,* 145–189.

Hill, J.P., Holmbeck, G.N., Marlow, L., Green, T.M., & Lynch, M.E. (1985). Pubertal status and parent-child relations in families of seventh-grade boys. *Journal of Early Adolescence, 5,* 31–44.

Hill, J.P., & Lynch, M.E. (1983). The intensification of gender-related role expectations during early adolescence. In J. Brooks-Gunn & A.C. Petersen (Eds.), *Girls at puberty: Biological and psychosocial perspectives.* New York: Plenum.

Hill, J.P., & Steinberg, L.D. (1976, April 26–30). *The development of autonomy in adolescence.* Paper presented at the Symposium on Research on Youth Problems, Fundacion Orbegoza Eizaquirre, Madrid, Spain.

Hill, K., Battin-Pearson, S., Hawkins, J.D., & Jie, G. (1999, June). *The role of social developmental processes in facilitating or disrupting the link between early offending and adult crimes in males and females.* Paper presented at the meeting of the Society for Prevention Research, New Orleans.

Hirsch, B.J., & Rapkin, B.D. (1987). The transition to junior high school: A longitudinal study of self-esteem, psychological symptomatology, school life, and social support. *Child Development, 58,* 1235–1243.

Hodges, E.V.E., & Perry, D.G. (1999). Personal and interpersonal antecedents and consequences of victimization by peers. *Journal of Personality and Social Psychology, 76,* 677–685.

Hodges, E.V.E., Boivin, M., Vitaro, F., & Bukowski, W.M. (1999). The power of friendship: Protection against an escalating cycle of peer victimization. *Developmental Psychology, 35,* 94–101.

Hoff, E., Laursen, B., & Tardif, T. (2002). Socioeconomic status and parenting. In M.H. Bornstein (Ed.), *Handbook of parenting* (2nd Ed.). Mahwah, NJ: Erlbaum.

Hofferth, S.L. (1990). Trends in adolescent sexual activity, contraception, and pregnancy in the United States. In J. Bancroft & J.M. Reinisch (Eds.), *Adolescence and puberty.* New York: Oxford University Press.

Hoff-Ginsberg, E., & Tardif, T. (1995). Socioeconomic status and parenting. In M.H. Bornstein (Ed.), *Children and parenting* (Vol. 2). Hillsdale, NJ: Erlbaum.

Hoffman, D., & Novak, T. (1999). *Computer access, socioeconomic status, and ethnicity.* Unpublished manuscript, Vanderbilt University, Nashville.

Hoffman, L.W. (1989). Effects of maternal employment in the two-parent family. *American Psychologist, 44,* 283–292.

Hoffman, L.W. (2000). Maternal employment: Effects of social context. In R.D. Taylor & M.C. Wang (Eds.), *Resilience across contexts.* Mahwah, NJ: Erlbaum.

Hoffman, M.L. (1970). Moral development. In P.H. Mussen (Ed.), *Manual of child psychology* (3rd ed., Vol. 2). New York: Wiley.

Hoffman, M.L. (1980). Moral development in adolescence. In J. Adelson (Ed.), *Handbook of adolescent psychology.* New York: Wiley.

Hoffman, M.L. (1988). Moral development. In M.H. Bornstein & M.E. Lamb (Eds.), *Developmental psychology: An advanced textbook* (2nd ed.). Hillsdale, NJ: Erlbaum.

Hoffman, S., Foster, E., & Furstenberg, F. (1993). Reevaluating the costs of teenage childbearing. *Demography, 30,* 1–13.

Hoffnung, M. (1984). Motherhood: Contemporary conflict for women. In J. Freeman (Ed.), *Women: A feminist perspective* (3rd ed.). Palo Alto, CA: Mayfield.

Holditch, P., Broomfield, K., Foster, J., Emshoff, J., & Adamczak, J. (2002, April). *Cool Girls, Inc.: Evaluating a developmentally sensitive intervention for at-risk girls.* Paper presented at the meeting of the Society for Research on Adolescence, New Orleans.

Holland, J.L. (1973). *Making vocational choices: A theory of careers.* Englewood Cliffs, NJ: Prentice Hall.

Holland, J.L. (1987). Current status of Holland's theory of careers: Another perspective. *Career Development Quarterly, 36,* 24–30.

Hollingshead, A.B. (1975). *Elmtown's youth and Elmtown revisited.* New York: Wiley.

Hollingworth, L.S. (1914). *Functional periodicity: An experimental study of the mental and motor abilities of women during menstruation.* New York: Columbia University, Teachers College.

Hollingworth, L.S. (1916). Sex differences in mental tests. *Psychological Bulletin 13,* 377–383.

Hollon, S.D. (2000). Cognitive therapy. In A. Kazdin (Ed.), *Encyclopedia of psychology.* Washington, DC, and New York: American Psychological Association and Oxford University Press.

Holmbeck, G., & Shapera, W. (1999). Research methods with adolescents. In P. Kendall, J. Butcher, & G. Holmbeck (Eds.), *Handbook of research methods in clinical psychology.* New York: Wiley.

Holmbeck, G.N. (1996). A model of family relational transformations during the transition to adolescence: Parent-adolescent conflict and adaptation. In J.A. Graber, J. Brooks-Gunn, & A.C. Petersen (Eds.), *Transitions in adolescence.* Mahwah, NJ: Erlbaum.

Holmbeck, G.N., Durbin, D., & Kung, E. (1995, March). *Attachment, autonomy, and adjustment before and after leaving home: Sullivan and Sullivan revisited.* Paper presented at the meeting of the Society for Research in Child Development, Indianapolis.

Holmes, L.D. (1987). *Quest for the real Samoa: The Mead-Freeman controversy and beyond.* South Hadley, MA: Bergin & Garvey.

Holtzmann, W. (1982). Cross-cultural comparisons of personality development in Mexico and the United States. In D. Wagner & H.W. Stevenson (Eds.), *Cultural perspectives on child development.* San Francisco: W.H. Freeman.

Hopkins, J.R. (2000). Erikson, E.H. In A. Kazdin (Ed.), *Encyclopedia of psychology.* Washington, DC, & New York: American Psychological Association and Oxford University Press.

Hops, H. (2002, April). *Multiple pathways to adolescent drug use and abuse.* Paper presented at the meeting of the Society for Research on Adolescence, New Orleans.

Hops, H., Davis, B., Alpert, A., & Longoria, N. (1997, April). *Adolescent peer relations and depressive symptomatology.* Paper presented at the meeting of the Society for Research in Child Development, Washington, DC.

Horney, K. (1967). *Feminine psychology.* New York: W.W. Norton.

Howe, M.J.A. (2000). Prodigies. In A. Kazdin (Ed.), *Encyclopedia of psychology.* Washington, DC, and New York: American Psychological Association and Oxford University Press.

Howe, N., & Strauss, W. (2000). *Millenials rising: The next great generation.* New York: Vintage.

Hoyt, S., & Scherer, D.G. (1998). Female juvenile delinquency. *Law and Human Behavior, 22,* 81–107.

Huang, L.N. (1989). Southeast Asian refugee children and adolescents. In J.T. Gibbs & L.N. Huang (Eds.), *Children of color.* San Francisco: Jossey-Bass.

Huang, L.N., and Ying, Y. (1989). Chinese American children and adolescents. In J.T. Gibbs and L.N. Huang, (Eds.), *Children of color.* San Francisco: Jossey-Bass.

Huebner, A.M., & Garrod, A.C. (1993). Moral reasoning among Tibetan monks: A study of Buddhist adolescents and young adults in Nepal. *Journal of Cross-Cultural Psychology, 24,* 167–185.

Huesmann, L.R. (1986). Psychological processes promoting the relation between exposure to media violence and aggressive behavior by the viewer. *Journal of Social Issues, 42,* 125–139.

Huges, M., Alfano, M., & Harkness, S. (2002, April). *The GEAR UP Project: Strenghtening academic transitions and attainment through relationship building.* Paper presented at the meeting of the Society for Research on Adolescence, New Orleans.

Hughes, D.L. (1997, April). *Racial socialization in urban African-American and Hispanic families.* Paper presented at the meeting of the Society for Research in Child Development, Washington, DC.

Hurtado, M.T. (1997, April). *Acculturation and planning among adolescents.* Paper presented at the meeting of the Society for Research in Child Development, Washington, DC.

Huston, A.C., & Alvarez, M. (1990). The socialization context of gender-role development in early adolescence. In R. Montemayor, G.R. Adams, & T.P. Gulotta (Eds.), *From childhood to adolescence: A transitional period?* Newbury Park, CA: Sage.

Huston, A.C., McLoyd, V.C., & Coll, C.G. (1994). Children and poverty: Issues in contemporary research. *Child Development, 65,* 275–282.

Huston, A.C., Siegle, J., & Bremer, M. (1983, April). *Family environment television use by preschool children.* Paper presented at the biennial meeting of the Society for Research in Child Development, Detroit.

Huston, A.C., & Wright, J.C. (1998). Mass media and children's development. In I.E. Siegel & K.A. Renninger (Eds.), *Handbook of child psychology* (5th ed., Vol. 4). New York: Wiley.

Huttenlocher, J., Haight, W., Bruk, A., Seltzer, M., & Lyons, T. (1991). Early vocabulary growth: Relation to language input and gender. *Developmental Psychology, 27,* 236–248.

Huttenlocher, P.R., & Dabholkar, A.S. (1997). Regional differences in synaptogenesis in human cerebral cortex. *Journal of Comparative Neurology, 37* (2), 167–178.

Hyde, J.M., & Delamater, J.D. (2000). Understanding human sexuality (7th ed.). New York: McGraw-Hill.

Hyde, J.S. (1985). *Half the human experience* (3rd ed.). Lexington, MA: D. C. Heath.

Hyde, J.S. (1993). Meta-analysis and the psychology of women. In F.L. Denmark & M.A. Paludi (Eds.), *Handbook on the psychology of women.* Westport, CT: Greenwood.

Hyde, J.S., & Delamater, J.D. (2000). *Human sexuality* (7th ed.). New York: McGraw-Hill.

Hyde, J.S., & Mezulis, A.H. (2001). Gender difference research: Issues and critique. In J. Worell (Ed.), *Encyclopedia of women and gender.* San Diego: Academic Press.

Hyde, J.S., & Plant, E.A. (1995). Magnitude of psychological gender differences: Another side of the story. *American Psychologist, 50,* 159–161.

I

Ianni, F.A.J., & Orr, M.T. (1996). Dropping out. In J.A. Graber, J. Brooks-Gunn, & A.C. Petersen (Eds.), *Transitions in adolescence.* Mahwah, NJ: Erlbaum.

Idol, L. (1997). Key questions related to building collaborative and inclusive schools. *Journal of Learning Disabilities, 30,* 384–394.

International Society for Technology in Education. (1999). *National educational technology standards for students document.* Eugene, OR: International Society for Technology in Education.

Irwin, C.E. (1993). The adolescent, health, and society: From the perspective of the physician. In S.G. Millstein, A.C. Petersen, & E.O. Nightingale (Eds.), *Promoting the health of adolescents.* New York: Oxford University Press.

J

Jackson, N., & Butterfield, E. (1996). A conception of giftedness designed to promote research. In R.J. Sternberg & J.E. Davidson (Eds.), *Conceptions of giftedness.* New York: Cambridge University Press.

Jacobs, J.E., & Potenza, M. (1990, March). *The use of decision-making strategies in late adolescence.* Paper presented at the meeting of the Society for Research in Adolescence, Atlanta.

Jacobs, J.K., Garnier, H.E., & Weisner, T. (1996, March). *The impact of family life on the process of dropping out of high school.* Paper presented at the meeting of the Society for Research on Adolescence, Boston.

Jacobson, K.C., & Crockett, L.J. (2000). Parental monitoring and adolescent adjustment: An ecological perspective. *Journal of Research on Adolescence, 10,* 65–97.

Jaffe, S., & Hyde, J.S. (2000). Gender differences in moral orientation. *Psychological Bulletin, 126,* 703–726.

Janz, N.K., Zimmerman, M.A., Wren, P.A., Israel, B.A., Freudenberg, N., & Carter, R.J. (1996). Evaluation of 37 AIDS prevention projects: Successful approaches and barriers to program effectiveness. *Health Education Quarterly, 23,* 80–97.

Jarrett, R.L. (1995). Growing up poor: The family experiences of socially mobile youth in low-income African-American neighborhoods. *Journal of Adolescent Research, 10,* 111–135.

Jensen, A.R. (1969). How much can we boost IQ and scholastic achievement? *Harvard Educational Review, 39,* 1–123.

Jessor, R., Turbin, M.S., & Costa, F. (in press). Risk and protection in successful outcomes among disadvantaged adolescents. *Applied Developmental Science.*

Jhally, S. (1990). *Dreamworlds: Desire/sex/power in rock video* (Video). Amherst: University of Massachusetts at Amherst, Department of Communications.

Jodl, K.M., Michael, A., Malanchuk, O., Eccles, J.S., & Sameroff, A. (2001). Parents' roles in shaping early adolescents' occupational aspirations. *Child Development, 72,* 1247–1265.

Johnson, D.W. (1990). *Teaching out: Interpersonal effectiveness and self-actualization.* Upper Saddle River, NJ: Prentice-Hall.

Johnson, D.W., & Johnson, R. (1991). *Teaching students to be peacemakers.* Edina, MN: Interaction Book Company.

Johnson, D.W., & Johnson, R.T. (1995, February). Why violence prevention programs don't work—and what does. *Educational Leadership,* pp. 63–68.

Johnson, J.G., Cohen, P., Pine, D.S., Klein, D.F., Kasen, S., & Brook, J.S. (2000). Association between cigarette smoking and anxiety disorders during adolescence and adulthood. *Journal of the American Medical Association, 284,* 348–2351.

Johnson, M.K., Beebe, T., Mortimer, J.T., & Snyder, M. (1998). Volunteerism in adolescence: A process perspective. *Journal of Research on Adolescence, 8,* 309–332.

Johnson, V.K. (2002). *Managing the transition to college: The role of families and adolescents' coping strategies.* Paper presented at the meeting of the Society for Research on Adolescence, New Orleans.

Johnston, J., Etteman, J., & Davidson, T. (1980). *An evaluation of "Freestyle": A television series to reduce sex-role stereotypes.* Ann Arbor: University of Michigan, Institute for Social Research.

Johnston, L.D., O'Malley, P.M., & Bachman, J.G. (1992, January 25). *Most forms of drug use decline among American high school and college students.* News release, Institute of Social Research, University of Michigan, Ann Arbor.

Johnston, L.D., O'Malley, P.M., & Bachman, J.G. (1999, December 17). *Drug trends in the United States are mixed* (Press Release). Ann Arbor, MI: Institute of Social Research, University of Michigan.

Johnston, L.D., O'Malley, P.M., & Bachman, J.G. (2000). *The monitoring of the future: National results on adolescent drug use.* Washington, DC: National Institute on Drug Abuse.

Johnston, L.D., O'Malley, P.M., & Bachman, J.G. (2001, December 19). *Monitoring the Future: 2001.* Ann Arbor, MI: Institute for Social Research, University of Michigan.

Jones, B.F., Rasmussen, C.M., & Moffit, M.C. (1997). *Real-life problem solving.* Washington, DC: American Psychological Association.

Jones, D.C., Costin, S.E., & Ricard, R.J. (1994, February). *Ethnic and sex differences in best friendship characteristics among African-American, Mexican-American, and White adolescents.* Paper presented at the meeting of the Society for Research on Adolescence, San Diego.

Jones, J.M. (1994). The African American: A duality dilemma? In W.J. Lonner & R. Malpass (Eds.), *Psychology and culture.* Needham Heights, MA: Allyn & Bacon.

Jones, L.V. (1984). White-black achievement differences: The narrowing gap. *American Psychologist, 39,* 1207–1213.

Jones, M.C. (1965). Psychological correlates of somatic development. *Child Development, 36,* 899–911.

Jones, S.E. (2000). Ethics in research. In A. Kazdin (Ed.). *Encyclopedia of psychology.* Washington, DC, & New York: American Psychological Association and Oxford University Press.

Josselson, R. (1994). Identity and relatedness in the life cycle. In H.A. Bosma, T.L.G. Graafsma, H.D. Grotevant, & D.J. De Levita (Eds.), *Identity and development.* Newbury Park, CA: Sage.

Joyner, K., & Udry, J.R. (2000). "You don't bring me anything but down: Adolescent romance and depression. *Journal of Health and Social Behavior, 41,* 369–391.

Jozefowicz, D.M.H. (2002, April). *Quantitative and qualitative perspectives on the transition to adulthood.* Paper presented at the meeting of the Society for Research on Adolescence, New Orleans.

Jozefowicz, D.M., Barber, B.L., & Mollasis, C. (1994, February). *Relations between maternal and adolescent values and beliefs: Sex differences and implications for occupational choice.* Paper presented at the meeting of the Society for Research on Adolescence, San Diego.

Juang, L.P., & Nguyen, H.H. (1997, April). *Autonomy and connectedness: Predictors of adjustment in Vietnamese adolescents.* Paper presented at the meeting of the Society for Research in Child Development, Washington, DC.

Jussim, L., & Eccles, J.S. (1993). Teacher expectations II: Construction and reflection of student achievement. *Journal of Personality and Social Psychology, 63,* 947–961.

K

Kagan, J. (1992). Yesterday's premises, tomorrow's promises. *Developmental Psychology, 28,* 990–997.

Kagan, J. (1998). *The power of parents.* Available on the World Wide Web: *http://www.Psychplace.com.*

Kagan, J., Snidman, N., & Arcus, D. (1995, August). *Antecedents of shyness.* Paper presented at the meeting of the American Psychological Association, New York City.

Kagan, S., & Madsen, M.C. (1972). Experimental analysis of cooperation and competition of Anglo-American and Mexican children. *Developmental Psychology, 6,* 49–59.

Kahn, S.E., & Richardson, A. (1983). Evaluation of a course in sex roles for secondary school students. *Sex Roles, 9,* 431–440.

Kail, R., & Hall, L.K. (2001). Distinguishing short-term memory from working memory. *Memory and Cognition, 29,* 1–9.

Kail, R., & Pellegrino, J.W. (1985). *Human intelligence.* New York: W.H. Freeman.

Kaiser Family Foundation. (1996). *Kaiser Family Foundation survey of 1,500 teenagers ages 12–18.* San Francisco: Kaiser Foundation.

Kalil, A., & Kunz, J. (2000, April). *Psychological outcomes of adolescent mothers in young adulthood.* Paper presented at the meeting of the Society for Research on Adolescence, Chicago.

Kamphaus, R.W. (2000). Learning disabilities. In A. Kazdin (Ed.), *Encyclopedia of psychology.* Washington, DC, and New York: American Psychological Association and Oxford University Press.

Kandel, D.B., & Lesser, G.S. (1969). Parent-adolescent relationships and adolescence independence in the United States and Denmark. *Journal of Marriage and the Family, 31,* 348–358.

Kandel, D.B., & Wu, P. (1995). The contributions of mothers and fathers to the intergenerational transmission of cigarette smoking. *Journal of Research on Adolescence, 5,* 225–252.

Kaplan, M.J., Middleton, T., Urdan, C., & Midgley, C. (2002). Achievement goals and goal structures. In C. Midgley (Ed.), *Goals, goal structures, and patterns of adaptive learning.* Mahwah, NJ: Erlbaum.

Kaplowitz, P.B., Slora, E.J., Wasserman, R.C., Pedlow, S.E., & Herman-Giddens, M.E. (2001). Earlier onset of puberty in girls: Relation to increased body mass index and race. *Pediatrics, 108,* 347–353.

Karniol, R., Gabay, R., Ochioin, Y., & Harari, Y. (1998). *Sex Roles, 39,* 45–58.

Kaufman, A.S. (2000a). Tests of intelligence. In R.J. Sternberg (Ed.), *Handbook of intelligence.* New York: Cambridge University Press.

Kaufmann, A.S. (2000b). Wechsler, David. In A. Kazdin (Ed.), *Encyclopedia of psychology.* Washington, DC, and New York: American Psychological Association and Oxford University Press.

Kaufman, A.S., & Lindenberger, E.O. (2002). *Assessing adolescence and adult intelligence* (2nd Ed.). Boston: Allyn & Bacon.

Keating, D.P. (1990). Adolescent thinking. In S.S. Feldman & G.R. Elliott (Eds.), *At the threshold: The developing adolescent.* Cambridge, MA: Harvard University Press.

Keel, P.K., Mitchell, J.E., Miller, K.B., Davis, T.L., & Crowe, S.J. (1999). Long-term outcome of bulimia nervosa. *Archives of General Psychiatry, 56,* 63–69.

Keener, D.C., & Boykin, K.A. (1996, March). *Parental control, autonomy, and ego development.* Paper presented at the meeting of the Society for Research on Adolescence, Boston.

Kelly, J. (2000). Sexually transmitted diseases. In A. Kazdin (Ed.), *Encyclopedia of psychology.* Washington, DC, and New York: American Psychological Association and Oxford University Press.

Kennedy, J.H. (1990). Determinants of peer social status: Contributions of physical appearance, reputation, and behavior. *Journal of Youth and Adolescence, 19,* 233–244.

Kenney, A.M. (1987, June). Teen pregnancy: An issue for schools. *Phi Delta Kappan,* pp. 728–736.

Kenniston, K. (1970). Youth: A "new" stage of life. *American Scholar, 39,* 631–654.

Kiess, W., Reich, A., Meyer, K., Glasow, A., Deutscher, J., Klammt, J., Yang, Y., Muller, G., & Kratzsch, J. (1999). A role for leptin in sexual maturation and puberty? *Hormone Research, 51,* 55–3.

Killen, M. (1991). Social and moral development in early childhood. In W.M. Kurtines & J.L. Gewirtz (Eds.), *Handbook of moral behavior and development* (Vol. 2). Mahwah, NJ: Erlbaum.

Killen, M., McGlothlin, H., & Lee-Kim, J. (in press). Between individuals and culture: Individuals' evaluations of exclusion from groups. In H. Keller, Y. Poortinga, & A. Schoelmerich (Eds.), *Between biology and culture: Perspectives on ontogenetic development.* Cambridge, UK: Cambridge University Press.

Kilmartin, C. (2000). *The masculine self.* New York: McGraw-Hill.

Kim, J. (2002, April). *"Cosmo chicks": The impact of contemporary women's magazines on readers' sexual attitudes and self perceptions.* Paper presented at the meeting of the Society for Research on Adolescence, New Orleans.

Kimmel, A. (1996). *Ethical issues in behavioral research.* Cambridge, MA: Blackwell.

Kindlundh, A.M.S., Isacson, D.G.L., Berlund, L., & Nyberg, F. (1999). Factors associated with adolescence use of doping agents: Anabolic-androgenic steroids. *Addiction, 94,* 543–553.

King, P. (1988). Heavy metal music and drug use in adolescents. *Postgraduate Medicine, 83,* 295–304.

King, P.M., & Kitchener, K.S. (1994). *Developing reflective judgment: Understanding and promoting intellectual growth and critical thinking in adolescents and adults.* San Francisco: Jossey-Bass.

Kinsey, A.C., Pomeroy, W.B., & Martin, C.E. (1948). *Sexual behavior in the human male.* Philadelphia: Saunders.

Kirby, D., Resnick, M.D., Downes, B., Kocher, T., Gunderson, P., Pothoff, S., Zelterman, D., & Blum, R.W. (1993). The effects of school-based health clinics in St. Paul on school-wide birthrates. *Family Planning Perspectives, 25,* 12–16.

Kirst, M.W. (1998, April). *A plan for the evaluation of California's class-size reduction initiative.* Paper presented at the meeting of the American Educational Research Association, San Diego.

Kitchener, K.S., & King, P.M. (1981). Reflective judgment: Concepts of justification and their relationship to age and education. *Journal of Applied Developmental Psychology, 2,* 89–111.

Klaczynski, P.A. (1997). Bias in adolescents' everyday reasoning and its relationship with intellectual ability, personal theories, and self-serving motivation. *Developmental Psychology, 33,* 273–283.

Klaczynski, P.A., & Narasimham, G. (1998). Development of scientific reasoning biases: Cognitive versus ego-protective explanations. *Developmental Psychology, 34,* 175–187.

Klaus, T. (1997, July). *Seven scary sexuality subjects for males . . . and how to address them.* Paper presented at the conference on Working with America's Youth, Pittsburgh.

Klaw, E., & Saunders, N. (1994). *An ecological model of career planning in pregnant African American teens.* Paper presented at the biennial meeting of the Society for Research on Adolescence, San Diego.

Klein, J.D., Allan, M.J., Elster, A.B., Stevens, D., Cox, C., Hedberg, V.A., & Goodman, R.A. (2001). Improving adolescent preventative care in community health centers. *Pediatrics, 107,* 318–327.

Knox, D., & Wilson, K. (1981). Dating behaviors of university students. *Family Relations, 30,* 255–258.

Kobak, R. (1999). The emotional dynamics of disruptions in attachment relationships: Implications for theory, research, and clinical intervention. In J. Cassidy & P. Shaver (Eds.), *Handbook of attachment.* New York: Guilford.

Koenig, L.J., & Faigeles, R. (1995, March). *Gender differences in adolescent loneliness and maladjustment.* Paper presented at the meeting of the Society for Research in Child Development, Indianapolis.

Kohlberg, L. (1958). *The development of modes of moral thinking and choice in the years 10 to 16.* Unpublished doctoral dissertation, University of Chicago.

Kohlberg, L. (1966). A cognitive-developmental analysis of children's sex-role concepts and attitudes. In E. E. Maccoby (Ed.), *The development of sex differences.* Palo Alto, CA: Stanford University Press.

Kohlberg, L. (1969). Stage and sequence: The cognitive-developmental approach to socialization. In D.A. Goslin (Ed.), *Handbook of socialization theory and research.* Chicago: Rand McNally.

Kohlberg, L. (1976). Moral stages and moralization: The cognitive-developmental approach. In T. Lickona (Ed.), *Moral development and behavior.* New York: Holt, Rinehart & Winston.

Kohlberg, L. (1981). *Essays on moral development: Vol. 1. The philosophy of moral development.* San Francisco: Harper & Row.

Kohlberg, L. (1984). *Essays on moral development: Vol. 2. The philosophy of moral development.* San Francisco: Harper & Row.

Kohlberg, L. (1986). A current statement on some theoretical issues. In S. Modgil & C. Modgil (Eds.), *Lawrence Kohlberg.* Philadelphia: Falmer.

Kohlberg, L., & Candee, D. (1979). *Relationships between moral judgment and moral action.* Unpublished manuscript, Harvard University.

Kohn, M.L. (1977). *Class and conformity: A study in values* (2nd ed.). Chicago: University of Chicago Press.

Koss, M.P. (1993). Rape: Scope, impact, interventions, and public policy responses. *American Psychologist, 48,* 1062–1069.

Koss-Chiono, J.D., & Vargas, L.A. (Eds.). (1999). *Working with Latino youth.* San Francisco: Jossey-Bass.

Kottak, C.P. (2002). *Cultural anthropology* (9th ed.). New York: McGraw-Hill.

Kounin, J.S. (1970). *Discipline and management in classrooms.* New York: Holt, Rinehart & Winston.

Kozol, J. (1991). *Savage inequalities.* New York: Crown.

Kozulin, A. (2000). Vygotsky. In A. Kazdin (Ed.), *Encyclopedia of psychology.* Washington, DC, and New York: American Psychological Association and Oxford University Press.

Kramer, L., & Lin, L. (1997, April). *Mothers' and fathers' responses to sibling conflict.* Paper presented at the meeting of the Society for Research in Child Development, Washington, DC.

Kremen, A.M., & Block, J. (2000, April). *Maladaptive pathways in adolescence.* Paper presented at the meeting of the Society for Research in Adolescence, Chicago.

Kreppner, K. (2001). Retrospect and prospect in the psychological study of families as systems. In J.P. McHale & W.S. Grolnick (Eds.), *Retrospect and prospect in the psychological study of families.* Mahwah, NJ: Erlbaum.

Kroger, J. (2000). *Identity development.* Thousand Oaks, CA: Sage.

Krupnik, C.G. (1985). Women and men in the classroom: Inequality and its remedies. *On Teaching and Learning: The Journal of the Harvard University Derek Bok Center, 10,* 18–25.

Ksir, C. (2000). Drugs. In A. Kazdin (Ed.), *Encyclopedia of psychology.* Washington, DC and New York: American Psychological Association and Oxford University Press.

Kuchenbecker, S. (2000). *Raising winners.* New York: Times Books/Random House.

Kuhn, D. (1998). Afterword to Volume 2: Cognition, perception, and language. In W. Damon (Ed.), *Handbook of child psychology* (5th ed., Vol. 2). New York: Wiley.

Kuhn, D. (1999). A developmental model of critical thinking. *Educational Researcher, 28,* 26–37.

Kuhn, D. (2000). Adolescence: Adolescent thought processes. In A. Kazdin (Ed.), *Encyclopedia of psychology.* Washington, DC, & New York: American Psychological Association and Oxford University Press.

Kuhn, D. (2000a). Adolescence: Adolescent thought processes. In A. Kazdin (Ed.), *Encyclopedia of psychology.* Washington, DC, & New York: American Psychological Association and Oxford University Press.

Kuhn, D. (2000b). Metacognitive development. In L. Balter & S. Tamis-LeMonda (Eds.), *Child psychology.* Philadelphia: Psychology Press.

Kulig, J.W., Mandel, L., Ruthazer, R., & Stone, D. (2001, March). *School-based substance use prevention for female students.* Paper presented at the meeting of the Society for Adolescent Medicine, San Diego.

Kuperminc, G., Jurkovic, G., Perilla, J., Murphy, A., Casey, S., Ibanez, G., Parker, J., & Urruzmendi, A. (2002, April). *Latino self, American self: Mexican and immigrant Latino adolescents' bicultural identity constructions.* Paper presented at the meeting of the Society for Research on Adolescence, New Orleans.

Kupersmidt, J.B., & Coie, J.D. (1990). Preadolescent peer status, aggression, and school adjustment as predictors of externalizing problems in adolescence. *Child Development, 61,* 1350–1363.

Kurdek, L.A., & Krile, D. (1982). A developmental analysis of the relation between peer acceptance and both interpersonal understanding and perceived social self-competence. *Child Development, 53,* 1485–1491.

Kurtz, D.A., Cantu, C.L., & Phinney, J.S. (1996, March). *Group identities as predictors of self-esteem among African American, Latino, and White adolescents.* Paper presented at the meeting of the Society for Research on Adolescence, Boston.

L

Labouvie-Vief, G., & Diehl, M. (1999). Self and personality development. In J.C. Kavanaugh & S.K. Whitbourne (Eds.), *Gerentology: An interdisciplinary perspective.* New York: Oxford University Press.

Ladd, G.W., & Kochenderfer, B.J. (in press). Parenting behaviors and parent-child relationship: Correlates of peer victimization in kindergarten. *Developmental Psychology.*

Ladd, G.W., & Le Sieur, K.D. (1995). Parents and children's peer relationships. In M.H. Bornstein (Ed.), *Children and parenting* (Vol. 4). Hillsdale, NJ: Erlbaum.

Ladd, G.W., & Pettit, G. (2002). Parents and children's peer relationships. In M. Bornstein (Ed.), *Handbook of parenting* (2nd ed., Vol. 5). Mahwah, NJ: Erlbaum.

LaFromboise, T., & Low, K.G. (1989). American Indian children and adolescents. In J.T. Gibbs & L.N. Huang (Eds.), *Children of color.* San Francisco: Jossey-Bass.

LaFromboise, T., Coleman, H.L.K., & Gerton, J. (1993). Psychological impact of biculturalism: Evidence and theory. *Psychological Bulletin, 114,* 393–412.

Lamb, M.E. (1997). Fatherhood then and now. In A. Booth & A.C. Crouter (Eds.), *Men in families.* Mahwah, NJ: Erlbaum.

Landry, D.J., Singh, S., & Darroch, J.E. (2000). Sexuality education in fifth and sixth grades in U.S. public schools, 1999. *Family Planning Perspectives, 32,* 212–219.

Lapsley, D.K. (1990). Continuity and discontinuity in adolescent social cognitive development. In R. Montemayor, G. Adams, & T. Gulotta (Eds.), *From childhood to adolescence: A transitional period?* Newbury Park, CA: Sage.

Lapsley, D.K. (1993). *Moral psychology after Kohlberg.* Unpublished manuscript, Department of Psychology, Brandon University, Manitoba.

Lapsley, D.K. (1996). *Moral psychology.* Boulder, CO: Westview Press.

Lapsley, D.K., Enright, R.D., & Serlin, R.C. (1985). Toward a theoretical perspective on the legislation of adolescence. *Journal of Early Adolescence, 5,* 441–466.

Lapsley, D.K., & Murphy, M.N. (1985). Another look at the theoretical assumptions of adolescent egocentrism. *Developmental Review, 5,* 201–217.

Lapsley, D.K., & Power, F.C. (Eds.). (1988). *Self, ego, and identity.* New York: Springer-Verlag.

Lapsley, D.K., Rice, K.G., & Shadid, G.E. (1989). Psychological separation and adjustment to college. *Journal of Counseling Psychology, 36,* 286–294.

Larose, S., & Boivin, M. (1998). Attachment to parents, social support expectations, and socioemotional adjustment during the high school–college transition. *Journal of Research on Adolescence, 8,* 1–28.

Larson, R.W. (1999, September). Unpublished review of J.W. Santrock's *Adolescence,* 8th ed. (New York: McGraw-Hill).

Larson, R.W. (2000). Toward a psychology of positive youth development. *American Psychologist, 55,* 170–183.

Larson, R.W., Clore, G.L., & Wood, G.A. (1999). The emotions of romantic relationships. In W. Furman, B.B. Brown, & C. Feiring (Eds.), *Contemporary perspectives on romantic relationships.* New York: Cambridge University Press.

Larson, R.W., Kubey, R., & Colletti, J. (1989). Changing channels: Early adolescent media choices and shifting investments. *Journal of Youth and Adolescence, 18,* 583–599.

Larson, R.W., & Richards, M. (1999). Waiting for the weekend: The development of Friday and Saturday nights as the emotional climax of the week. In A.C. Crouter & R.W. Larson (Eds.), *Temporal rhythms in the lives of adolescents: Themes and variations.* San Francisco: Jossey-Bass.

Larson, R.W., Richards, M.H., Moneta, G., Holmbeck, G., & Duckett, E. (1996). Changes in adolescents' daily interactions with their families from 10 to 18: Disengagement and transformation. *Developmental Psychology, 32,* 744–754.

Larson, R.W., & Verman, S. (1999). How children and adolescents spend time across the world. *Psychological Bulletin, 125,* 701–736.

Lauren, B., Coy, K.C., & Collins, W.A. (1998). Reconsidering changes in parent-child conflict across adolescence: A meta-analysis. *Child Development, 69,* 817–832.

Laursen, B. (1995). Conflict and social interaction in adolescent relationships. *Journal of Research on Adolescence, 5,* 55–70.

LaVoie, J. (1976). Ego identity formation in middle adolescence. *Journal of Youth and Adolescence, 5,* 371–385.

Law, T.C. (1992, March). *The relationship between mothers' employment status and perception of child behavior.* Paper presented at the meeting of the Society for Research on Adolescence, Washington, DC.

Lazarus, R.S. (1991). *Emotion and adaptation.* New York: Oxford University Press.

Leadbeater, B.J. (1994, February). *Re-conceptualizing social supports for adolescent mothers: Grandmothers, babies, fathers, and beyond.* Paper presented at the meeting of the Society for Research on Adolescence, San Diego.

Leadbeater, B.J. & Way, N. (2000). *Growing up fast.* Mahwah, NJ: Erlbaum.

Leadbeater, B.J., Way, N., & Raden, A. (1994, February). *Barriers to involvement of fathers of the children of adolescent mothers.* Paper presented at the meeting of the Society for Research on Adolescence, San Diego.

Learner-Centered Principles Work Group. (1997). *Learner-centered psychological principles: A framework for school reform and redesign.* Washington, DC: American Psychological Association.

Lebra, T.S. (1994). Mother and child in Japanese socialization: A Japan-U.S. comparison. In P. Greenfield & R. Cocking (Eds.), *Cross-cultural roots of minority child development* (pp. 259–274). Hillsdale, NJ: Erlbaum.

Leinhardt, G., Crowley, K., Knutson, K. (Eds.) (2002). *Learning conversations in museums.* Mahwah, NJ: Erlbaum.

Lee, C.C. (1985). Successful rural black adolescents: A psychological profile. *Adolescence, 20,* 129–142.

Lee, V.E., Croninger, R.G., Linn, E., & Chen, X. (1995, March). *The culture of sexual harassment in secondary schools.* Paper presented at the meeting of the Society for Research in Child Development, Indianapolis.

Leffert, N., & Blyth, D.A. (1996, March). *The effects of community contexts on early adolescents.* Paper presented at the meeting of the Society for Research on Adolescence, Boston.

Lefkowitz, E.S., Afifi, T.L., Sigman, M., & Au, T.K. (1999, April). *He said, she said: Gender differences in mother-adolescent conversations about sexuality.* Paper presented at the meeting of the Society for Research in Child Development, Albuquerque.

Leinhardt, G., Crowley, K., & Knutson, K. (Eds.) (2002). *Learning conversations in museums.* Mahwah, NJ: Erlbaum.

Leitenberg, H., Detzer, M.J., & Srebnik, D. (1993). Gender differences in masturbation and the relation of masturbation experience in preadolescence and/or early adolescence to sexual behavior and adjustment in young adulthood. *Archives of Sexual Behavior, 22,* 87–98.

Leong, F.T.L. (1995). Introduction and overview. In F.T.L. Leong (Ed.), *Career development and vocational behavior in racial and ethnic minorities.* Hillsdale, NJ: Erlbaum.

Leong, F.T.L. (2000). Cultural pluralism. In A. Kazdin (Ed.), *Encyclopedia of psychology.* Washington, DC, and New York: American Psychological Association and Oxford University Press.

Lerner, J.V., Jacobson, L., & del Gaudio, A. (1992, March). *Maternal role satisfaction and family variables as predictors of adolescent adjustment.* Paper presented at the meeting of the Society for Research on Adolescence, Washington, DC.

Lerner, R.M. (1993). Early adolescence: Toward an agenda for the integration of research, policy, and intervention. In R.M. Lerner (Ed.), *Early adolescence.* Hillsdale, NJ: Erlbaum.

Lerner, R.M. (1998). Theories of human development: Contemporary perspectives. In W. Damon (Ed.), *Handbook of child psychology* (5th ed., Vol. 1). New York: Wiley.

Lerner, R.M. (2000). Developmental psychology: Theories. In A. Kazdin (Ed.), *Encyclopedia of psychology.* Washington, DC, & New York: American Psychological Association and Oxford University Press.

Lerner, R.M., Fisher, C.B., & Weinberg, R.A. (2000). Toward a science for and of the people: Promoting civil society through the application of developmental science. *Child Development, 71* 11–20.

Lerner, R.M., Lerner, J.V., von Eye, A., Ostrum, C.W., Nitz, K., Talwar-Soni, R., & Tubman, J. (1996). Continuity and discontinuity across the transition of early adolescence: A developmental contextual perspective. In J.A. Graber, J. Brooks-Gunn, & A.C. Petersen (Eds.), *Transitions through adolescence: Interpersonal domains and context.* Mahwah, NJ: Erlbaum.

Lerner, R.M., & Olson, C.K. (1995, February). "My body is so ugly." *Parents,* pp. 87–88.

Levant, R.F. (1995). *Masculinity reconstructed: Changing rules of manhood.* New York: Dutton.

Levant, R.F. (1999, August). *Boys in crisis.* Paper presented at the meeting of the American Psychological Association, Boston.

Levant, R.F., & Brooks, G.R. (1997). *Men and sex: New psychological perspectives.* New York: Wiley.

LeVay, S. (1991). A difference in hypothalamic structure between heterosexual and homosexual men. *Science, 253,* 1034–1037.

Leventhal, T., & Brooks-Gunn, J. (2000). The neighborhoods they live in: The effects of neighborhood residence on child and adolescent outcomes. *Psychological Bulletin, 126,* 309–337.

Leventhal, T., & Brooks-Gunn, J. (2003). Moving up: Neighborhood effects on children and families. In M.H. Bornstein & R.H. Bradley (Eds.), *Socioeconomics status, parenting, and child development.* Mahwah, NJ: Erlbaum.

Leventhal, T., Graber, J.A., & Brooks-Gunn, J. (2001). *Adolescent transitions into young adulthood.* Unpublished manuscript, Center for Children and Families, Columbia University, New York.

Levesque, J., & Prosser, T. (1996). Service learning connections. *Journal of Teacher Education, 47,* 325–334.

Lewis, C.G. (1981). How adolescents approach decisions: Changes over grades seven to twelve and policy implications. *Child Development, 52,* 538–554.

Lewis, R. (1997). With a marble and telescope: Searching for play. *Childhood Education, 36,* 346.

Lewis, R. (2002). *Human genetics* (4th ed.). New York: McGraw-Hill.

Lewis, V.G., Money, J., & Bobrow, N.A. (1977). Idiopathic pubertal delay beyond the age of 15: Psychological study of 12 boys. *Adolescence, 12,* 1–11.

Lieberman, M., Doyle, A., & Markiewicz, D. (1999). Developmental patterns in security of attachment to mother and father in late childhood and early adolescence: Associations with peer relations. *Child Development, 70,* 202–213.

Limber, S.P. (1997) Preventing violence among school children. *Family Futures, 1,* 27–28.

Lindner-Gunnoe, M. (1993). *Noncustodial mothers' and fathers' contributions to the adjustment of adolescent stepchildren.* Unpublished doctoral dissertation. University of Virginia.

Linn, M.C. (1991). Scientific reasoning, adolescent. In R.M. Lerner, A.C. Petersen, & J. Brooks-Gunn (Eds.), *Encyclopedia of adolescence* (Vol. 2). New York: Garland.

Liprie, M.L. (1993). Adolescents' contributions to family decision making. In B.H. Settles, R.S. Hanks, & M.B. Sussman (Eds.), *American families and the future: Analyses of possible destinies.* New York: Haworth Press.

Lipsitz, J. (1980, March). *Sexual development in young adolescents.* Invited speech given at the American Association of Sex Educators, Counselors, and Therapists, New York City.

Lipsitz, J. (1983, October). *Making it the hard way: Adolescents in the 1980s.* Testimony presented at the Crisis Intervention Task Force, House Select Committee on Children, Youth, and Families, Washington, DC.

Lipsitz, J. (1984). *Successful schools for young adolescents.* New Brunswick, NJ: Transaction Books.

Livesley, W.J., & Bromley, D.B. (1973). *Person perception in childhood and adolescence.* New York: Wiley.

Lochman, J.E., & Dodge, K.A. (1998). Distorted perceptions in dyadic interactions of aggressive and nonaggresive boys: Effects of prior expectations, context, and boys' age. *Development and Psychopathology, 10,* 495–512.

Loeber, R., Farrington, D.P., Stouthamer-Loeber, M., Moffitt, T., & Caspi, A. (1998). The development of male offending: Key findings from the first decade of the Pittsburgh Youth Study. *Studies in Crime and Crime Prevention, 7,* 141–172.

Loehlin, J. (1995, August). *Heritability of intelligence.* Paper presented at the meeting of the American Psychological Association, New York City.

Loehlin, J.C. (2000). Group differences in intelligence. In R. J. Sternberg (Ed.), *Handbook of intelligence.* New York: Cambridge University Press.

Loewen, I.R., & Leigh, G.K. (1986). *Timing of transition to sexual intercourse: A multivariate analysis of white adolescent females ages 15–17.* Paper presented at the meeting of the Society for the Scientific Study of Sex, St. Louis.

Logan, G. (2000). Information processing theories. In A. Kazdin (Ed.), *Encyclopedia of psychology.* Washington, DC, and New York: American Psychological Association and Oxford University Press.

Long, T., & Long, L. (1983). *Latchkey children.* New York: Penguin.

Lonner, W.J. (1990). An overview of cross-cultural testing and assessment. In R.W. Brislin (Ed.), *Applied cross-cultural psychology.* Newbury Park, CA: Sage.

Lopez, N. (2001, March). *Gender and culture.* Invited presentation at the Center on Women's Studies, University of Texas at Dallas.

Lord, S. (1995, March). *Parent psychological experiences as mediators of the influence of economic conditions on parenting in low income urban contexts.* Paper presented at the meeting of the Society for Research in Child Development, Indianapolis.

Lord, S.E., & Eccles, J.S. (1994, February). *James revisited: The relationship of domain self-concepts and values to Black and White adolescents' self-esteem.* Paper presented at the meeting of the Society for Research on Adolescence, San Diego.

Lowe, B., Zipfel, S., Buchholz, C., Dupont, Y., Reas, D.L., & Herzog, W. (2001). Long-term outcome of anorexia nervosa in a prospective 21-year follow-up study. *Psychology and Medicine, 31,* 881–890.

Luborsky, L.B. (2000) Psychoanalysis: Psychoanalytic psychotherapies. In A. Kazdin (Ed.), *Encyclopedia of psychology.* Washington, DC, & New York: American Psychological Association and Oxford University Press.

Luo, Q., Fang, X., & Aro, P. (1995, March). *Selection of best friends by Chinese adolescents.* Paper presented at the meeting of the Society for Research in Child Development, Indianapolis.

Luria, A., & Herzog, E. (1985, April). *Gender segregation across and within settings.* Paper presented at the biennial meeting of the Society for Research in Child Development, Toronto.

Luster, T.J., Perlstadt, J., McKinney, M.H., & Sims, K.E. (1995, March). *Factors related to the quality of the home environment adolescents provide for their infants.* Paper presented at the meeting of the Society for Research in Child Development, Indianapolis.

Luthar, S.S., Cicchetti, D., & Becker, B. (2000). The construct of resilience: A critical evaluation and guidelines for future work. *Child Development, 71,* 543–562.

Lyendecker, B., Carlson, V., Ascencio, M., & Miller, A. (2002). Parenting among Latino families in the United States. In M. Bornstein (Ed.), *Handbook of parenting* (2nd ed., Vol. 4). Mahwah, NJ: Erlbaum.

Lynch, M.E. (1991). Gender intensification. In R.M. Lerner, A.C. Petersen, & J. Brooks-Gunn (Eds.), *Encyclopedia of adolescence* (Vol. 1). New York: Garland.

Lyon, G.R. (1996). Learning disabilities. In *Special education for students with disabilities.* Los Altos, CA: Packard Foundation.

Lyon, G.R., & Moats, L.C. (1997). Critical conceptual and methodological considerations in reading intervention research. *Journal of Learning Disabilities, 30,* 578–588.

Lyons, M.J., True, W.R., Eisen, S.A., Goldberg, J., Meyer, J.M., Farone, S.V., Eaves, L.J., & Tsuang, M.T. (1995). Differential heritability of adult and juvenile antisocial traits. *Archives of General Psychiatry, 52,* 906–915.

Lyons, N.P. (1990). Listening to voices we have not heard. In C. Gilligan, N.P. Lyons, & T.J. Hanmer (Eds.), *Making connections.* Cambridge, MA: Harvard University Press.

M

Maas, H.S. (1954). The role of members in clubs of lower-class and middle-class adolescents. *Child Development, 25,* 241–251.

Maccoby, E.E. (1984). Middle childhood in the context of the family. In W.A. Collins (Ed.), *Development during middle childhood.* Washington, DC: National Academy Press.

Maccoby, E.E. (1987, November). Interview with Elizabeth Hall: All in the family. *Psychology Today,* pp. 54–60.

Maccoby, E.E. (1992). Trends in the study of socialization: Is there a Lewinian heritage? *Journal of Social Issues, 48,* 171–185.

Maccoby, E.E. (1995). The two sexes and their social systems. In P. Moen, G.H. Elder, & K. Luscher (Eds.), *Examining lives in context.* Washington, DC: American Psychological Association.

Maccoby, E.E. (1996). Peer conflict and intrafamily conflict: Are there conceptual bridges? *Merrill-Palmer Quarterly, 42,* 165–176.

Maccoby, E.E. (1998). *The two sexes.* Cambridge, MA: Harvard University Press.

Maccoby, E.E., & Jacklin, C.N. (1974). *The psychology of sex differences.* Palo Alto, CA: Stanford University Press.

Maccoby, E.E., & Mnookin, R.H. (1992). *Dividing the child: Social and legal dilemmas of custody.* Cambridge, MA: Harvard University Press.

MacDermid, S., & Crouter, A.C. (1995). Midlife, adolescence, and parental employment in family systems. *Journal of Youth and Adolescence, 24,* 29–54.

MacDonald, K. (1987). Parent-child physical play with rejected, neglected, and popular boys. *Developmental Psychology, 23,* 705–711.

MacLean, M.G., & Paradise, M.J. (1997, April). *Substance use and psychological health in homeless adolescents.* Paper presented at the meeting of the Society for Research in Child Development, Washington, DC.

Maddux, C.D., Johnson, D.L., & Willis, J.W. (1997). *Educational computing.* Boston: Allyn & Bacon.

Mader, S. (1999). *Biology* (6th ed.). New York: McGraw-Hill.

Madison, B.E., & Foster-Clark, F.S. (1996, March). *Pathways to identity and intimacy: Effects of gender and personality.* Paper presented at the meeting of the Society for Research on Adolescence, Boston.

Maehr, M.L. (2001). Goal theory is *not* dead—not yet, anyway: A reflection on the special issue. *Educational Psychology Review, 13,* 177–186.

Maehr, M.L., & Midgley, C. (1996). *Transforming school cultures.* Boulder, CO: Westview Press.

Magee, J., Gordon, J.I., & Whelan, A. (2001). Bringing the human genome and the revolution in bioinformatics to the medical school classroom. *Academic Medicine, 76,* 852–855.

Maggs, J.L., Schulenberg, J., & Hurrelmann, K. (1997). Developmental transitions in adolescence: Health promotion implications. In J. Schulenberg, J.L. Maggs, & K. Hurrelmann (Eds.), *Health risks and developmental transitions during adolescence.* New York: Cambridge University Press.

Magnuson, K.A., & Duncan, G.J. (2002). Parents in poverty. In M. Bornstein (Ed.), *Handbook of parenting* (2nd ed., Vol. 4). Mahwah, NJ: Erlbaum.

Magnuson, K.A., & Duncan, G.J. (2002). Poverty and parenting. In M.H. Bornstein (Ed.), *Handbook of parenting.* Mahwah, NJ: Erlbaum.

Magnusson, D. (1988). *Individual development from an interactional perspective: A longitudinal study.* Hillsdale, NJ: Erlbaum.

Maguin, E., Zucker, R.A., & Fitzgerald, H.E. (1995). The path to alcohol problems through conduct problems: A family-based approach to very early intervention with risk. In G.M. Boyd, J. Howard, & R.A. Zucker (Eds.), *Alcohol problems among adolescents.* Hillsdale, NJ: Erlbaum.

Main, M. (2000). Attachment theory. In A. Kazdin (Ed.), *Encyclopedia of psychology.* Washington, DC, & New York: American Psychological Association and Oxford University Press.

Majhanovich, S. (1998, April). *Unscrambling the semantics of Canadian multiculturalism.* Paper presented at the meeting of the American Educational Research Association, San Diego.

Male, M. (2003). *Technology for inclusion* (3rd Ed.). Boston: Allyn & Bacon.

Malik, N.M., & Furman, W. (1993). Practitioner review: Problems in children's peer relations: What can the clinician do? *Journal of Child Psychology and Psychiatry, 34,* 1303–1326.

Malina, R.M. (2001). Physical activity and fitness: Pathways from childhood to adulthood. *American Journal of Human Biology, 13,* 162–172.

Manis, F.R., Keating, D.P., & Morrison, F.J. (1980). Developmental differences in the allocation of processing capacity. *Journal of Experimental Child Psychology, 29,* 156–169.

Manke, B., & Pike, A. (1997, April). *The search for new domains of nonshared environmental experience: Looking outside the family.* Paper presented at the meeting of the Society for Research in Child Development, Washington, DC.

Mantzoros, C.S. (2000). Role of leptin in reproduction. *Annals of the New York Academy of Sciences, 900,* 174–83.

Mantzoros, C.S., Flier, J.S., & Rogol, A.D. (1997). A longitudinal assessment of hormonal and physical alterations during normal puberty in boys. V. Rising leptin levels may signal the onset of puberty. *Journal of Clinical Endocrinology and Metabolism, 82,* 1066–1070.

Maracek, J. (1995). Gender, politics, and psychology's ways of knowing. *American Psychologist, 50,* 162–163.

Marcell, AV., & Millstein, S.G. (2001, March). *Quality of adolescent preventive services: The role of physician attitudes and self-efficacy.* Paper presented at the meeting of the Society for Adolescent Medicine, San Diego.

Marcia, J. (1980). Ego identity development. In J. Adelson (Ed.), *Handbook of adolescent psychology.* New York: Wiley.

Marcia, J. (1987). The identity status approach to the study of ego identity development. In T. Honess & K. Yardley (Eds.), *Self and identity: Perspectives across the lifespan.* London: Routledge & Kegan Paul.

Marcia, J. (1989). Identity and intervention. *Journal of Adolescence, 12,* 401–410.

Marcia, J. (1994). The empirical study of ego identity. In H.A. Bosma, T.L.G. Graafsma, H.D. Grotevant, & D.J. De Levita (Eds.), *Identity and development.* Newbury Park, CA: Sage.

Marcia, J. (1996). Unpublished review of J.W. Santrock's *Adolescence,* 7th ed. (Dubuque, IA: Brown & Benchmark).

Marklein, M.B. (1998, November 24). An eye-level meeting of the minds. *USA Today,* p. 9D.

Markstrom, C.A., & Tryon, R.J. (1997, April). *Resiliency, social support, and coping among poor African-American and European-American Appalachian adolescents.* Paper presented at the meeting of the Society for Research in Child Development, Washington, DC.

Markus, H., & Nurius, P. (1986). Possible selves. *American Psychologist, 41,* 954–969.

Markus, H.R., & Kitayama, S. (1994). The cultural construction of self and emotion: Implications for social behavior. In S. Kitayama & H.R. Markus (Eds.), *Emotion and culture.* Washington, DC: American Psychological Association.

Markus, H.R., Mullally, P.R., & Kitayama, S. (1999). *Selfways: Diversity in modes of cultural participation.* Unpublished manuscript, Department of Psychology, University of Michigan.

Marmorstein, N.R., & Shiner, R.L. (1996, March). *The family environments of depressed adolescents.* Paper presented at the meeting of the Society for Research on Adolescence, Boston.

Marsh, H.W. (1991). Employment during high school: Character building or a subversion of academic goals? *Sociology of Education, 64,* 172–189.

Marshall, S., Adams, G.R., Ryan, B.A., & Keating, L.J. (1994, February). *Parental influences on adolescent empathy.* Paper presented at the meeting of the Society for Research on Adolescence, San Diego.

Martella, R.C., Nelson, J.R., & Marchand-Martella, N.E. (2003). *Managing disruptive behaviors in the classroom.* Boston: Allyn & Bacon.

Martin, E.W., Martin, R., & Terman, D.L. (1996). The legislative and litigation history of special education. *Future of Children, 6* (1), 25–53.

Martin, J. (1976). *The education of adolescents.* Washington, DC: U.S. Department of Education.

Martin, N.C. (1997, April). *Adolescents' possible selves and the transition to adulthood.* Paper presented at the meeting of the Society for Research in Child Development, Washington, DC.

Masten, A.S., & Coatsworth, J.D. (1998). The development of competence in favorable and unfavorable environments: Lessons from research on successful children. *American Psychologist, 53,* 205–220.

Masten, A.S., Hubbard, J.J., Gest, S.D., Tellegen, A., Garmezy, N., & Ramirez, M. (in press). Adaptation in the context of adversity: Pathways to resilience and maladaptation from childhood to late adolescence. *Development and Psychopathology.*

Mathes, P.G., Howard, J.K., Allen, S.H., & Fuchs, D. (1998). Peer-assisted learning strategies for first-grade readers: Responding to the needs of diverse learners. *Reading Research Quarterly, 33,* 62–94.

Matlin, M.W. (1993). *The psychology of women* (2nd ed.). San Diego: Harcourt Brace Jovanovich.

Matsumoto, D. (2000). Cross-cultural communication. In A. Kazdin (Ed.), *Encyclopedia of psychology.* Washington, DC, and New York: American Psychological Association and Oxford University Press.

Mayer, J.D., Caruso, D., & Salovy, P. (2000). Competing models of emotional intelligence. In R. Sternberg (Ed.), *Handbook of human intelligence.* New York: Cambridge University Press.

Mayes L.C., & Truman, S.D. (2002). Substance abuse and parenting. In M. Bornstein (Ed.), *Handbook of parenting* (2nd ed., Vol. 4). Mahwah, NJ: Erlbaum.

McAdoo, H.P. (1996). *Black families* (3rd ed.). Newbury Park, CA: Sage.

McAdoo, H.P. (2002). African-American parenting. In M. Bornstein (Ed.), *Handbook of parenting* (2nd ed., Vol. 4). Mahwah, NJ: Erlbaum.

McAlister, A., Perry, C., Killen, J., Slinkard, L.A., & Maccoby, N. (1980). Pilot study of smoking, alcohol, and drug abuse prevention. *American Journal of Public Health, 70,* 719–721.

McCormick, C.B., & Pressley, M. (1997). *Educational psychology.* New York: Longman.

McDougall, P., Schonert-Reichl, K., & Hymel, S. (1996, March). *Adolescents at risk for high school dropout: The role of social factors.* Paper presented at the meeting of the Society for Research on Adolescence, Boston.

McHale, J.P., & Grolnick, W.S. (Eds.). (2001). *Retrospect and prospect in the psychological study of families.* Mahwah, NJ: Erlbaum.

McHale, S.M. (1995). Lessons about adolescent development from the study of African-American youth. In L.J. Crockett & A.C. Crouter (Eds.), *Pathways through adolescence.* Hillsdale, NJ: Erlbaum.

McLanahan, S., & Sandefur, G. (1994). *Growing up with a single parent: What hurts, what helps?* Cambridge, MA: Harvard University Press.

McLoyd, V.C. (1990). The impact of economic hardship on Black families and children: Psychological distress, parenting, and socioemotional development. *Child Development, 61,* 311–346.

McLoyd, V.C. (1993, March). *Sizing up the future: Economic stress, expectations, and adolescents' achievement motivation.* Paper presented at the biennial meeting of the Society for Research in Child Development, New Orleans.

McLoyd, V.C. (1998). Children in poverty. In I.E. Siegel & K.A. Renninger (Eds.), *Handbook of child psychology* (5th ed., Vol. 4). New York: Wiley.

McLoyd, V.C. (2000). Poverty. In A. Kazdin (Ed.), *Encyclopedia of psychology.* Washington, DC, and New York: American Psychological Association and Oxford University Press.

McMillan, J.H. (2000). *Educational research* (3rd ed.). New York: HarperCollins.

McMillan, J.H., & Wergin, J.F. (2002). *Understanding and evaluating educational research* (2nd Ed.). Upper Saddle River, NJ: Prentice-Hall.

McNally, D. (1990). *Even eagles need a push.* New York: Dell.

McPartland, J.M., & McDill, E.L. (1976). *The unique role of schools in the causes of youthful crime.* Baltimore: Johns Hopkins University Press.

McRee, J.N., & Gebelt, J.L. (2001, April). *Pubertal development, choice of friends, and adolescent male tobacco use.* Paper presented the meeting of the Society for Research in Child Development, Minneapolis.

Mead, M. (1928). *Coming of age in Samoa.* New York: Morrow.

Mead, M. (1978, Dec. 30–Jan. 5). The American family: An endangered species. *TV Guide.*

Medler, S.M. (2000, April). *Adolescent and best friend smoking behavior: What role does attitude play?* Paper presented at the meeting of the Society for Research on Adolescence, Chicago.

Medrich, E.A., Rosen, J., Rubin, V., & Buckley, S. (1982). *The serious business of growing up.* Berkeley: University of California Press.

Meece, J.L., & Kurtz-Costes, B. (2001). Introduction: The schooling of ethnic minority children. *Educational Psychologist, 36,* 1–8.

Meichenbaum, D., & Butler, L. (1980). Toward a conceptual model of the treatment of test anxiety: Implications for research and treatment. In I.G. Sarason (Ed.), *Test anxiety.* Mahwah, NJ: Erlbaum.

Mekos, E., Hetherington, E.M., & Reiss, D. (1996). Sibling differences in problem behavior: The role of differential treatment in nondivorced and remarried families. *Child Development, 67,* 148–165.

Melby, J.N. (1995, March). *Early family and peer predictors of later adolescent tobacco use.* Paper presented at the meeting of the Society for Research in Child Development, Indianapolis.

Merrell, K.W., & Gimpel, G.A. (1997). *Social skills of children and adolescents.* Mahwah, NJ: Erlbaum.

Messinger, J.C. (1971). Sex and repression in an Irish folk community. In D.S. Marshal & R.C. Suggs (Eds.), *Human sexual behavior: Variations in the ethnographic spectrum* (pp. 3–37). New York: Basic Books.

Metz, E., & McLellan, J.A. (2000, April). *Challenging community service predicts civic engagement and social concerns.* Paper presented at the meeting of the Society for Research on Adolescence, Chicago.

Meyer-Bahlburg, H.F., Ehrhart, A.A., Rosen, L.R., Gruen, R.S., Veridiano, N.P., Vann, F.H., & Neuwalder, H.F. (1995). Prenatal estrogens and the development of homosexual orientation. *Developmental Psychology, 31,* 12–21.

Michael, R.T., Gagnon, J.H., Laumann, E.O., & Kolata, G. (1994). *Sex in America.* Boston: Little, Brown.

Midgley, C. (Ed.), *Goals, goal structures, and patterns of adaptive learning.* Mahwah, NJ: Erlbaum.

Midgley, C., & Urdan, T. (1995). Predictors of middle school students' use of self-handicapping strategies. *Journal of Early Adolescence, 15,* 389–411.

Miller, B.C., Benson, B., & Galbraith, K.A. (2001). Family relationships and adolescent pregnancy risk: A research synthesis. *Developmental Review, 21,* 1–38.

Miller, J.G. (1995, March). *Culture, context, and personal agency: The cultural grounding of self and morality.* Paper presented at the meeting of the Society for Research in Child Development, Indianapolis.

Miller, M.A., Alberts, J.K., Hecht, M.L., Trost, M.R., & Krizek, R.L. (2000). *Adolescent relationships and drug use.* Mahwah, NJ: Erlbaum.

Miller, P.J. (2001, April). *New insights from developmental cultural psychology: What the study of intra-cultural variation can contribute.* Paper presented at the meeting of the Society for Research on Child Development, Minneapolis.

Miller, S.K., & Slap, G.G. (1989). Adolescent smoking: A review of prevalence and prevention. *Journal of Adolescent Health Care, 10,* 129–135.

Miller-Jones, D. (1989). Culture and testing. *American Psychologist, 44,* 360–366.

Millstein, S.G. (1993). A view of health from the adolescent's perspective. In S.G. Millstein, A.C. Petersen, & E.O. Nightingale (Eds.), *Promoting the health of adolescents.* New York: Oxford University Press.

Minuchin, P. (2002). Looking toward the horizon: Present and future in the study of family systems. In J.P. McHale & W.S. Grolnick (Eds.), *Retrospect and prospect in the study of families.* Mahwah, NJ: Erlbaum.

Minuchin, P.P., & Shapiro, E.K. (1983). The school as a context for social development. In P.H. Mussen (Ed.), *Handbook of child psychology* (4th ed., Vol. 4). New York: Wiley.

Mischel, W. (1973). Toward a cognitive social learning reconceptualization of personality. *Psychological Review, 80,* 252–283.

Mischel, W. (1995, August). *Cognitive-affective theory of person-environment psychology.* Paper presented at the meeting of the American Psychological Association, New York City.

Mischel, W., & Mischel, H. (1975, April). *A cognitive social-learning analysis of moral development.* Paper presented at the meeting of the Society for Research in Child Development, Denver.

Mizes, J.S., & Miller, K.J. (2000). Eating disorders. In M. Herson & R.T. Ammerman (Eds.), *Advanced abnormal child psychology* (2nd ed.). Mahwah, NJ: Erlbaum.

Moje, E., Ciechanowski, K.M., Ellis, L., & Carrillo, R. (2002, April). *"I'm not White": Racial and ethnic identity representations among Latino/a youth.* Paper presented at the meeting of the Society for Research on Adolescence, New Orleans.

Moldin, S. (1999). Research methods in behavior genetics. In P. Kendall, J. Butcher, & G. Holmbeck (Eds.), *Handbook of research methods in clinical psychology.* New York: Wiley.

Monteith, M. (2000). Prejudice. In A. Kazdin (Ed.), *Encyclopedia of psychology.* Washington, DC, and New York: American Psychological Association and Oxford University Press.

Montemayor, R. (1982). The relationship between parent-adolescent conflict and the amount of time adolescents spend with parents, peers, and alone. *Child Development, 53,* 1512–1519.

Montemayor, R., & Flannery, D.J. (1991). Parent-adolescent relations in middle and late adolescence. In R.M. Lerner, A.C. Petersen, & J. Brooks-Gunn (Eds.), *Encyclopedia of adolescence* (Vol. 2). New York: Garland.

Montemayor, R., Adams, G.R., & Gulotta, T.P. (Eds.). (1990). *From childhood to adolescence: A transitional period?* Newbury Park, CA: Sage.

Monti, P.M., Colby, S.M., & O'Leary, T.A. (Eds.). (2001). *Adolescents, alcohol, and substance abuse.* New York: Guilford.

Moore, D. (1998, Fall). Gleanings: Focus on work-based learning. *CenterWork Newsletter* (NCRVE, University of California, Berkeley), pp. 1–4.

Moos, R.H., Finney, J.W., & Cronkite, R.C. (1990). *Alcoholism treatment: Context, process, and outcome.* New York: Oxford University Press.

Morales, J., & Roberts, J. (2002, April). *Developmental pathways from peer competence to romantic relationships.* Paper presented at the meeting of the Society for Research on Adolescence, New Orleans.

Morgan, M. (1984). Reward-induced decrements and increments in intrinsic motivation. *Review of Educational Research, 54,* 5–30.

Morgan, M. (1987). Television, sex-role attitudes, and sex-role behavior. *Journal of Early Adolescence, 7,* 269–282.

Morris, L., Warren, C.W., & Aral, S.O. (1993, September). Measuring adolescent sexual behaviors and related health outcomes. *Public Health Reports, 108,* 31–36.

Morrison, L.L., & L'Heureux, J. (2001). Suicide and gay/lesbian/bisexual youth: Implications for clinicians. *Journal of Adolescence, 24,* 39–50.

Morrow, L. (1988, August 8). Through the eyes of children. *Time,* pp. 32–33.

Mortimer, J., & Lorence, J. (1979). Work experience and occupational value socialization: A longitudinal study. *American Journal of Sociology, 84,* 1361–1385.

Mortimer, J., Finch, M., Ryu, S., Shanahan, M., & Call, K. (1996). The effects of work intensity on adolescent mental health, achievement, and behavioral adjustment: New evidence from a prospective study. *Child Development, 67,* 1243–1261.

Mortimer, J.T., Finch, M., Shanahan, M., & Ryu, S. (1992). Work experience, mental health, and behavioral adjustment in adolescence. *Journal of Research on Adolescence, 2,* 24–57.

Mortimer, J.T., Harley, C., & Johnson, M.K. (1998, February). *Adolescent work quality and the transition to adulthood.* Paper presented at the meeting of the Society for Research on Adolescence, San Diego, CA.

Moss, R., & Reyes, O. (2000, April). *The effects of exposure to community violence on urban youth and relevant protective factors.* Paper presented at the meeting of the Society for Research on Adolescence, Chicago.

Mosteller, F. (1995, Summer/Fall). The Tennessee study of class size in the early school grades. *Future of Children, 5* (2), 113–127.

Mott, F.L., & Marsiglio, W. (1985, September/October). Early childbearing and completion of high school. *Family Planning Perspectives,* p. 234.

Mullis, I.V.S., Martin, M.O., Beaton, A.E., Gonzales, E.J., Kelly, D.L., & Smith, T.A. (1998). *Mathematics and science achievement in the final year of secondary school.* Chestnut Hill, MA: Boston College, TIMSS International Study Center.

Munsch, J., Woodward, J., & Darling, N. (1995). Children's perceptions of their relationships with coresiding and non-custodial fathers. *Journal of Divorce and Remarriage, 23,* 39–54.

Murdock, B.B. (1999). Working memory and conscious awareness. In A.F. Collins, S.E. Gatherhole, M.A. Conway, & P.E. Morris (Eds.), *Theories of memory.* Mahwah, NJ: Erlbaum.

Murphy, K., & Schneider, B. (1994). Coaching socially rejected early adolescents regarding behaviors used by peers to infer liking: A dyad-specific intervention. *Journal of Early Adolescence, 14,* 83–95.

Murray, J.P. (2000). Media effects. In A. Kazdin (Ed.), *Encyclopedia of psychology.* Washington, DC, and New York: American Psychological Association and Oxford University Press.

Murrell, A.J. (2000). Discrimination. In A. Kazdin (Ed.), *Encyclopedia of psychology.* Washington, DC, and New York: American Psychological Association and Oxford University Press.

Myers, D.L. (1999). *Excluding violent youths from juvenile court: The effectiveness of legislative waiver.* Doctoral dissertation, University of Maryland, College Park.

N

Nagata, D.K. (1989). Japanese American children and adolescents. In J.T. Gibbs & L.N. Huang (Eds.), *Children of color.* San Francisco: Jossey-Bass.

Naglieri, J. (2000). The Stanford-Binet tests. In A. Kazdin (Ed.), *Encyclopedia of psychology.* Washington, DC, and New York: American Psychological Association and Oxford University Press.

Nansel, T., & Overpeck, M. (2002, April). *The relationship of bullying and being bullied to aggression/violence in a nationally representative sample of U.S. youth.* Paper presented at the meeting of the Society for Research on Adolescence, New Orleans.

Nansel, T.R., Overpeck, M., Pilla, R., Ruan, W., Simons-Morton, B., & Scheidt, P. (2001). Bullying behaviors among U.S. youth. *Journal of the American Medical Association, 285,* 2094–2100.

Nash, J.M. (1997, February 3). Fertile minds. *Time,* pp. 50–54.

National and Community Service Coalition. (1995). *Youth volunteerism.* Washington, DC: Author.

National Assessment of Educational Progress. (1976). *Adult work skills and knowledge* (Report No. 35-COD-01). Denver: National Assessment of Educational Progress.

National Assessment of Educational Progress. (1996). Gender Differences in motivation and strategy use in science. *Journal of Research in Science Teaching, 33,* 393–406.

National Assessment of Educational Progress. (1997). *NAEP 1996 mathematics report card for the nation and the states.* Washington, DC: National Center for Education Statistics.

National Center for Addiction and Substance Abuse. (2001). *2000 teen survey.* New York: Author.

National Center for Education Statistics. (1997). *School-family linkages* [Unpublished manuscript]. Washington, DC: U.S. Department of Education.

National Center for Education Statistics. (1998). *Violence and discipline problems in U.S. public schools.* Washington, DC: Author.

National Center for Education Statistics. (2000). *The condition of education.* Washington, DC: U.S. Department of Education, Office of Educational Research and Improvement.

National Center for Health Statistics. (2000). *Adolescent Health Chartbook in Health, United States, 2000.* Hyattsville, MD: U.S. Department of Health and Human Services.

National Center for Health Statistics. (2000). *Health United States, 2000, with adolescent health chartbook.* Bethesda, MD: U.S. Department of Health and Human Services.

National Center for Health Statistics. (2001). *Health, United States, socioeconomic status.* Atlanta, GA: Centers for Disease Control and Prevention.

National Clearinghouse for Alcohol and Drug Information. (1999). *Physical and psychological effects of anabolic steroids.* Washington, DC: Substance Abuse and Mental Health Services Administration.

National Vital Statistics Reports. (2001). Deaths and death rates for the 10 leading causes of death in specified age groups. *National Vital Statistics Reports, 48* (No. 11), Table 8.

Neemann, J., Hubbard, J., & Masten, A.S. (1995). The changing importance of romantic relationship involvement to competence from childhood to late adolescence. *Development and Psychopathology, 7,* 727–750.

Neimark, E.D. (1982). Adolescent thought: Transition to formal operations. In B.B. Wolman (Ed.), *Handbook of developmental psychology.* Englewood Cliffs, NJ: Prentice Hall.

Neisser, U., Boodoo, G., Bouchard, T.J., Boykin, A.W., Brody, N., Ceci, S.J., Halpern, D.F., Loehlin, J.C., Perloff, R., Sternberg, R.J., & Urbina, S. (1996). Intelligence: Knowns and unknowns. *American Psychologist, 51,* 77–101.

Neugarten, B.L. (1988, August). *Policy issues for an aging society.* Paper presented at the meeting of the American Psychological Association, Atlanta.

Newby, T.J., Stepich, D.A., Lehman, J.D., & Russell, J.D. (2000). *Instructional technology for teaching and learning* (2nd ed.). Upper Saddle River, NJ: Prentice Hall.

Newcomb, M.D., & Bentler, P.M. (1989). Substance use and abuse among children and teenagers. *American Psychologist, 44,* 242–248.

Newcomer, S.F., & Udry, J.R. (1985). Oral sex in an adolescent population. *Archives of Sexual Behavior, 14,* 41–46.

Newman, B.S., & Muzzonigro, P.G. (1993). The effects of traditional family values on the coming out process of gay male adolescents. *Adolescence, 28,* 213–226.

Newman, J.W. (2002). *America's teachers.* Boston: Allyn & Bacon.

Nicholas, G., & Daniel, J.H. (2000, April). *Music videos: Influential or entertaining?* Paper presented at the meeting of the Society for Research on Adolescence, Chicago.

Nicholls, J.G. (1979). Development of perception of own attainment and causal attribution for success and failure in reading. *Journal of Educational Psychology, 71,* 94–99.

Niederjohn, D.M., Welsh, D.P., & Scheussler, M. (2000, April). *Adolescent romantic relationships: Developmental influences of parents and peers.* Paper presented at the meeting of the Society for Research on Adolescence, Chicago.

Nottelmann, E.D., Susman, E.J., Blue, J.H., Inoff-Germain, G., Dorn, L.D., Loriaux, D.L., Cutler, G.B., & Chrousos, G.P. (1987). Gonadal and adrenal hormone correlates of adjustment in early adolescence. In R.M. Lerner & T.T. Foch (Eds.), *Biological-psychological interactions in early adolescence.* Hillsdale, NJ: Erlbaum.

Nucci, L. (1996). Morality and the personal sphere of actions. In E. Reed, E. Turiel, & T. Brown (Eds.), *Values and knowledge.* Mahwah, NJ: Erlbaum.

Nucci, L. (2001). *Education in the moral domain.* Cambridge, UK: Cambridge University Press.

O

O'Brien, R.W. (1990, March). *The use of family members and peers as resources during adolescence.* Paper presented at the meeting of the Society for Research in Adolescence, Atlanta.

O'Connor, T.G. (1994, February). *Patterns of differential parental treatment.* Paper presented at the meeting of the Society for Research on Adolescence, San Diego.

O'Connor, T.G., Hetherington, E.M., Reiss, D., & Plomin, R. (1995). A twin-sibling study of observed parent-adolescent interactions. *Child Development, 66,* 812–829.

O'Quin, K., & Dirks, P. (1999). Humor. In M.A. Runco & S. Pritzker (Eds.), *Encyclopedia of creativity.* San Diego: Academic Press.

Oakes, J., & Lipton, M. (2003). *Teaching to change the world* (2nd Ed.). New York: McGraw-Hill.

Oden, S.L., & Asher, S.R. (1975, April). *Coaching children in social skills for friendship making.* Paper presented at the meeting of the Society for Research in Child Development, Denver.

Offer, D., Ostrov, E., Howard, K.I., & Atkinson, R. (1988). *The teenage world: Adolescents' self-image in ten countries.* New York: Plenum.

Office of Juvenile Justice and Prevention. (1998). *Arrests in the United States under age 18: 1997.* Washington, DC: Author.

Ogbu, J.U. (1989, April). *Academic socialization of black children: An inoculation against future failure?* Paper presented at the meeting of the Society for Research in Child Development, Kansas City.

Ogbu, J., & Stern, P. (2001). Caste status and intellectual development. In R.J. Sternberg & E.L. Grigorenko (Eds.). *Environmental effects on cognitive abilities.* Mahwah, NJ: Erlbaum.

Olivardia, R., Pope, H.G., Mangweth, B., & Hudson, J.I. (1995). Eating disorders in college men. *American Journal of Psychiatry, 152,* 1279–1284.

Olweus, D. (1980). Bullying among schoolboys. In R. Barnen (Ed.), *Children and violence.* Stockholm: Acaemic Litteratur.

Olweus, D. (1993). *Bullying at school.* Cambridge, MA: Blackwell.

Olweus, D. (1994). Development of stable aggressive reaction patterns in males. *Advances in the study of aggression* (Vol. 1). Orlando: Academic Press.

Orlofsky, J. (1976). Intimacy status: Relationship to interpersonal perception. *Journal of Youth and Adolescence, 5,* 73–88.

Orlofsky, J., Marcia, J., & Lesser, I. (1973). Ego identity status and the intimacy vs. isolation crisis of young adulthood. *Journal of Personality and Social Psychology, 27,* 211–219.

Orthner, D.K., Giddings, M., & Quinn, W. (1987). *Youth in transition: A study of adolescents from Air Force and civilian families.* Washington, DC: U.S. Air Force.

Oser, F., & Gmünder, P. (1991). *Religious judgment: A developmental perspective.* Birmingham, AL: Religious Education Press.

Osipow, S.H., & Littlejohn, E.M. (1995). Toward a multicultural theory of career development: Prospects and dilemmas. In F.T.L. Leong (Ed.), *Career development and vocational behavior of racial and ethnic minorities.* Hillsdale, NJ: Erlbaum.

Osofsky, J.D. (1990, Winter). Risk and protective factors for teenage mothers and their infants. *SRCD Newsletter,* pp. 1–2.

Overton, W.F., & Byrnes, J.P. (1991). Cognitive development. In R.M. Lerner, A.C. Petersen, & J. Brooks-Gunn (Eds.), *Encyclopedia of adolescence* (Vol. 1). New York: Garland.

Owens, T., Stryker, S., & Goodman, N. (Eds.) (2001). *Extending self-esteem theory and research.* New York: Cambridge University Press.

P

Paige, K.E., & Paige, J.M. (1985). *Politics and reproductive rituals.* Berkeley: University of California Press.

Paikoff, R.L., Parfenoff, S.H., Williams, S.A., McCormick, A., Greenwood, G.L., & Holmbeck, G.N. (1997). Parenting, parent-child relationships, and sexual possibility situations among urban African American preadolescents: Preliminary findings and implications for HIV prevention. *Journal of Family Psychology, 11,* 11–22.

Paloutzian, R. (2000). *Invitation to the psychology of religion* (3rd ed.). Boston: Allyn & Bacon.

Paloutzian, R., & Santrock, J.W. (2000). The psychology of religion. In J.W. Santrock, *Psychology* (6th ed.). New York: McGraw-Hill.

Paludi, M.A. (1998). *The psychology of women.* Upper Saddle River, NJ: Prentice-Hall.

Papini, D., & Sebby, R. (1988). Variations in conflictual family issues by adolescent pubertal status, gender, and family member. *Journal of Early Adolescence, 8,* 1–15.

Parcel, G.S., Simons-Morton, G.G., O'Hara, N.M., Baranowski, T., Kolbe, L.J., & Bee, D.E. (1987). School promotion of healthful diet and exercise behavior: An integration of organizational change and social learning theory interventions. *Journal of School Health, 57,* 150–156.

Paris, S.G., & Paris, A.H. (2001). Classroom applications of research on self-regulated learning. *Educational Psychologist, 36,* 89–102.

Parke, R.D. (1995). Fathers and families. In M.H. Bornstein (Ed.), *Children and parenting* (Vol. 3). Hillsdale, NJ: Erlbaum.

Parke, R.D. (2001). Parenting in the new millennium: Prospects, promises, and pitfalls. In J.P. McHale & W.S. Grolnick (Eds.), *Retrospect and prospect in the psychological study of families.* Mahwah, NJ: Erlbaum.

Parke, R.D. (2002). Fathers and families. In M. Bornstein (Ed.), *Handbook of parenting* (2nd ed., Vol. 3). Mahwah, NJ: Erlbaum.

Parke, R.D., & Buriel, R. (1998). Socialization in the family. In N. Eisenberg (Ed.), *Handbook of child psychology* (5th ed., Vol. 3). New York: Wiley.

Parke, R.D., McDowell, D.J., Kim, M., Killian, C., Dennis, J., Flyr, M.L., & Wild, M.N. (2002). Fathers' contributions to chlidren's peer relationships. In C.S. Tamis-LeMonda & N. Cabrera (Eds.), *The handbook of father involvement.* Mahwah, NJ: Erlbaum.

Parker, A., & Fischhoff, B. (2002, April). *Individual differences in decision-making competence.* Paper presented at the meeting of the Society for Research on Adolescence, New Orleans.

Parker, L. (2002, April). *A correlational analysis of factors associated with bullying.* Paper presented at the meeting of the Society for Research on Adolescence, New Orleans.

Pate, R.R., Trost, S.G., Levin, S., & Dowda, M. (2000). Sports participation and health-related behaviors of U.S. youth. *Archives of Pediatric and Adolescent Medicine, 154,* 904–911.

Patterson, C.J. (1995). Sexual orientation and human development: An overview. *Developmental Psychology, 31,* 3–11.

Patterson, G.R., & Stouthamer-Loeber, M. (1984). The correlation of family management practices and delinquency. *Child Development, 55,* 1299–1307.

Patterson, G.R., DeBaryshe, B.D., & Ramsey, E. (1989). A developmental perspective on antisocial behavior. *American Psychologist, 44,* 329–335.

Patterson, S.J., Sochting, I., & Marcia, J.E. (1992). The inner space and beyond: Women and identity. In G.R. Adams, T.P. Gullotta, & R. Montemayor (Eds.), *Adolescent identity formation.* Newbury Park, CA: Sage.

Paul, E.L. (2000). *Taking Sides: Controversial issues in sex and gender.* New York: McGraw-Hill.

Paul, E.L., & White, K.M. (1990). The development of intimate relationships in late adolescence. *Adolescence, 25,* 375–400.

Peak, L. (1996). *Pursuing excellence: A study of U.S. eighth-grade mathematics and science teaching, learning, curriculum, and achievement in international context.* Washington, DC: U.S. Department of Education, National Center for Educational Statistics.

Pellegrini, A.D. (2000, April). *Longitudinal study of bullying, victimization, and peer affiliation during the transition to middle school.* Paper presented at the meeting of the Society for Research on Adolescence, Chicago.

Pentz, M.A. (1994). Primary prevention of adolescent drug abuse. In C. Fisher & R. Lerner (Eds.), *Applied developmental psychology.* New York: McGraw-Hill.

Peplau, L.A., & Perlman, D. (Eds.). (1982). *Loneliness: A sourcebook of current theory, research, and therapy.* New York: Wiley.

Perkins, D. (1999). The many faces of constructivism. *Educational Leadership, 57* (3), 6–11.

Perry, C., Hearn, M., Murray, D., & Klepp, K. (1988). *The etiology and prevention of adolescent alcohol and drug abuse.* Unpublished manuscript, University of Minnesota.

Perry, C.L., Kelder, S.H., & Komro, K.A. (1993). The social world of adolescents: Families, peers, schools, and the community. In S.G. Millstein, A.C. Petersen, & E.O. Nightingale (Eds.), *Promoting the health of adolescents.* New York: Oxford University Press.

Perry, W.G. (1970). *Forms of intellectual and ethical development in the college years.* New York: Holt, Rinehart & Winston.

Perry, W.G. (1999). *Forms of ethical and intellectual development in the college years: A scheme.* San Francisco: Jossey-Bass.

Perry-Jenkins, M., Payne, J., & Hendricks, E. (1999, April). *Father involvement by choice or necessity: Implications for parents' well-being.* Paper presented at the meeting of the Society for Research in Child Development, Albuquerque.

Peskin, H. (1967). Pubertal onset and ego functioning. *Journal of Abnormal Psychology, 72,* 1–15.

Peters, K.F., Menaker, T.J., Wilson, P.L., & Hadley, D.W. (2001). The Human Genome Project: An update. *Cancer and Nursing, 24,* 287–292.

Petersen, A. C. (1993). Creating adolescents: The role of context and process in developmental trajectories. *Journal of Research on Adolescence, 3,* 1–18.

Petersen, A.C. (1979, January). Can puberty come any faster? *Psychology Today,* pp. 45–56.

Petersen, A.C. (1987, September). Those gangly years. *Psychology Today,* pp. 28–34.

Petersen, A.C., & Crockett, L. (1985). Pubertal timing and grade effects on adjustment. *Journal of Youth and Adolescence, 14,* 191–206.

Petersen, A.C., Sarigiani, P.A., & Kennedy, R.E. (1991). Coping with adolescence. In M.E. Colte & S. Gore (Eds.), *Adolescent stress: Causes and consequences.* New York: Aldine de Gruyter.

Peterson, K.A. (1997, September 3). In high school, dating is a world unto itself. *USA Today,* pp. 1–2D.

Peterson, P.L., Hawkins, J.D., Abbott, R.D., & Catalano, R.F. (1994). Disentangling the effects of parent drinking, family management, and parental alcohol norms on current drinking by Black and White adolescents. *Journal of Research on Adolescence, 4,* 203–228.

Petraitis, J., Flay, B.R., & Miller, T.Q. (1995). Reviewing theories of adolescent substance use: Organizing pieces of the puzzle. *Psychological Bulletin, 17,* 67–86.

Pettit, G.S., Bates, J.E., Dodge, K.A., & Meece, D.W. (1999). The impact of after-school peer contact on early adolescent externalizing problems is moderated by parental monitoring, perceived neighborhood safety, and prior adjustment. *Child Development, 70,* 768–778.

Pettit, G.S., Laird, R.D., Dodge, K.A., Bates, J.A., & Criss, M.M. (2001). Antecedents and behavior-problem outcomes of parental monitoring and psychological control in early adolescence. *Child Development, 72,* 583–598.

Pfefferbaum, A., Mathalon, D.H., Sullivan, E.V., Rawles, J.M., Zipursky, R.B., & Lim, K.O. (1994). A quantitative magnetic resonance imaging study of changes in brain morphology from infancy to late adulthood. *Archives of Neurology, 51,* 874.

Philpot, C.L., Brooks, G.R., Lusterman, D., & Nutt, R.L. (1997). *Bridging separate gender worlds.* Washington, DC: American Psychological Association.

Phinney, J.S. (1989). Stages of ethnic identity development in minority group adolescents. *Journal of Early Adolescence, 9,* 34–49.

Phinney, J.S. (1996). When we talk about American ethnic groups, what do we mean? *American Psychologist, 51,* 918–927.

Phinney, J.S. (2000). Ethnic identity. In A. Kazdin (Ed.), *Encyclopedia of psychology.* Washington, DC, and New York: American Psychological Association and Oxford University Press.

Phinney, J.S. (2000, April). *Family obligations and life satisfaction among adolescents from immigrant families.* Paper presented at the meeting of the Society for Research on Adolescence, Chicago.

Phinney, J.S., & Alipuria, L.L. (1990). Ethnic identity in college students from four ethnic groups. *Journal of Adolescence, 13,* 171–183.

Phinney, J.S., & Devich-Navarro, M. (1997). Variations in bicultural identification among African American and Mexican American adolescents. *Journal of Research on Adolescence, 7,* 3–32.

Phinney, J.S., Ferguson, D.L., & Tate, J.D. (1997). Intergroup attitudes among ethnic minority adolescents: A causal model. *Child Development, 68,* 955–969.

Phinney, J.S., & Landin, J. (1998). Research paradigms for studying ethnic minority families within and across groups. In V.C. McLoyd & L. Steinberg (Eds.), *Studying minority adolescents.* Mahwah, NJ: Erlbaum.

Phinney, J.S., Madden, T., & Ong, A. (2000). Cultural values and intergenerational discrepancies in immigrant and non-immigrant families. *Child Development, 71,* 528–539.

Phinney, J.S., & Rosenthal, D.A. (1992). Ethnic identity in adolescence: Process, context, and outcome. In G.R. Adams, T.P. Gullotta, & R. Montemayor (Eds.), *Adolescent identity formation.* Newbury Park, CA: Sage.

Piaget, J. (1932). *The moral judgment of the child.* New York: Harcourt Brace Jovanovich.

Piaget, J. (1952). *The origins of intelligence in children.* New York: International Universities Press.

Piaget, J. (1954). *The construction of reality in the child.* New York: Basic Books.

Piaget, J. (1972). Intellectual evolution from adolescence to adulthood. *Human Development, 15,* 1–12.

Pintrich, P.R., & Schunk, D.H. (2002). *Motivation in education.* (2nd Ed.). Boston: Allyn & Bacon.

Pisani, E. (2001). AIDS in the 21st century: Some critical considerations. *Reproductive Health Matters, 8,* 63–76.

Pittman, L.D. (2000, April). *Links to parenting practices of African American mothers in impoverished neighborhoods.* Paper presented at the meeting of the Society for Research on Adolescence, Chicago.

Place, D.M. (1975). The dating experience for adolescent girls. *Adolescence, 38,* 157–173.

Pleck, J.H. (1981). *The myth of masculinity.* Beverly Hills, CA: Sage.

Pleck, J.H. (1983). The theory of male sex role identity: Its rise and fall, 1936–present. In M. Lewin (Ed.), *In the shadow of the past: Psychology portrays the sexes.* New York: Columbia University Press.

Pleck, J.H. (1995). The gender-role strain paradigm: An update: In R.F. Levant & W.S. Pollack (Eds.), *A new psychology of men.* New York: Basic.

Pleck, J.H. (1997). Paternal involvement: Levels, sources, and consequences. In M.E. Lamb (Ed.), *The role of the father in child development.* New York: Wiley.

Pleck, J.H., Sonnenstein, F., & Ku, L. (1991). Adolescent males' condom use. Relationships between perceived cost benefits and consistency. *Journal of Marriage and the Family, 53,* 733–745.

Pleck, J.H., Sonnenstein, F., & Ku, L. (1994). Problem behaviors and masculine ideology in adolescent males. In R. Ketterlinus & M.E. Lamb (Eds.), *Adolescent problem behaviors.* Hillsdale, NJ: Erlbaum.

Pleiss, M.K., & Feldhusen, J.F. (1995). Mentors, role models, and heroes in the lives of gifted children. *Educational Psychologist, 30,* 159–169.

Plomin, R. (1993, March). *Human behavioral genetics and development: An overview and update.* Paper presented at the biennial meeting of the Society for Research in Child Development, New Orleans.

Plomin, R., DeFries, J.C., McClearn, G.E., & Rutter, M. (1997). *Behavioral genetics* (3rd ed.). New York: W. H. Freeman.

Plomin, R., Reiss, D., Hetherington, E.N., & Howe, G.W. (1994). Nature and nurture: Contributions to measures of family environment. *Developmental Psychology, 30,* 32–43.

Poll finds racial tension decreasing. (1990, June 29). *Asian Week,* p. 4.

Pollack, W. (1999). *Real boys.* New York: Henry Holt.

Poortinga, Y.H. (2000). Cross-cultural test adaptation. In A. Kazdin (Ed.), *Encyclopedia of psychology.* Washington, DC, and New York: American Psychological Association and Oxford University Press.

Popper, S.D., Ross, S., & Jennings, K.D. (2000). Development and psychopathology. In M. Herson & R.T. Ammerman (Eds.), *Advanced abnormal child psychopathology.* Mahwah, NJ: Erlbaum.

Porter, M. (2000, April). *Social-cognitive development and friendship competence in adolescence.* Paper presented at the meeting of the Society for Research on Adolescence, Chicago.

Potvin, L., Champagne, F., & Laberge-Nadeau, C. (1988). Mandatory driver training and road safety: The Quebec experience. *American Journal of Public Health, 78,* 1206–1212.

Powell, A.G., Farrar, E., & Cohen, D.K. (1985). *The shopping mall high school: Winners and losers in the educational marketplace.* Boston: Houghton Mifflin.

Powers, S.I., Welsh, D.P., & Wright, V. (1994). Adolescents' affective experience of family behaviors: The role of subjective understanding. *Journal of Research in Adolescence, 4,* 585–600.

Presidential Task Force on Psychology and Education. (1992). *Learner-centered psychological principles: Guidelines for school redesign and reform (draft).* Washington, DC: American Psychological Association.

Pressley, M. (1983). Making meaningful materials easier to learn. In M. Pressley & J.R. Levin (Eds.), *Cognitive strategy research: Educational applications* (pp. 239–266). New York: Springer-Verlag.

Pressley, M. (1995). More about the development of self-regulation: Complex, long-term, and thoroughly social. *Educational Psychologist, 30,* 207–212.

Pressley, M., & Roehrig, A. (2002). Educational psychology in the modern period. In B.J. Zimmerman & D.H. Schunk (Eds.), *Educational psychology.* Mahwah, NJ: Erlbaum.

Pressley, M., & Schneider, W. (1997). *Introduction to memory development during childhood and adolescence.* Mahwah, NJ: Erlbaum.

Price, J.H. (2001). Violence, mental health, and youths. *American Journal of Health Education, 32,* 130–131.

Price, R.H., Cioci, M., Penner, W., & Trautlein, B. (1990). *School and community support programs that enhance adolescent health and education.* Washington, DC: Carnegie Council on Adolescent Development.

Prinsky, L.E., & Rosenbaum, J.L. (1987). Leerics or lyrics? *Youth and Society, 18,* 384–394.

Prinstein, M.J., Fetter, M.D., & La Greca, A.M. (1996, March). *Can you judge adolescents by the company they keep? Peer group membership, substance use, and risk-taking behaviors.* Paper presented at the meeting of the Society for Research on Adolescence, Boston.

Psathas, G. (1957). Ethnicity, social class, and adolescent independence. *Sociological Review, 22,* 415–523.

Quadrel, M.J., Fischoff, B., & Davis, W. (1993). Adolescent (in)vulnerability. *American Psychologist, 48,* 102–116.

Quinton, D., Rutter, M., & Gulliver, L. (1990). Continuities in psychiatric disorders from childhood to adulthood in the children of psychiatric patients. In L. Robins & M. Rutter (Eds.), *Straight and devious pathways from childhood to adulthood.* New York: Cambridge University Press.

Raffaelli, M., & Ontai, L. (in press). "She's sixteen years old and there's boys calling over to the house": An exploratory study of sexual socialization in Latino families. *Culture, Health, and Sexuality.*

Rainey, R. (1965). The effects of directed vs. non-directed laboratory work on high school chemistry achievement. *Journal of Research in Science Teaching, 3,* 286–292.

Rajapakse, J.C., DeCarli, C., McLaughlin, A., Giedd, J.N., Krain, A.L., Hamburger, S.D., & Rapoport, J.L. (1996). Cerebral magnetic resonance image segmentation using data fusion. *Journal of Computer Assisted Tomography, 20,* 206.

Ramey, S.L., & Ramey, C.T. (2000). Early childhood experiences and developmental competence. In S. Danzinger & J. Waldfogel (Eds.), *Securing the future: Investing in children from birth to college.* New York: Russell Sage Foundation.

Ramirez, O. (1989). Mexican American children and adolescents. In J.T. Gibbs & L.N. Huang (Eds.), *Children of color.* San Francisco: Jossey-Bass.

Raskin, P.M. (1985). Identity in vocational development. In A.S. Waterman (Ed.), *Identity in adolescence.* San Francisco: Jossey-Bass.

Raymore, L.A., Barber, B.L., & Eccles, J.S. (2001). Leaving home, attending college, partnership, and parenthood: The role of life transition events in leisure pattern stability from adolescence to early adulthood. *Journal of Youth and Adolescence, 30,* 197–223.

Regnerus, M.D. (2001). *Making the Grade: The Influence of Religion upon the Academic Performance of Youth in Disadvantaged Communities.* Report 01-04, Center for Research on Religion and Urban Civil Society, University of Pennsylvania.

Reinherz, H.Z., Giaconia, R.M., Silverman, A.B., & Friedman, A.C. (1994, February). *Early psychosocial risks for adolescent suicidal ideation and attempts.* Paper presented at the meeting of the Society for Research on Adolescence, San Diego.

Reinisch, J.M. (1990). *The Kinsey Institute new report on sex: What you must know to be sexually literate.* New York: St. Martin's Press.

Remafedi, G., French, S., Story, M., Resnick, M.D., & Blum, R. (1998). The relationship between suicide risk and sexual orientation: Results of a population-based study. *American Journal of Public Health, 88,* 57–60.

Remez, L. (2000). Oral sex among adolescents: Is it sex or is it abstinence? *Family Planning Perspectives, 32,* 212–226.

Repinski, D.J., & Leffert, N. (1994, February). *Adolescents' relationships with friends: The effects of a psychoeducational intervention.* Paper presented at the biennial meeting of the Society for Research on Adolescence, San Diego.

Reschly, D. (1996). Identification and assessment of students with disabilities. *Future of children, 6* (1), 40–53.

Resnick, L., & Nelson-Gall, S. (1997). Socializing intelligence. In L. Smith, J. Dockrell, & P. Tomlinson (Eds.), *Piaget, Vygotsky, and beyond.* London: Routledge Paul.

Resnick, M.D., Wattenberg, E., & Brewer, R. (1992, March). *Paternity avowal/disavowal among partners of low income mothers.* Paper presented at the meeting of the Society for Research on Adolescence, Washington, DC.

Rest, J.R. (1986). *Moral development: Advances in theory and research.* New York: Praeger.

Rest, J.R., Narvaez, D., Bebeau, M.J., & Thoma, S.J. (1999). *Postconventional moral thinking.* Mahwah, NJ: Erlbaum.

Reuter, M.W., & Biller, H.B. (1973). Perceived paternal nurturance-availability and personality adjustment among college males. *Journal of Consulting and Clinical Psychology, 40,* 339–342.

Reynolds, D. (2000). School effectiveness and improvement. In A. Kazdin (Ed.), *Encyclopedia of psychology.* Washington, DC, and New York: American Psychological Association and Oxford University Press.

Richards, M., Suleiman, L., Sims, B., & Sedeno, A. (1994, February). *Experiences of ethnically diverse young adolescents growing up in poverty.* Paper presented at the meeting of the Society for Research on Adolescence, San Diego.

Richards, M.H., Crowe, P.A., Larson, R., & Swarr, A. (1998). Developmental patterns and gender differences in the experience of peer companionship during adolescence. *Child Development, 69,* 154–163.

Richards, M.H., & Duckett, E. (1994). The relationship of maternal employment to early adolescent daily experiences with and without parents. *Child Development, 65,* 225–236.

Richards, M.H., & Larson, R. (1990, July). *Romantic relations in early adolescence.* Paper presented at the Fifth International Conference on Personal Relations, Oxford University, England.

Richardson, J.L., Dwyer, K., McGrugan, K., Hansen, W.B., Dent, C., Johnson, C.A., Sussman, S.Y., Brannon, B., & Glay, B. (1989). Substance use among eighth-grade students who take care of themselves after school. *Pediatrics, 84,* 556–566.

Rickards, T. (1999). Brainstorming. In M.A. Runco & S. Pritzker (Eds.), *Encyclopedia of creativity.* San Diego: Academic Press.

Rimberg, H.M., & Lewis, R.J. (1994). Older adolescents and AIDS: Correlates of self-reported safer sex practices. *Journal of Research on Adolescence, 4,* 453–464.

Roberts, D., Jacobson, L., & Taylor, R.D. (1996, March). *Neighborhood characteristics, stressful life events, and African-American adolescents' adjustment.* Paper presented at the meeting of the Society for Research on Adolescence, Boston.

Roberts, D.F. (1993). Adolescents and the mass media: From "Leave It to Beaver" to "Beverly Hills 90210." In R. Takanishi (Ed.), *Adolescence in the 1990s.* New York: Teachers College Press.

Roberts, G.C., Treasure, D.C., & Kavussanu, M. (1997). Motivation in physical activity contexts: An achievement goal perspective. *Advances in Motivation and Achievement, 10,* 413–447.

Robinson, D.P., & Greene, J.W. (1988). The adolescent alcohol and drug problem: A practical approach. *Pediatric Nursing, 14,* 305–310.

Robinson, N.S. (1995). Evaluating the nature of perceived support and its relation to perceived self-worth in adolescents. *Journal of Research on Adolescence, 5,* 253–280.

Roblyer, M.D., & Edwards, J. (2000). *Integrating educational psychology into teaching.* (2nd ed.). Upper Saddle River, NJ: Prentice Hall.

Rockhill, C.M., & Greener, S.M. (1999, April). *Development of the Meta-Mood Scale for elementary-school children.* Paper presented at the meeting of the Society for Research in Child Development, Albuquerque.

Rodgers, C. (2000). Gender schema. In A. Kazdin (Ed.), *Encyclopedia of psychology.* Washington, DC, and New York: American Psychological Association and Oxford University Press.

Rodriquez, M.L., & Quinlan, S.L. (2002, April). *Searching for a meaningful identity: Self/ethnic representations and family beliefs in Latino youth.* Paper presented at the meeting of the Society for Research on Adolescence, New Orleans.

Roe, A. (1956). *The psychology of occupations.* New York: Wiley.

Roemmich, J.N., Clark, P.A., Berr, S.S., Mai, V., Mantzoros, C.S., Flier, J.S., Weltman, A., & Rogol, A.D. (1999). Gender differences in leptin levels during puberty are related to the subcutaneous fat depot and sex steroids. *American Journal of Physiology, 275,* E543–551.

Roff, M., Sells, S.B., & Golden, M.W. (1972). *Social adjustment and personality development in children.* Minneapolis: University of Minnesota Press.

Rog, E., Hunsberger, B., & Alisat, S. (2002, April). *Bridging the gap between high-school and college through a social support intervention: A long-term evaluation.* Paper presented at the meeting of the Society for Research on Adolescence, New Orleans.

Rogatch, F.A., Cicchetti, D., Shields, A., & Toth, S.L. (1995). Parenting dysfunction in child maltreatment. In M.H. Bornstein (Ed.), *Handbook of parenting* (Vol. 4). Hillsdale, NJ: Erlbaum.

Rogers, A. (1987). *Questions of gender differences: Ego development and moral voice in adolescence.* Unpublished manuscript, Department of Education, Harvard University.

Rogers, C.R. (1950). The significance of the self regarding attitudes and perceptions. In M.L. Reymart (Ed.), *Feelings and emotions.* New York: McGraw-Hill.

Rogoff, B. (1990). *Apprenticeship in thinking.* New York: Oxford University Press.

Rogoff, B. (1998). Cognition as a collaborative process. In W. Damon (Ed.), *Handbook of child psychology* (5th ed., Vol. 2). New York: Wiley.

Rogoff, B., Baker-Sennett, J., Lacasa, P., & Goldsmith, D. (1995). Development through participation in sociocultural activity. *Cultural practices as contexts for development: New Directions for Child Development, 67* (Spring), 45–65.

Rogol, A.D., Roemmich, J.N., & Clark, P.A. (1998, September). *Growth at Puberty.* Paper presented at a workshop, Physical Development, Health Futures of Youth II: Pathways to Adolescent Health, Maternal and Child Health Bureau, Annapolis, MD.

Rohner, R.P., & Rohner, E.C. (1981). Parental acceptance-rejection and parental control: Cross-cultural codes. *Ethnology, 20,* 245–260.

Romo, H. (2000, April). *Keeping Latino youth in school.* Paper presented at the meeting of the Society for Research on Adolescence, Chicago.

Rose, H.A., & Rodgers, K.B. (2000, April). *Suicide ideation in adolescents who are confused about sexual orientation: A risk and resiliency approach.* Paper presented at the meeting of the Society for Research in Adolescence, Chicago.

Rose, S., & Frieze, I.R. (1993). Young singles' contemporary dating scripts. *Sex Roles, 28,* 499–509.

Rose, S.A., Feldman, J.F., McCarton, C.M., & Wolfson, J. (1988). Information processing in seven-month-old infants as a function of risk status. *Child Development, 59,* 489–603.

Rosenbaum, E., & Kandel, D.B. (1990). Early onset of adolescent sexual behavior and drug involvement. *Journal of Marriage and the Family, 52,* 783–798.

Rosenberg, M. (1979). *Conceiving the self.* New York: Basic Books.

Rosenthal, R. (2000). Expectancy effects. In A. Kazdin (Ed.), *Encyclopedia of psychology.* Washington, DC, & New York: American Psychological Association and Oxford University Press.

Rosner, B.A., & Rierdan, J. (1994, February). *Adolescent girls' self-esteem: Variations in developmental trajectories.* Paper presented at the meeting of the Society for Research on Adolescence, San Diego.

Rosnow, R.L. (2000). Longitudinal research. In A. Kazdin (Ed.), *Encyclopedia of psychology.* Washington, DC, & New York: American Psychological Association and Oxford University Press.

Rosselli, H.C. (1996, Feb/Mar). Gifted students. *National Association for Secondary School Principals,* pp. 12–17.

Rotenberg, K.J. (1993, March). *Development of restrictive disclosure to friends.* Paper presented at the biennial meeting of the Society for Research in Child Development, New Orleans.

Roth, J., & Brooks-Gunn, J. (2000). What do adolescents need for healthy development? Implications for youth policy. *Social Policy Report, Society for Research in Child Development, XIV* (No. 1), 1–19.

Roth, J., Brooks-Gunn, J., Murray, L., & Foster, W. (1998). Promoting healthy adolescents: Synthesis of youth development program evaluations. *Journal of Research on Adolescence, 8,* 423–459.

Rothbaum, F., Poll, M., Azuma, H., Miyake, K., & Weisz, J. (2000). The development of close relationships in Japan and the United States: Paths of symbiotic harmony and generative tension. *Child Development, 71,* 1121–1142.

Rubin, K.H. (2000). Middle childhood: Social and emotional development. In A. Kazdin (Ed.), *Encyclopedia of psychology*. Washington, DC, and New York: American Psychological Association and Oxford University Press.

Rubin, K.H., Bukowski, W., & Parker, J.G. (1998). Peer interactions, relationships, and groups. In N. Eisenberg (Ed.), *Handbook of child psychology* (5th ed., Vol. 3). New York: Wiley.

Rubin, K.H., Mills, R.S.L., & Rose-Krasnor, L. (1989). Maternal beliefs and children's competence. In B. Schneider, G. Attili, J. Nadel, & R. Weissberg (Eds.), *Social competence in developmental perspective*. Amsterdam: Kluwer Academic.

Rubin, Z., & Solman, J. (1984). How parents influence their children's friendships. In M. Lewis (Ed.), *Beyond the dyad*. New York: Plenum.

Ruble, D.N., & Martin, C.L. (1998). Gender development. In N. Eisenberg (Ed.), *Handbook of child psychology* (5th ed., Vol. 3). New York: Wiley.

Ruble, D.N., Boggiano, A.K., Feldman, N.S., & Loebl, J.H. (1980). Developmental analysis of the role of social comparison in self evaluation. *Developmental Psychology, 16*, 105–115.

Rudolph, K.D., Lambert, S.F., Clark, A.G., & Kurlakowsky, K.D. (2001). Negotiating the transition to middle school: The role of self-regulatory processes. *Child Development, 72*, 929–946.

Rumberger, R.W. (1983). Dropping out of high school: The influence of race, sex, and family background. *American Educational Research Journal, 20*, 199–220.

Rumberger, R.W. (1995). Dropping out of middle school: A multilevel analysis of students and schools. *American Educational Research Journal, 3*, 583–625.

Runco, M. (2000). Creativity: Research on the processes of creativity. In A. Kazdin (Ed.), *Encyclopedia of psychology*. Washington, DC, and New York: American Psychological Association and Oxford University Press.

Russell, S.T., & Truong, N.L. (2002, April). *Adolescent sexual orientation, family relationships, and emotional health*. Paper presented at the meeting of the Society for Research on Adolescence, New Orleans.

Rutter, M. (2002). Family influences on behavior and development. In J.P. McHale & W.S. Grolnick (Eds.), *Retrospect and prospect in the study of families*. Mahwah, NJ: Erlbaum.

Rutter, M., Maughan, B., Mortimore, P., & Ouston, J. (1979). *Fifteen thousand hours: Secondary schools and their effects on children*. Cambridge, MA: Harvard University Press.

Ryan, A.M. (2001). The peer group as a context for development of adolescent motivation and achievement. *Child Development, 72*, 1135–1150.

Ryan, A.M., & Patrick, H. (1996, March). *Positive peer relationships and psychosocial adjustment during adolescence*. Paper presented at the meeting of the Society for Research on Adolescence, Boston.

Ryan-Finn, K.D., Cause, A.M., & Grove, K. (1995, March). *Children and adolescents of color: Where are you? Selection, recruitment, and retention in developmental research*. Paper presented at the meeting of the Society for Research in Child Development, Indianapolis.

Saarni, C. (1988). Children's understanding of the interpersonal consequences of dissemblance of nonverbal emotional-expressive behavior. *Journal of Nonverbal Behavior, 12*, 275–294.

Saarni, C. (1999). *The development of emotional competence*. New York: Guilford.

Sadeh, A., Raviv, A., & Gruber, R. (2000). Sleep patterns and sleep disruptions in school-age children. *Developmental Psychology, 36*, 291–301.

Sadker, M., & Sadker, D. (1986, March). Sexism in the classroom: From grade school to graduate school. *Phi Delta Kappan*, pp. 512–515.

Sadker, M., & Sadker, D. (1994). *Failing at fairness*. New York: Touchstone.

Sadker, M., & Sadker, D. (2003). *Teachers, schools, and society* (6th Ed.). New York: McGraw-Hill

Salas, J. (2000, April). *Special relationships with teachers facilitate school success: Perspectives of Mexican American students from poor and working-class families*. Paper presented at the meeting of the Society for Research on Adolescence, Chicago.

Saliba, J.A. (1996). *Understanding new religious movements*. Grand Rapids, MI: William B. Erdmans.

Salovy, P., & Mayer, J.D. (1990). Emotional intelligence. *Imagination, Cognition, and Personality, 9*, 185–211.

Salovy, P., & Woolery, A. (2000). Emotional intelligence: Categorization and measurement. In G. Fletcher & M.S. Clark (Eds.), *The Blackwell handbook of social psychology* (Vol. 2). Oxford, UK: Blackwell.

Santelli, J.S., Rogin, L., Brener, N.D., & Lowry, R. (2001, March). *Timing of alcohol and other drug use and sexual risk behaviors among unmarried adolescents*. Paper presented at the meeting of the Society for Research on Adolescence, San Diego.

Santilli, N.R., Falbo, M.C., & Harris, J.T. (2002, April). *The role of volunteer services, self perceptions, and relationships with others on prosocial development*. Paper presented at the meeting of the Society for Research on Adolescence, New Orleans.

Santrock, J.W. (2001). *Educational psychology*. New York: McGraw-Hill.

Santrock, J.W. (2002). *Life-span development* (8th ed.). New York: McGraw-Hill.

Santrock, J.W. (2003). *Psychology* (7th ed.). New York: McGraw-Hill.

Santrock, J.W., & Halonen, J.A. (2002). *Your guide to college success* (2nd ed.). Belmont, CA: Wadsworth.

Santrock, J.W., Sitterle, K.A., & Warshak, R.A. (1988). Parent-child relationships in stepfather families. In P. Bronstein & C.P. Cowan (Eds.), *Fatherhood today: Men's changing roles in the family*. New York: Wiley.

Sarigiani, P.A., & Petersen, A.C. (2000). Adolescence: Puberty and biological maturation. In A. Kazdin (Ed.), *Encyclopedia of psychology*. Washington, DC, & New York: American Psychological Association and Oxford University Press.

Sarrel, P., & Masters, W. (1982). Sexual molestation of men by women. *Archives of Human Sexuality, 11*, 117–131.

Savin-Williams, R.C. (1995). An exploratory study of pubertal maturation timing and self-esteem among gay and bisexual male youths. *Developmental Psychology, 31*, 56–64.

Savin-Williams, R.C. (1998). The disclosure to families of same-sex attractions by lesbian, gay, and bisexual youth. *Journal of Research on Adolescence, 8*, 49–68.

Savin-Williams, R.C. (2001). *Mom, dad, I'm gay*. Washington, DC: American Psychological Association.

Savin-Williams, R.C., & Demo, D.H. (1983). Conceiving or misconceiving the self: Issues in adolescent self-esteem. *Journal of Early Adolescence, 3*, 121–140.

Savin-Williams, R.C., & Rodriguez, R.G. (1993). A developmental, clinical perspective on lesbian, gay male, and bisexual youths. In T.P. Gullotta, G.R. Adams, & R. Montemayor (Eds.), *Adolescent sexuality*. Newbury Park, CA: Sage.

Sax, L.J., Astin, A.W., Korn, W.S., & Mahoney, K.M. (1999). *The American college freshman: Norms for fall 1999*. Los Angeles: Higher Education Research Institute, UCLA.

Sax, L.J., Astin, A.W., Korn, W.S., & Mahoney, K.M. (2000). *The American freshman; National norms for 2000*. Los Angeles: Higher Education Research Institute, UCLA.

Sax, L.J., Lindholm, J.A., Atin, A.W., Korn, W.S., & Mahoney, K.M. (2001). *The American Freshman: National norms for fall 2001*. Los Angeles: Higher Education Research Institute, UCLA.

Scarr, S. (1986). Best of human genetics. *Contemporary Psychology, 41*, 149–150.

Scarr, S. (1993). Biological and cultural diversity: The legacy of Darwin for development. *Child Development, 64*, 1333–1353.

Scarr, S., & Weinberg, R.A. (1980). Calling all camps! The war is over. *American Sociological Review, 45*, 859–865.

Scarr, S., & Weinberg, R.A. (1983). The Minnesota adoption studies: Genetic differences and malleability. *Child Development, 54*, 253–259.

Schaie, K.W. (2000). Review of Santrock *Life-span development*, 8th ed. (Boston: McGraw-Hill).

Scharf, M., & Shulman, S. (2000, April). *Adolescents' socio-emotional competence and parental representations of peer relationships in adolescence*. Paper presented at the meeting of the Society for Research on Adolescence, Chicago.

Scheer, S.D. (1996, March). *Adolescent to adult transitions: Social status and cognitive factors*. Paper presented at the meeting of the Society for Research on Adolescence, Boston.

Scheer, S.D., & Unger, D.G. (1994, February). *Adolescents becoming adults: Attributes for adulthood*. Paper presented at the meeting of the Society for Research on Adolescence, San Diego.

Schiever, S.W., & Maker, C.J. (1997). Enrichment and acceleration: An overview and new directions. In N. Colangelo & G.A. Davis (Eds.), *Handbook of gifted education*. Boston: Allyn & Bacon.

Schiff, J.L., & Truglio, R.T. (1995, March). *In search of the ideal family: The use of television family portrayals during early adolescence*. Paper presented at the meeting of the Society for Research in Child Development, Indianapolis.

Schneider, B., & Stevensen, D. (1999). *The ambitious generation*. New Haven, CT: Yale University.

Schneider, W., & Bjorklund, D. (1998). Memory. In W. Damon (Ed.), *Handbook of child psychology* (5th ed., Vol. 2). New York: Wiley.

Scholte, R., & Dubas, J.S. (2002, April). *The social context of early, on-time, and late maturing Dutch boys: Implications for adjustment*. Paper presented at the meeting of the Society for Research on Adolescence, New Orleans.

Schorr, L.B. (1989, April). *Within our reach: Breaking the cycle of disadvantage*. Paper presented at the biennial meeting of the Society for Research in Child Development, Kansas City.

Schulenberg, J. (June, 1999). *Binge drinking trajectories before, during, and after college: More reasons to worry from a developmental perspective*. Invited paper presented at the meeting of the American Psychological Society, Denver, Colorado.

Schulenberg, J., & Maggs, J.L. (in press). A developmental perspective on alcohol use and heavy drinking during adolescence and the transition to early adulthood. *NIAAA Monographs*.

Schulenberg, J., Maggs, J.L., Steinman, K.J., & Zucker, R.A. (2001). Development matters: Taking the long view on substance abuse etiology and intervention during adolescence. In P.M. Monti, S.M. Colbyk, & T.A. O'Leary (Eds.), *Adolescents, alcohol, and substance abuse*. New York: Guilford.

Schulenberg, J., O'Malley, P.M., Bachman, J.G., & Johnson, L.D. (2000). "Spread your wings and fly": The course of health and well-being during the transition to young adulthood. In L. Crockett & R. Silbereisen (Eds.), *Negotiating adolescence in times of social change*. New York: Cambridge University Press.

Schunk, D.H. (1989). Self-efficacy and academic motivation. *Educational Psychologist, 25*, 71–86.

Schunk, D.H. (1991). Self-efficacy and cognitive skill learning. In C. Ames & R. Ames (Eds.), *Research on motivation and education* (Vol. 3). Orlando: Academic Press.

Schunk, D.H. (2001). Social cognitive theory and self-regulated learning. In B.J. Zimmerman & D.H. Schunk (Eds.), *Self-regulated learning and academic achievement* (2nd ed.). Mahwah, NJ: Erlbaum.

Schunk, D.H., & Ertmer, P.A. (2000). Self-regulation and academic learning: Self-efficacy enhancing interventions. In M. Boekaerts, P.R. Pintrich, & M. Zeidner (Eds.), *Handbook of self-regulation*. San Diego: Academic Press.

Schunk, D.H., & Zimmerman, B.J. (Eds.). (1994). *Self-regulation of learning and performance*. Mahwah, NJ: Erlbaum.

Schuster, M. (2000, November 16). Commentary on the increase in oral sex in adolescence. *USA Today*, p. 2D.

Scott-Jones, D. (1995, March). *Incorporating ethnicity and socioeconomic status in research with children*. Paper presented at the meeting of the Society for Research in Child Development, Indianapolis.

Search Institute. (1995). *Barriers to participation in youth programs*. Unpublished manuscript, the Search Institute, Minneapolis.

Seginer, R. (1998). Adolescents' perception of relationships with older sibling in the context of other close relationships. *Journal of Research on Adolescence, 8*, 287–308.

Seidman, E. (2000). School transitions. In A. Kazdin (Ed.), *Encyclopedia of psychology*. Washington, DC, and New York: American Psychological Association and Oxford University Press.

Seiffge-Krenke, I. (1998). *Adolescents' health: A developmental perspective*. Mahwah, NJ: Erlbaum.

Seligman, M.E.P., & Csikszentmihalyi, M. (2000). Positive psychology. *American Psychologist, 55*, 5–14.

Selman, R. (1976). Social-cognitive understanding. In T. Lickona (Ed.), *Moral development and behavior*. New York: Holt, Rinehart & Winston.

Selman, R. (1980). *The growth of interpersonal understanding*. New York: Academic Press.

Selman, R.L., & Adalbjarnardottir, S. (2000). Developmental method to analyze the personal meaning adolescents make of risk and relationship: The case of "drinking." *Applied Developmental Science, 4*, 47–65.

Selman, R.L., & Schultz, L.H. (1999, August). *The GSID approach to developmental evaluation of conflict resolution and violence prevention programs*. Paper presented at the meeting of the American Psychological Association, Boston.

Semaj, L.T. (1985). Afrikanity, cognition, and extended self-identity. In M.B. Spencer, G.K. Brookins, & W.R. Allen (Eds.), *Beginnings: The social and affective development of Black children*. Hillsdale, NJ: Erlbaum.

Serow, R.C., Ciechalski, J., & Daye, C. (1990). Students as volunteers. *Urban Education, 25*, 157–168.

Sesma, A. (2000, April). *Friendship intimacy, adversity, and psychological well-being in adolescence*. Paper presented at the meeting of the Society for Research on Adolescence, Chicago.

Sewell, T.E. (2000). School dropout. In A. Kazdin (Ed.), *Encyclopedia of psychology*. Washington, DC, and New York: American Psychological Association and Oxford University Press.

Shade, S.C., Kelly, C., & Oberg, M. (1997). *Creating culturally responsive schools*. Washington, DC: American Psychological Association.

Shaffer, L. (2000, April). *From the mouths of babes and dudes: Pros and cons of different types of adolescent peer relationships*. Paper presented at the meeting of the Society for Research on Adolescence, Chicago.

Shaie, K.W. (2000). Review of Santrock *Life-span development*, 8th ed. (Boston: McGraw-Hill).

Sharp, V. (1999). *Computer education for teachers* (3rd ed.). New York: McGraw-Hill.

Sheeber, L., Hops, H., & Davis, B. (2001). Family processes in adolescent depression. *Clinical Child and Family Psychology Review, 4*, 19–32.

Sheeber, L., Hops, H., Andrews, J.A., & Davis, B. (1997, April). *Family support and conflict: Prospective relation to adolescent depression*. Paper presented at the meeting of the Society for Research in Child Development, Washington, DC.

Sheffield, V.C. (1999, May). *Application of genetic strategies and human genome project resources for the identification of human disease genes*. Paper presented at the meeting of the Society for Pediatric Research, San Francisco.

Sheidow, A.J., Groman-Smith, D., Henry, D.B., & Tolan, P.H. (2000, April). *Family and community characteristics: Risk factors for violence exposure in inner-city youth*. Paper presented at the meeting of the Society for Research on Adolescence, Chicago.

Sherman, B.L., & Dominick, J.R. (1986). Violence and sex in music videos: TV and rock 'n' roll. *Journal of Communication, 36*, 79–93.

Sherrod, L., & Brabek, K. (2002, April). *Community service and youths' political views*. Paper presented at the meeting of the Society for Research on Adolescence, New Orleans.

Shields, S.A. (1991). Gender in the psychology of emotion: A selective research review. In K.T. Strongman (Ed.), *International review of studies on emotion* (Vol. I). New York: Wiley.

Shin, H.S. (2001). A review of school-based drug prevention program evaluations in the 1990s. *American Journal of Health Education, 32*, 139–147.

Shonkoff, J.P. (2000). Science, policy, and practice: Three cultures in search of a shared mission. *Child Development, 71*, 181–187.

Short, R.J., & Talley, R.C. (1997). Rethinking psychology and the schools. *American Psychologist, 52*, 234–240.

Shulman, S., & Collins, W.A. (Eds.) (1998). *New directions for child development: Adolescent romantic relationships*. San Francisco: Jossey-Bass.

Shulman, S., & Seiffge-Krenke, I. (2001). Adolescent romance: Between experience and relationships. *Journal of Adolescence, 35*, 417–428.

Shweder, R.A. (1991). *Thinking through cultures: Expeditions in cultural psychology*. Cambridge, MA: Harvard University Press.

Sidhu, K.K. (2000, April). *Identity formation among second generation Canadian Sikh adolescent males*. Paper presented at the meeting of the Society for Research in Adolescence, Chicago.

Sieber, J.E. (2000). Ethics in research. In A. Kazdin (Ed.). *Encyclopedia of psychology*. Washington, DC, & New York: American Psychological Association and Oxford University Press.

SIECUS. (1999). *Public support for sexuality education*. Washington, DC: Author.

Siegel, L.S., & Wiener, J. (1993, Spring). Canadian special education policies: Children with learning disabilities in a bilingual and multicultural society. *Social Policy Report, Society for Research in Child Development, 7*, 1–16.

Siegler, R.S. (1996). Information processing. In J.W. Santrock, *Child development* (7th ed.). Dubuque, IA: Brown & Benchmark.

Siegler, R.S. (1998). *Children's thinking* (3rd ed.). Upper Saddle River, NJ: Prentice-Hall.

Siegler, R.S. (2000). Developmental research: Microgenetic method. In K. Lee (Ed.), *Childhood cognitive development*. Malden, MA: Blackwell.

Sieving, R.E., McNelly, C.S., & Blum, R.W. (2000). *Maternal expectations, mother-child connectedness, and adolescent sexual debut*. Unpublished manuscript, Department of Pediatrics, Medical School, University of Minnesota.

Silberg, J.L., & Rutter, M.L. (1997, April). *Pubertal status, life stress, and depression in juvenile twins: A genetic investigation*. Paper presented at the meeting of the Society for Research in Child Development, Washington, DC.

Silver, M.E. (1995, March). *Late adolescent-parent relations and the high school to college transition*. Paper presented at the meeting of the Society for Research in Child Development, Indianapolis.

Silver, M.E., Levitt, M.J., Santos, J., & Perdue, L. (2002, April). *Changes in family relationships as adolescents become young adults*. Paper presented at the meeting of the Society for Research on Adolescence, New Orleans.

Silver, S. (1988, August). *Behavior problems of children born into early-childbearing families*. Paper presented at the meeting of the American Psychological Association, Atlanta.

Silverberg, S.B., & Steinberg, L. (1990). Psychological well-being of parents with early adolescent children. *Developmental Psychology, 26*, 658–666.

Silverman, J.G., Raj, A., Mucci, L.A., & Hathaway, J.E. (2001). Dating violence against adolescent girls and associated substance use, unhealthy weight control, sexual risk behavior, pregnancy, and suicidality. *Journal of the American Medical Association, 386*, 572–579.

Silverman, L.K. (1993). A developmental model for counseling the gifted. In L.K. Silverman (Ed.), *Counseling the gifted and the talented*. Denver: Love.

Simmons, A.M., & Avery, P.G. (in press). Civic life as conveyed in U.S. civics and history textbooks. *Journal of Social Education*.

Simmons, R.G., & Blyth, D.A. (1987). *Moving into adolescence*. Hawthorne, NY: Aldine.

Simons, J.M., Finlay, B., & Yang, A. (1991). *The adolescent and young adult fact book*. Washington, DC: Children's Defense Fund.

Simons, J.S., Walker-Barnes, C., & Mason, C.A. (2001, April). *Predicting increases in adolescent drug use: A longitudinal investigation*. Paper presented at the meeting of the Society for Research in Child Development, Minneapolis.

Simons-Morton, B., Haynie, D.L., Crump, A.D., Eitel, P., & Saylor, K.E. (2001). Peer and parent influences on smoking and drinking among early adolescents. *Health Education & Behavior, 28*, 95–107.

Singh, S., Wulf, D., Samara, R., & Cuca, Y.P. (2000). Gender differences in the timing of first intercourse: Data from 14 countries. *International Family Planning Perspectives, 26*, 21–28, 43.

Sitlington, P.L., Clark, G.M., & Kolstoe, O.P. (2000). *Transition education and services for adolescents with disabilities* (3rd ed.). Boston: Allyn & Bacon.

Skinner, B.F. (1938). *The behavior of organisms: An experimental analysis*. New York: Appleton-Century-Crofts.

Skoe, E.E., & Gooden, A. (1993). Ethic of care and real-life moral dilemma content in male and female early adolescents. *Journal of Early Adolescence, 13*, 154–167.

Skoe, E.E., & Marcia, J.E. (1988). *Ego identity and care-based moral reasoning in college women*. Unpublished manuscript, Acadia University.

Slavin, R.E. (1995). *Cooperative learning: Theory, research, and practice* (2nd ed.). Boston: Allyn & Bacon.

Slee, P.T., & Taki, M. (1999, April). *School bullying*. Paper presented at the meeting of the Society for Research in Child Development, Albuquerque.

Slomkowski, C., Rende, R., Conger, K.J., Simons, R.L., & Conger, R.D. (2001). Sisters, brothers, and delinquency: Social influence during early and middle adolescence. *Child Development, 72*, 271–283.

Small, S.A. (1990). *Preventive programs that support families with adolescents*. Washington, DC: Carnegie Council on Adolescent Development.

Smetana, J. (1988). Concepts of self and social convention: Adolescents' and parents' reasoning about hypothetical and actual family conflicts. In M. Gunnar (Ed.), *21st Minnesota symposium on child psychology*. Hillsdale, NJ: Erlbaum.

Smetana, J. (1993, March). *Parenting styles during adolescence: Global or domain-specific?* Paper presented at the biennial meeting of the Society for Research in Child Development, New Orleans.

Smetana, J. (1997, April). *Parenting reconceptualized: A social domain analysis*. Paper presented at the meeting of the Society for Research in Child Development, Washington, DC.

Smetana, J., & Gaines, C. (1999). Adolescent-parent conflict in middle-class African-American families. *Child Development, 70*, 1447–1463.

Smetana, J.G. (1995). Parenting styles and conceptions of parental authority during adolescence. *Child Development, 66*, 299–316.

Smetana, J.G., Abernethy, A., & Harris, A. (2000). Adolescent-parent interactions in middle-class African-American families: Longitudinal change and contextual variations. *Journal of Family Psychology, 14*, 458–474.

Smith, R.C., & Crockett, L.J. (1997, April). *Positive adolescent peer relations: A potential buffer against family adversity*. Paper presented at the meeting of the Society for Research in Child Development, Washington, DC.

Smith, R.E., & Smoll, F.L. (1997). Coaching the coaches: Youth sports as a scientific and applied behavioral setting. *Current Directions in Psychological Science, 6*, 16–21.

Snarey, J. (1987, June). A question of morality. *Psychology Today*, pp. 6–8.

Snider, B.A., & Miller, J.P. (1993). The land-grant university system and 4-H: A mutually beneficial relationship of scholars and practitioners in youth development. In R.M. Lerner (Ed.), *Early adolescence*. Hillsdale, NJ: Erlbaum.

Snyder, H.N., & Sickmund, M. (1999, October). *Juvenile offenders and victims: 1999 national report*. Washington, DC: National Center for Juvenile Justice.

Sommer, B.B. (1978). *Puberty and adolescence*. New York: Oxford University Press.

Sonenstein, F.L., Pleck, J.H., & Ku, L.C. (1989). Sexual activity, condom use, and AIDS awareness among adolescent males. *Family Planning Perspectives, 21* (4), 152–158.

Sorensen, R.C. (1973). *Adolescent sexuality in contemporary America*. New York: World.

Spade, J.Z., & Reese, C.A. (1991). We've come a long way, maybe: College students' plans for work and family. *Sex Roles, 24*, 309–321.

Spear, L.P. (2000). Neurobehavioral changes. *Current Directions in Psychological Science, 9*, 111–114.

Spearman, C.E. (1927). *The abilities of man*. New York: Macmillan.

Spence, J.T., & Helmreich, R. (1972). The Attitudes Toward Women Scale: An objective instrument to measure the rights and roles of women in contemporary society. *JSAS Catalog of Selected Documents in Psychology, 2*, 66.

Spencer, M.B. (1999). Social and cultural influences on school adjustment: The application of an identity-focused cultural ecological perspective. *Educational Psychologist, 34*, 43–57.

Spencer, M.B. (2000). Ethnocentrism. In A. Kazdin (Ed.), *Encyclopedia of psychology*. Washington, DC, and New York: American Psychological Association and Oxford University Press.

Spencer, M.B., & Dornbusch, S.M. (1990). Challenges in studying minority youth. In S.S. Feldman & G.R. Elliott (Eds.), *At the threshold: The developing adolescent*. Cambridge, MA: Harvard University Press.

Spencer, M.B., Noll, E., Stoltzfuz, J., & Harpalani, V. (2001). Identity and school adjustment: Revisiting the "acting white" assumption. *Educational Psychologist, 36*, 21–30.

Spokane, A.R. (2000). Career choice. In A. Kazdin (Ed.), *Encyclopedia of psychology*. Washington, DC, and New York: American Psychological Association and Oxford University Press.

Spring, J. (2002). *American education* (10th ed.). New York: McGraw-Hill.

Spring, J. (2000). *The intersection of cultures*. New York: McGraw-Hill.

Sputa, C.L., & Paulson, S.E. (1995, March). *A longitudinal study of changes in parenting across adolescence*. Paper presented at the meeting of the Society for Research in Child Development, Indianapolis.

Sroufe, L.A. (1996). *Emotional development*. New York: Cambridge University Press.

Sroufe, L.A. (2001). From infant attachment to adolescent autonomy: Longitudinal data on the role of parents in development. In J. Borkowski, S. Ramey, & M. Bristol-Power (Eds.), *Parenting and your child's world*. Mahwah, NJ: Erlbaum.

Sroufe, L.A., Egeland, B., & Carlson, E.A. (1999). One social world: The integrated development of parent-child and peer relationships. In W.A. Collins & B. Laursen (Eds.), *Minnesota symposium on child psychology* (Vol. 31). Mahwah, NJ: Erlbaum.

St. Pierre, R., Layzer, J., & Barnes, H. (1996). *Regenerating two-generation programs*. Cambridge, MA: Abt Associates.

Stake, J.E. (2000). When situations call for instrumentality and expressiveness: Resource appraisal, coping strategy choice, and adjustment. *Sex Roles, 42*, 865–885.

Stanovich, K.E. (1998). *How to think straight about psychology* (4th ed.). New York: Longman.

Stattin, H., & Magnusson, D. (1990). *Pubertal maturation in female development: Paths through life* (Vol. 2). Hillsdale, NJ: Erlbaum.

Steinberg, L.D. (1986). Latchkey children and susceptibility to peer pressure: An ecological analysis. *Developmental Psychology, 22*, 433–439.

Steinberg, L.D. (1988). Reciprocal relation between parent-child distance and pubertal maturation. *Developmental Psychology, 24*, 122–128.

Steinberg, L.D., & Cauffman, E. (1999). A developmental perspective on jurisdictional boundary. In J. Fagan & F. Zimring (Eds.), *A developmental perspective on jurisdictional boundary*. Chicago: University of Chicago Press.

Steinberg, L.D., Fegley, S., & Dornbusch, S.M. (1993). Negative impact of part-time work on adolescent adjustment: Evidence from a longitudinal study. *Developmental Psychology, 29*, 171–180.

Steinberg, L.D., & Silk, J.S. (2002). Parenting adolescents. In M. Bornstein (Ed.), *Handbook of parenting* (2nd ed., Vol. 1). Mahwah, NJ: Erlbaum.

Stepp, L.S. (2000). *Our last best shot: Guiding our children through early adolescence*. New York: Riverhead Books.

Stern, D., & Hallinan, M.T. (1997, Summer). The high schools, they are a-changin'. *CenterWork Newsletter* (NCRVE, University of California, Berkeley), pp. 4–7.

Stern, D., & Rahn, M. (1998, Fall). How health career academies provide work-based learning. *CenterWork Newsletter* (NCRVE, University of California, Berkeley), pp. 5–8.

Sternberg, R.J. (1977). *Intelligence, information processing, and analogical reasoning: The componential analysis of human abilities*. Hillsdale, NJ: Erlbaum.

Sternberg, R.J. (1985, December). Teaching critical thinking, Part 2: Possible solutions. *Phi Delta Kappan*, pp. 277–280.

Sternberg, R.J. (1986). *Intelligence applied*. San Diego: Harcourt Brace Jovanovich.

Sternberg, R.J. (1997). Educating intelligence: Infusing the triarchic theory into instruction. In R.J. Sternberg & E. Grigorenko (Eds.), *Intelligence, heredity, and environment*. New York: Cambridge University Press.

Sternberg, R.J. (1999). Intelligence. In M.A. Runco & S. Pritzker (Eds.), *Encyclopedia of creativity*. San Diego: Academic Press.

Sternberg, R.J. (2000). Looking back and looking forward on intelligence: Toward a theory of successful intelligence. In M. Bennett (Ed.), *Developmental psychology*. Philadelphia: Psychology Press.

Sternberg, R.J., & Clinkenbeard, P.R. (1995, May/June). The triarchic model applied to identifying, teaching, and assessing gifted children. *Roeper Review*, 255–260.

Sternberg, R.J., & Nigro, C. (1980). Developmental patterns in the solution of verbal analogies. *Child Development, 51*, 27–38.

Sternberg, R.J., & Rifkin, B. (1979). The development of analogical reasoning processes. *Journal of Experimental Child Psychology, 27*, 195–232.

Sternberg, R.J., Torff, B., & Grigorenko, E. (1998, May). Teaching for successful intelligence raises school achievement. *Phi Delta Kappan*, pp. 667–669.

Steur, F.B., Applefield, J.M., & Smith, R. (1971). Televised aggression and the interpersonal aggression of preschool children. *Journal of Experimental Child Psychology, 11*, 442–447.

Stevens, J.H. (1984). Black grandmothers' and black adolescent mothers' knowledge about parenting. *Developmental Psychology, 20*, 1017–1025.

Stevens, V., De Bourdeaudhuij, & Van Oost, P. (2001). Anti-bullying interventions at school. *Health Promotion International, 16*, 155–167.

Stevenson, D.L., Kochanek, J., & Schneider, B. (1998). Making the transition from high school: Recent trends and policies. In K. Borman & B. Schneider (Eds.), *The adolescent years: Social influences and educational challenges*. Chicago: University of Chicago Press.

Stevenson, H.C. (1997). Managing anger: Protective, proactive, or adaptive racial socialization identity profiles and African-American manhood development. *Journal of Prevention & Intervention in the Community, 16*, 35–61.

Stevenson, H.C. (1998). Raising safe villages: Cultural-ecological factors that influence the emotional adjustment of adolescents. *Journal of Black Psychology, 24*, 44–59.

Stevenson, H.W. (1992, December). Learning from Asian schools. *Scientific American*, pp. 6, 70–76.

Stevenson, H.W. (1995). Mathematics achievement of American students: First in the world by the year 2000? In C.A. Nelson (Ed.), *Basic and applied perspectives on learning, cognition, and development*. Minneapolis: University of Minnesota Press.

Stevenson, H.W., Hofer, B.K., & Randell, B. (2000). Middle childhood: Education and schooling. In W. Damon (Ed.), *Encyclopedia of psychology*. Washington, DC, & New York: American Psychological Association and Oxford University Press.

Stevenson, H.W., Lee, S., Chen, C., Stigler, J.W., Hsu, C., & Kitamura, S. (1990). Contexts of achievement. *Monograph of the Society for Research in Child Development, 55* (Serial No. 221).

Stipek, D.J. (1996). Motivation and instruction. In D.C. Berliner & R.C. Calfee (Eds.), *Handbook of educational psychology*. New York: Macmillan.

Stipek, D.J. (2002). *Motivation to learn* (4th Ed.). Boston: Allyn & Bacon.

Stone, M.R., Barber, B.L., & Eccles, J.S. (2001, April). *How to succeed in high school by really trying: Does activity participation benefit students at all levels of social self-concept?* Paper presented at the meeting of the Society for Research in Child Development, Minneapolis.

Strahan, D.B. (1983). The emergence of formal operations in adolescence. *Transcendence, 11*, 7–14.

Strasburger, V.C., & Donnerstein, E. (1999). Children, adolescents, and the media: Issues and solutions. *Pediatrics, 103*, 129–137.

Streigel-Moore, R.H., Silberstein, L.R., & Rodin, J. (1993). The social self in bulimia nervosa: Public self-consciousness, social anxiety, and perceived fraudulence. *Journal of Abnormal Psychology, 102*, 297–303.

Streitmatter, J. (1993). Gender differences in identity development: An examination of longitudinal data. *Adolescence, 28*, 55–66.

Strickland, B.R. (1995). Research on sexual orientation and human development: A commentary. *Developmental Psychology, 31*, 137–140.

Strober, M., Freeman, R., & Morrell, W. (1997). The long-term course of severe anorexia nervosa in adolescents: Survival analysis of recovery, relapse, and outcome predictors over 10–15 years in a prospective study. *International Journal of Eating Disorders, 22*, 339–360.

Studer, M., & Thornton, A. (1987). Adolescent religiosity and contraceptive usage. *Journal of Marriage and the Family, 49*, 117–128.

Studer, M., & Thornton, A. (1989). The multifaceted impact of religiosity on adolescent sexual experience and contraceptive usage: A reply to Shornack and Ahmed. *Journal of Marriage and the Family, 51*, 1085–1089.

Stunkard, A.J. (2000). Obesity. In A. Kazdin (Ed.), *Encyclopedia of psychology*. Washington, DC, and New York: American Psychological Association and Oxford University Press.

Suárez-Orozco, C. (1999, August). *Conceptual considerations in our understanding of immigrant adolescent girls*. Paper presented at the meeting of the American Psychological Association, Boston.

Suárez-Orozco, C. (2002). Afterward: Understanding and serving the children of immigrants. *Harvard Educational Review, 71*, 579–589.

Suárez-Orozco, M., & Suárez-Orozco, C. (2002, April). *Global engagement: Immigrant youth and the social process of schooling.* Paper presented at the meeting of the Society for Research on Adolescence, New Orleans.

Sue, S. (1990, August). *Ethnicity and culture in psychological research and practice.* Paper presented at the meeting of the American Psychological Association, Boston.

Sue, S., & Okazaki, S. (1990). Asian-American educational achievements: A phenomenon in search of an explanation. *American Psychologist, 45,* 913–920.

Sullivan, H.S. (1953). *The interpersonal theory of psychiatry.* New York: W. W. Norton.

Sullivan, K., & Sullivan, A. (1980). Adolescent-parent separation. *Developmental Psychology, 16,* 93–99.

Suomi, S.J., Harlow, H.F., & Domek, C.J. (1970). Effect of repetitive infant-infant separations of young monkeys. *Journal of Abnormal Psychology, 76,* 161–172.

Super, D.E. (1967). *The psychology of careers.* New York: Harper & Row.

Super, D.E. (1976). *Career education and the meanings of work.* Washington, DC: U.S. Office of Education.

Susman, E.J. (1997). Modeling developmental complexity in adolescence: Hormones and behavior in context. *Journal of Research on Adolescence, 7,* 283–306.

Susman, E.J. (2001). Review of Santrock's *Adolescence,* 9th ed. (New York: McGraw-Hill).

Susman, E.J., Dorn, L.D., & Schiefelbein, V.L. (in press). Puberty, sexuality, and health. In R.M. Lerner, M.A. Easterbrooks, & J. Mistry (Eds.), *Comprehensive handbook of psychology: Developmental psychology* (Vol. 6). New York: Wiley.

Susman, E.J., Finkelstein J.W., Chinchilli, V.M., Schwab, J., Liben, L.S., D'Arcangelo, M.R., Meinke, J., Demers, L.M., Lookingbill, G., & Kulin, H.E. (1987). The effect of sex hormone replacement therapy on behavior problems and moods in adolescents with delayed puberty. *Journal of Pediatrics, 133* (4), 521–525.

Susman, E.J., Murowchick, E., Worrall, B.K., & Murray, D.A. (1995, March). *Emotionality, adrenal hormones, and context interactions during puberty and pregnancy.* Paper presented at the meeting of the Society for Research in Child Development, Indianapolis.

Susman, E.J., Schiefelbein, V., & Heaton, J.A. (2002, April). *Cortisol attenuations, puberty, and externalizing behavior: Family adjustment mediators.* Paper presented at the meeting of the Society for Research on Adolescence, New Orleans.

Sussman, A.L. (2001). Reality monitoring of performed and imagined interactive events: Developmental and contextual effects. *Journal of Experimental Child Psychology, 79,* 115–138.

Sutton-Smith, B. (1982). Birth order and sibling status effects. In M.E. Lamb & B. Sutton-Smith (Eds.), *Sibling relationships: Their nature and significance across the life span.* Hillsdale, NJ: Erlbaum.

Swanson, D.P. (1997, April). *Identity and coping styles among African-American females.* Paper presented at the meeting of the Society for Research in Child Development, Washington, DC.

Swanson, H.L. (1999). What develops in working memory? A life-span perspective. *Developmental Psychology, 35,* 986–1000.

Swarr, A.E., & Richards, M.H. (1996). Longitudinal effects of adolescent girls' pubertal development, perceptions of pubertal timing, and parental relations. *Developmental Psychology, 32,* 636–646.

Swim, J.K., Aikin, K.J., Hall, W.S., & Hunter, B.A. (1995). Sexism and racism: Old-fashioned and modern prejudices. *Journal of Personality and Social Psychology, 67,* 199–214.

T

Takahashi, K., & Majima, N. (1994). Transition from home to college dormitory: The role of preestablished affective relationships in adjustment to a new life. *Journal of Research on Adolescence, 4,* 367–384.

Takanishi, R., & DeLeon, P.H. (1994). A Head Start for the 21st century. *American Psychologist, 49,* 120–122.

Tamis-LeMonda, C.S., & Cabrera, N. (Eds.) (2002). *The handbook of father involvement.* Mahwah, NJ: Erlbaum.

Tanaka-Matsumi, J. (2001). Abnormal psychology and culture. In D. Matsumoto (Ed.), *The handbook of culture and psychology.* New York: Oxford University Press.

Tannen, D. (1990). *You just don't understand!* New York: Ballantine.

Tapert, S., Brown, G.S., Kindermann, S.S., Cheung, E.H., Frank, L.R., & Brown, S.A. (2001). fMRI measurement of brain dysfunction in alcohol-dependent young women. *Alcoholism: Clinical & Experimental Research, 25,* 236–245.

Tappan, M.B. (1998). Sociocultural psychology and caring psychology: Exploring Vygotsky's "hidden curriculum." *Educational Psychologist, 33,* 23–33.

Tavris, C., & Wade, C. (1984). *The longest war: Sex differences in perspective* (2nd ed.). San Diego: Harcourt Brace Jovanovich.

Taylor, J. McLean, Gilligan, C., & Sullivan, A.M. (1996). *Between voice and silence: Women and girls, race and relationship.* Cambridge, MA: Harvard University Press.

Taylor, J.H., & Walker, L.J. (1997). Moral climate and the development of moral reasoning: The effects of dyadic discussions between young offenders. *Journal of Moral Education, 26,* 21–43.

Taylor, R.D., & Wang, M.C. (2000). *Resilience across contexts.* Mahwah, NJ: Erlbaum.

Terman, D.L., Larner, M.B., Stevenson, C.S., & Behrman, R.E. (1996). Special education for students with disabilities: Analysis and recommendations. *Future of Children, 6* (1), 4–24.

Tesser, A., Fleeson, R.B., & Suls, J.M. (2000). *Psychological perspectives on self and identity.* Washington, DC: American Psychological Association.

Teti, D.M. (2002). Retrospect and prospect in the study of sibling relationships. In J.P. McHale & W.S. Grolnick (Eds.), *Retrospect and prospect in the study of families.* Mahwah, NJ: Erlbaum.

Tetreault, M.K.T. (1997). Classrooms for diversity: Rethinking curriculum and pedagogy. In J.A. Banks & C.A. Banks (Eds.), *Multicultural education* (3rd ed.). Boston: Allyn & Bacon.

Thomas, C.W., Coffman, J.K., & Kipp, K.L. (1993, March). *Are only children different from children with siblings? A longitudinal study of behavioral and social functioning.* Paper presented at the biennial meeting of the Society for Research in Child Development, New Orleans.

Thomas, K. (1998, November 4). Teen cyberdating is a new wrinkle for parents, too. *USA Today,* p. 9D.

Thompson, L., & Walker, A.J. (1989). Gender in families: Women and men in marriage, work, and parenthood. *Journal of Marriage and the Family, 51,* 845–871.

Thompson, P.M., Giedd, J.N., Woods, R.P., MacDonald, D., Evans, A.C., & Toga, A.W. (2000). Growth patterns in the developing brain detected by using continuum mechanical tensor maps. *Nature, 404,* 190–193.

Thompson, R.A., & Nelson, C.A. (2001). Developmental science and the media. *American Psychologist, 56,* 5–15.

Thornburg, H.D. (1981). Sources of sex education among early adolescents. *Journal of Early Adolescence, 1,* 171–184.

Thorton, A., & Camburn, D. (1989). Religious participation and sexual behavior and attitudes. *Journal of Marriage and the Family, 49,* 117–128.

Thurstone, L.L. (1938). *Primary mental abilities.* Chicago: University of Chicago Press.

Tilton-Weaver, L., & Leighter, S. (2002, April). *Peer management behavior: Linkages to parents' beliefs about adolescents and adolescents' friends.* Paper presented at the meeting of the Society for Research on Adolescence, New Orleans.

Tirozzi, G.N., & Uro, G. (1997). Education reform in the United States. *American Psychologist, 52,* 241–249.

Tolan, P.H. (2001). Emerging themes and challenges in understanding youth violence. *Journal of Clinical Child Psychology, 30,* 233–239.

Tolan, P.H., Guerra, N.G., & Kendall, P.C. (1995). A developmental-ecological perspective on antisocial behavior in children and adolescents: Toward a unified risk and intervention framework. *Journal of Consulting and Clinical Psychology, 63,* 579–584.

Tomlinson-Keasey, C. (1972). Formal operations in females from 11 to 54 years of age. *Developmental Psychology, 6,* 364.

Tomlinson-Keasey, C., Warren, L.W., & Elliott, J.E. (1986). Suicide among gifted women: A prospective study. *Journal of Abnormal Psychology, 95,* 123–130.

Torff, B. (2000). Multiple intelligences. In A. Kazdin (Ed.), *Encyclopedia of psychology.* Washington, DC, and New York: American Psychological Association and Oxford University Press.

Triandis, H.C. (1994). *Culture and social behavior.* New York: McGraw-Hill.

Triandis, H.C. (2000). Cross-cultural psychology. In A. Kazdin (Ed.), *Encyclopedia of psychology*. Washington, DC, & New York: American Psychological Association and Oxford University Press.

Trickett, E.J., & Moos, R.H. (1974). Personal correlates of contrasting environments: Student satisfaction in high school classrooms. *American Journal of Community Psychology, 2*, 1–12.

Trimble, J.E. (1989, August). *The enculturation of contemporary psychology*. Paper presented at the meeting of the American Psychological Association, New Orleans.

Tubman, J.G., Windle, M., & Windle, R.C. (1996). The onset and cross-temporal patterning of sexual intercourse in middle adolescence: Prospective relations with behavioral and emotional problems. *Child Development, 67*, 327–343.

Tucker, C.J., McHale, S.M., & Crouter, A.C. (2001). Conditions of sibling support in adolescence. *Journal of Family Psychology, 15*, 254–271.

Tucker, L.A. (1987). Television, teenagers, and health. *Journal of Youth and Adolescence, 16*, 415–425.

Tuckman, B.W., & Hinkle, J.S. (1988). An experimental study of the physical and psychological effects of aerobic exercise on schoolchildren. In B.G. Melamed & others (Eds.), *Child health psychology*. Hillsdale, NJ: Erlbaum.

Tudge, J.R.H., & Scrimsher, S. (2002). Lev S. Vygotsky on education. In B.J. Zimmerman & D.H. Schunk (Eds.), *Educational psychology*. Mahwah, NJ: Erlbaum.

Tupuola, A. (2000, April). *Shifting notions of personal identity for Samoan youth in New Zealand*. Paper presented at the meeting of the Society for Research on Adolescence, Chicago.

Turiel, E. (1998). The development of morality. In N. Eisenberg. (Ed.), *Handbook of child psychology* (5th ed., Vol. 3). New York: Wiley.

U

U.S. Bureau of the Census. (2000). *Statistical abstracts of the United States, 1999*. Washington, DC: U.S. Government Printing Office.

U.S. Department of Education. (1996). *Number and disabilities of children and youth served under IDEA*. Washington, DC: Office of Special Education Programs, Data Analysis System.

U.S. Department of Energy. (2001). *The Human Genome Project*. Washington, DC: Author.

Udry, J.R. (1990). Hormonal and social determinants of adolescent sexual initiation. In J. Bancroft & J.M. Reinisch (Eds.), *Adolescence and puberty*. New York: Oxford University Press.

Underwood, M.K., & Hurley, J.C. (1997, April). *Children's responses to angry provocation as a function of peer status and aggression*. Paper presented at the meeting of the Society for Research in Child Development, Washington, DC.

Underwood, M.K., & Hurley, J.C. (2000). Emotion regulation in peer relationships in middle childhood. In L. Balter & C.S. Tamis-LeMonda (Eds.), *Child psychology*. Philadelphia: Psychology Press.

Underwood, M.K., Kupersmidt, J.B., & Coie, J.D. (1996). Childhood peer sociometric status and aggression as predictors of adolescent childbearing. *Journal of Research on Adolescence, 6*, 201–223.

Unger, R., & Crawford, M. (1992). *Women and gender* (2nd ed.). New York: McGraw-Hill.

UNICEF. (2000). *Educating girls, transforming the future*. Geneva: UNICEF.

Updegraff, K.A. (1999, April). *Mothers' and fathers' involvement in adolescents' peer relationships: Links to friendship adjustment and peer competence*. Paper presented at the meeting of the Society for Research in Child Development, Albuquerque.

Urberg, K.A. (1999). Introduction: Some thoughts about studying the influence of peers on children and adolescents. *Merrill-Palmer Quarterly, 45*, 1–12.

Urberg, K.A., Degirmencioglu, S.M., Tolson, J.M., & Halliday-Scher, K. (1995). The structure of adolescent peer networks. *Developmental Psychology, 31*, 540–547.

Urberg, K.A., Goldstein, M.S., & Toro, P. (2002, April). *Social moderators of the effects of parent and peer drinking on adolescent drinking*. Paper presented at the meeting of the Society for Research on Adolescence, New Orleans.

Urdan, T., & Midgley, C. (2001). Academic self-handicapping: What we know, what more is there to learn. *Educational Psychology Review, 13*, 115–138.

Urdan, T., Midgely, C., & Anderman, E.M. (1998). The role of classroom goal structure in students' use of self-handicapping strategies. *American Educational Research Journal, 35*, 101–122.

Usher, B., Zahn-Waxler, C., Finch, C., & Gunlicks, M. (2000, April). *The relation between global self-esteem, perceived competence, and risk for psychopathology in adolescence*. Paper presented at the meeting of the Society for Research on Adolescence, Chicago.

V

Valisner, J. (2000). Cultural psychology. In A. Kazdin (Ed.), *Encyclopedia of psychology*. Washington, DC, and New York: American Psychological Association and Oxford University Press.

van Dijk, T.A. (1987). *Communicating racism*. Newbury Park, CA: Sage.

Van Goozen, S.H.M., Matthys, W., Cohen-Kettenis, P.T., Thisjssen, J.H.H., & van Engeland, H. (1998). Adrenal androgens and aggression in conduct disorder prepubertal boys and normal control. *Biological Psychiatry, 43*, 156–158.

Van Hoof, A. (1999). The identity status field re-reviewed: An update of unresolved and neglected issues with a view on some alternative approaches. *Developmental Review, 19*, 497–565.

Vandell, D.L., Minnett, A., & Santrock, J.W. (1987). Age differences in sibling relationships during middle childhood. *Applied Developmental Psychology, 8*, 247–257.

Ventura, S.J., Mosher, W.D., Curtin, S.C., Abma, J.C., & Henshaw, S. (2001). Trends in pregnancy rates for the United States, 1976–1997: An update. *National Vital Statistics Reports, 49*, 1–9.

Vernberg, E.M. (1990). Psychological adjustment and experience with peers during early adolescence: Reciprocal, incidental, or unidirectional relationships? *Journal of Abnormal Child Psychology, 18*, 187–198.

Vernberg, E.M., Ewell, K.K., Beery, S.H., & Abwender, D.A. (1994). Sophistication of adolescents' interpersonal negotiation strategies and friendship formation after relocation: A naturally occurring experiment. *Journal of Research on Adolescence, 4*, 5–19.

Vicary, J.R., Klingaman, L.R., & Harkness, W.L. (1995). Risk factors associated with date rape and sexual assault of adolescent girls. *Journal of Adolescence, 18*, 289–306.

Vidal, F. (2000). Piaget, Jean. In A. Kazdin (Ed.), *Encyclopedia of psychology*. Washington, DC, and New York: American Psychological Association and Oxford University Press.

Vondracek, F.W. (1991). Vocational development and choice in adolescence. In R.M. Lerner, A.C. Petersen, & J. Brooks-Gunn (Eds.), *Encyclopedia of adolescence* (Vol. 2). New York: Garland.

Vygotsky, L. (1962). *Thought and language*. Cambridge, MA: MIT Press.

W

Wagennar, A.C. (1983). *Alcohol, young drivers, and traffic accidents*. Lexington, MA: D.C. Heath.

Wagner, R.K. (2000). Practical intelligence. In A. Kazdin (Ed.), *Encyclopedia of psychology*. Washington, DC, & New York: American Psychological Association and Oxford University Press.

Wahlsten, D. (2000). Behavioral genetics. In A. Kazdin (Ed.), *Encyclopedia of psychology*. Washington, DC, & New York: American Psychological Association and Oxford University Press.

Waldron, H.B., Brody, J.L., & Slesnick, N. (2001). Integrative behavioral and family therapy for adolescent substance abuse. In P.M. Monti, S.M. Colbyk, & T.A. O'Leary (Eds.), *Adolescents, alcohol, and substance abuse*. New York: Guilford.

Walker, H. (1998, May 31). Youth violence: Society's problem. *Eugene Register Guard*, p. 1C.

Walker, L.J. (1984). Sex differences in the development of moral reasoning: A critical review. *Child Development, 51*, 131–139.

Walker, L.J. (1991). Sex differences in moral development. In W.M. Kurtines & J. Gewirtz (Eds.), *Moral behavior and development* (Vol. 2). Hillsdale, NJ: Erlbaum.

Walker, L.J. (1993, March). *Is the family a sphere of moral growth for children?* Paper presented at the biennial meeting of the Society for Research in Child Development, New Orleans.

Zimmerman, B.J. (2000). Attaining self-regulation: A social cognitive perspective. In M. Boekaerts, P.R. Pintrich, & M. Zeidner (Eds.), *Handbook of self-regulation*. San Diego: Academic Press.

Zimmerman, B.J. (2002). Achieving academic excellence: A self-regulatory perspective. In M. Ferrari (Ed.), *The prusuit of excellence through education*. Mahwah, NJ: Erlabaum.

Zimmerman, B.J., Bonner, S., & Kovach, R. (1996). *Developing self-regulated learners*. Washington, DC: American Psychological Association.

Walker, L.J. (1996). Unpublished review of J.W. Santrock's *Child development*, 8th ed. (Dubuque, IA: Brown & Benchmark).

Walker, L.J., deVries, B., & Trevethan, S.D. (1987). Moral stages and moral orientation in real-life and hypothetical dilemmas. *Child Development, 58*, 842–858.

Walker, L.J., Hennig, K.H., & Krettenauer, R. (2000). Parent and peer contexts for children's moral reasoning development. *Child Development, 71*, 1033–1048.

Walker, L.J., & Pitts, R.C. (1998). Naturalistic conceptions of moral maturity. *Developmental Psychology, 34*, 403–419.

Walker, L.J., & Taylor, J.H. (1991). Family interaction and the development of moral reasoning. *Child Development, 62*, 264–283.

Wallace-Broscious, A., Serafica, F.C., & Osipow, S.H. (1994). Adolescent career development: Relationships to self-concept and identity status. *Journal of Research on Adolescence, 4*, 127–150.

Wallis, C. (1985, December 9). Children having children. *Time*, pp. 78–88.

Walter, C.A. (1986). *The timing of motherhood.* Lexington, MA: D.C. Heath.

Walters, E., & Kendler, K.S. (1994). Anorexia nervosa and anorexia-like symptoms in a population based twin sample. *American Journal of Psychiatry, 152*, 62–71.

Walther-Thomas, C., Korinek, L., McLaughlin, V.L., & Williams, B.T. (2000). *Collaboration for inclusive education.* Boston: Allyn & Bacon.

Wang, J.Q. (2000, November). *A comparison of two international standards to assess child and adolescent obesity in three populations.* Paper presented at the meeting of American Public Health Association, Boston.

Ward, L.M. (1994, February). *The nature and prevalence of sexual messages in the television programs adolescents view most.* Paper presented at the meeting of the Society for Research on Adolescence, San Diego.

Ward, L.M. (2000, April). *Does television exposure affect adolescents' sexual attitudes and expectations? Correlational and experimental confirmation.* Paper presented at the meeting of the Society for Research on Adolescence, Chicago.

Wartella, E., Heintz, K., Aidman, A., & Mazzarella, S. (1990). Television and beyond: Children's video media in one community. *Communications Research, 17*, 45–64.

Wass, H., Miller, M.D., & Redditt, C.A. (1991). Adolescents and destructive themes in rock music: A follow-up. *Omega, 23*, 199–206.

Waterman, A.S. (1985). Identity in the context of adolescent psychology. In A.S. Waterman (Ed.), *Identity in adolescence: Processes and contents.* San Francisco: Jossey-Bass.

Waterman, A.S. (1989). Curricula interventions for identity change: Substantive and ethical considerations. *Journal of Adolescence, 12*, 389–400.

Waterman, A.S. (1992). Identity as an aspect of optimal psychological functioning. In G.R. Adams, T.P. Gullotta, & R. Montemayor (Eds.), *Adolescent identity formation.* Newbury Park, CA: Sage.

Waterman, A.S. (1999). Identity, the identity statuses, and identity status development: A contemporary statement. *Developmental Review, 19*, 591–621.

Waters, G.S., & Caplan, D. (2001). Age, working memory, and on-line syntactic processing in sentence comprehension. *Psychology & Aging, 16*, 128–144.

Way, N. (1997, April). *Father-daughter relationships in urban families.* Paper presented at the meeting of the Society for Research in Child Development, Washington, DC.

Wechsler, H., Davenport, A., Sowdall, G., Moetykens, B., & Castillo, S. (1994). Health and behavioral consequences of binge drinking in college. *Journal of the American Medical Association, 272*, 1672–1677.

Weineke, J.K., Thurston, S.W., Kelsey, K.T., Varkonyi, A., Wain, J.C., Mark, E.J., & Christiani, D.C. (1999). Early age at smoking initiation and tobacco carcinogen DNA damage in the lung. *Journal of the National Cancer Institute, 91*, 614–619.

Weiner, B. (1986). *An attributional theory of motivation and emotion.* New York: Springer.

Weiner, B. (1992). *Human motivation: Metaphors, theories, and research.* Newbury Park, CA: Sage.

Weiner, B. (2000). Motivation: An overview. In A. Kazdin (Ed.), *Encyclopedia of psychology.* Washington, DC, and New York: American Psychological Association and Oxford University Press.

Weinstein, C.S. (2003). *Secondary classroom management* 2nd ed. New York: McGraw-Hill.

Weiss, R.S. (1973). *Loneliness: The experience of emotional and social isolation.* Cambridge, MA: MIT Press.

Weissberg, R., & Caplan, M. (1989, April). *A follow-up study of a school-based social competence program for young adolescents.* Paper presented at the meeting of the Society for Research in Child Development, Kansas City.

Weissberg, R.P., & Greenberg, M.T. (1998). School and community competence—Enhancement and prevention interventions. In I.E. Siegel & K.A. Renninger (Eds.), *Handbook of child psychology* (5th ed., Vol. 4). New York: Wiley.

Weist, M.D., & Cooley-Quille, M. (2001). Advancing efforts to address youth violence involvement. *Journal of Clinical Child Psychology, 30*, 147–151.

Welsh, D.P., Vickerman, R., Kawaguschi, M.C., & Rostosky, S.S. (1998). *Discrepancies adolescent romantic couples' and observers' perceptions of couple interaction and their relationship to mental health.* Unpublished manuscript, Dept. of Psychology, University of Massachusetts, Amherst.

Weng, A., & Montemayor, R. (1997, April). *Conflict between mothers and adolescents.* Paper presented at the meeting of the Society for Research in Child Development, Washington, DC.

Wentzel, K.R., & Asher, S.R. (1995). The academic lives of neglected, rejected, popular, and controversial children. *Child Development, 66*, 754–763.

Wentzel, K.R., & Erdley, C.A. (1993). Strategies for making friends: Relations to social behavior and peer acceptance in early adolescence. *Developmental Psychology, 29*, 819–826.

Wertsch, J. (2000). Cognitive development. In M. Bennett (Ed.), *Developmental psychology.* Philadelphia: Psychology Press.

Westen, D. (2000). Psychoanalytic theories. In A. Kazdin (Ed.), *Encyclopedia of psychology.* Washington, DC, & New York: American Psychological Association and Oxford University Press.

Whalen, C.K. (2001). ADHD treatment in the 21st century: Pushing the envelope. *Journal of Clinical Child Psychology, 30*, 136–140.

Whalen, C.O. (2000). Attention deficit hyperactivity disorder. In A. Kazdin (Ed.), *Encyclopedia of psychology.* Washington, DC, and New York: American Psychological Association and Oxford University Press.

White, K.M., Speisman, J.C., Costos, D., & Smith, A. (1987). Relationship maturity: A conceptual and empirical approach. In J. Meacham (Ed.), *Interpersonal relations: Family, peers, friends.* Basel, Switzerland: Karger.

White, L., & Gilbreth, J.G. (2001). When children have two fathers: Effects of relationships with stepfathers and noncustodial fathers on adolescent outcomes. *Journal of Marriage and the Family, 63*, 155–167.

White, M. (1993). *The material child: Coming of age in Japan and America.* New York: Free Press.

Whiting, B.B. (1989, April). *Culture and interpersonal behavior.* Paper presented at the biennial meeting of the Society for Research in Child Development, Kansas City.

Whiting, B.B., & Edwards, C.P. (1988). *Children of different worlds.* Cambridge, MA: Harvard University Press.

Whitman, F.L., Diamond, M., & Martin, J. (1993). Homosexual orientation in twins: A report on 61 pairs and three triplet sets. *Archives of Sexual Behavior, 22*, 187–206.

Wigfield, A., & Eccles, J.S. (1989). Test anxiety in elementary and secondary school students. *Journal of Educational Psychology, 24*, 159–183.

Wigfield, A., & Eccles, J.S. (Eds.) (2001). *Development of achievement motivation.* San Diego: Academic Press.

William T. Grant Foundation Commission on Work, Family, and Citizenship. (1988, February). *The forgotten half: Noncollege-bound youth in America.* New York: William T. Grant Foundation.

Williams, C., & Bybee, J. (1994). What do children feel guilty about? Developmental and gender differences? *Developmental Psychology, 30*, 617–623.

Williams, J.E., & Best, D.L. (1982). *Measuring sex stereotypes: A thirty-nation study.* Newbury Park, CA: Sage.

Williams, J.E., & Best, D.L. (1989). *Sex and psyche: Self-concept viewed cross-culturally.* Newbury Park, CA: Sage.

Williams, T.M., & Cox, R. (1995, March). *Informative versus other children's TV programs: Portrayals of ethnic diversity, gender, and aggression.* Paper presented at the meeting of the Society for Research in Child Development, Indianapolis.

Williams, T.M., Baron, D., Phillips, S., David, L., & Jackson, D. (1986, August). *The portrayal of sex roles on Canadian and U.S. television.* Paper presented at the conference of the International Association for Mass Media Research, New Delhi, India.

Wills, T.A., Sandy, J.M., Yaeger, A., & Shinar, O. (2001). Family risk factors and adolescent substance use: Moderation effects for temperament dimensions. *Developmental Psychology, 37,* 283–297.

Wilson, B.J., & Gottman, J.M. (1995). Marital interaction and parenting. In M.H. Bornstein (Ed.), *Children and parenting* (Vol. 4). Hillsdale, NJ: Erlbaum.

Wilson, J.W. (1987). *The truly disadvantaged: The inner city, the underclass, and public policy.* Chicago: University of Chicago Press.

Wilson, M.N. (2000). Cultural diversity. In A. Kazdin (Ed.), *Encyclopedia of psychology.* Washington, DC, and New York: American Psychological Association and Oxford University Press.

Wilson, M.N., Cook, D.Y., & Arrington, E.G. (1997). African-American adolescents and academic achievement: Family and peer influences. In R.D. Taylor & M.C. Wang (Eds.), *Social and emotional adjustment and relation ethnic minority families.* Mahwah, NJ: Erlbaum

Wilson-Shockley, S. (1995). *Gender differences adolescent depression: The contribution of negative affect.* M.S. thesis, University of Illinois at Urbana-Champaign.

Windle, M. (1989). Substance use and abuse adolescent runaways: A four-year follow-up study. *Journal of Youth and Adolescence, 18,* 331–341.

Windle, M., & Dumenci, L. (1998). An investigation of maternal and adolescent depressed mood using a latent trait-state model. *Journal of Research on Adolescence, 8,* 461–484.

Winne, P.H. (1995). Inherent details in self-regulated learning. *Educational Psychologist,* 173–187.

Winne, P.H. (1997). Experimenting to bootstrap self-regulated learning. *Journal of Educational Psychology, 89,* 397–410.

Winne, P.H., & Perry, N.E. (2000). Measuring self-regulated learning. In M. Boekaerts, P. Pintrich, & M. Zeidner (Eds.), *Handbook regulation.* San Diego: Academic Press.

Winner, E. (1996). *Gifted children: Myths realities.* New York: Basic Books.

Winner, E. (2000). The origins and ends giftedness. *American Psychologist, 55,*

Wodarski, J.S., & Hoffman, S.D. (1984). education for adolescents. *Social Work Education, 6,* 69–92.

Wolery, M. (2000). Special education. (Ed.), *Encyclopedia of psychology.* DC, and New York: American Psy... Association and Oxford Universit...

Advancemen...
Cartoon, pg....
Zedonek. **Fig...**
Educational...
Eyes of Adol...
pp. 55–73.

CHAPTER 8

Cartoon, pg. ...
Reprinted wit...
pg. 274: Jason...
1997.

CHAPTER 9

Images of Adol...
"Self and Identi...
and G.R. Elliott...
Developing Adol...
1990. Reprinted...
Figure 9.1: From...
Demo, "Conceivi...
in Adolescent Sel...
Adolescence, 2, pp...
by Sage Publicati...
of Sage Publicati...
BLEACHERS © S...
permission of Uni...
reserved. **Cartoon...**
New Yorker Collec...
cartoonbank.com.

CHAPTER 10

Figure 10.1: Adapte...
"Sexism and Racism...
Prejudices," *Journal...*
Psychology, 68: 212, ...
"Modern Racism Sc...
Gaertner (eds.), *Prej...*
Racism, 1986 Acade...
J.S. Hyde, "Gender D...
Performance," *Psych...*
Copyright © 1990 by...
Association. Reprinte...
10.3: L.J. Sax, A.W. As...
1999. *The American F...*
Fall 1999. Higher Edu...

SUBJECT INDEX